Public Policies
toward
Business

Readings and Cases

The Irwin Series in Economics

Consulting Editor

LLOYD G. REYNOLDS *Yale University*

Public Policies toward Business

Readings and Cases

Edited by

WILLIAM G. SHEPHERD

Professor of Economics
University of Michigan

1975

RICHARD D. IRWIN, INC. Homewood, Illinois 60430

Irwin-Dorsey International London, England WC2H 9NJ
Irwin-Dorsey Limited Georgetown, Ontario L7G 4B3

First Printing, May 1975

ISBN 0-256-01749-2
Library of Congress Catalog Card No. 74–29752
Printed in the United States of America

PREFACE

The literature of public policies toward business has several main parts: (1) *scientific research* into the concepts and actual nature of industry and into the forms and criteria for applying public policies; (2) the content and details of *actual* policies, including agencies, cases, precedents, and the like; (3) studies of the *effects* of these policies; and (4) *proposals* to reform, extend, abolish or otherwise change existing policies. The issues involve art and judgment, as well as science. In each area, the best writings are surrounded by much debate and assertion, stuff and nonsense.

This collection offers excerpts from the more important and perceptive sources in all four areas, so that the student sinks roots directly into the literature and prepares to use it further. I have tried to let the literature come alive by presenting many of the remarkable characters (scholars, judges, officials, and others) who have created it. The selections also are meant to show the depth and evolution of the field. Many of the important ideas and lessons have been around for a long time, to be rediscovered by the young—and their seniors, too!—every generation or so. Each section also includes a bank of review questions.

In trying for reasonably wide coverage, I have leaned toward variety and excerpts rather than a full reprinting of a relatively few pieces. The editing is meant to convey the content and tone of each piece, whetting the reader's thirst for more.

The sequence of topics complements Clair Wilcox and William G. Shepherd, *Public Policies toward Business*, 5th ed. (Homewood, Ill.: Richard D. Irwin, 1975), but this collection can also be used quite effectively with other texts or on its own.

I am greatly indebted to the authors, journals, and publishers for permissions to reprint.

April 1975   WILLIAM G. SHEPHERD

vii

CONTENTS

Part I

THE SETTING FOR POLICIES

One needs clear concepts of competition and monopoly; of market structure, behavior, and performance. Competition may be defined as "perfect," or as a turbulent process of rivals' moves, or as reasonable degrees of choice, or in other ways. Five views on the nature and importance of competition follow. Then the efficiency effects of monopoly are defined. The next four readings consider actual conditions of competition and technology. Then three readings treat specific problems of reaching "optimal" policies.

Adam Smith (1723–90)

THE WEALTH OF NATIONS*

Smith not only founded modern economics at one great stroke, but also attacked the Mercantilist system of restraints on competition in local and international markets.

A monopoly granted either to an individual or to a trading company has the same effect as a secret in trade or manufactures. The monopolists, by keeping the market constantly under-stocked, by never fully supplying the effectual demand, sell their commodities much above the natural price, and raise their emoluments, whether they consist in wages or profit, greatly above their natural rate.

The price of monopoly is upon every occasion the highest which can be got. The natural price, or the price of free competition, on the contrary, is the lowest which can be taken, not upon every occasion indeed, but for any considerable time together. The one is upon every occasion the highest which can be squeezed out of the buyers, or which, it is supposed, they will consent to give: The other is the lowest which the sellers can commonly afford to take, and at the same time continue their business.

✻　✻　✻　✻　✻

People of the same trade seldom meet together, even for merriment and diversion, but the conversation ends in a conspiracy against the public, or in some contrivance to raise prices. It is impossible indeed to prevent such meetings, by any law which either could be executed, or would be consistent with liberty and justice. But though the law cannot hinder people of the same trade from sometimes assembling together, it ought to do nothing to facilitate such assemblies; much less to render them necessary.

✻　✻　✻　✻　✻

* Adam Smith, *The Wealth of Nations* (New York: Modern Library edition, 1937), pp. 61, 128, 612, 712.

But the cruellest of our revenue laws, I will venture to affirm, are mild and gentle, in comparison of some of those which the clamour of our merchants and manufacturers has extorted from the legislature, for the support of their own absurd and oppressive monopolies. Like the laws of Draco, these laws may be said to be all written in blood.

✻   ✻   ✻   ✻   ✻

By a perpetual monopoly, all the other subjects of the state are taxed very absurdly in two different ways; first, by the high price of goods, which, in the case of a free trade, they could buy much cheaper; and, secondly, by their total exclusion from a branch of business, which it might be both convenient and profitable for many of them to carry on. It is for the most worthless of all purposes too that they are taxed in this manner. It is merely to enable the company to support the negligence, profusion, and malversation of their own servants, whose disorderly conduct seldom allows the dividend of the company to exceed the ordinary rate of profit in trades which are altogether free, and very frequently makes it fall even a good deal short of that rate. . . .

Henry C. Simons (1901–47)

<h1 style="text-align:center">A POSITIVE PROGRAM FOR
LAISSEZ FAIRE*</h1>

A cofounder of the original "Chicago School" of economics, Simons applied classical liberal analysis unstintingly, even radically.

Much significance has been, and should be, attached to the simultaneous development of capitalism and democracy. Indeed, it seems clear that *none of the precious "freedoms" which our generation has inherited can be extended, or even maintained, apart from an essential freedom of enterprise—apart from a genuine "division of labor" between competitive and political controls.* The existence (and preservation) of a competitive situation in private industry makes possible a minimizing of the

* Henry C. Simons, *Economic Policy for a Free Society* (Chicago: University of Chicago Press, 1949), pp. 41–44, 49–58. These passages were written in 1935, when the issues appeared to be particularly urgent. Most Chicagoans presently are much more optimistic about the prevalence of competition.

responsibilities of the sovereign state. It frees the state from the obligation of adjudicating endless, bitter disputes among persons as participants in different industries and among owners of different kinds of productive services. In a word, it makes possible a political policy of laissez faire. . . .

It seems clear, at all events, that there is an intimate connection between freedom of enterprise and freedom of discussion and that political liberty can survive only within an effectively competitive economic system. Thus, *the great enemy of democracy is monopoly, in all its forms:* gigantic corporations, trade associations and other agencies for price control, trade-unions—or, in general, organization and concentration of power within functional classes. Effectively organized functional groups possess tremendous power for exploiting the community at large and even for sabotaging the system. The existence of competition within such groups, on the other hand, serves to protect the community as a whole and to give an essential flexibility to the economy. The disappearance of competition would almost assure the wrecking of the system in the economic struggle of organized minorities; on the political side, it would present a hopeless dilemma. If the organized economic groups were left to exercise their monopoly powers without political restraint, the result would be a usurpation of sovereignty by these groups—and, perhaps, a domination of the state by them. On the other hand, if the state undertakes to tolerate (instead of destroying) such organizations and to regulate their regulations, it will have assumed tasks and responsibilities incompatible with its enduring in a democratic form.

* * * * *

The gains from monopoly organization in general are likely, of course, to accrue predominantly to the strong and to be derived at the expense of the weak. Among producers, organization is least expensive and most easily achieved, as well as most effective, within groups whose members are unusually large and prosperous at the outset. Among workers, the bias is not less striking. . . .

Another major factor in the inefficient allocation of resources is to be found in government regulation and interference. Tariff legislation is again the main case in point, for the protective tariff is essentially a device for forcing resources from uses of higher to uses of lower productivity. Moreover, there are good reasons for believing that political controls will generally work out in this way. Government interference with relative prices is in the nature of arbitration of conflicts of interest between minority producer groups and consumers (the whole community); and such interference inevitably involves decisions which have regard primarily for the interests of the minorities. Producers are, from a political point of view, organized, articulate groups; and it is in the nature of the political process to conciliate such groups. Anyone may detect the notorious economic fallacies, and thus see the dictates of sound policy, if he will look at every issue from the viewpoint of consumers; but no politician can be expected to do this, or to act on his conclusions if he does, except in a world where legislators are motivated primarily by the desire to be retired at the next election. People as consumers are unorganized and inarticulate, and, representing merely the interests of the community as a whole, they always will be. This fact, perhaps, suggests the decisive argument for laissez faire and against "planning" of the now popular sort. . . .

Public regulation of private monopoly would seem to be, at best, an anomalous arrangement, tolerable only as a temporary expedient. Half-hearted, sporadic, principle-less regulation is a misfortune for all concerned; and systematic regulation, on the basis of any definite and adequate principle, would leave private ownership almost without a significant function or responsibility to discharge. Analysis of the problem, and examination of experience to date, would seem to indicate the wisdom of abandoning the existing scheme of things with respect to the railroads and utilities, rather than of extending the system to include other industries as well. Political control of utility charges is imperative, to be sure, for competition simply cannot function effectively as an agency of control. We may endure regulation for a time, on the dubious assumption that governments are more nearly competent to regulate than to operate. *In general, however, the state should face the necessity of actually taking over, owning, and managing directly, both the railroads and the utilities, and all other industries in which it is impossible to maintain effectively competitive conditions.* For industries other than the utilities, there still remains a real alternative to socialization, namely, the establishment and preservation of competition as the regulative agency. . . .

There must be outright dismantling of our gigantic corporations and persistent prosecution of producers who organize, by whatever methods, for price maintenance or output limitation. There must be explicit and unqualified repudiation of the so-called "rule of reason." Legislation must prohibit, and administration effectively prevent, the acquisition by any private firm, or group of firms, of substantial monopoly power, regardless of how reasonably that power may appear to be exercised. The Federal Trade Commission must become perhaps the most powerful of our governmental agencies; and the highest standards must be maintained, both in the appointment of its members and in the recruiting of its large technical staff. In short, restraint of trade must be treated as a major crime and prosecuted unremittingly by a vigilant administrative body.

*   *   *   *   *

Joseph A. Schumpeter (1883–1950)

THE PROCESS OF CREATIVE DESTRUCTION*

To Schumpeter, competition was a turbulent sequence of disequilibria (innovation breeds monopoly breeds profit breeds another firm's innovation breeds new monopoly . . .) which yield progress, not an equilibrium with fine-tuned optimal conditions. Is he right? Does the process occur in all or parts of the economy?

. . . The fundamental impulse that sets and keeps the capitalist engine in motion comes from the new consumers' goods, the new methods of production or transportation, the new markets, the new forms of industrial organization that capitalist enterprise creates.

. . . The opening up of new markets, foreign or domestic, and the organizational development from the craft shop and factory to such concerns as U.S. Steel illustrate the same process of industrial mutation—if I may use that biological term—that incessantly revolutionizes the economic structure *from within*, incessantly destroying the old one, incessantly creating a new one. This process of Creative Destruction is the essential fact about capitalism. It is what capitalism consists in and what every capitalist concern has got to live in. This fact bears upon our problem in two ways.

First, since we are dealing with a process whose every element takes considerable time in revealing its true features and ultimate effects, there is no point in appraising the performance of that process *ex visu* of a given point of time; we must judge its performance over time, as it unfolds through decades or centuries. A system—any system, economic or other —that at *every* given point of time fully utilizes its possibilities to the best advantage may yet in the long run be inferior to a system that does so at *no* given point of time, because the latter's failure to do so may be a condition for the level or speed of long-run performance.

* From pp. 83–85, 99, *Capitalism, Socialism and Democracy*, 3d Edition by Joseph Schumpeter. Copyright 1942, 1947 by Joseph A. Schumpeter. Copyright 1950 by Harper & Row, Publishers, Inc. Reprinted by permission of the publisher. An erudite, cosmopolitan, and socially ambitious Viennese, Schumpeter became Harvard's leading theorist and wrote the monumental *History of Economic Analysis*. Fatalistic about Marxian predictions of the trend toward monopoly, he stressed the vitality even of "monopolistic" industry.

Second, since we are dealing with an organic process, analysis of what happens in any particular part of it—say, in an individual concern or industry—may indeed clarify details of mechanism but is inconclusive beyond that. Every piece of business strategy acquires its true significance only against the background of that process and within the situation created by it. It must be seen in its role in the perennial gale of creative destruction; it cannot be understood irrespective of it or, in fact, on the hypothesis that there is a perennial lull.

But economists who, *ex visu* of a point of time, look for example at the behavior of an oligopolist industry—an industry which consists of a few big firms—and observe the well-known moves and countermoves within it that seem to aim at nothing but high prices and restrictions of output are making precisely that hypothesis. They accept the data of the momentary situation as if there were no past or future to it and think that they have understood what there is to understand if they interpret the behavior of those firms by means of the principle of maximizing profits with reference to those data. The usual theorist's paper and the usual government commission's report practically never try to see that behavior, on the one hand, as a result of a piece of past history and, on the other hand, as an attempt to deal with a situation that is sure to change presently—as an attempt by those firms to keep on their feet, on ground that is slipping away from under them. In other words, the problem that is usually being visualized is how capitalism administers existing structures, whereas the relevant problem is how it creates and destroys them. As long as this is not recognized, the investigator does a meaningless job. As soon as it is recognized, his outlook on capitalist practice and its social results changes considerably.

The first thing to go is the traditional conception of the *modus operandi* of competition. Economists are at long last emerging from the stage in which price competition was all they saw. As soon as quality competition and sales effort are admitted into the sacred precincts of theory, the price variable is ousted from its dominant position. However, it is still competition within a rigid pattern of invariant conditions, methods of production and forms of industrial organization in particular, that practically monopolizes attention. But in capitalist reality as distinguished from its textbook picture, it is not that kind of competition which counts but the competition from the new commodity, the new technology, the new source of supply, the new type of organization (the largest-scale unit of control for instance)—competition which commands a decisive cost or quality advantage and which strikes not at the margins of the profits and the outputs of the existing firms but at their foundations and their very lives. This kind of competition is as much more effective than the other as a bombardment is in comparison with forcing a door, and so much more important that it becomes a matter of comparative indifference whether competition in the ordinary sense functions more or less promptly; the powerful lever that in the long run expands output and brings down prices is in any case made of other stuff.

It is hardly necessary to point out that competition of the kind we now have in mind acts not only when in being but also when it is merely an ever-present threat. It disciplines before it attacks.

. . . [P]ure cases of long-run monopoly must be of the rarest occurrence and . . . even tolerable approximations to the requirements of the concept must be still rarer than are cases of perfect competition. The power to exploit at pleasure a given pattern of demand—or one that changes independently of the monopolist's action and of the reactions it provokes— can under the conditions of intact capitalism hardly persist for a period long enough to matter for the analysis of total output, unless buttressed by public authority, for instance, in the case of fiscal monopolies. A modern business concern not *so* protected—i.e., even if protected by import duties or import prohibitions—and yet wielding that power (except temporarily) is not easy to find or even to imagine. Even railroads and power and light concerns had first to create the demand for their services and, when they had done so, to defend their market against competition. Outside the field of public utilities, the position of a single seller can in general be conquered—and retained for decades—only on the condition that he does not behave like a monopolist. . . .

Corwin D. Edwards (1901–)

MAINTAINING COMPETITION*

*Competition may be neither "perfect," nor Schumpe-
terian, nor a magic solution to all ills. Yet, Edwards
notes, it can be effective—and often powerful—even in
modest doses, if it is given reasonable policy support.*

This competition consists in access by buyers and sellers to a substantial number of alternatives and in their ability to reject those which are

---

* Corwin D. Edwards, *Maintaining Competition* (New York: McGraw-Hill, 1949), pp. 9–12, 14–15. A life-long opponent of monopoly in various government and academic posts, Edwards has done landmark studies of international cartels, Japanese combines, and "conglomerate power." Yet, evidently, his criteria are not doctrinaire or rigid.

relatively unsatisfactory. Its structural characteristics in a particular market are as follows:

1. There must be an appreciable number of sources of supply and an appreciable number of potential customers for substantially the same product or service. Suppliers and customers do not need to be so numerous that each trader is entirely without individual influence, but their number must be great enough that persons on the other side of the market may readily turn away from any particular trader and may find a variety of other alternatives.

2. No trader must be so powerful as to be able to coerce his rivals, nor so large that the remaining traders lack the capacity to take over at least a substantial portion of his trade.

3. Traders must be responsive to incentives of profit and loss; that is, they must not be so large, so diversified, so devoted to political rather than commercial purposes, so subsidized, or otherwise so unconcerned with results in a particular market that their policies are not affected by ordinary commercial incentives arising out of that market.

4. Matters of commercial policy must be decided by each trader separately without agreement with his rivals.

5. New traders must have opportunity to enter the market without handicap other than that which is automatically created by the fact that others are already well established there.

6. Access by traders on one side of the market to those on the other side of the market must be unimpaired except by obstacles not deliberately introduced, such as distance or ignorance of the available alternatives.

7. There must be no substantial preferential status within the market for any important trader or group of traders on the basis of law, politics, or commercial alliances.

Where markets are so organized, competition affords a rough and limited but effective safeguard for certain interests of those immediately involved and for certain aspects of the public interest. . . .

Thus conceived, competition is not, of course, a complete basis for public policy. It cannot be expected to assure full production, distributive justice, protection against widespread economic distress, or stability in contrast to the swings of the business cycle. Although it affords flexibility in the use of resources, it cannot be expected to overcome the lags and frictions of folkways and of human ignorance. Its function with reference to all such problems is to prevent the defects of social organization from being made worse by deliberate adoption of restrictive policies designed to serve private interests. It minimizes planned restrictions of output, deliberate exploitation of the weak, and deliberate refusal to adopt new methods. It eliminates extremes of inefficiency. These are the limits of its usefulness. To accomplish these purposes competition is an appropriate part of any public policy. If constructive programs can be developed which improve the performance of the economic system, there is strong ground for adopting them; but there will still be need to provide safeguards against onerous bargains and to guarantee opportunities for economic progress. Although not means to an economic utopia, these safeguards, like garbage collection, are necessary, if insufficient, for the public health. . . .

To preserve competition in a mixed economy requires two programs. One is to prevent anticompetitive private forces from destroying competition or seriously impairing its effectiveness in those areas in which it is the basis of public policy. This requires activities designed to prevent the rise of large monopolistic organizations, to keep the differentials of size and power in business within such limits that certain concerns may not coercively jeopardize the independence of others, to assure that important points of business policy are determined separately rather than jointly, and to safeguard opportunities for access to the market both by established concerns and by newcomers.

The other program is to make certain that the controls over the noncompetitive areas of the economy are applied in such a way as to avoid public sabotage of competition in the supposedly competitive areas. In this latter task, three dangers must be avoided: first, that the private groups desiring to set aside competition will capture the machinery of the state and use it to set up schemes of public control that do not differ in purpose and effect from those of a private monopoly; second, that the boundaries between competitive and noncompetitive areas will be badly defined so that competition is ineffective where it is supposed to prevail or so that no man's lands are created subject neither to competition nor to public control; third, that in the noncompetitive areas the controls established by the state will fail to provide adequate substitutes for the safeguards of competition that have been done away with.

✻   ✻   ✻   ✻   ✻

Carl Kaysen (1920–   )

THE CORPORATION: HOW MUCH
POWER? WHAT SCOPE?*

*Kaysen notes that "corporate power" does raise seri-
ous social issues, on local as well as national levels. The
issues have intensified, not abated.*

When the invisible hand of the competitive market is, in turn, dis-
placed to a significant extent by the increasingly visible hand of powerful
corporate management, the question "Quo warranto?" is bound to arise,
whatever decisions are in fact made. And the fact is that the power of
corporate management is, in the political sense, irresponsible power, an-
swerable ultimately only to itself. No matter how earnestly management
strives to "balance" interests in making its decisions—interests of stockholders, of employees, of customers, of the "general public," as well as
the institutional interests of the enterprise—it is ultimately its own conception of these interests and their desirable relations that rules. When
the exercise of choice is strongly constrained by competitive forces, and
the power of decision of any particular management is narrow and pro-
portioned to the immediate economic needs of the enterprise, the political question of the warrant of management authority and its proper scope
does not arise. When, as we have argued, the scope of choice is great and
the consequences reach widely into the economy and far into the future,
the problem of the authority and responsibility of the choosers is bound
to become pressing. . . .

It is when we step down from the level of national politics to the state
and local levels that the political power of the large corporation is seen
in truer perspective. The large national-market firm has available to it
the promise of locating in a particular area or expanding its operations
there, the threat of moving or contracting its operations as potent bargaining points in its dealings with local and even state political leaders.
The branch manager of the company whose plant is the largest employer
in a town or the vice-president of the firm proposing to build a plant
which will become the largest employer in a small state treats with local

* Carl Kaysen, "The Corporation: How Much Power? What Scope?" in E. S. Mason,
ed., *The Corporation in Modern Society* (Cambridge: Harvard University Press, 1959),
pp. 99–101. Kaysen was a leading expert on the monopoly problem in the 1950s. Since
1964 he has been Director of the Institute for Advanced Studies at Princeton.

government not as a citizen but as a quasi-sovereign power. Taxes, zoning laws, roads, and the like become matters of negotiation as much as matters of legislation. Even large industrial states and metropolitan cities may face similar problems: the largest three employers in Michigan account for probably a quarter of the state's industrial employment; in Detroit the proportion is more nearly a third. At this level, the corporation's scope of choice, its financial staying power, its independence of significant local forces are all sources of strength in dealing with the characteristically weak governments at the local and often at the state levels.

William S. Comanor (1937–   ) and
Harvey Leibenstein (1922–   )

ALLOCATIVE EFFICIENCY, X-EFFICIENCY AND THE MEASUREMENT OF WELFARE LOSSES*

Monopoly may cause two main forms of inefficiency.
Here they are defined, diagrammed, and compared.

In estimating the loss from monopoly,[1] it has been common to assume that inputs are used as efficiently as in competitive markets. The presumed reason for this assumption is that firms have a clear interest in minimizing costs per unit of output. While the "carrot" of greater profits may well be a major determinant of firm behaviour, the competitive "stick" may be equally important, and to this extent, monopoly will affect costs as well as prices. In this context, the welfare loss from monopoly should include the reduction in what one of the authors has called "X-efficiency"[2] as well as the extent of allocative inefficiency, and therefore the

---

* William S. Comanor and Harvey Leibenstein, "Allocative Efficiency, X-Efficiency and the Measurement of Welfare Losses," *Economica*, August 1969, pp. 304–07. Comanor is a leading expert on antitrust policy and on advertising's effect on competition. Leibenstein, *inter alia*, originated the term "X-efficiency."

[1] In this paper it is recognized that monopoly does not depend entirely on the size distribution of firms but rather rests on the entire set of factors which permits firms to behave differently from what would be enforced in purely competitive markets with similar cost and demand conditions.

[2] Harvey Leibenstein, "Allocative Efficiency vs. 'X-Efficiency,'" *American Economic Review*, vol. LVI (1966), pp. 392–415.

combined welfare loss from monopoly may be very much larger than the usually calculated loss.

Competition may have an important impact on costs because it serves as a major source of disciplinary pressure on firms in the market, which, to a greater or lesser degree, affects all firms in competitive industries. In the first place, the process of competition tends to eliminate high-cost producers, while the existence of substantial market power often allows such firms to remain in business. This is due to the oft-noted fact that the high price-cost margins, which are established by firms with substantial market power, often serve as an umbrella which protects their high-cost rivals. Second, the process of competition, by mounting pressures on firm profits, tends to discipline managements *and employees* to utilize their inputs, and to put forth effort, more energetically and more effectively than is the case where this pressure is absent.[3] Thus, a shift from monopoly to competition has two possible effects: (1) the elimination of monopoly rents, and (2) the reduction of unit costs.[4]

Although both of these effects should be included in estimating the welfare losses which result from monopoly, in fact, frequently only the first has been examined. By assuming that actual costs equal minimum costs, Harberger[5] and others have estimated the welfare loss which results from monopoly by calculating approximately the total consumer surplus which is lost. This is illustrated in Figure 1 by the triangle ABC where this area equals $\frac{1}{2}\Delta p \Delta q$, where Δp is the difference between price and actual unit costs and Δq is the corresponding difference in quantities. It is in these computations where actual costs are assumed to represent economic costs, for Δp is also considered to represent the difference in price between monopolistic and competitive equilibrium.

Now let us suppose that a shift from monopoly to competition not only lowers price but also lowers costs (i.e., increases X-efficiency). What are the welfare losses under these circumstances which are due to monopoly? We show below that there is a simple mathematical relation, in the case of linear demand functions, which relates the full reduction in allocative efficiency to that estimated under the limiting assumption noted above.

---

[3] Cf. R. M. Cyert and J. G. March, *A Behavioral Theory of the Firm*, Englewood Cliffs, N.J., 1963, where the related concept of "organizational slack" is used to describe the process whereby costs rise above minimum levels.

[4] The hypothesized cost effect of competition is not original to this article but originated as long ago as 1897 in an article in the *Atlantic Monthly* of that year by A. T. Hadley. See Oliver E. Williamson, "A Dynamic Stochastic Theory of Managerial Behavior," in A. Phillips and O. Williamson (eds.), *Prices: Issues in Theory, Practice and Public Policy*, p. 23. A more recent statement of this hypothesis was made by Tibor Scitovsky in "Economic Theory and the Measurement of Concentration," in NBER, *Business Concentration and Price Policy*, Princeton, 1955, pp. 106–8.

[5] Arnold Harberger, "Monopoly and Resource Allocation," *American Economic Review, Papers and Proceedings*, vol. XLIV (1954), pp. 77–92.

FIGURE 1.

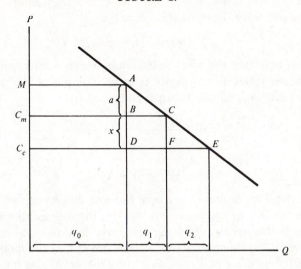

The important implication of our result is that the actual degree of *allocative inefficiency* may be very much larger than the level as heretofore calculated. Furthermore, to this larger sum must be added the volume of *X-inefficiency* for the monopolistically used inputs to obtain the total welfare loss from monopoly.

In Figure 1, we assume that a shift from monopoly to competition will reduce the monopoly rent per unit of output by a units but that it will reduce unit costs by x units. On this basis, we can distinguish the various components of welfare loss which result from monopoly. W_a is the partial welfare loss which results from allocative inefficiency associated with monopoly, and is illustrated by the triangle ABC in Figure 1. This is the standard measure of the welfare loss which has been calculated in earlier studies. W_{ax}, on the other hand, describes the full measure of allocative inefficiency which results from monopoly under the view that competition affects the level of costs as well as prices. It is measured by the triangle ADE. At the same time, W_x is the welfare loss from X-inefficiency resulting from monopoly, and refers to the higher costs used to produce the restricted level of output. This loss has no allocative component since it is concerned with no change in output levels, and is the rectangle C_mC_cDB.

The quantity a is the price-cost margin which exists under monopoly, while the quantity x is the cost difference between monopoly and competition; q_1 is the difference in quantity which results from a shift from monopoly to competition exclusive of the cost effect, while q_2 is the difference in quantity directly associated with the cost reduction. Now let X equal the cost difference in units of a, i.e., X is equal to x/a, which is the ratio of the cost difference to the price-cost margin under monopoly.

As indicated above, $W_a = aq_1/2$, while

(1) $$W_{ax} = (a + Xa)(q_1 + q_2)/2.$$

We can then note that the total welfare loss which results from the allocative inefficiency due to monopoly is some multiple of the welfare loss as measured earlier, and this factor is indicated by

(2) $$\frac{W_{ax}}{W_a} = \frac{aq_1 + aq_2 + Xaq_1 + Xaq_2}{aq_1},$$

and hence[6]

(3) $$W_{ax}/W_x = (1 + X)^2.$$

This relationship implies that where the cost difference due to monopoly is large relative to the price-cost margin, the loss in allocative inefficiency may be far greater than the allocative loss as usually measured. For example, in the diagram above, it is assumed that the monopoly rent and the cost effect are equal, and, as a consequence, W_{ax} is four times the usual measure of welfare loss. If, on the other hand, the ratio of x to a were three, then we would need to multiply the conventional welfare loss by a factor of sixteen.

A numerical example may illustrate the implications of this relationship. Suppose that actual costs are 6 percent below the monopoly price, and that one half of the total output of the economy is produced in monopolized sectors. If the price elasticity were equal to two, the welfare loss W_a would be approximately 0·18 percent of the net national product. Now, suppose that the cost-effect differential is 18 percent, which does not appear to be an impossible figure. In that case, the full allocative welfare loss W_{ax} is nearly 3 percent of the net national product—a not insubstantial sum.

The pure X-efficiency effect, apart from the allocative effect, is, of course, likely to be the largest of all. In the numerical illustration above, the welfare loss W_x would be one half of 18 percent, i.e., 9 percent, of the net national product. Furthermore, it should be noted that in fact W_x is likely to be even larger relatively to W_{ax}, since we have assumed a high price-elasticity of demand.

---

[6] We note that $q_2/q_1 = x/a = X$, by similar triangles. Therefore $W_{ax}/W_a = 1 + 2X + X^2$.

John Moody (1868–1958)

DOMINATING INFLUENCES IN
THE TRUSTS*

Moody presented the full scope of the hundreds of new industrial "trusts" (some mighty, many trivial) which had arisen during 1890–1901. He then assessed the larger setting of financial power as follows, and concluded that antitrust was already irrelevant!

That remarkable group of men known as the "Standard Oil," or Rockefeller financiers . . . either entirely control or make their influence felt to a marked degree in all the Greater Trusts. They are in fact the real fathers of the Trust idea in this country, and, of course, have always been the controlling factors in that most far-reaching and successful of all Trusts, the Standard Oil Company. . . .

But it is not merely in oil and its allied industries that the Rockefeller interests are dominant. They are the controlling factors in the Copper Trust and the Smelters' Trust, and are also closely identified with the mammoth Tobacco Trust, which now practically encircles the globe. Furthermore, while not entirely dominant, they are interested in and display a marked influence in the great Morgan properties, such as the United States Steel Corporation. In the hundreds of smaller Industrial Trusts, the Rockefeller interests are also conspicuous in many ways. . . .

The great Rockefeller alliances in the railroad and industrial fields are supplemented and welded together, as it were, through the New York city financial interests of the group. Their banking influence is of very great importance, and their ramifications are far-reaching and of great effectiveness. . . .

The Morgan group of industries and transportation companies is, next to the Standard Oil interests, by far the most important. In fact, the only gigantic interests or groups which can in any sense be considered as on the same plane are the Rockefeller and Morgan groups. There are, it is true, a number of other large groups in special lines, but these two are the only distinctively great interests that dominate immense areas in all

---

* John Moody, *The Truth about the Trusts* (New York: Moody Publishing, 1904, reprinted 1968), pp. 491–501. Moody, an acute and meticulous observer, founded the major financial reporting service which still flourishes.

lines, steam transportation, public service, industrial, financial, banking, insurance and so forth. The great Morgan enterprises in the industrial world are the Steel and Shipping Trusts, the Electrical Supply Trust, the Rubber Trust, and a score or more of smaller aggregations. In the public utility field the Morgan interests dominate a series of lesser enterprises, but have never been so conspicuous in these lines as have the Rockefeller financiers. . . .

It should not be supposed, however, that these two great groups of capitalists and financiers are in any real sense rivals or competitors for power, or that such a thing as "war" exists between them. For, as a matter of fact, they are not only friendly, but they are allied to each other by many close ties, and it would probably require only a little stretch of the imagination to describe them as a single great Rockefeller-Morgan group. It is felt and recognized on every hand in Wall Street to-day, that they are harmonious in nearly all particulars, and that instead of there being danger of their relations ever becoming strained, it will be only a matter of a brief period when one will be more or less completely absorbed by the other, and a grand close alliance will be the natural outcome of conditions which, so far as human foresight can see, can logically have no other result.

Around these two groups, or what must ultimately become one greater group, all the other smaller groups of capitalists congregate. They are all allied and intertwined by their various mutual interests.

. . . Therefore, viewed as a whole, we find the dominating influences in the Trusts to be made up of an intricate network of large and small groups of capitalists, many allied to one another by ties of more or less importance, but all being appendages to or parts of the greater groups, which are themselves dependent on and allied with the two mammoth or Rockefeller and Morgan groups. These two mammoth groups jointly (for, as pointed out, they really may be regarded as one) constitute the heart of the business and commercial life of the nation, the others all being the arteries which permeate in a thousand ways our whole national life, making their influence felt in every home and hamlet, yet all connected with and dependent on this great central source, the influence and policy of which dominates them all. . . .

The modern Trust is the natural outcome or evolution of societary conditions and ethical standards which are recognized and established among men to-day as being necessary elements in the development of civilization. . . .

In view of the foregoing facts, it is plain to see that the Sherman Anti-Trust law has not been a success. As statistics show, nearly all the great Trusts, transportation and other, have been created since the passage of this anti-trust law, and in spite of it. As has been recently pointed out by a capable observer, this statute "seems to have not even the slightest tendency, either to do away with Trusts after they are created, or to prevent their creation. We may, therefore, be excused for wondering what such a statute is good for, or whether it is good for anything." . . .

In view of these facts, the anti-trust legislation which has thus far been tried or broached in this country would appear to be singularly inefficient and beside the point. It does not seem to be in any sense in conformity to the spirit of modern tendencies and conditions. It aims merely to prick the pimples of the social problem rather than to go to the root of things. For when we realize what monopoly is, its depth and width and general importance in modern industrial and commercial life, we can readily see that any kind of legislation aiming to abolish or materially retrench monopoly would have to be far-reaching and radical in its effects and would constitute a practical revolution in the bases of modern society. Whether one may regard monopoly as a curse or a blessing it is too deeply rooted in civilized society to be whisked away with a broom. This being so, there would seem to be no immediate prospect of "effective" legislation touching the Trust problem.

John M. Blair (1914–   )

ECONOMIC CONCENTRATION*

What forces shape market structure? Does modern technology "dictate" high concentration, as Moody urged 70 years ago? Blair says it does not; the trend toward economies of large scale has reversed.

Although from the dawn of the Industrial Revolution through the first third of this century the general direction of technological change was toward a larger scale of operations, technology, like a great river, is always in motion; its only constant is change. And, like a river, technology can completely reverse its course. When an easier and simpler route presents itself, it can move in a direction opposite to what had been true of

---

* Excerpted from *Economic Concentration* by John M. Blair, copyright © 1972 by Harcourt Brace Jovanovich, Inc., and reprinted with their permission. Blair has labored for several decades to expose specious arguments for monopoly and to illumine the benefits of competition. Chief economist of the Kefauver and Hart Committee during 1954–70, he led attacks on administered pricing and drug pricing. He organized lengthy hearings on economic concentration during 1964–68; his book gives much of the findings.

the past and would be logically expected for the future. Up to the 1930s, observers of the industrial scene could be forgiven for having failed to foresee that what had been true of the past would not be true of the future. There was little warning that the effect on size of the emerging new technologies would be quite different from the technologies of the past. By making possible economic production with a smaller capital outlay, these new technologies have lowered the barriers to entry, thus creating a potential stimulus to competition. By enabling small plants to match, or even exceed, the productive efficiency of large plants, they have brought about a radical geographic decentralization of production.

The early "capital-saving" or "decentralizing" technologies have occurred in much the same areas as the improvements that underlay the Industrial Revolution—power, machines, and transportation. Just as steam had replaced water wheels as the primary source of industrial power, so was steam replaced by electricity; as single-purpose, highly specialized machines operating in sequence had replaced skilled craftsmen, so were they replaced by newer, more flexible and adaptable multipurpose machines; and as railroads had replaced the canal, the wagon, and the ox-cart, so have railroads suffered from the inroads of truck and automobile.

Electrification has been the essential prerequisite to industrial decentralization. While steam had a centripetal effect by drawing industrial plants in around the source of power, electricity has had a centrifugal effect by diffusing power to the plants, thereby making possible their location in terms of markets and other economic factors. . . .

By greatly widening the area in which plants can be located, by freeing the individual machines from the long line shafts, by making possible the introduction of the individual, independently operated, multipurpose machine, and by permitting the use of industrial measuring, recording, and controlling instruments and controls, electricity set in motion a profound transformation of the whole structure of industry. . . .

Decentralizing technologies also began to appear in the areas of machinery and processes. The most important mechanical capital-saving technique is the independently operated, multipurpose machine. Powered by electricity and practically independent of its surroundings, the multipurpose machine can operate intermittently and quickly change the nature of its product, thereby enabling the small plant to adapt its output to changes in demand. . . . As measured by the three basic criteria of machine operations—speed, precision, and versatility—one multipurpose machine with automatic adjustments may represent the equivalent of a whole series of specialized machines; a few multipurpose machines may replace whole factories.

The world of chemistry also gave rise to a number of processes that speeded operations, reduced waste, and improved the value of products with only a relatively small capital expenditure. . . .

The decentralizing technologies received a tremendous impetus from a revolution in transportation which made it possible for the small plant to obtain supplies and get its products to the market. With the advent of the motor truck it was no longer necessary to channel raw materials over great distances from a relatively small number of rich sources into a few giant clusters of industrial facilities located along railroad routes. And no longer was the mass distribution served only by the railroads. In essence, the truck tended to transform the inflow of materials and the outflow of finished products from a giant national pattern into smaller regional and local patterns. . . .

Quite apart from the truck, the automobile had its own decentralizing effects. No longer was it necessary for a plant to be located within a large industrial center in order to be assured of an adequate supply of labor. Rather, the workers, using their automobiles, could commute over long distances between their homes and the plant. By means of the automobile, workers have been enabled to come to the plant, wherever it is, instead of the plant's being brought to the workers. Indeed, because of the growing problem of traffic congestion the location of large plants within a major city has become a rarity. . . .

The effect of these new technologies on the mind of man has, if anything, proved to be greater than their impact on industry structure itself. To "the early Victorian economists, marvelling over the mechanical efficiency of the monster textile mills," size came to be equated with efficiency. But they were also strong believers in competition, so the attribution of efficiency to size gave rise to a conceptual dilemma that moved even the most reserved of British economists to describe it as "vexatious" and as the "dilemma which has given rise to all this pother." . . .

Beginning with the new technologies of the Industrial Revolution, the veneration of size has come to take on the character of a mystique, and, like most mystiques, it has come to enjoy an independent life of its own. The danger is that the size mystique will continue to grip men's minds long after the circumstances that originally gave rise to it have disappeared. In this case the circumstances have not only disappeared but are being replaced by forces operating in the opposite direction—the new decentralizing technologies.

❖   ❖   ❖   ❖   ❖

John Jewkes (1902–   ) and others

THE SOURCES OF INVENTION[*]

This book shows in detail that small-scale operators have made many important inventions and continue to do so. It and parallel studies have placed the burden against the claim that only large-scale corporate "R&D" can create progress.

In the nineteenth century there was apparently a stronger link between science and invention and a much more closely knit society of men concerned with technical progress than is frequently supposed. The next obvious step is to try to ascertain what has been happening in the present century and, for this purpose, a study has been made of some sixty inventions which can reasonably be considered modern. In these case histories no attempt has been made to enter upon detailed technical matters; the purpose has been to identify the individual or individuals who appear to have made the greatest contribution to ultimate success, to determine the conditions under which the work was carried out and generally to try to isolate the factors which contributed to, or impeded, the advance. The information for each case was collected from printed records, which are plentiful but scattered and often conflicting; from inventors themselves wherever possible or those closely connected with them; or from scientists and technologists whose views and judgments should carry most authority.

It might at first sight be supposed that, by collecting facts and opinions in this way, it ought to be possible to assemble a body of knowledge sufficient to test any general statement about the circumstances under which modern inventions have arisen. Yet, although the evidence seems to support, often strongly, some general inferences, the element of personal judgment that has necessarily gone into them should not be overlooked.

The cases which were chosen for examination are listed below; from this list 50 of the most interesting histories are printed in Part II.

---

[*] John Jewkes and others, *The Sources of Invention* (New York: St. Martin's Press, rev. ed., 1969), excerpted from pp. 71–90 and 247–49. Jewkes is a leading conservative, classical liberal economist in Britain of long standing. The book includes detailed case studies of each invention.

1. Acrylic Fibres: Orlon, etc.
2. Air Conditioning
3. Automatic Transmissions
4. Bakelite
5. Ball-Point Pen
6. Catalytic Cracking of Petroleum
7. Cellophane
8. Cellophane Tape
9. Chromium Plating
10. Cinerama
11. Continuous Casting of Steel
12. Continuous Hot-Strip Rolling
13. Cotton Picker
14. Crease-Resisting Fabrics
15. Cyclotron
16. DDT
17. Diesel-Electric Railway Traction
18. Domestic Gas Refrigeration
19. Duco Lacquers
20. Electric Precipitation
21. Electron Microscope
22. Fluorescent Lighting
23. Freon Refrigerants
24. Gyro-Compass
25. Hardening of Liquid Fats
26. Helicopter
27. Insulin
28. Jet Engine
29. Kodachrome
30. Krilium
31. Long-Playing Record
32. Magnetic Recording
33. Methyl Methacrylate Polymers: Perspex, etc.
34. Modern Artificial Lighting
35. Neoprene
36. Nylon and Perlon
37. Penicillin
38. "Polaroid" Land Camera
39. Polyethylene
40. Power Steering
41. Quick Freezing
42. Radar
43. Radio
44. Rockets
45. Safety Razor
46. Self-Winding Wrist-Watch
47. Shell Molding
48. Silicones
49. Stainless Steels
50. Streptomycin
51. Sulzer Loom
52. Synthetic Detergents
53. Synthetic Light Polariser
54. Television
55. "Terylene" Polyester Fibre
56. Tetraethyl Lead
57. Titanium
58. Transistor
59. Tungsten Carbide
60. Xerography
61. Zip Fastener

All these cases can be held to belong to the twentieth century; the year 1900, that is to say, has been taken as the dividing line between old and modern inventions. It is, of course, arbitrary to slice history into neat sections in this way. But there are some reasons for adopting this division. The turn of the century witnessed the rapid growth of new technologies, especially in the chemical field; and it was then that the first large-scale industrial research laboratories, so often taken as a symbol of a new era in technology, began to make their appearance. A number of inventions originating in the second quarter of this century have been included.

The choice of what might be regarded as "important" inventions has also had to be largely arbitrary. . . .

Taken together the items chosen, with certain exceptions such as atomic energy and the electronic devices employed in "automation," seem to constitute a representative cross section of the technical progress of this century. . . .

Turning now to the sixty-one case histories. Each was an intricate skein which refused to shake out into simple lines and which tended to become the more complicated the more thoroughly it was examined. Some of the histories, indeed, appear more sharp cut than others. Firmer contours, for instance, can perhaps be given to the story in the case of nylon, penicillin, insulin, bakelite, titanium, the transistor, and the jet engine than in the case of stainless steel, the electron microscope, chromium plating, fluorescent lighting, the acrylic fibres, or radio. But, at every point, the contributions of even the most outstanding workers are clearly bound up with the speculations, reasoning, guesses and mistakes of others. . . .

From what has been said, it was not to be expected that all, or even most, of the cases would fall into neat and watertight groups. All that can be indicated, in each instance, is where the balance lies between autonomous and institutional research, between the work of research institutions of different types and different sizes, between the achievements of large teams and of individuals. . . .

More than one half of the cases can be ranked as individual invention in the sense that much of the pioneering work was carried through by men who were working on their own behalf without the backing of research institutions and usually with limited resources and assistance or, where the inventors were employed in institutions, these institutions were, as in the case of universities, of such a kind that the individuals were autonomous, free to follow their own ideas without hindrance. Into this group it seems proper to place:

Air Conditioning; Automatic Transmissions; Bakelite; Ball-Point Pen; Catalytic Cracking of Petroleum; Cellophane; Chromium Plating; Cinerama; Cotton Picker; Cyclotron; Domestic Gas Refrigeration; Electric Precipitation; Electron Microscope; Gyro-Compass; Hardening of Liquid Fats; Helicopter; Insulin; Jet Engine; Kodachrome; Magnetic Recording; Penicillin; "Polaroid" Land Camera; Power Steering; Quick Freezing; Radio; Safety Razor; Self-Winding Wrist-Watch; Streptomycin; Sulzer Loom; Synthetic Light Polarizer; Titanium; Xerography; Zip Fastener. . . .

The inventions, some of them of outstanding importance, which seem to have had their origin largely in the research laboratories of manufacturing companies are:

Acrylic Fibres; Cellophane Tape; Continuous Hot-Strip Rolling; Crease Resisting; DDT; Diesel-Electric Locomotive; Duco Lacquers; Fluorescent Lighting; Freon Refrigerants; Krilium; Methyl Methacrylate Polymers; Modern Artificial Lighting; Neoprene; Nylon; Polyethylene; Silicones; Synthetic Detergents; Television; Terylene; Tetraethyl Lead; Transistor.

This list can be subdivided in a number of ways. Some of the inventions have arisen in the research organisations of very large firms; others have been produced by much smaller firms. A few have been the outcome of "directed" research where the target has been set for the research workers by the firm; others have had an element of accident about them in the sense that important and unpredictable discoveries have been made in the course of basic research work where no specific problem had been set. In some instances the firm must take the whole of the credit, in others individual inventors have independently been in competition with the firms and have made important contributions. In some cases, although the discovery was made in a firm, it was not a firm in the industry where such a discovery might normally have been expected.

The list contains several important inventions emerging from firms much smaller than those mentioned above. Terylene was discovered by a small research group in the laboratory of a firm which had no direct interest in the production of new fibres. The continuous hot strip rolling of steel sheets was conceived of by an inventor who might well be considered an individual inventor and perfected in one of the smaller American steel companies. The crease-resisting process emerged from a medium-sized firm in the Lancashire cotton industry. Cellophane tape was the product of what was virtually a one-man effort in a then small American firm. The virtues of DDT were found by a Swiss chemical firm which, for that industry, was of modest dimensions. . . .

Even where inventions have arisen in the research laboratories of firms, the team responsible for it seems often to have been quite small. It is usually found that one outstanding figure has been surrounded by, and has stimulated, a few devoted colleagues in an intimate relation with his manner of thought and speculations. . . .

To sum up: A significant proportion of 20th-century inventions have not come from institutions where research will tend to be guided toward defined ends. There are many similarities between the present and the past century in the type of men who invent and the conditions under which they do so. Many of the twentieth-century stories could be transplanted to the nineteenth without appearing incongruous to the time or the circumstances; far too many, indeed, to render tenable the idea of a sharp and complete break between the periods. The novelty of this century appears to lie in the relative decline of invention of the individual type in certain industries, industries in which the large industrial research laboratory is most commonly to be found. . . .

The range of experiment into the best possible ways of utilising the funds of industry for enlisting the assistance of the more inventive brains of the community would be narrowed if manufacturing became more monopolistically organised, either in the sense that one firm or a few large firms dominated an industry or if all the firms within one industry frustrated competition by fixing common prices and associated such cartel arrangements with a common research centre. Yet here we are confronted with a modern, and by now widely held, opinion that monopoly encourages, and may even be a condition precedent to, innovation.

Some of the reasons for assuming that monopoly and progress are bound together are simply shallow thinking. Thus it may be said: this is the age of the large monopolistic or oligopolistic firm, it is also the great age of technical invention, therefore the two must be cause and effect. Big firms go to great pains to bring to the public notice the part they have played in technical advance and they rarely say anything about the work of others which preceded their own development efforts: and the public is disposed to accept the expurgated stories at their face value. It is symptomatic that in these days no firm ever boasts about its high profits, which are the real test of its achievement, but will vaunt its inventions.

There are, however, reasons which go deeper. One of these is the spurious parallel often drawn between monopoly powers as embodied in the patent right and the monopoly possessed by a firm as the only producer in its field of manufacture. Most people regard the patent as, on the whole, a beneficial institution; why, then, it may be argued, boggle at the logical extension of it in the form of industrial monopoly? They are, in fact, not the same kind of thing. The patent right is conferred upon the inventor after the invention has been made, a reward for services actually rendered; it is limited in time and conditioned in other ways. The privilege of industrial monopolising is claimed for services to be rendered in the form of more rapid innovation and is not dependent upon proof of delivery; nor is it limited in time or area.

It may be that the attempt to correlate monopoly and innovation is the latest manifestation of that ingrained belief in the virtues of size which has run through so much economic thinking about industrial organisation since the beginning of this century. In the earlier years it took the form of a claim that very large factories or firms would inevitably be more efficient in *manufacturing* than smaller, that there was an inner "logic" of this kind in the structure of industry. Less is now heard of this form of argument; it has largely been replaced by the conviction that research on a very large scale is the all-important advantage that the large firm or the large group of firms has over the smaller. Certain economists, who are themselves highly individualist by nature and would probably be horrified by the suggestion that they would do better work as members of a large team, confidently assert the merits of scale of operation in other branches of knowledge. But in earlier pages it has been suggested that the correlation between the size of research institutes and their inventive achievements is not clearly established.

It seems impossible to establish scientifically any final conclusion concerning the relation between monopoly and innovation. The arguments in favour of monopoly are not very good arguments, and they do not wholly fit the facts. On the other hand, the case made for competition is certainly not conclusive. In the last resort, those who have to frame public policy must judge whether competition, with its stimulus but its uncertainty, will be a more effective force than monopoly with its security but its absence of the driving force of rivalry.

Clair Wilcox (1898–1970)

COMPETITION AND MONOPOLY
IN AMERICAN INDUSTRY*

Summing up a deep and brilliant survey of U.S. markets in the 1930s, Wilcox found both monopoly and competition, plus strong forces which breed competition if they are not obstructed. Much the same is true today. But is the balance shifting?

The major categories of business activity may be divided roughly into two groups. The first of these groups includes agriculture, wholesale and retail distribution, personal service, building construction, and a miscellany of smaller trades. The second includes transportation, public utilities, manufacturing, mining, and finance. In the first group business enterprises are numerous, the typical enterprise is small, the degree of concentration is low, and prices are relatively flexible. In the second, enterprises are less numerous, the typical enterprise is larger, the degree of concentration is higher, and prices are relatively rigid. Among the industries in the first group, it is probable that competition is more usual than monopoly. Among those in the second, it is possible that monopoly is as usual as competition. . . .

In those industries which appear normally to be competitive, competition is constantly breaking down. Competitors continually seek to limit competition and to obtain for themselves some measure of monopoly power. They enter into agreements governing prices and production. They set up associations to enforce such agreements. They procure the

---

* Clair Wilcox, *Competition and Monopoly in American Industry*, Monograph 21, Temporary National Economic Committee (Washington, D.C.: 1940), excerpted from pages 307–15. Though the TNEC's vast studies came to naught, thanks to World War II, Wilcox went on to write *Public Policies Toward Business*, based on his grasp of real industrial conditions.

enactment of restrictive legislation. For a time they may succeed in bringing competition under control. But these arrangements, too, are constantly breaking down. Competitors violate the agreements. Associations lack the power to enforce them. New enterprises come into the field. Restrictive statutes are invalidated by the courts or repealed by the legislatures. The lines of control are repeatedly broken and reformed. The facts that describe the situation existing in such an industry today may not apply to the one in which it will find itself tomorrow.

In those industries that appear at any time to be monopolized, likewise, monopoly is constantly tending to break down. Human wants may be satisfied in many different ways. Shifts in consumer demand may rob the monopolist of his market. Invention may develop numerous substitutes for his product. . . .

The monopolist may suffer, too, from the lack of the stimulus to efficiency which is afforded by active competition. His originality may give way to inertia, his energy to lethargy. He may be inclined to play safe and let well enough alone. He is likely to devote more attention to the conservation of investment values than he does to the improvement of materials, machines, processes, and products. In such a situation vigorous competitors may arise to dispute his exclusive occupancy of the field. Government, finally, may intervene. Legislation may forbid practices that were once allowed. Enforcement may catch up with violations of the law. For one or another of these reasons, few of the great trusts that were formed near the turn of the century now possess anything approaching absolute monopoly power. But few of the fields that were then monopolized have become effectively competitive. Combinations have been dissolved, new competitors have arisen, and competition has been restored, only to give way to a succession of devices designed for the purpose of dividing markets and maintaining prices. Here, again, the lines of control are repeatedly broken and repeatedly reformed. . . .

In those industries where the nature of the product, the market, the supply of materials, and the technology of production is such as to encourage it, competition reasserts itself in the face of collusive agreements and restrictive legislation. Commodities that cannot be identified with their producers may be provided by many firms. Goods whose sale depends upon their style, articles of distinctive design, products that are made to order, and services that must be rendered in person, since they do not lend themselves to standardization, mechanization, or mass production, are likely to be sold by several establishments no one of which controls a major part of the supply. Markets that are large and those that are growing invite the entrance of numerous concerns. Markets so limited that a small scale of operations holds down the capital required for admission may also prove to be hospitable to newcomers. An abundance of materials and a wide dispersion of the sources of supply facilitate the erection of many plants. A technology that is simple presents no obstacle to new enterprises. Processes that depend upon highly skilled labor, those that resist mechanization, and those that permit a small establishment to produce at a low cost, since they do not necessitate a large investment in a single plant, favor the formation of a multitude of small concerns. Each of these factors contributes to the preservation of competitive conditions in a trade.

In other fields the characteristics of the product, the market, the supply of materials, and the technology of production are conducive to monopoly. A service whose adequate performance requires unified operation is better rendered by a single concern. Goods that can be standardized and manufactured in quantity lend themselves to mass production which, in turn, may sometimes lead to concentration of control. Products that can be associated with brand names may be removed, in some degree, from competition. The great width of markets for standardized, machine-made goods may enlarge the scale of production and thus increase the possibility of concentration. The narrowness of markets for the products of difficult and costly processes may deliver them into the hands of a few firms. Scarcity of materials and paucity of the sources of supply facilitate unified ownership. A technology which necessitates the acquisition of extensive properties, the construction of huge plants, and the installation of expensive equipment may prevent the establishment of new concerns. Ability to cut unit costs by increasing the scale of production may reduce the number of competitors. Heavy fixed charges and fear of the consequences of competitive warfare may inhibit competition on the basis of price.

But monopoly cannot be attributed to natural factors alone. It is the product of formal agreements and secret understandings; of combinations, intercorporate stockholdings, and interlocking directorates; of the ruthless employment of superior financial resources and bargaining power; of unequal representation before legislatures, courts, and administrative agencies; of the exclusion of competitors from markets, materials, and sources of investment funds; of restrictive contracts and discriminatory prices; of coercion, intimidation, and violence. It is the product, too, of institutions of property which permit private enterprises to take exclusive title to scarce resources; of franchises, permits, and licenses which confer upon their holders exclusive privileges in the employment of limited facilities and the performance of important services; of patents which grant to their owners the exclusive right to control the use of certain machines and processes and the manufacture and sale of certain goods; of tariffs which exclude foreign producers from domestic markets; of statutes which exclude out-of-state producers and ordinances which exclude out-of-town producers from local markets; of legislation which limits output, fixes minimum prices, and handicaps strong competitors; and of inadequate enforcement, over many years, of the laws that are designed to preserve competition. In nearly every case in which monopoly persists, it will be found that artificial factors are involved.

Walton H. Hamilton (1881–   )

THE POLITICS OF INDUSTRY*

In this lean and incisive book, Hamilton shows the main defects of using "the law" to "control" industry. (Compare his broad critique of administrative agencies with Cramton's and Nicholas Johnson's comments on regulation in Part IV.)

As the separation between industry and Government has been effected, each has acted and reacted upon the other so that the line between private and public has ceased to be sharply drawn. Yet the breakdown of separation has not brought union and has not stripped from either the business economy or the political state its own identity. They exist side by side as aspects of, rather than as distinct dominions within, a single culture. Each of the two is still in transition, the economy moving much faster than the state. The problem of their relationship needs an almost continuous restatement. . . . The problem is to make sure that the corporation, through the best possible series of compromises, will adequately serve all of the interests dependent upon it. It is imperative that no specific claim be exalted to the detriment of other interests, and that private interest be served within the limits of the general welfare. . . .

A resort to judicial process is an essential of a system of justice. But an attempt to amend or revise the structure and practices of an industry by resort to judicial process is a task fraught with uncertainty. The legal process was intended to do justice in the instant case, to end conflict between two belligerent individuals. It was never shaped for so stupendous and alien a task as causing the channels of commerce to run straight, or

---

* From *The Politics of Industry*, by Walton H. Hamilton. Copyright © 1957 by The Regents of The University of Michigan. Reprinted by permission of Alfred A. Knopf, Inc. Hamilton is an extraordinary critic, whom all students should read (for pleasure as well as content). Probably no expert today can match his brevity, wit, and sophistication about industrial policies.

fitting an industry out with a new and different set of practices. It is in its nature a bothersome and interminable technique beset with ceremonial and irrelevance. It is possessed of all the frailties which attach to the use of a procedure ill-fitted for the work at hand.

In antitrust we are meeting the great economy with a weapon of control designed for petty trade. . . .

It is little short of a fiction to state an antitrust case in terms of the innocence or guilt of a corporation and of its executives. The real question is whether its activities are moving toward objectives of which the law approves. To cloak the inquiry as a research for personal and corporate guilt is to blur the issue of holding a going concern within channels which serve the public interest.

In recent times a new mythology has been improvised as a weapon of resistance to antitrust. Its purpose has remained steadfast in spite of its hurried creation, its ephemeral materials, and its inner contradictions. It has invented a distinction between hard and soft competition; has assigned the former role to the Sherman and the latter to the Robinson-Patman Act; and has pitted them against each other. A realistic court has pointed out that price discriminations, which are offenses under the Robinson-Patman Act, are themselves the instruments by which a corporation may flaunt the Sherman Act.

A second myth is the invocation of the rhetoric of good faith. It is held to be fit and proper for a corporation to bestow a lower price upon a favored customer even though it cannot be justified by any showing of costs. The sanctioning proviso is that it is made in good faith to meet an equally low price of a competitor. Here no account is taken of the effect of discriminatory prices upon the process of competition or the health of the economy. For the administration of the antitrust laws, no more uncertain and evasive standard of judgment could be found than that of good faith.

A third myth is the creation of a concept of effective competition. It holds that the acts and things done by the accused are to be judged in terms of their ultimate and far-flung effects. Such a test blurs all standards of judgment, for a stream of business conduct is played upon by a multiplex of forces which it is impossible to isolate and evaluate. As a result, there is an invitation to the use of standards so uncertain as to provide an easy escape for even the most flagrant violation of the law.

*   *   *   *   *

The administrative agency is not the most brilliant of political inventions. In the last several years a library of findings and orders attest the activities of the several agencies. Yet to this body of fact no searching analysis in functional terms has as yet been brought. Although an administrative agency is not neatly adapted to its regulatory office and has not been tailored to the specific demands of diverse public policies, its employment has become almost general.

* * * * *

The task of the administrative agency is to correct the lapses of management from public duty and to direct the stream of executive conduct to legitimate goals. In general, its work is in the nature of a review. It usually does not intrude until management has acted. Yet it brings to its task a procedure which has the decorous characteristics of a process at law. The course of business cannot be arrested until challenged decisions are referred to the administrative agency, and the correctives finally arrived at cannot be carried back through time to be inserted at the points where they belong. The two processes are completely out of step, and the difference in tempo is a shortcoming which is ever present. It thus happens that a course of conduct is well on its way, or a policy of the regulated has come to be established, before the question of its validity is entertained by the agency of Government.

* * * * *

In practice, the initiative in most such matters has come to be left to the companies which are being regulated. . . . In these and like cases the prescribed area of regulation has been narrowed by the failure of administrative bodies to assert and maintain dominion. As a result, an unexpected paradox emerges. As the Congress becomes increasingly sensitive to the need for more pervasive controls and acts upon this belief, the agencies themselves tend to allow areas of their domains to lie fallow.

Yet such surrender does not take from the commission the opportunity to be eternally busy. It invites and entertains complaints from parties which have been, or think they have been, injured by the activities or policies of the regulated concerns. It soon discovers that the number of complaints is legion, far in excess of the time, patience, and receptivity to printed word and verbal barrage of even the most Job-like of officials.

The result is that the commission on all its levels becomes busy, in fact overbusy, but largely with detailed problems of the moment, problems which have been raised by complaining parties. It has adequate legal authority to raise questions on its own motion, but amid all the bustle of everyday activity there is very little leisure in which to do it. The larger questions of holding the regulated industry to its function, of improving its capacity to serve the public, of looking to the hazards ahead and guarding against them, and of making of it a more effective instrument of the general welfare are neglected. Matters of policy get immersed in the quagmire of detail. The agency fails to direct the activities of the industry to public objectives, and the industry is left to effect for itself such structure and practices as serve its purpose.

Richard A. Posner (1937–   )

LAW ENFORCEMENT*

Agencies often grow preoccupied with small cases, letting the big ones slide. This may be rational bureaucratic strategy and even socially efficient, Posner urges. Is he correct?

§ 26.2. *Choice of cases by the public agency.* The process by which a law enforcement agency decides where to concentrate its resources is of great interest in view of the monopoly position in law enforcement that public agencies so frequently occupy. We explore the process here on the assumption that the agency acts as a rational maximizer, comparing expected returns and expected costs with alternative uses of its resources. . . .

Discussions of the allocation of resources within public agencies typically emphasize the importance of the agency's devoting its major resources to the most important cases. Agencies are commonly lambasted for devoting disproportionate resources to trivial cases. Economic analysis suggests that this type of criticism is superficial. The importance of the case—the stakes to the agency of a successful outcome—is only one criterion of the efficient allocation of agency resources and it is frequently dominated by others.

The expected utility of a case to the agency is the stakes, if it prevails, discounted (multiplied) by the probability that it will prevail. To simplify the analysis, we will assume initially that the agency has just two cases it is interested in, A and B, and the decision it must make is how to allocate a fixed budget between them. A is the more important case. If the agency wins it, the agency's utility will increase by 100 units; a victory in B is worth only 50 units. A loss in either case is worth zero.

Since the probability of a successful outcome, and hence the expected utility, is in both cases a function in part of how much the agency spends on prosecution, it is tempting to suggest that the agency devote all or most of its resources to trying to win A. But this would be correct only

---

* Richard A. Posner, *Economic Analysis of Law* (Boston: Little, Brown, 1973), pp. 379–83. Posner is a leading, perceptive "Chicago School" critic of harmful policies. He has proposed sharp revisions in antitrust and regulation. A member of a Bar Association study group on the FTC in 1969, he recommended abolition. On the staff of the Solicitor General's Office in 1965–67, he argued the Procter & Gamble-Clorox and other cases before the Supreme Court.

if the agency's outlays were the *only* factor affecting the probability of the outcome in either case, and plainly they are not. The defendant's outlays are critical, as is the relative effectiveness of the agency's and the defendant's outlays in influencing the outcome. Let us examine these two factors more closely.

(1) If the case is very important to the defendant, then, other things being equal, he will spend a large amount on its defense. The more he spends, either the less effective the agency's outlays will be in influencing the outcome in its favor or the more the agency itself will spend in order to neutralize the defendant's expenditures. In either event the expected utility of the case to the agency, net of its costs of prosecution, will be smaller. Thus, other things being equal, the rational maximizing agency will prefer to invest resources in a case that is relatively unimportant to the defendant. To be sure, if the stakes to plaintiff and defendant were always the same in a case, the reduction in cost to the agency from bringing a case that was unimportant to the defendant would be offset by the reduction in the agency's expected utility due to the unimportance of the outcome to it. But the stakes of the parties often diverge. A case may be important to the agency but not to the defendant because, although the monetary stakes—which are all the defendant cares about—are small, the case, if won by the agency, will constitute a useful precedent that will increase the effectiveness of its litigation outlays in future cases and deter some future violations altogether. Yet the case may seem trivial to observers who ignore its precedent-setting significance.

(2) If outcome were a function solely of the parties' litigation expenditures, whenever they spent the same amount on the case the probability of the agency's winning would be 50 percent. But we know that agencies win on average a good deal more often than 50 percent of the time and that defendants on average probably spend more per case than agencies. Plainly, outcome also depends on the relative skill and experience of counsel, the state of the precedents, and how the law allocates the burdens of production and persuasion between the parties. Other things being equal, the agency will prefer to bring cases in which its expenditures are relatively more effective than the defendant's, especially since the less effective the defendant's expenditures are the less he will spend on the litigation; this will increase the impact of the agency's outlays still further.

Once it is accepted that the probability of the agency's prevailing varies across cases, it becomes easy to show that the agency may prefer the easier case to the harder even if the easier case is substantially less important to it. Suppose that, starting from an initial allocation of equal resources to cases A and B, the agency can increase the probability of prevailing in A from 60 to 65 percent by spending $1,000 more on A and $1,000 less on B and that this reduces the probability of its prevailing in B from, say, 80 percent to 70 percent. Suppose further that the agency can increase the probability of prevailing in B from 80 percent to 95 percent by spending $1,000 more on B and $1,000 less on A and that this reduces the probability of its prevailing in A from 60 to 55 percent. The expected utility generated by its initial allocation was $100 \times .60 + 50 \times .80$, or 100. Its expected utility from reallocating $1,000 from B to A would be $100 \times .65 + 50 \times .70$, or 100. But its expected utility from reallocating $1,000 from A to B—the big case to the small one—would be $100 \times .55 + 50 \times .95$, or 102.5, which is greater than under the alternative allocations.

If we enrich our simple model, the result is to confirm that the rational maximizing agency will often exhibit a strong, and perfectly sensible, preference for small cases. We assumed that the number of cases brought by the agency was a given; but number of cases brought, like expenditure per case, is one of the agency's choice variables. As an agency brings more and more cases of a particular type, its total expected utility will rise, but probably at a diminishing rate. It becomes more difficult to find cases that are easy to win. The probability of success therefore declines. The higher the rate at which the probability of success declines with the number of cases brought, the fewer cases will be brought, other things being equal. Probably the rate will be higher in classes of relatively important cases than in classes of relatively unimportant cases. The universe of minor violations is ordinarily larger than the universe of major ones: one does not "run out" of cases that are easy to win so soon.

We also assumed that the budget of the agency was independent of its performance. This is clearly wrong: the agency that won no cases one year could expect a reduction in its appropriation the next. The legislature will withhold appropriations when it thinks the agency is failing to use its resources efficiently and we have seen that an exclusive concentration on large cases could be an inefficient use of resources.

Finally, we ignored settlements, although most criminal and administrative as well as most ordinary civil cases are settled rather than litigated. This fact is likely to make small cases even more attractive to the agency. A defendant will not contest a case if the cost of his defense would exceed his stakes in the case. Such cases are therefore easy for the plaintiff to win unless the plaintiff's stakes are also no greater than his costs, in which event the plaintiff's threat to sue (and thereby compel the defendant to incur litigation costs) will not be credible. If the stakes of the parties are not equal, and the stakes to the plaintiff are greater than his litigation expenses but the defendant's stakes are less than the defendant's litigation expenses, the plaintiff should be able, at trivial cost, to induce the defendant to capitulate. This will be a class of small cases since the defendant's stakes must be smaller than his litigation costs. (The plaintiff's stakes must be larger but presumably the disparity is normally confined within a fairly narrow range.) Here then is another reason why we would expect to find the rational maximizing agency concentrating a seemingly disproportionate amount of resources on small cases. In sum, the agency that took its critics' advice to "reorder its priorities" by allocating a larger part of its resources to big cases would often experience diminished effectiveness.

George J. Stigler (1911–   )

THE THEORY OF ECONOMIC REGULATION*

Stigler analyzes the proposition that private interests use policy perhaps more than policy controls private interests. To get "good" regulation, regulators must be given the right kind of incentives. These are presently lacking, he argues.

The state—the machinery and power of the state—is a potential resource or threat to every industry in the society. With its power to prohibit or compel, to take or give money, the state can and does selectively help or hurt a vast number of industries. That political juggernaut, the petroleum industry, is an immense consumer of political benefits, and simultaneously the underwriters of marine insurance have their more modest repast. The central tasks of the theory of economic regulation are to explain who will receive the benefits or burdens of regulation, what form regulation will take, and the effects of regulation upon the allocation of resources.

Regulation may be actively sought by an industry, or it may be thrust upon it. A central thesis of this paper is that, as a rule, regulation is acquired by the industry and is designed and operated primarily for its benefit. There are regulations whose net effects upon the regulated industry are undeniably onerous; a simple example is the differentially heavy taxation of the industry's product (whiskey, playing cards). These onerous regulations, however, are exceptional and can be explained by

* Copyright 1971, American Telephone and Telegraph Company, 195 Broadway, New York, New York 10007. Reprinted with permission from *The Bell Journal of Economics and Management Science*. A leading theorist, Stigler originated the effort to test the "real" effects of regulation, an effort which has flowered at Chicago into a vigorous cottage industry. He is Walgreen Professor at the University of Chicago and a former President of the American Economic Association.

the same theory that explains beneficial (we may call it "acquired") regulation.

Two main alternative views of the regulation of industry are widely held. The first is that regulation is instituted primarily for the protection and benefit of the public at large or some large subclass of the public. In this view, the regulations which injure the public—as when the oil import quotas increase the cost of petroleum products to America by $5 billion or more a year—are costs of some social goal (here, national defense) or, occasionally, perversions of the regulatory philosophy. The second view is essentially that the political process defies rational explanation: "politics" is an imponderable, a constantly and unpredictably shifting mixture of forces of the most diverse nature, comprehending acts of great moral virtue (the emancipation of slaves) and of the most vulgar venality (the congressman feathering his own nest).

❋ ❋ ❋ ❋ ❋

This question, why does an industry solicit the coercive powers of the state rather than its cash, is offered only to illustrate the approach of the present paper. We assume that political systems are rationally devised and rationally employed, which is to say that they are appropriate instruments for the fulfillment of desires of members of the society. This is not to say that the state will serve any person's concept of the public interest: indeed the problem of regulation is the problem of discovering when and why an industry (or other group of like-minded people) is able to use the state for its purposes, or is singled out by the state to be used for alien purposes.

The state has one basic resource which in pure principle is not shared with even the mightiest of its citizens: the power to coerce. The state can seize money by the only method which is permitted by the laws of a civilized society, by taxation. The state can ordain the physical movements of resources and the economic decisions of households and firms without their consent. These powers provide the possibilities for the utilization of the state by an industry to increase its profitability. The main policies which an industry (or occupation) may seek of the state are four.

The most obvious contribution that a group may seek of the government is a direct subsidy of money. The domestic airlines received "air mail" subsidies (even if they did not carry mail) of $1.5 billion through 1968. The merchant marine has received construction and operation subsidies reaching almost $3 billion since World War II. The education industry has long shown a masterful skill in obtaining public funds: for example, universities and colleges have received federal funds exceeding $3 billion annually in recent years, as well as subsidized loans for dormitories and other construction. The veterans of wars have often received direct cash bonuses.

*   *   *   *   *

We have already sketched the main explanation for the fact that an industry with power to obtain governmental favors usually does not use this power to get money: unless the list of beneficiaries can be limited by an acceptable device, whatever amount of subsidies the industry can obtain will be dissipated among a growing number of rivals. The airlines quickly moved away from competitive bidding for air mail contracts to avoid this problem. On the other hand, the premier universities have not devised a method of excluding other claimants for research funds, and in the long run they will receive much-reduced shares of federal research monies.

The second major public resource commonly sought by an industry is control over entry by new rivals. There is considerable, not to say excessive, discussion in economic literature of the rise of peculiar price policies (limit prices), vertical integration, and similar devices to retard the rate of entry of new firms into oligopolistic industries. Such devices are vastly less efficacious (economical) than the certificate of convenience and necessity (which includes, of course, the import and production quotas of the oil and tobacco industries).

*   *   *   *   *

We propose the general hypothesis: every industry or occupation that has enough political power to utilize the state will seek to control entry. In addition, the regulatory policy will often be so fashioned as to retard the rate of growth of new firms. For example, no new savings and loan company may pay a dividend rate higher than that prevailing in the community in its endeavors to attract deposits. The power to limit selling expenses of mutual funds, which is soon to be conferred upon the Securities and Exchange Commission, will serve to limit the growth of small mutual funds and hence reduce the sales costs of large funds.

*   *   *   *   *

A third general set of powers of the state which will be sought by the industry are those which affect substitutes and complements. Crudely put, the butter producers wish to suppress margarine and encourage the production of bread. The airline industry actively supports the federal subsidies to airports; the building trade unions have opposed labor-saving materials through building codes. We shall examine shortly a specific case of inter-industry competition in transportation.

The fourth class of public policies sought by an industry is directed to price-fixing. Even the industry that has achieved entry control will often want price controls administered by a body with coercive powers. If the number of firms in the regulated industry is even moderately large, price discrimination will be difficult to maintain in the absence of public support. The prohibition of interest on demand deposits, which is probably effective in preventing interest payments to most non-business depositors, is a case in point. Where there are no diseconomies of large scale for the individual firm (e.g., a motor trucking firm can add trucks under a given license as common carrier), price control is essential to achieve more than competitive rates of return.

＊　＊　＊　＊　＊

Conclusion

The idealistic view of public regulation is deeply imbedded in professional economic thought. So many economists, for example, have denounced the ICC for its pro-railroad policies that this has become a cliché of the literature. This criticism seems to me exactly as appropriate as a criticism of the Great Atlantic and Pacific Tea Company for selling groceries, or as a criticism of a politician for currying popular support. The fundamental vice of such criticism is that it misdirects attention: it suggests that the way to get an ICC which is not subservient to the carriers is to preach to the commissioners or to the people who appoint the commissioners. The only way to get a different commission would be to change the political support for the Commission, and reward commissioners on a basis unrelated to their services to the carriers.

Until the basic logic of political life is developed, reformers will be ill-equipped to use the state for their reforms, and victims of the pervasive use of the state's support of special groups will be helpless to protect themselves. Economists should quickly establish the license to practice on the rational theory of political behavior.

I. Questions for Review: Basic Issues of Markets and Policies

What does "efficient allocation under perfect competition" mean, in analytical terms?

Contrast efficiency in a system of competitive market reaching equilibrium with the disequilibrium-monopoly sequence envisaged by Schumpeter. Does either of them best describe all or part of the U.S. economy?

What are the main elements of market structure? How do we know this?

Why is the distinction between loose and tight oligopoly likely to be an important one?

In what manner might market power make it more difficult to achieve full employment in the entire economy?

In what manner might market power make the distribution of economic rewards less "equitable"?

How may imperfections in financial markets tend to increase market power in other markets?

What causes barriers to entry?

Why is it difficult to evaluate the effects of market power on (1) profitability and (2) technological change?

How can you distinguish between pecuniary and technical scale economies (*a*) in theory and (*b*) in fact?

There are few industrial markets in which horizontal pure monopoly (one firm controlling all) has been achieved and maintained. Analyse possible reasons (*other* than the antitrust laws) for this lack of monopoly, which is surprising in light of the enormous rewards for monopolizing.

Apex, Inc., controls 100 percent of the U.S. production of apexes. Under what conditions might it be found that Apex, though a "monopolist," doesn't have much *market power*?

What is X-inefficiency? Is it exclusively an effect of high market shares?

"Concentration ratios are useful in describing industries, but they tell little about how the leading firms will behave." Do you agree? Explain.

If firms are sales maximizers, what main implications follow for behavior in (*a*) oligopolies and (*b*) dominant-firm cases?

"Dominant firms" normally can choose among a range of pricing strategies. Analyse the proposition that "dominant firms decline," in light of theory and of evidence.

Firm A increases its market share from 30 to 40 percent. Has the market power of Firm A, and of the industry, risen?

"The stock market keeps managers—even in the biggest monopolies—on a treadmill." Explain if and how this might be so.

Consider the following facts:

	Industry X	Industry Y
Concentration (4-firm)	80	50
Entry barriers	Low	High
Profit rate on equity	25%	20%
Internal efficiency of firms	Moderate	Poor
Growth rate per year	5%	10%
New products per year	5	2

Which industry is more competitive? Which has the better performance?

Industry X has a national Census concentration ratio of 14, regional concentration ratios of 50, 48, 63, and 98 in four regions, and imports at 30 percent of U.S. production. What other *kinds* of information would you need in order to measure the true degree of concentration in such an industry?

An industry has 999 firms, but the 8 leading firms have market shares of 21, 17, 13, 10, 7, 5, 4, and 3 percent respectively. Is the structure of this industry competitive?

In industry A there are hundreds of equally small competitors. In industry B, there are just two firms with 50 percent each. Give at least three reasons (or "determinants") which might explain such great differences in structure.

The following are local markets which you face. For each one, estimate whether it is a monopoly, tight oligopoly, or loose oligopoly. Explain as fully as you can. *(a)* Movies, *(b)* Banking, *(c)* Newspapers, *(d)* Textbooks, *(e)* Sports Events.

"The rate of profit on sales in the gazooka industry is only 2.3 percent. This proves that the industry is extremely competitive." Do you agree?

What is "loose oligopoly"? Is it the prevalent, "natural" structure of markets?

Does tight oligopoly structure tend to persist, once it occurs? What are the main factors tending to perpetuate it? What tends to erode it?

Would you expect concentration to be lower—industry by industry—in Great Britain than in the United States? Why?

How does market structure in U.S. industries compare with that in industrial economies abroad?

"The rising share of the largest firms in the total economy means that market power is increasing." Is this correct?

Briefly summarize what the evidence about economies of scale shows about the possible differences between optimum structure and natural structure in the broad range of U.S. industries. Illustrate with facts from three or four industries, if you can.

If both large and small firms survive in an industry, does this show that both sizes of firms are within the range of "optimum size"?

It is often said that technological trends increasingly favor large scale, and that is why industrial concentration is rising. Do you agree with all or part of this?

Does market power foster technological progress? Be very precise in defining the possible relationships.

"The critical policy question for antitrust is the rate at which market power naturally fades away." Do you agree?

What are the main *defects* of benefit-cost analysis as a basis for choosing policies toward market power?

How does precedent multiply the yields from any one case?

What main kinds of costs might policy actions impose?

Why is the burden of proof often critical in policy choices?

Part II

❧

POLICIES TO PROMOTE COMPETITION

"Antitrust" includes a range of specific tools, agencies, cases, and precedents, some working at cross-purposes with others. One must first understand the laws and agencies, and why they usually operate below potential. Then one can digest the cases and try to appraise what the effects of it all may have been. And then one can form sensible judgments about the various proposals for "reforming" or extending antitrust that have recently proliferated. These readings follow that sequence of topics.

Walton H. Hamilton (1881–   ) and
Irene Till (1906–   )

ANTITRUST IN ACTION*

By 1940 it was widely argued that the Sherman Act was a weak law, enforced only by a corporal's guard. Why had this happened? Has it continued?

THE CHARTER OF FREEDOM
Scruples and the Constitution

The Sherman Act is a weapon of policy from another age. As the eighties became the nineties, the Nation was becoming uncomfortably conscious of an industrial revolution. Although dinky little railways were a commonplace, the trunk line was still a novelty. The land was dotted with factories using simple mechanical processes; yet chemistry and biology had not been subdued into technologies and electricity had just ceased to be a toy. The telephone was still a novelty; the electric light had just passed its eleventh birthday; the wonders that lie within the vacuum tube were still to be explored. The automobile was a rather impious hope; the airplane, an adventurous flight in wishful thinking. The motion picture and the radio broadcast were as yet hardly tangible enough to be subjects of fancy. Agriculture, once the foundation of national wealth, was being driven back country. Petty trade had been forced to make a place beside itself for a big business which seemed to masses of the people to be strange, gigantic, powerful.

The unruly times offered opportunity to the swashbuckling captains of industry, whose ways were direct, ruthless, and not yet covered over by the surface amenities of a later age. In sugar, nails, tobacco, copper, jute, cordage, borax, slate pencils, oilcloth, gutta percha, barbed fence wire, castor oil they bluntly staked out their feudal domains. The little man caught in a squeeze play—the independent crowded to the wall by "the

---

* Walton H. Hamilton and Irene Till, *Antitrust in Action*, Monograph No. 16, Temporary National Economic Committee (Washington, D.C.: U.S. Government Printing Office, 1941), excerpted from pages 5–11 and 23–26. Till has worked for several public units promoting competition (see also her analysis of drugs, below).

Octopus"—the farmer selling his wheat, corn, or tobacco under the tyranny of a market he did not understand—the craftsman stripped of his trade by the machine—the consumer forced to take the ware at an artificial price or go without—here were dramatic episodes. Industry was in the clutch of radical forces—and of iniquity. It was a period in which the ordinary man was confused, disturbed, resentful.

Of this confusion, disturbance, resentment, Congress became aware. It was led by protest and petition to the necessity of doing something about it. Yet a number of obstacles blurred the vision and arrested the action of the Fifty-first Congress. At the time there had been little experience with administration. The regulatory commission was almost unknown. The Interstate Commerce Commission, but 3 years old, had not yet found its footing; the dominant purpose behind it was not to regulate the railroads but to put an end to rebates and discriminations upon which favored shippers thrived. Some of the State commissions were a bit older, but they had little to offer in the way of usage, device, invention. Just as little was known about industry, whose curious ways had not yet become a subject of detailed study; a speculative account of how competition was supposed to work was enough. Since, barring collusion, the general theory was applicable to any ware of trade, the bewildering variety of industrial activity was hardly suspected. . . .

In direct attack a great many bills were introduced. In Senate and House Member after Member, with his ear to the ground and his head full of scruples, put on paper his own proposal for banning monopoly from the land. As their authors were unlike in courage, vision, knowledge, forthrightness, so did the bills differ in orbit of influence, range of remedy, agency of enforcement, making life mildly uncomfortable or distinctly disagreeable for enemies to the public good. Directness went straight to the mark with prison sentences for "malefactors of great wealth"; decorum countered with the proposal of a constitutional amendment to ease the way for "a strong measure." Nor could "the thumbscrew of monopoly" be considered as a question apart. As a possible "mother of trusts," at least to free-trade Senators, the protective tariff became a new-born iniquity. Thrusts at scarce money, at high money, at the money trust, at high finance, were constantly in evidence. The urge to trust busting went forward to overtones of the currency, investment banking, the tariff, options in grain, the sins of the other party. . . .

Back to the Common Law

As a creature of such currents of thought the statute took shape. The original Sherman bill was a very tentative proposal. It professed to outlaw all arrangements which prevented "full and free competition," to open the Federal courts to suits by parties damnified by such agreements, to provide for the forfeiture of the charter of the offending corporation. Its terms were uncertain, it invited constitutional attack, its author was timid in its defense. Twice it was rewritten by the Committee on Finance; yet it remained the target for the kind of shafts which the statesmen of that generation loved to hurl. The author, confused, yielding, anxious to placate, time after time would concede objection and accept amendment. As thus from many desks rather incongruous bits came into place, members became quite uncertain as to the objective and content of the proposed measure. After running the gauntlet of "the habitudes of the lawyer," the bill retained its legal ban upon interference with competition and its right of private suit for double the amount of damages and costs. As for implementation, a clause—really a broad sheet of paper whereon judges might freely write—gave to the circuit courts of the United States jurisdiction over "all suits of a civil nature at common law or in equity" and authority to "issue all remedial process, orders or writs proper or necessary to enforce its provisions." A postscript granted a limited exception to trade unions in their resort to collective action to shorten hours and to raise wages, and to farmers' cooperatives in the sale of their own products.

But a posse of Senators on the warpath was not enthusiastic about so lukewarm a measure. Nor were statesmen from the Grain Belt content to let slip the opportunity to have the law on processors and speculators. . . .

[Various strengthening changes were made.]

Step by step all seemed right. Yet somehow the whole of the resolve seemed different from the sum of the motions. A majority had gone along, yet only a straggling of supporters remained faithful to the completed work. Once—and then again—a motion had been made to recommit the bill, not to the Finance Committee whence in lean form it had come, but to the Judiciary Committee. On former occasions the proposal "to deliver the child for nurture to persons who have most interest in its death" had been voted down and for the time the measure was saved from "this great mausoleum of senatorial literature." Now for the third time the motion for reference was put and carried; and the Judiciary Committee—stung by criticism or avid to exploit an opportunity—within 6 days returned to the Senate a bill with the same caption. The committee had scrapped all that had been sent along; and, with Senator Hoar, of Massachusetts, as draftsman, had written its own law.

The new bill simply recited for "commerce among the several States," the rule of the common law against restraint of trade. This recitation was deemed necessary for it was believed that there was no "Federal common law." A statute was regarded as necessary to bring the body of ancient usage within reach of the United States courts. The statement was framed in familiar legal symbols, not in the language of industry or the idiom of public policy. The prohibitions, which had grown out of the experience with petty trade, were taken over intact. . . .

After the briefest of discussions the Senate adopted the Hoar bill. Its sponsors were apologetic for the very little distance the statute went; but the zeal for argument had long since been spent. It was accepted as a "first installment," presently to be amended as experience pointed the way. In the House a time limit forced an early vote; leave to print crowded the inaudible debate from the floor into the Congressional Record. A single amendment led to a struggle in conference and was eventually abandoned; the text was left intact. There was no enthusiasm; but here was something at least for the people back home—and the congressional campaign was warming up. Besides there were matters of real consequence, such as the McKinley Tariff Act, which wanted legislative attention. So, with only a single vote in dissent—though in both Houses Members answered "present" or were conveniently absent—on the 2d of July 1890, the bill became the law of the land. It is to this day strangely enough called the Sherman Act—for no better reason, according to its author, than that Senator Sherman had nothing to do with it whatever.

The Intent—If Any—Of Congress

A great deal has been said about the purpose of Congress in passing the act. At best legislative intent is an evasive thing. It is wrapped in the conditions, the problems, the attitudes, the very atmosphere of an era that is gone. But aside from saying that the act reflects its date, there is little more in the way of concretion to recite. Instead, as a creation of the process of legislation, the statute bears the confused marks of its origin. . . .

In a search for intent the record has been thumbed through with meticulous care and to little purpose. The debates exhibit heat, passion, righteous indignation against the devil of monopoly. The bills proposed went much farther than the Hoar Act. In learned books and before learned judges, passage after passage has been cited to prove what the framers did—and did not—have in mind. The great bother is that the bill which was arduously debated was never passed, and that the bill which was passed was never really discussed. The House, in fact, never had a chance at the measure which provoked discussion.

A ruse, whose cleverness only legislative experts can appreciate, drove a barrier between debate and eventual statute. The matter went to a committee notoriously hostile to the legislation. The committee turned a deaf ear to all that the Senate had said and done and went its own way. Intent, therefore, forsakes the Congressional Record for the capacious recesses of that flexible corpus called the common law. When the bill was reported back the session was late, interest had died, apathy ruled. Yet the statute —untouched except for the Miller-Tydings amendment of 1937—has for 50 years remained the basic act for the control of American industry.

The Fifty-first Congress sensed the rush of an oncoming industrialism. Its task, facing the future, was to create a barrier against shock, a road to order, a guaranty of justice. In debate it laid bare evils within the emerging national economy, but could bring itself to do something about it only in a babble of voices. Except for words, it made no thrust at present dangers; it came to no grip with the trends of the times; it made no attempt to chart a course for American industry. When the voters would no longer tolerate delay, it acted. When the need was to shape the future, it looked to the past. On the eve of the greatest of industrial revolutions, the National Government was fitted out with a weapon forged to meet the problems of petty trade. Out of an inability of Congress to face the economic problems of its day the "charter of freedom" for American industry was born.

BIG ACT LITTLE STICK
The Shortage of Funds

A statute lives by appropriations—and from the first the demands of Antitrust have fallen upon the deaf ear of Congress. Not until its fiftieth year was as much as $1,000,000 appropriated to the purposes of the Sherman Act. For more than a decade no separate staff was charged with its enforcement; and when in 1903 Antitrust became a division in the Department of Justice, it was given only half a million dollars, to be expended at the rate of $100,000 a year over a period of 5 years. Between 1908 and 1935 the appropriation varied between $100,000 and $300,000. In 1936 the figure was increased to $435,000; in 1939, to about $800,000, and for the fiscal years of 1940 and 1941 to an all-high of $1,300,000 and $1,325,000.

It is obvious that the staff has been inadequate to police against restraint the whole of American business. In the famous trust-busting campaign of Theodore Roosevelt, the average number of attorneys in active service was 5. In the Wilson administration, when the World War had caused prices to skyrocket, the number had risen to 18. In the twenties, when the corporation was evolved into an intricate and evasive structure, and merger, amalgamation, integration, holding company was the order of the day, the number engaged did not exceed 25. Not until 1938 were as many as 50 lawyers actually employed; not until 1939 did professional personnel reach 200 attorneys and a half dozen economists.

For almost its whole life Antitrust has been a kind of a corporal's guard —a small section tucked away in the intricacies of a Government department. . . . The contrast between the miniature staff on duty and the enormity of the job to be done speaks for itself. As well attempt to maintain law and order in Boston, Philadelphia, or San Francisco with the bold police force of Oshkosh or Annapolis.

. . . In fixing its appropriations, year by year, Congress customarily uses as its standard the sums allotted in previous years. Legislative custom has it that this year's appropriation is about right. The sum is a norm, with every presumption in its favor; the burden of proof is upon the demand for more money. Thus ancient thought, frozen into a figure, stands as an obstacle against the appropriation which current knowledge and a later understanding suggest.

But the folkways of the Budget cannot fully account for the neglect. The trickle of funds is symptom as well as fact and cause. In the hurly-burly of industrial movement there has been little conscious appreciation of the character and magnitude of the task Antitrust has to perform. The public can understand a chivalrous adventure in trust-busting in the grand manner. And when a champion of the people rides into the wind, seeks out the octopus in his lair, and brings home the scalp of a trust, it applauds. But it has little appreciation of the detailed, day-by-day drudgery essential to the assertion of the public interest in everyday business. With the shift from market to management, authority can be met only with authority. Thus the safeguarding of the public interest in business becomes a continuous and watchful task. In Antitrust old style, heroic victories were now and then to be won upon the open field. In Antitrust new style, a detail of pedestrian work must be done day by day and a multitude of decisions be made back of the line.

The cause of Antitrust lacks that massed support which causes congressional purse strings to loosen. Its appeal is greatest to the man on the outside who wants to barge in on a trade and needs its help in making his way. It is least to persons who, already established, are wary of interference. The support of labor is not easily enlisted. In many industries it has a vested interest in the maintenance of restraints; the power of its leaders depends upon the maintenance of things as they are. It is more prone to view the Sherman Act as a weapon to be used against the trade-union than as an instrument of a better living. The group of men—and women—of good will, who busy themselves more than most over public affairs, are well disposed; but to them Antitrust is only one among many worthy causes to which fitfully they give their attention. A general opinion may favor all the money needed to put teeth into the act; and interested groups may be lukewarm or even hostile to appropriations. But, under our Government, the pressure of the many is difficult. It is the few who understand how to concentrate their pressure at the focal points that count.

The act, throughout the political community, is held in least favor where power and influence are greatest. A rather instinctive suspicion of Antitrust prevails in high industrial quarters. As a symbol the Sherman Act is grand. It sets down a lofty profession of economic faith; it proclaims industry to be the instrument of the common good; it preached the philosophy which makes the market the rightful agency of business control. The statute holds enough of the raw material of thought, out of which the creed of laissez-faire was formulated, to have high ceremonial value in financial circles. It serves its function best, however, as a generality, left in Olympian aloofness, unsullied by contact with mundane affairs. As a control which might do active duty in his own industry, the ordinary man of affairs views it as suspect. As a scheme of regulation it moves toward diffusion of power and runs directly against the trend toward concentration.

The leanness of the budget has left its lines on the national economy. In 1890 free competition as the way of order for industry was not seriously questioned. Conformity to this standard was an obvious expression of public policy. In the years to come the pattern of industry was to be beaten upon by a continuous industrial revolution; turbulent forces were at large which the law said should be subdued. Yet at no time did Congress choose to do more than equip a few knights to go forth to romantic combat. The negligent oversight under which industry was left to its own devices has confused the problem and multiplied the modern task of Antitrust. Industry might once have been held to its competitive norms; it is now too late to restore the primitive design. The recession of the market, as an instrument of industrial control, has obscured the norms of reference provided by the common law. The situation was allowed to get out of hand before the agency was equipped for its task. Antitrust has never been accorded its chance.

Robert H. Bork (1929–   )

VERTICAL INTEGRATION AND THE SHERMAN ACT: THE LEGAL HISTORY OF AN ECONOMIC MISCONCEPTION*

Bork here assembles the case that vertical mergers do not—cannot—reduce competition. Since they may also yield large economies, Bork maintains that antitrust should keep hands off all vertical mergers. Only horizontal factors or imperfect capital markets create monopoly; vertical integration cannot extend it.

The utility of the vertical-integration concept for antitrust law seems a much easier subject than is the law that has been built around that concept. Yet there is hardly more agreement about the one than the other. It is the

* Robert H. Bork, "Vertical Integration and the Sherman Act: The Legal History of an Economic Misconception," *The University of Chicago Law Review*, vol. 22, 1954, excerpted from pp. 194–200. Bork has extended this classical-style analysis to other antitrust issues, as a law professor at Yale. In 1973, as Solicitor-General, he ended the "Saturday night massacre" by dismissing Archibald Cox as Special Watergate Prosecutor.

thesis here that the concept is almost entirely lacking in significance as an analytical tool for differentiating between competition and monopoly, and that, with one exception, its only proper use is as a term descriptive of corporate structure. . . .

Monopoly power is usually defined as the ability to alter the market price for a product or service. A firm effects the alteration of market price through changes in its own output that significantly change the total output of the industry. Thus monopoly power depends upon the percentage of the market occupied by the firm, and the ease of entry into that market. Vertical integration does not increase the percentage of the market controlled by a firm. It should be equally apparent that such integration does not impede entry into a market. Even though almost all of the myths concerning the ways in which vertical integration confers market power upon a firm, or facilitates the exploitation of such power, have been discredited, the theory that vertical integration prolongs monopoly by imposing greater capital requirements upon potential entrants is still confidently advanced in the literature as though it, too, had not been badly shaken. Of course, vertical integration could affect entry only if two levels or stages of operation were monopolized by the integrated firm or cartel, so that entrants would have to come in on both levels at once. This would indeed require greater capital than would entrance upon one level. If there are greater-than-competitive profits being made in the industry, however, there seems no reason why the increased capital necessary for entry would not be forthcoming, unless there are impediments in the capital market that prevent capital from flowing to areas where it can most profitably be employed. Until such impediments have been shown to exist, the fact that increased capital is required for vertical integration must be assumed to have no adverse effect upon entry into monopolized markets. Therefore, since vertical integration does not increase the percentage of a market supplied by a firm and cannot be shown to impede entry into that market, such integration can be said to add nothing to monopoly power.

Nor does vertical integration affect a firm's pricing policy. If, for example, a firm operates at both the manufacturing and retail levels, it maximizes over-all profit by setting the output at each level as though the levels were independent. Where both levels are competitive, the firm maximizes by equating marginal cost and price at each level; each level makes the competitive return. Where the firm has a monopoly at the manufacturing level but is competitive in retailing, it will, of course, exact a monopoly profit at the first level. And the manufacturing level will sell to the retail level at the same price as it sells to outside retailers. If the integrated firm has monopolies at both the manufacturing and retail levels, however, the levels will not maximize independently. It has already been explained that vertically integrated monopolies can take but one monopoly profit. Therefore, if the manufacturing level charged a monopoly price, the retail level would not act independently and further restrict output, but would attempt to sell all of the manufacturing level's output at a competitive margin.

The above analysis supports the thesis that it is always horizontal market power, and not integration into other levels, which is important. This thesis has recently been attacked with the argument that, since the horizontal monopoly power may be impregnable (because it arises from a patent, natural monopoly in a basic supply, etc.), there may be no alternative but to dissolve the vertical integration which transmits the monopoly power from one level to another. The answer to this argument is clear from what has gone before. Suppose a monopolist at one level does not integrate vertically. He will charge the monopoly price to his customers, and that toll will be passed on to the ultimate consumers. What has already been said shows that the gaining of a second monopoly vertically related to the first would not alter price, output, or the allocation of productive resources on the second level monopolized. Therefore, dissolving the vertical integration accomplishes precisely nothing.

There is, however, one advantage a monopolist might not otherwise enjoy which he may obtain by vertical integration: the ability to discriminate in price between different classes of customers. A monopolist may have two classes of customers making different products, one of which is willing to pay more than the other, and yet, because of reselling between the classes, be unable to take advantage of the situation by discrimination. If, however, the monopolist should integrate with one of the classes, leakage would stop and discrimination become possible. It is not at all clear that this result is socially undesirable. One result of the discrimination is an increased profit for the monopolist. But the objection to monopoly is not that some people make too much money. It is that monopoly leads to a misallocation of society's resources through a restriction of output. In many cases, when a monopolist price-discriminates he tends to increase his output, and the resultant output is more like that dictated by competition than if he had not discriminated. In some cases this result may not occur, but on balance it seems more likely. Therefore, if the horizontal monopoly is legal, there should be no objection to price discrimination, and hence none to vertical integration employed to effect discrimination. The real problem, once more, is horizontal, not vertical.

This brief statement makes clear the position from which the use of the vertical-integration concept is criticized. With this analysis in mind we turn to an examination of some of the more common judicial notions concerning vertical integration. (The italicized statements are abstracted from the cases.)

Vertical integration may be used to gain a monopoly at one level. This notion appears in the cases but the mechanism by which it operates is rarely mentioned. There is no such mechanism unless a monopoly at another level is already held. In that case the important issue is the first monopoly, not the vertical integration. In any event, the second monopoly adds no power the first did not confer.

Vertical integration makes possible, or lends itself to, the price "squeeze" by which a monopolist at one level drives out competitors at another. The "squeeze" does not automatically result from any internal efficiencies of integration, for the competitive unit does not maximize profit by reflecting cost savings in its selling price but by selling at the price established by its competitors. Nor does vertical integration confer any unique ability to "squeeze" as a monopolizing technique. A "squeeze" is nothing more than a price-cutting campaign at one level. A nonintegrated firm can just as easily wage this sort of warfare by selling its goods at the cost of the raw materials as can the second level of a vertically integrated firm. The use of the term "squeeze" serves only to make the practice seem peculiar to vertical integration and thus lend an undeserved sinister coloration to that form of organization.

The vertically integrated firm can monopolize one level by cutting prices there because it can offset its losses by advancing prices at another level. The theory of recoupment has been exploded many times. If both levels are competitive, prices can be advanced at neither; if either level is monopolistic, prices would already have been advanced there to make the maximum profit. In either case, recoupment of losses incurred in price-cutting is impossible. Leaving out the notion of recoupment, it is possible to say that predation in one market may be continued longer if money is being made elsewhere. But this applies to horizontal and diversified, as well as to vertical, integration.

By eliminating profit at one level the vertically integrated firm can undersell competition at the next. This myth has been as thoroughly discredited as recoupment. The firm can do this only if it is willing to forgo the return on part of its invested capital. Any firm, integrated or not, may do the same thing.

A variation of the above, which appears in the District Court *A & P* opinion, is particularly interesting. *Profit is eliminated at the retail level, and, consequently, increased volume is achieved. The increased volume raises the profits of the manufacturing level. The firm, therefore, not only undersells its competitors at the retail level, but it sacrifices no profits in doing so.* This argument must assume that the manufacturing level had been operating at an inefficient scale so that the increase in volume made up for the loss of retail profits. Of course the firm could have made more money by allowing its manufacturing units to sell to outsiders, thus obtaining increased volume at that level without sacrificing any of its retail profits. When this is seen it becomes apparent that the mechanism described by the court is merely the sacrifice of profit in order to cut prices. Vertical integration is not relevant.

Money earned at one level gives a vertically integrated firm an ad-

*vantage over its nonintegrated competitors at another level. This is espe-
cially true where the money is paid by the nonintegrated competitors.* The
advantage is said to be derived from the fact that the money paid in raises
the costs of the competitors and lowers the costs of the integrated company.
Of course, money received can never lower costs. The competitors' costs
are not raised since they would have to pay for essential goods or services
at that level in any event. Since output is determined by marginal cost and
price (or marginal revenue where there is monopoly power), and since
neither is altered by the situation described, the vertically integrated firm
derives no competitive advantage.

*One level of a vertically integrated firm may harm another of its own
levels by charging it too high prices.* The higher-than-market price to the
second level would cause that level to decrease its output. So long as the
market is competitive (or regulated) no one is damaged by this except the
integrated firm which finds itself failing to maximize profits. If the market
in which the second level sells is monopolistic, a restriction of output would
occur anyway. The problem is then the monopoly and not the bookkeeping
transactions between the two levels.

*Walter Adams (1922–) and
Joel B. Dirlam (1915–)*

STEEL IMPORTS AND VERTICAL
OLIGOPOLY POWER*

*In real markets, vertical integration does cause mo-
nopoly behavior and results, according to Adams and
Dirlam. The steel industry is important in itself. Also,
its conditions are found in many others. If Adams' and
Dirlam's reasoning is correct, it does away with much
of Bork's case, which, they say, holds only in a "hermetically sealed world." Where does the truth lie?*

It is our contention that a vertically integrated oligopoly must maintain
its administered price structure with all the economic and political weap-

* Walter Adams and Joel B. Dirlam, "Steel Imports and Vertical Oligopoly Power,"
American Economic Review, June 1964, excerpted from pp. 626–27, 628–29, 639–40,
645–46, and 651–53. Both authors have been leading specialists on industrial conditions and critics of wayward policies since 1950. Adams is at Michigan State University and Dirlam at the University of Rhode Island.

ons at its disposal. It must defend *à outrance* the vertical succession of keystone prices on which the entire price system rests. It must, therefore, contain, insulate, neutralize, and sterilize imports, especially when they threaten the vertically interwoven strategic prices. It cannot allow imports to have more than a sporadic, peripheral, nonstructural impact. Conversely, if the entire noncompetitive price structure is to be eroded, this must be done through an attack on strategic prices. Only if imports are pinpointed at the focus of vertical price policy (i.e., strategic prices) can they trigger price competition in the unconcentrated segments of the industry. . . .

Some of the prices in the vertical steel price structure are of more importance than others. These are what we have earlier called strategic prices. They are the keystone on which a portion of the price edifice rests. If they change, it will be necessary to shift the entire structure. Like the Gulf Coast or Group 3 spot prices for gasoline, they serve as a "peg to hang the price structure on." Thus the price for wire rods is strategic because it is the base on which the superstructure of wire and wire-products prices is built.

If the steel oligopoly lived in a hermetically sealed world, it could maintain what it regards as the appropriate relations among prices in the vertical sequences with little difficulty. But no such world exists. The oligopoly has to permit the price structure to respond to outside stimuli, which constantly threaten it at various points. Some of the exogenous forces can be ignored as temporary aberrations. Others may be "contained" by minor adjustments. When a strategic price is threatened, however, the threat must be dealt with at almost any cost, not simply because of the necessity for reevaluating the specific price, but because of the danger to the market structure depending upon it.

The vertically organized giants in the steel industry, therefore, seldom consider a price in isolation. A change in any price introduces uncertainties up and down the line. If a product price is reduced, sales of semifinished steel may fall off because fabricators' margins have been compressed. The same consequence can result from an increase in prices of semifinished materials while product prices remain unchanged. The vertically integrated firms must consider these aspects of policy because they sell varying proportions of their products to nonintegrated firms at different stages of production. Their own customers may compete directly or indirectly with them on the finished product. Yet, for a variety of reasons associated with the individuality of customers and vagaries of location and technology, it does not ordinarily pay to eliminate all outside sales. For all these reasons, a decision to meet or not meet the lower price of a semifinished steel product cannot be made by integrated giants simply on the facts about direct costs and extent of unutilized capacity for that product alone.

The nonintegrated fabricator, on the other hand, lives in an entirely different world. He is aware of the vertical structure of prices only insofar as it affects his margin. When the margin is disturbed—increasing or decreasing—he will respond. But in normal times he lives within the margins permitted by the structure and cooperates with its preservation by not undercutting the prices of fabricated products published by his suppliers of raw or semifinished materials.

. . . Given the tapered integration and dual distribution in the wire segment of the steel industry, the majors had to compete with their nonintegrated customers. Before reducing rod prices, therefore, they had to consider not only the implications for rod revenues, but also the impact of this "cost" reduction on the independent fabricators and the indirect impact on the level of product prices. As long as the independent fabricators continued to buy domestic rod—and most of them used a 50/50 mix of imported and domestic rods in order not to cut themselves off from domestic supply sources—the majors felt that price cutting in the products markets would not get out of hand. On the other hand, if the majors had matched the lower price of imported rods, this would have lowered costs for the nonintegrated fabricators and served as a carte blanche invitation to cut product prices further than they had already been cut. In short, if the integrated steel companies were at all rational, we must presume that they concluded during the 1957–62 period that their losses from cuts in wire-rod prices, including the effect on products prices, would exceed the losses they suffered from relinquishing part of the noncaptive wire-rod market to imports. And this had to be a decision in which vertical considerations were paramount.

*   *   *   *   *

The Spengler-Adelman-Bork position is not in accord with the facts of life in the steel industry. To be sure, the nonintegrated fabricators responded to lower import prices on the individual products they produced because failure to do so would have meant extinction. As producers of a single product—or, at most, a handful of products—they had no alternative than to meet the price reductions precipitated by imports. In addition, they responded to the compression of their fabricating margins by turning in ever-increasing numbers to imported wire rods—that is, to lower-priced supplies of their basic raw material. Their reaction in both the product and raw-material markets, therefore, was roughly in accord with the profit-maximizing calculus applied in a horizontal context.

The integrated firms, by contrast, in a calculated effort to protect the industry's price structure, refused to meet the import prices either of products or rods. On some products, the integrated giants lowered prices to meet price cuts of their domestic nonintegrated competitors. Elsewhere, they preferred to abandon the field to imports altogether rather than to reduce their product prices. . . .

At the wire-rod level, the integrated firms seemed to react perversely to the import threat. They first raised prices (1955–58) and then maintained them with catatonic insensitivity (1958–63.)[1] They did so, not only because of their addiction to cost-plus, target-rate-of-return pricing, but more importantly in an attempt to maintain the vertical relationship between wire-rod and wire-product prices.

---

[1] According to the Spengler theory on vertical integration, rational monopolists or oligopolists would transfer semifinished products from one stage to another at prices free from monopolistic profits, thereby permitting the final price to be set at a lower figure than a price resulting from a series of transactions between independent bilateral oligopolists. If the steel industry conformed to Spengler's hypothesis, the transfer price for wire rods should have been affected by, if not identical with, the cost of imported rods of commensurate quality. The consequent reduction in the cost of wire-rod inputs to the wire divisions should have depressed the price of wire and, ultimately, wire-products prices.

That prices did not behave as the hypothesis suggests is obvious. It is instructive to inquire why. First, the structure of the industry was not that envisaged by Spengler. Integration is not complete, but is tapered forward, so that prices for wire rod and wire are not merely accounting transfer prices, but have a function vis-a-vis independent customers. Second, these prices are fixed by an administrative process, in the course of which a number of forces are brought to bear on price determination. Not only do the industry leaders take into account target return, but also the possible interactions of prices of wire rod, wire, and wire products, and the attitudes of customers to changes in accustomed differentials. Third, we may doubt whether, in any event, Spengler's optimism is warranted. There is little to show that transfer prices within a vertically integrated firm would, in actuality, be set at lower levels than market prices. In most U.S. industries, oligopolistic pricing policies, which might be expected to set prices in the market, would be regarded as proper procedures by managers responsible for transfer pricing within a vertically integrated firm. Hence, we would not anticipate that a shift to vertical integration in an industry already characterized by horizontal oligopoly would be reflected in appreciable price reductions because of elimination of interstitial profits. In fact, the probabilities would seem to lie in the opposite direction. While a horizontal oligopoly might be immediately affected by import competition, and forced to modify its pricing procedures and standards, a partially vertically integrated industry could continue to resist such pressures at one level, maintaining "cost" constituents that a horizontal oligopoly would have been forced to abandon.

Richard A. Smith (1911–   )

GENERAL ELECTRIC: A CRISIS OF ANTITRUST*

The biggest price-fixing case in U.S. history embraced some eight conspiracies among electrical equipment companies, which had become "a way of life" well before 1950. Smith conveys the flavor and form of these hotel-room connivances. There were fines, jail sentences, and large damage claims. Has price collusion in this industry disappeared? How widely do these shenanigans occur in other industries?

Roughly $650 million in sales was involved, according to Justice Department estimates, from 1951 through 1958. The annual total amounted to about $75 million and was broken down into two categories, sealed bids and open bids. The sealed-bid business (between $15 million and $18 million per year) was done with public agencies, city, state, and federal. The private-sector business was conducted with private utilities and totaled $55 million to $60 million per annum.

The object of the conspiracy, in so far as the sealed-bid business was concerned, was to rotate that business on a fixed-percentage basis among four participating companies, then the only circuit-breaker manufacturers in the United States. G.E. got 45 percent, Westinghouse 35, Allis-Chalmers 10, Federal Pacific 10. Every ten days to two weeks working-level meetings were called in order to decide whose turn was next. Turns were determined by the "ledger list," a table of who had got what in recent weeks, and after that the only thing left to decide was the price that the company picked to "win" would submit as the lowest bid.

Above this working-level group was a second tier of conspirators who dealt generally with the over-all scheme of rigging the sealed bids but whose prime purpose was maintenance of book prices (quoted prices) and market shares in the yearly $55 million to $60 million worth of private-sector business. Once each week, the top executives (general managers and vice-presidents) responsible for carrying out the conspiracy would get the word to each other via intercompany memo. A different executive would

---

* Richard A. Smith, "General Electric: A Crisis of Antitrust," excerpted from *Corporations in Crisis* (New York: Doubleday, 1962), pp. 125–27, 134, and 148–51. Smith is a *Fortune* staff writer.

have the "duty" over each thirty-day period. That involved initiating the memos, which all dealt with the same subject matter; the jobs coming up that week, the book price each company was setting, comments on the general level of equipment prices.

The conspiracies had their own lingo and their own standard operating procedures. The attendance list was known as the "Christmas-card list," meetings as "choir practices." Companies had code numbers—G.E. 1, Westinghouse 2, Allis-Chalmers 3, Federal Pacific 7—which were used in conjunction with first names when calling a conspirator at home for price information ("This is Bob, what is 7's bid?"). At the hotel meetings it was S.O.P. not to list one's employer when registering and not to have breakfast with fellow conspirators in the dining room. The G.E. men observed two additional precautions: never to be the ones who kept the records and never to tell G.E.'s lawyers anything.

But things were not always smooth even inside this well-oiled machine, for the conspirators actually had no more compunction at breaking the rules of the conspiracy than at breaching the Sherman Act. "Everyone accused the others of not living up to the agreement," Clarence Burke recalled, "and the ones they complained about tried to shift the blame onto someone else." The most constant source of irritation occurred in the sealed-bid business, where chiseling was difficult to detect. But breaks in book price to the utilities in the open-bid business also generated ill will and vituperation. Indeed, one of the many ironies of the whole affair is that the conspiracy couldn't entirely suppress the competitive instinct. Every so often some company would decide that cutthroat competition outside was preferable to the throat-cutting that went on in the cartel; they would break contact and sit out the conspiracy for a couple of years.

*   *   *   *   *

G.E. was involved in at least seven other conspiracies during the time the circuit-breaker cartel was inoperative. The one in power transformers (G.E. Vice-President Raymond W. Smith) was going, for G.E. had yet to develop the "black box" (a design breakthrough using standard components to produce tailor-made transformers), which two years later would enable it to take price leadership away from Westinghouse. The one in turbine generators (G.E. Vice-President William S. Ginn) was functioning too. In the fall of 1957 it was agreed at the Barclay Hotel to give G.E. "position" in bidding on a 500,000-kilowatt TVA unit.

The question that naturally arises, the cartels being so numerous, is why didn't G.E.'s top management stop them? Cordiner has been criticized within the company, and rightly so, for sitting aloofly in New York and sending out "pieces of paper"—his 20.5 antitrust directive—rather than having 20.5 personally handed to the local staff by the local boss. But there was also a failure in human relations. . . .

The first grand jury was looking into conspiracies in insulators, switchgear, circuit breakers, and several other products. The second grand jury was hearing four transformer cases and one on industrial controls. With a score of Justice men working on them, cases proliferated, and from December on lawyers began popping up trying to get immunity for their clients in return for testimony. Scarcely a week went by that Bicks and company didn't get information on at least two new cases. But what they still needed was decisive data that would break a case wide open. In January 1960, at just about the time Ralph Cordiner was making an important speech to G.E.'s management corps ("every company and every industry—yes, and every country—that is operated on a basis of cartel systems is liquidating its present strength and future opportunities"), the trust busters hit the jackpot in switchgear.

"The Phases of the Moon." Switchgear had been particularly baffling to the Antitrust Division, so much that in trying to establish a cartel pattern in the jumble of switchgear prices the trust busters got the bright idea they might be in code. A cryptographer was brought in to puzzle over the figures and try to crack the secret of how a conspirator could tell what to bid and when he'd win. But the cryptographer was soon as flummoxed as everyone else. One of the government attorneys in the case, however, had made a point of dropping in on a college classmate who was the president of a small Midwestern electrical-equipment company. This executive didn't have chapter and verse on the switchgear cartel but what he did have was enough for Justice to throw a scare into a bigger company, I-T-E Circuit Breaker. Indicating that subpoenas would follow, antitrust investigators asked I-T-E's general counsel, Franklyn Judson, to supply the names of sales managers in specific product lines. Judson decided to conduct an investigation of his own. When the subpoenas did come, a pink-cheeked blond young man named Nye Spencer, the company's sales manager for switchgear, was resolutely waiting—his arms loaded with data. He had decided he wasn't about to commit another crime by destroying the records so carefully laid away in his cellar.

There were pages on pages of notes taken during sessions of the switchgear conspiracy—incriminating entries like "Potomac Light & Power, O.K. for G.E." and "Before bidding on this, check with G.E."; neat copies of the ground rules for meetings of the conspirators: no breakfasting together, no registering at the hotel with company names, no calls to the office, no papers to be left in hotel-room wastebaskets. Spencer, it seems, had been instructed to handle some of the secretarial work of the cartel and believed in doing it right; he'd hung onto the documents to help in training an assistant. But the most valuable windfall from the meticulous record keeper was a pile of copies of the "phases of the moon" pricing formula for as far back as May 1958.

Not much to look at—just sheets of paper, each containing a half-dozen columns of figures—they immediately solved the enigma of switchgear prices in commercial contracts. One group of columns established the bidding order of the seven switchgear manufacturers—a different company, each with its own code number, phasing into the priority position every two weeks (hence "phases of the moon"). A second group of columns, keyed into the company code numbers, established how much each company was to knock off the agreed-upon book price. For example, if it were No. 1's (G.E.'s) turn to be low bidder at a certain number of dollars off book, then all Westinghouse (No. 2) or Allis-Chalmers (No. 3) had to do was look for their code number in the second group of columns to find how many dollars they were to bid *above* No. 1. These bids would then be fuzzed up by having a little added to them or taken away by companies 2, 3, etc. Thus there was not even a hint that the winning bid had been collusively arrived at.

With this little device in hand, the trust busters found they could light up the whole conspiracy like a switchboard. The new evidence made an equally profound impression on the grand juries. On February 16 and 17, 1960, they handed down the first seven indictments. Forty companies and eighteen individuals were charged with fixing prices or dividing the market on seven electrical products. Switchgear led the list.

CASES

Details of Typical Cases. A "case" usually involves two parties, "plaintiff" (who first filed a complaint) and "respondent" (the defendant). Trial in District Court involves arguments about facts and points of law, after careful pretrial preparation (often lasting years). Either side may appeal the Court's decision to the Appeals Court in its region or ultimately to the U.S. Supreme Court. Appeals can involve only points of law, not new facts: the trial record is the sole source of facts. The decision is announced in an "opinion," written by a member of the majority.* It reviews previous steps, facts, points of law, and anything else which explains the decision to "reverse" or "affirm" the court below. If there is a conviction, the case may be remanded down to the original court for devising a suitable "remedy" (or "relief"). Minority members often write "dissenting opinions," commonly in sharp, even sarcastic, tones. The decision sets "precedent" for future cases which may fit the facts and legal status of the case under review. The dissent often defines the limits of the precedent or even sets the stage for future reversals.

The title of District Court decisions lists the original plaintiff first. Most Antitrust Division suits are cited as "U.S. *versus* Alleged Offender, Inc." (the defendant company). On appeal appellate courts *often* and the Supreme Court *always* lists the appealing party first.

Opinions in important antitrust cases often run 20 to 50 pages or even longer, and some of them make very heavy reading indeed. The excerpts here focus only on the key facts and legal points. Structural and merger cases come first (roughly, Sherman Act Section 2 and Clayton Act Section 7). Restrictive practice cases then follow (roughly, Sherman Act Section 1).

---

* Actually, most opinions are drafted by the judge's law clerk, usually a young lawyer just out of law school!

Section 2 Cases

United States v. Standard Oil Co.
221 U.S. 1, 59 (1911)

The Standard Oil Company achieved its monopoly of the U.S. oil industry during 1870–1880, by various pricing tactics, railroad rebates, and other means. By 1910 it was slipping but still dominant, and its 40-year monopoly had been extraordinarily lucrative. A government antitrust case succeeded in winning conviction and an order to dissolve the trust. The Supreme Court affirmed. But Chief Justice White, who had awaited this opportunity, wrote a majority opinion advancing the "rule of reason." (The wording, incidentally, is tortured and obscure, hard reading for everyone.) "Unreasonable" acts, the specific intent of Standard Oil, and the role of Section 1 were stressed. Despite Harlan's dissent, this greatest stroke of "trustbusting" was also a statement virtually withdrawing future actions except in extreme instances.

. . . In other words, having by the 1st section forbidden all means of monopolizing trade, that is, unduly restraining it by means of every contract, combination, etc., the 2d section seeks, if possible, to make the prohibitions of the act all the more complete and perfect by embracing all attempts to reach the end prohibited by the 1st section, that is, restraints of trade, by any attempt to monopolize, or monopolization thereof, even although the acts by which such results are attempted to be brought about or are brought about be not embraced within the general enumeration of the 1st section. And, of course, when the 2d section is thus harmonized with and made as it was intended to be the complement of the 1st, it becomes obvious that the criteria to be resorted to in any given case for the purpose of ascertaining whether violations of the section have been committed, is the rule of reason guided by the established law and by the plain duty to enforce the prohibitions of the act, and thus the public policy which its restrictions were obviously enacted to subserve. . . .

In substance, the propositions urged by the Government are reducible to this: That the language of the statute embraces every contract, combination, etc., in restraint of trade, and hence its text leaves no room for the exercise of judgment, but simply imposes the plain duty of applying its prohibitions to every case within its literal language. The error involved lies in assuming the matter to be decided. This is true because as the acts which may come under the classes stated in the 1st section and the restraint of trade to which that section applies are not specifically enumerated or defined, it is obvious that judgment must in every case be called into play in order to determine whether a particular act is embraced within the statutory classes, and whether if the act is within such classes its nature or effect causes it to be a restraint of trade within the intendment of the act. To hold to the contrary would require the conclusion either that every contract, act, or combination of any kind or nature, whether it operated a restraint on trade or not, was within the statute, and thus the statute would be destructive of all right to contract or agree or combine in any respect whatever as to subjects embraced in interstate trade or commerce, or if this conclusion were not reached, then the contention would require it to be held that as the statute did not define the things to which it related and excluded resort to the only means by which the acts to which it relates could be ascertained—the light of reason—the enforcement of the statute was impossible because of its uncertainty. The merely generic enumeration which the statute makes of the acts to which it refers and the absence of any definition of restraint of trade as used in the statute leaves room for but one conclusion, which is, that it was expressly designed not to unduly limit the application of the act by precise definition, but while clearly fixing a standard, that is, by defining the ulterior boundaries which could not be transgressed with impunity, to leave it to be determined by the light of reason, guided by the principles of law and the duty to apply and enforce the public policy embodied in the statute, in every given case whether any particular act or contract was within the contemplation of the statute.

. . . [T]he very genius for commercial development and organization which it would seem was manifested from the beginning soon begot an intent and purpose to exclude others which was frequently manifested by acts and dealings wholly inconsistent with the theory that they were made with the single conception of advancing the development of business power by usual methods, but which, on the contrary, necessarily involved the intent to drive others from the field and to exclude them from their right to trade and thus accomplish the mastery which was the end in view. And, considering the period from the date of the trust agreements of 1879 and 1882, up to the time of the expansion of the New Jersey corporation, the gradual extension of the power over the commerce in oil which ensued, the decision of the supreme court of Ohio, the tardiness or reluctance in conforming to the commands of that decision, the methods first adopted and that which finally culminated in the plan of the New Jersey corporation, all additionally serve to make manifest the continued existence of the intent which we have previously indicated, and which, among other things, impelled the expansion of the New Jersey corporation. The exercise of the power which resulted from that organization fortifies the foregoing conclusions, since the development which came, the acquisition here and there which ensued of every efficient means by which competition could have been asserted, the slow but resistless methods which followed by which means of transportation were absorbed and brought under control, the system of marketing which was adopted by which the country was divided into districts and the trade in each district in oil was turned over to a designated corporation within the combination, and all others were excluded, all lead the mind up to a conviction of a purpose and intent which we think is so certain as practically to cause the subject not to be within the domain of reasonable contention.

. . . As penalties which are not authorized by law may not be inflicted by judicial authority, it follows that to meet the situation with which we are confronted the application of remedies two-fold in character becomes essential: 1st. To forbid the doing in the future of acts like those which we have found to have been done in the past which would be violative of the statute. 2d. The exertion of such measure of relief as will effectually dissolve the combination found to exist in violation of the statute, and thus neutralize the extension and continually operating force which the possession of the power unlawfully obtained has brought and will continue to bring about.

In applying remedies for this purpose, however, the fact must not be overlooked that injury to the public by the prevention of an undue restraint on, or the monopolization of, trade or commerce, is the foundation upon which the prohibitions of the statute rest, and moreover that one of the fundamental purposes of the statute is to protect, not to destroy, rights of property. . . .

Justice Harlan, concurring in part and dissenting in part:

. . . On reading the opinion just delivered, the first inquiry will be, that as the court is unanimous in holding that the particular things done by the Standard Oil Company and its subsidiary companies, in this case, were illegal under the Anti-Trust Act, whether those things were in reasonable or unreasonable restraint of interstate commerce, why was it necessary to make an elaborate argument, as is done in the opinion, to show that according to the "rule of reason" the act as passed by Congress should be interpreted as if it contained the word "unreasonable" or the word "undue"? The only answer which, in frankness, can be given to this question, is, that the court intends to decide that its deliberate judgment, fifteen years ago, to the effect that the act permitted no restraint whatever of interstate commerce, whether reasonable or unreasonable, was not in accordance with the "rule of reason." In effect the court says that it will now, for the first time, bring the discussion under the "light of reason," and apply the "rule of reason" to the questions to be decided. I have the authority of this court for saying that such a course of proceeding on its part would be "judicial legislation." . . .

. . . To overreach the action of Congress merely by judicial construction, that is, by indirection, is a blow at the integrity of our governmental system, and in the end will prove most dangerous to all. Mr. Justice Bradley wisely said, when on this bench, that illegitimate and unconstitutional practices get their first footing by silent approaches and slight deviations from legal modes of legal procedure. . . .

United States v. U.S. Steel Corp.
251 U.S. 417 (1920)

> *Formed in 1901 with two thirds of the industry, U.S. Steel was the greatest of the "trust" consolidations. It established cooperative pricing (the "Gary dinners") and reinforced the basing-point system. But its share dwindled and its predatory behavior was tame compared to many other trusts. By 1920, also, the "rule of reason" stood as precedent and World War I had transmuted trusts into patriotic producers. Even so, the Supreme Court vote to acquit U.S. Steel was only 4 to 3. Was U.S. Steel a "good" trust? Should the Court have looked at 1901–10 rather than 1920?*

. . . Our present purpose is, not retrospect for itself, however instructive, but practical decision upon existing conditions that we may not by their disturbance produce, or even risk, consequences of a concern that cannot now be computed. In other words, our consideration should be of not what the Corporation had power to do or did, but what it has now power to do and is doing, and what judgment should be now pronounced —whether its dissolution, as the government prays, or the dismissal of the suit, as the Corporation insists. . . .

The power attained was much greater than that possessed by any one competitor—it was not greater than that possessed by all of them. Monopoly, therefore, was not achieved, and competitors had to be persuaded by pools, associations, trade meetings, and through the social form of dinners, all of them, it may be, violations of the law, but transient in their purpose and effect. They were scattered through the years from 1901 (the year of the formation of the Corporation), until 1911, but, after instances of success and failure, were abandoned nine months before this suit was brought. . . .

What, then, can now be urged against the Corporation? Can comparisons in other regards be made with its competitors and by such comparisons guilty or innocent existence be assigned it? It is greater in size and productive power than any of its competitors, equal or nearly equal to them all, but its power over prices was not and is not commensurate with its power to produce.

It is true there is some testimony tending to show that the Corporation had such power, but there was also testimony and a course of action tending strongly to the contrary. The conflict was by the judges of the District Court unanimously resolved against the existence of that power, and in doing so they but gave effect to the greater weight of the evidence. It is certain that no such power was exerted. On the contrary, the only attempt at a fixation of prices was, as already said, through an appeal to and confederation with competitors, and the record shows besides that when competition occurred it was not in pretense, and the Corporation declined in productive powers—the competitors growing either against or in consequence of the competition. If against the competition we have an instance of movement against what the Government insists was an irresistible force; if in consequence of competition, we have an illustration of the adage that "competition is the life of trade" and is not easily repressed. The power of monopoly in the Corporation under either illustration is an untenable accusation. . . .

We have pointed out that there are several of the Government's contentions which are difficult to represent or measure, and the one we are now considering—that is, the power is "unlawful regardless of purpose" —is another of them. It seems to us that it has for its ultimate principle and justification that strength in any producer or seller is a menace to the public interest and illegal, because there is potency in it for mischief. The regression is extreme, but short of it the Government cannot stop. The fallacy it conveys is manifest.

The Corporation was formed in 1901, no act of aggression upon its competitors is charged against it, it confederated with them at times in offense against the law, but abandoned that before this suit was brought, and since 1911 no act in violation of law can be established against it, except its existence be such an act. . . . The Corporation is undoubtedly of impressive size and it takes an effort of resolution not to be affected by it or to exaggerate its influence. But we must adhere to the law, and the law does not make mere size an offense, or the existence of unexerted power an offense. It, we repeat, requires overt acts, and trusts to its prohibition of them and its power to repress or punish them. It does not compel competition nor require all that is possible. . . .

But there are countervailing considerations. We have seen whatever there was of wrong intent could not be executed; whatever there was of evil effect was discontinued before this suit was brought, and this, we think, determines the decree. . . . [A] court of equity . . . is not expected to enforce abstractions, and do injury thereby, it may be, to the purpose of the law. . . . And it is certainly a matter for consideration that there was no legal attack on the Corporation until 1911, 10 years after its formation and the commencement of its career. We do not, however, speak of the delay simply as to its time, or say that there is estoppel in it because of its time but on account of what was done during that time—the many millions of dollars spent, the development made, and the enterprises undertaken; the investments by the public that have been invited and are not to be ignored. . . .

In conclusion, we are unable to see that the public interest will be served by yielding to the contention of the Government respecting the dissolution of the company or the separation from it of some of its subsidiaries; and we do see in a contrary conclusion a risk of injury to the public interest, including a material disturbance of, and, it may be serious detriment to, the foreign trade. And in submission to the policy of the law and its fortifying prohibitions the public interest is of paramount regard.

We think, therefore, that the decree of the District Court should be affirmed. . . .

Justice Day, dissenting:

For many years, as the record discloses, this unlawful organization exerted its power to control and maintain prices by pools, associations, trade meetings, and as the result of discussion and agreements at the so-called "Gary Dinners," where the assembled trade opponents secured cooperation and joint action through the machinery of special committees of competing concerns, and by prudent prevision took into account the possibility of defection, and the means of controlling and perpetuating that industrial harmony which arose from the control and maintenance of prices.

It inevitably follows that the corporation violated the law in its formation and by its immediate practices. The power, thus obtained from the combination of resources almost unlimited in the aggregation of competing organizations, had within its control the domination of the trade, and the ability to fix prices and restrain the free flow of commerce upon a scale heretofore unapproached in the history of corporate organization in this country.

These facts established, as it seems to me they are by the record, it follows that, if the Sherman Act is to be given efficacy, there must be a decree undoing so far as is possible that which has been achieved in open, notorious, and continued violation of its provisions. . . .

From the earliest decisions of this court it has been declared that it was the effective power of such organizations to control and restrain competition and the freedom of trade that Congress intended to limit and control. That the exercise of the power may be withheld, or exerted with forbearing benevolence, does not place such combinations beyond the authority of the statute which was intended to prohibit their formation, and when formed to deprive them of the power unlawfully attained.

It is said that a complete monopolization of the steel business was never attained by the offending combinations. To insist upon such result would be beyond the requirements of the statute and in most cases practicably impossible. . . .

United States v. Aluminum Company of America

United States Circuit Court of Appeals, Second Circuit, 1945. 148 F.2d 416.

This "big" case aimed at a 45-year-old monopoly, which was then the 28th largest U.S. industrial firm. The decision rejected the rule of reason, treating the conscious maintenance of monopoly as critical. Judge Hand's comment about 90, 60, and 30 percent market shares is still the usual rule of thumb. This "landmark" case actually resulted, on remand, in very modest relief: mainly, disposal of World War II aluminum plants to new firms rather than to Alcoa.

Before L. Hand, Swan, and Augustus N. Hand, Circuit Judges.

L. Hand, J. . . . The action was brought . . . to adjudge that the defendant, Aluminum Company of America, was monopolizing interstate and foreign commerce, particularly in the manufacture and sale of "virgin" aluminum ingot, and that it be dissolved; and further to adjudge that that company and the defendant, Aluminum Limited, had entered into a conspiracy in restraint of such commerce. It also asked incidental relief. . . .

The action came to trial on June 1, 1938, and proceeded without much interruption until August 14, 1940, when the case was closed after more than 40,000 pages of testimony had been taken. The judge took time to consider the evidence, and delivered an oral opinion which occupied him from September 30, to October 9, 1941. Again he took time to prepare findings of fact and conclusions of law which he filed on July 14, 1942; and he entered final judgment dismissing the complaint on July 23rd, of that year. The petition for an appeal, and assignments of error, were filed on September 14, 1942, and the petition was allowed on the next day. On June 12, 1944, the Supreme Court, declaring that a quorum of six justices qualified to hear the case was wanting, referred the appeal to this court. . . .

There are various ways of computing "Alcoa's" control of the aluminum market—as distinct from its production—depending upon what one regards as competing in that market. The judge figured its share—during the years 1929–1938, inclusive—as only about thirty-three percent; to do so he included "secondary," and excluded that part of "Alcoa's" own production which it fabricated and did not therefore sell as ingot. If, on the other hand, "Alcoa's" total production, fabricated and sold, be included, and balanced against the sum of imported "virgin" and "secondary," its share of the market was in the neighborhood of sixty-four percent for that period. The percentage we have already mentioned—over ninety— results only if we both include all "Alcoa's" production and exclude "secondary." That percentage is enough to constitute a monopoly; it is doubtful whether sixty or sixty-four percent would be enough; and certainly thirty-three percent is not. Hence it is necessary to settle what he shall treat as competing in the ingot market.

. . . Thus, in the case at bar "Alcoa" always knew that the future supply of ingot would be made up in part of what it produced at the time, and, if it was as far-sighted as it proclaims itself, that consideration must have had its share in determining how much to produce. How accurately it could forecast the effect of present production upon the future market is another matter. Experience, no doubt, would help; but it makes no difference that it had to guess; it is enough that it had an inducement to make the best guess it could, and that it would regulate that part of the future supply, so far as it should turn out to have guessed right. The competition of "secondary" must therefore be disregarded, as soon as we consider the position of "Alcoa" over a period of years; it was as much within "Alcoa's" control as was the production of the "virgin" from which it had been derived. This can be well illustrated by the case of a lawful monopoly: e.g. a patent or a copyright. The monopolist cannot prevent those to whom he sells from reselling at whatever prices they please. . . .

We conclude therefore that "Alcoa's" control over the ingot market must be reckoned at over ninety percent; that being the proportion which its production bears to imported "virgin" ingot. If the fraction which it did not supply were the produce of domestic manufacture there could be no doubt that this percentage gave it a monopoly—lawful or unlawful, as the case might be. The producer of so large a proportion of the supply has complete control within certain limits. . . .

. . . But the whole issue is irrelevant anyway, for it is no excuse for "monopolizing" a market that the monopoly has not been used to extract from the consumer more than a "fair" profit. The Act has wider purposes. Indeed, even though we disregarded all but economic considerations, it would by no means follow that such concentration of producing power is to be desired, when it has not been used extortionately. Many people believe that possession of unchallenged economic power deadens initiative, discourages thrift and depresses energy; that immunity from competition is a narcotic, and rivalry is a stimulant, to industrial progress; that the spur of constant stress is necessary to counteract an inevitable disposition to let well enough alone. Such people believe that competitors, versed in the craft as no consumer can be, will be quick to detect opportunities for saving and new shifts in production, and be eager to profit by them. In any event the mere fact that a producer, having command of the domestic market, has not been able to make more than a "fair" profit, is no evidence that a "fair" profit could not have been made at lower prices.

. . . True, it might have been thought adequate to condemn only those monopolies which could not show that they had exercised the highest possible ingenuity, had adopted every possible economy, had anticipated every conceivable improvement, stimulated every possible demand. No doubt, that would be one way of dealing with the matter, although it would imply constant scrutiny and constant supervision, such as courts are unable to provide. Be that as it may, that was not the way that Congress chose; it did not condone "good trusts" and condemn "bad" ones; it forbad all. Moreover, in so doing it was not necessarily actuated by economic motives alone. It is possible, because of its indirect social or moral effect, to prefer a system of small producers, each dependent for his success upon his own skill and character, to one in which the great mass of those engaged must accept the direction of a few. These considerations, which we have suggested only as possible purposes of the Act, we think the decisions prove to have been in fact its purposes.

. . . Throughout the history of these statutes it has been constantly assumed that one of their purposes was to perpetuate and preserve, for its own sake and in spite of possible cost, an organization of industry in small units which can effectively compete with each other. We hold that "Alcoa's" monopoly of ingot was of the kind covered by § 2.

It does not follow because "Alcoa" had such a monopoly, that it "monopolized" the ingot market: it may not have achieved monopoly; monopoly may have been thrust upon it. If it had been a combination of existing smelters which united the whole industry and controlled the production of all aluminum ingot, it would certainly have "monopolized" the market. In several decisions the Supreme Court has decreed the dissolution of such combinations, although they had engaged in no unlawful trade practices. . . .

A market may, for example, be so limited that it is impossible to produce at all and meet the cost of production except by a plant large enough to supply the whole demand. Or there may be changes in taste or in cost which drive out all but one purveyor. A single producer may be the survivor out of a group of active competitors, merely by virtue of his superior skill, foresight and industry. In such cases a strong argument can be made that, although the result may expose the public to the evils of monopoly, the Act does not mean to condemn the resultant of those very forces which it is its prime object to foster: finis opus coronat. The successful competitor, having been urged to compete, must not be turned upon when he wins. . . .

It would completely misconstrue "Alcoa's position in 1940 to hold that it was the passive beneficiary of a monopoly, following upon an involuntary elimination of competitors by automatically operative economic forces. Already in 1909, when its last lawful monopoly ended, it sought to strengthen its position by unlawful practices, and these concededly continued until 1912.

. . . We need charge it with no moral derelictions after 1912; we may assume that all it claims for itself is true. The only question is whether it falls within the exception established in favor of those who do not seek, but cannot avoid, the control of a market. It seems to us that that question scarcely survives its statement. It was not inevitable that it should always anticipate increases in the demand for ingot and be prepared to supply them. Nothing compelled it to keep doubling and redoubling its capacity before others entered the field. It insists that it never excluded competitors; but we can think of no more effective exclusion than progressively to embrace each new opportunity as it opened, and to face each newcomer with new capacity already geared into a great organization, having the advantage of experience, trade connections and the elite of personnel. Only in case we interpret "exclusion" as limited to manoeuvres not honestly industrial, but actuated solely by a desire to prevent competition, can such a course, indefatigably pursued, be deemed not "exclusionary." So to limit it would in our judgment emasculate the Act; would permit just such consolidations as it was designed to prevent. . . .

In order to fall within § 2, the monopolist must have both the power to monopolize, and the intent to monopolize. To read the passage as demanding any "specific," intent, makes nonsense of it, for no monopolist monopolizes unconscious of what he is doing. So here, "Alcoa" meant to keep, and did keep, that complete and exclusive hold upon the ingot market with

which it started. That was to "monopolize" that market, however inno-
cently it otherwise proceeded. So far as the judgment held that it was not
within § 2, it must be reversed.

United States v. United Shoe Machinery Corp.

United States District Court, District of
Massachusetts, 1953. 110 F.Supp. 205,
affirmed per curiam 347 U.S. 521, 74 S.Ct. 699,
98 L.Ed. 910 (1954).

> *This case refined the reasons by which even a good
> monopolist could be convicted if it had (1) high market
> share plus (2) some specific actions to get or keep the
> share. USM's extensive price discrimination was one
> such action. Judge Wyzanski, a leading jurist on anti-
> trust matters, retained Carl Kaysen as an expert eco-
> nomic assistant. The remedy was modest, and USM
> was, in any case, small. In 1969 further steps had to be
> negotiated to end USM's now-tiny monopoly.*

Wyzanski, J.   December 15, 1947 the Government filed a complaint
against United Shoe Machinery Corporation . . . in order to restrain alleged
violations of §§ 1 and 2 of [the Sherman Act].

Stripped to its essentials, the 52-page complaint charged, *first*, that since
1912 United had been "monopolizing interstate trade and commerce in the
shoe machinery industry of the United States."

. . . The facts show that (1) defendant has, and exercises, such overwhelming strength in the shoe machinery market that it controls that market, (2) this strength excludes some potential, and limits some actual,
competition, and (3) this strength is not attributable solely to defendant's
ability, economies of scale, research, natural advantages, and adaptation
to inevitable economic laws.

In estimating defendant's strength, this Court gives some weight to the
75 plus percentage of the shoe machinery market which United serves. But
the Court considers other factors as well. In the relatively static shoe machinery market where there are no sudden changes in the style of machines
or in the volume of demand, United has a network of long-term, complicated leases with over 90 percent of the shoe factories. These leases assure
closer and more frequent contacts between United and its customers than
would exist if United were a seller and its customers were buyers. Beyond

this general quality, these leases are so drawn and so applied as to strengthen United's power to exclude competitors. Moreover, United offers a long line of machine types, while no competitor offers more than a short line. Since in some parts of its line United faces no important competition, United has the power to discriminate, by wide differentials and over long periods of time, in the rate of return it procures from different machine types. Furthermore, being by far the largest company in the field, with by far the largest resources in dollars, in patents, in facilities, and in knowledge, United has a marked capacity to attract offers of inventions, inventors' services, and shoe machinery businesses. And, finally, there is no substantial substitute competition from a vigorous secondhand market in shoe machinery.

To combat United's market control, a competitor must be prepared with knowledge of shoemaking, engineering skill, capacity to invent around patents, and financial resources sufficient to bear the expense of long developmental and experimental processes. The competitor must be prepared for consumers' resistance founded on their long-term, satisfactory relations with United, and on the cost to them of surrendering United's leases. Also, the competitor must be prepared to give, or point to the source of, repair and other services, and to the source of supplies for machine parts, expendable parts, and the like. Indeed, perhaps a competitor who aims at any large-scale success must also be prepared to lease his machines. These considerations would all affect *potential* competition, and have not been without their effect on *actual* competition.

Not only does the evidence show United has control of the market, but also the evidence does not show that the control is due entirely to excusable causes. The three principal sources of United's power have been the original constitution of the company, the superiority of United's products and services, and the leasing system. The first two of these are plainly beyond reproach. . . .

But United's control does not rest solely on its original constitution, its ability, its research, or its economies of scale. There are other barriers to competition, and these barriers were erected by United's own business policies. Much of United's market power is traceable to the magnetic ties inherent in its system of leasing, and not selling, its more important machines. The lease-only system of distributing complicated machines has many "partnership" aspects, and it has exclusionary features such as the 10-year term, the full capacity clause, the return charges, and the failure to segregate service charges from machine charges. Moreover, the leasing system has aided United in maintaining a pricing system which discriminates between machine types. . . .

They are contracts, arrangements, and policies which, instead of encouraging competition based on pure merit, further the dominance of a particular firm. In this sense, they are unnatural barriers; they unnecessarily exclude actual and potential competition; they restrict a free market. While the law allows many enterprises to use such practices, the Sherman Act is now construed by superior courts to forbid the continuance of effective market control based in part upon such practices. Those courts hold that market control is inherently evil and constitutes a violation of § 2 unless economically inevitable, or specifically authorized and regulated by law. . . .

Although leasing should not now be abolished by judicial decree, the Court agrees with the Government that the leases should be purged of their restrictive features. In the decree filed herewith, the term of the lease is shortened, the full capacity clause is eliminated, the discriminatory commutative charges are removed, and United is required to segregate its charges for machines from its charges for repair service.

. . . Some price discrimination, if not too rigid, is inevitable. Some may be justified as resting on patent monopolies. Some price discrimination is economically desirable, if it promotes competition in a market where several multiproduct firms compete. And while price discrimination has been an evidence of United's monopoly power, a buttress to it, and a cause of its perpetuation, its eradication cannot be accomplished without turning United into a public utility, and the Court into a public utility commission, or requiring United to observe a general injunction of nondiscrimination between different products—an injunction which would be contrary to sound theory, which would require the use of practices not followed in any business known to the Court, and which could not be enforced. . . .

United States v. E. I. du Pont de Nemours & Co.

Supreme Court of the United States, 1956.
351 U.S. 377, 76 S.Ct. 994, 100 L.Ed. 1264.

Du Pont's virtual monopoly of cellophane did display clear intent and high profits, but the majority chose to define the market broadly. The Court was soon defining markets much more closely (see Grinnell and the merger cases below). What was the "correct" market boundary here?

Reed, J.   The United States brought this civil action under § 4 of the Sherman Act against E. I. du Pont de Nemours and Company. The complaint . . . charged du Pont with monopolizing, attempting to monopolize and conspiracy to monopolize interstate commerce in cellophane and cellulosic caps and bands in violation of § 2 of the Sherman Act. . . . After a lengthy trial, judgment was entered for du Pont on all issues. . . . The appeal, as specifically stated by the Government, "attacks only the ruling that du Pont has not monopolized trade in cellophane." At issue for determination is only this alleged violation by du Pont of § 2 of the Sherman Act.

During the period that is relevant to this action, du Pont produced almost 75 percent of the cellophane sold in the United States, and cellophane constituted less than 20 percent of all "flexible packaging material" sales.

. . . In considering what is the relevant market for determining the control of price and competition, no more definite rule can be declared than that commodities reasonably interchangeable by consumers for the same purposes make up that "part of the trade or commerce," monopolization of which may be illegal. As respects flexible packaging materials, the market geographically is nationwide.

. . . Cellophane costs more than many competing products and less than a few. But whatever the price, there are various flexible wrapping materials that are bought by manufacturers for packaging their goods in their own plants or are sold to converters who shape and print them for use in the packaging of the commodities to be wrapped.

Cellophane differs from other flexible packaging materials. From some it differs more than from others. The basic materials from which the wrappings are made and the advantages and disadvantages of the products to the packaging industry are summarized in Findings 62 and 63. They are aluminum, cellulose acetate, chlorides, wood pulp, rubber hydrochloride, and ethylene gas. It will adequately illustrate the similarity in characteristics of the various products by noting here Finding 62 as to glassine. Its use is almost as extensive as cellophane and many of its characteristics equally or more satisfactory to users.

It may be admitted that cellophane combines the desirable elements of transparency, strength and cheapness more definitely than any of the others. . . .

But, despite cellophane's advantages, it has to meet competition from other materials in every one of its uses. . . . Food products are the chief outlet, with cigarettes next. The Government makes no challenge to Finding 283 that cellophane furnishes less than 7 percent of wrappings for bakery products, 25 percent for candy, 32 percent for snacks, 35 percent for meats and poultry, 27 percent for crackers and biscuits, 47 percent for fresh produce, and 34 percent for frozen foods. Seventy-five to eighty percent of cigarettes are wrapped in cellophane. Thus, cellophane shares the packaging market with others. The over-all result is that cellophane accounts for 17.9 percent of flexible wrapping materials, measured by the wrapping surface. . . .

The facts above considered dispose also of any contention that competitors have been excluded by du Pont from the packaging material market.

That market has many producers and there is no proof du Pont ever has possessed power to exclude any of them from the rapidly expanding flexible packaging market. . . . Nor can we say that du Pont's profits, while liberal (according to the Government 15.9 percent net after taxes on the 1937–1947 average), demonstrate the existence of a monopoly without proof of lack of comparable profits during those years in other prosperous industries. Cellophane was a leader, over 17 percent, in the flexible packaging materials market. There is no showing that du Pont's rate of return was greater or less than that of other producers of flexible packaging materials. . . .

The "market" which one must study to determine when a producer has monopoly power will vary with the part of commerce under consideration. The tests are constant. That market is composed of products that have reasonable interchangeability for the purposes for which they are produced —price, use and qualities considered. While the application of the tests remains uncertain, it seems to us that du Pont should not be found to monopolize cellophane when that product has the competition and interchangeability with other wrappings that this record shows.

On the findings of the District Court, its judgment is affirmed.

Warren, C. J., with whom Black and Douglas, JJ., join, dissenting:

. . . We cannot agree that cellophane, in the language of Times-Picayune Publishing Co. v. United States, 345 U.S. 594, 613, 73 S.Ct. 872, 883, 97 L.Ed. 1277, is " 'the self-same product' " as glassine, grease-proof and vegetable parchment papers, waxed papers, sulphite papers, aluminum foil, cellulose acetate, and Pliofilm and other films.

If the conduct of buyers indicated that glassine, waxed and sulphite papers and aluminum foil were actually "the self-same products" as cellophane, the qualitative differences demonstrated by the comparison of physical properties in Finding 59 would not be conclusive. But the record provides convincing proof that businessmen did not so regard these products. During the period covered by the complaint (1923–1947) cellophane enjoyed phenomenal growth. Du Pont's 1924 production was 361,249 pounds, which sold for $1,306,662. Its 1947 production was 133,502,858 pounds, which sold for $55,339,626. Findings 297 and 337. Yet throughout this period the price of cellophane was far greater than that of glassine, waxed paper or sulphite paper. Finding 136 states that in 1929 cellophane's price was seven times that of glassine; in 1934, four times, and in 1949 still more than twice glassine's price. Reference to DX–994, the graph upon which Finding 136 is based, shows that cellophane had a similar price relation to waxed paper and that sulphite paper sold at even less than glassine and waxed paper. We cannot believe that buyers, practical businessmen, would have bought cellophane in increasing amounts over a quarter of a century if close substitutes were available at from one seventh to one half cellophane's price. That they did so is testimony to cellophane's distinctiveness.

The inference yielded by the conduct by cellophane buyers is reinforced by the conduct of sellers other than du Pont. Finding 587 states that Sylvania, the only other cellophane producer, absolutely and immediately followed every du Pont price change, even dating back its price list to the effective date of du Pont's change. Producers of glassine and waxed paper, on the other hand, displayed apparent indifference to du Pont's repeated and substantial price cuts. DX–994 shows that from 1924 to 1932 du Pont dropped the price of plain cellophane 84 percent, while the price of glassine remained constant. And during the period 1933–1946 the prices for glassine and waxed paper actually increased in the face of a further 21 percent decline in the price of cellophane. If "shifts of business" due to "price sensitivity" had been substantial, glassine and waxed paper producers who wanted to stay in business would have been compelled by market forces to meet du Pont's price challenge just as Sylvania was. . . .

Certainly du Pont itself shared our view. From the first, du Pont recognized that it need not concern itself with competition from other packaging materials. For example, when du Pont was contemplating entry into cellophane production, its Development Department reported that glassine "is so inferior that it belongs in an entirely different class and has hardly to be considered as a competitor of cellophane." This was still du Pont's view in 1950 when its survey of competitive prospects wholly omitted reference to glassine, waxed paper or sulphite paper and stated that "Competition for du Pont cellophane will come from competitive cellophane and from noncellophane films made by us or by others."

. . . A confidential du Pont report shows that during the period 1937–1947, despite great expansion of sales, du Pont's "operative return" (before taxes) averaged 31 percent, while its average "net return" (after deduction of taxes, bonuses, and fundamental research expenditures) was 15.9 percent. Such profits provide a powerful incentive for the entry of competitors.

Yet from 1924 to 1951 only one new firm, Sylvania, was able to begin cellophane production. And Sylvania could not have entered if La Cellophane's secret process had not been stolen. . . .

The foregoing analysis of the record shows conclusively that cellophane is the relevant market. Since du Pont has the lion's share of that market, it must have monopoly power, as the majority concede. This being so, we think it clear that, in the circumstances of this case, du Pont is guilty of "monopolization." The briefest sketch of du Pont's business history precludes it from falling within the "exception to the Sherman Act prohibitions of monopoly power" (majority opinion, 76 S.Ct. 1004) by successfully asserting that monopoly was "thrust upon" it. Du Pont was not "the passive beneficiary of a monopoly" within the meaning of United States v. Aluminum Co. of America, supra, 148 F.2d at pages 429–430. It sought and maintained dominance through illegal agreements dividing the world market, concealing and suppressing technological information, and restricting its licensee's production by prohibitive royalties, and through numerous maneuvers which might have been "honestly industrial" but whose necessary effect was nevertheless exclusionary. . . .

United States v. Grinnell Corp.
Supreme Court of the United States, 1966.
384 U.S. 563, 86 S.Ct. 1698, L.Ed.2d 778.

> Grinnell *contrasts with* Cellophane: *the Warren Court grew more sensitive to the existence of significant monopoly. Grinnell was next acquired by ITT and then divested into genuinely competitive conditions in 1971. Its performance is reported to be sharply improved.*

Douglas, J.   This case presents an important question under § 2 of the Sherman Act, which makes it an offense for any person to "monopolize . . . any part of the trade or commerce among the several States." This is a civil suit brought by the United States against Grinnell Corporation (Grinnell), American District Telegraph Co. (ADT), Holmes Electric Protective Co. (Holmes) and Automatic Fire Alarm Co. of Delaware (AFA). . . .

Grinnell manufactures plumbing supplies and fire sprinkler systems. It also owns 76 percent of the stock of ADT, 89 percent of the stock of AFA, and 100 percent of the stock of Holmes. ADT provides both burglary and fire protection services; Holmes provides burglary services alone; AFA supplies only fire protection service. Each offers a central station service under which hazard-detecting devices installed on the protected premises automatically transmit an electric signal to a central station. The central station is manned 24 hours a day. Upon receipt of a signal, the central station, where appropriate, dispatches guards to the protected premises and notifies the police or fire department direct. There are other forms of protective services. But the record shows that subscribers to accredited central station service (i.e., that approved by the insurance underwriters) receive reductions in their insurance premiums that are substantially greater than the reduction received by the users of other kinds of protection service. In 1961 accredited companies in the central station service business grossed $65,000,000. ADT, Holmes, and AFA are the three largest companies in the business in terms of revenue: ADT (with 121 central stations in 115 cities) has 73 percent of the business; Holmes (with 12 central stations in three large cities) has 12.5 percent; AFA (with three central stations in three large cities) has 2 percent. Thus the three companies that Grinnell controls have over 87 percent of the business. . . .

ADT over the years reduced its minimum basic rates to meet competition and renewed contracts at substantially increased rates in cities where it had a monopoly of accredited central station service. ADT threatened retaliation against firms that contemplated inaugurating central station service. And the record indicates that, in contemplating opening a new central station, ADT officials frequently stressed that such action would deter their competitors from opening a new station in that area.

The offense of monopoly under § 2 of the Sherman Act has two elements: (1) the possession of monopoly power in the relevant market and (2) the willful acquisition or maintenance of that power as distinguished from growth or development as a consequence of a superior product, business acumen, or historic accident. We shall see that this second ingredient presents no major problem here, as what was done in building the empire was done plainly and explicitly for a single purpose. . . . In the present case, 87 percent of the accredited central station service business leaves no doubt that the congeries of these defendants have monopoly power—power which, as our discussion of the record indicates, they did not hesitate to wield—if that business is the relevant market. The only remaining question therefore is, what is the relevant market? . . .

The District Court treated the entire accredited central station service business as a single market and we think it was justified in so doing. Defendants argue that the different central station services offered are so diverse that they cannot under *du Pont* be lumped together to make up the relevant market. For example, burglar alarm services are not interchangeable with fire alarm services. They further urge that *du Pont* requires that protective services other than those of the central station variety be included in the market definition.

But there is here a single use, i.e., the protection of property, through a central station that receives signals. It is that service, accredited, that is unique and that competes with all the other forms of property protection. We see no barrier to combining in a single market a number of different products or services where that combination reflects commercial realities. To repeat, there is here a single basic service—the protection of property through use of a central service station—that must be compared with all other forms of property protection. . . .

Burglar alarm service is in a sense different from fire alarm service; from waterflow alarms; and so on. But it would be unrealistic on this record to break down the market into the various kinds of central station protective services that are available. Central station companies recognize that to compete effectively, they must offer all or nearly all types of service. The different forms of accredited central station service are provided from a single office and customers utilize different services in combination.

Fortas, J., with whom Stewart, J., joins, dissenting:

The trial court's definition of the "product" market even more dramatically demonstrates that its action has been Procrustean—that it has tailored the market to the dimensions of the defendants. It recognizes that a person seeking protective services has many alternative sources. It lists "watchmen, watchdogs, automatic proprietary systems confined to one site (often, but not always), alarm systems connected with some local police or fire station, often unaccredited CSPS [central station protective services], and often accredited CSPS." The court finds that even in the same city a single customer seeking protection for several premises may "exercise its option" differently for different locations. It may choose accredited CSPS for one of its locations and a different type of service for another.

But the court isolates from all of these alternatives only those services in which defendants engage. It eliminates all of the alternative sources despite its conscientious enumeration of them. Its definition of the "relevant market" is not merely confined to "central station" protective services, but to those central station protective services which are "accredited" by insurance companies.

There is no pretense that these furnish peculiar services for which there is no alternative in the market place, on either a price or a functional basis. The court relies solely upon its finding that the services offered by accredited central stations are of better quality, and upon its conclusion that the insurance companies tend to give "noticeably larger" discounts to policyholders who are accredited central station protective services. This Court now approves this strange red-haired, bearded, one-eyed man-with-a-limp classification.

I do not suggest that wide disparities in quality, price and customer appeal could never affect the definition of the market. But this follows only where the disparities are so great that they create separate and distinct categories of buyers and sellers. The record here and the findings do not approach this standard. They fall far short of justifying the narrowing of the market as practiced here. I need refer only to the exclusion of nonaccredited central stations, which the court seeks to justify by reference to differentials in insurance discounts. This differential may indeed affect the relative cost to the consumer of the competing modes of protection. But, in the absence of proof that it results in eliminating the competing services from the category of those to which the purchaser "can practicably turn" for supplies, it does not justify their total exclusion. This sort of exclusion of the supposedly not-quite-so-attractive service from the basic definition of the kinds of business and service against which defendants' activity will be measured, is entirely unjustified on this record.

United States v. International Business Machines Corporation

United States District Court
for the Southern District of New York
Civil Action No. 69 CIV. 200

Filed under melodramatic conditions on January 17, 1969, this briefly worded suit climaxed a three-year investigation and set up what may be the big Section 2 case of the 1970s. The alleged market share is about 70 percent: the plus is pervasive price discrimination. Trial was finally set to begin over six years later. If the case ran the full course, any remedy could take at least ten years more.

. . . IBM was originally organized as the Computer-Tabulating-Recording Co. and from 1911 to 1933 it owned a majority of the capital stock of, and controlled, The Tabulating Machine Company, a corporation organized in 1905 under the laws of the State of New Jersey. During this period IBM operated in the tabulating field through The Tabulating Machine Company, which was merged with IBM in 1933. The tabulating business continued to represent the major product line of IBM until the advent of the electronic computer in the 1950s.

11. In 1932 the United States filed a civil antitrust suit against IBM and Remington Rand, Inc., charging that they had unreasonably restrained and monopolized interstate trade and commerce in tabulating machines and tabulating cards by entering into agreements in which they agreed:

a.   To lease only and not sell tabulating machines.
b.   To adhere to minimum prices for the rental of tabulating machines as fixed by IBM.
c.   To require customers to purchase their cards and requirements from the lessor or pay a higher price for the rental of machines.

The agreements between IBM and Remington Rand, Inc. were cancelled in 1934 prior to the trial of that suit, and the issues presented by the agreements were withdrawn from the case. The lease provision requiring the lessees to purchase cards from the lessor was adjudged to be illegal by this Court.

12. On January 21, 1952, the United States filed another civil antitrust suit against IBM charging that it had violated Sections 1 and 2 of the Sherman Act by attempting to monopolize and monopolizing interstate trade and commerce in the tabulating industry. The complaint alleged that IBM owned more than 90 percent of all the tabulating machines in the United States and manufactured and sold about 90 percent of all tabulating cards sold in the United States. This suit was terminated by the entry of a consent judgment by this Court on January 25, 1956. . . .

16. IBM's total revenues from the sale or lease of general purpose digital computers in the United States increased from $506,668,000 in 1961 to $2,311,353,000 in 1967. During this period of time IBM's share of total industry revenues of these products varied from approximately 69 percent to approximately 80 percent. In 1967 IBM's share of such revenues was approximately 74 percent. Its nearest competitor in 1967 had revenues of approximately $156,000,000 or 5 percent of the total.

17. Approximately 76 percent of the value of all general purpose digital computers shipped in the United States in 1967 were shipped by IBM while its two nearest competitors together accounted for about 8 percent of such shipments. At the end of the same year, approximately 67 percent of the value of all installed general purpose digital computers in the United States was represented by machines that had been manufactured by IBM.

18. IBM manufactures general purpose digital computers at its plants located in Poughkeepsie and Endicott, New York, and manufactures parts, components and subassemblies at numerous other plants in the United States. Such computers and related products are shipped to customers located throughout the United States. . . .

20. Pursuant to and in furtherance of the aforesaid attempt to monopolize and the monopolization, the defendant has pursued a manufacturing and marketing policy that has prevented competing manufacturers of general purpose digital computers from having an adequate opportunity effectively to compete for business in the general purpose digital computer market, and has done, among other acts, the following:

a. Maintained a pricing policy whereby it quotes a single price for hardware, software and related support and, thereunder, (i) discriminated among customers by providing certain customers with extensive software and related support in a manner that unreasonably inhibited the entry or growth of competitors; and (ii) limited the development and scope of activities of an independent software and computer support industry as a result of which the ability of its competitors to compete effectively was unreasonably impaired.

b. Used its accumulated software and related support to preclude its competitors from effectively competing for various customer accounts.

c. Restrained and attempted to restrain competitors from entering or remaining in the general purpose digital computer market by introducing selected computers, with unusually low profit expectations, in those segments of the market where competitors had or appeared likely to have unusual competitive success, and by announcing future production of new models for such markets when it knew that it was unlikely to be able to complete production within the announced time.

d. Dominated the educational market for general purpose digital computers, which was of unusual importance to the growth of competitors both by reason of this market's substantiality and by reason of its ultimate impact on the purchasing decisions in the commercial market, by granting exceptional discriminatory allowances in favor of universities and other educational institutions. . . .

United States of America before
Federal Trade Commission
in the matter of
Xerox Corporation
Docket No. 8909

The premier new dominant firm of the 1960s, Xerox has strong patent protection until at least 1978. This action was part of the FTC "revival" after 1970. It seeks mainly to loosen the patent barriers, rather than change structure. Tentative agreement on modest relief was announced in late 1974 but reversed in 1975.

COMPLAINT

The Federal Trade Commission, having reason to believe that Xerox Corporation, hereinafter referred to as Xerox or respondent, has violated and is violating Section 5 of the Federal Trade Commission Act, and that a proceeding in respect thereof would be in the public interest, issues this complaint, stating its charges as follows: . . .

In 1971, Xerox's total revenues were approximately $2 billion, net income after taxes was approximately $213 million, and total assets were approximately $2.2 billion. Xerox's after-tax return on stockholders' equity averaged 21.2 percent for the period 1967 through 1971. In 1971, approximately 50 percent of Xerox's total revenues were derived from its domestic business in office copiers and supplies and approximately 25 percent of Xerox's total revenues were derived from Rank Xerox. In 1971, Xerox was approximately the 52nd largest domestic industrial firm in terms of total revenues and approximately the 17th most profitable such firm based on return on stockholders' equity. . . .

IV. Nature of Trade and Commerce

The relevant market is the sale and lease of office copiers in the United States, hereinafter referred to as the office copier market. This market includes as a relevant submarket the sale and lease of plain paper office copiers in the United States, hereinafter referred to as the plain paper submarket. The office copier market is dominated by the plain paper submarket and Xerox dominates the plain paper submarket.

a. In 1971, revenues from the sale and lease of office copiers were approximately $1.1 billion and total revenues from the sale and lease of office copiers and supplies were approximately $1.7 billion; Xerox accounted for approximately 86 percent of the former and 60 percent of the latter. In 1971, revenues from the sale and lease of plain paper copiers and supplies were approximately $1.0 billion; Xerox accounted for approximately 95 percent of said revenues.

The office copier market has had and continues to have high barriers to entry and barriers to effective competition among existing competitors. . . .

VI. Violations

a. Xerox has monopoly power in the relevant market and submarket.

b. Xerox has the power to inhibit, frustrate, and hinder effective competition among firms participating in the relevant market and submarket.

Xerox has engaged in marketing acts, practices and methods of competition including, but not limited to,

a. following a lease only policy pursuant to which Xerox refuses to sell and discourages the sale of its office copiers,

b. using package leasing plans and quantity discount rental price plans,

c. discriminating in price among customers,

d. maintaining a stock of depreciated copiers and planning to use or using such copiers to inhibit, frustrate, or hinder price competition,

e. announcing new copier models and taking orders thereon before availability of such copiers in response to introduction of competing copiers by actual or potential competitors,

f. requiring that it be the exclusive source of maintenance and repair service for leased Xerox office copiers,

g. falsely disparaging competitive supplies,

h. tying supplies to the lease of office copiers.

Xerox has engaged in acts, practices and methods of competition relating to patents including, but not limited to,

a. monopolizing and attempting to monopolize patents applicable to office copiers,

b. maintaining a patent barrier to competition by attempting to recreate a patent structure which would be equivalent in scope to expired patents,

c. developing and maintaining a patent structure of great size, complexity, and obscurity of boundaries,

d. using its patent position to obtain access to technology owned by actual or potential competitors.

e. entering into cross-license arrangements with actual or potential competitors.

f. including in licenses under United States Patent Number 3,121,006 provisions having the effect of limiting licenses to the manufacture and sale of only coated paper copiers,

g. offering patent licenses applicable to plain paper copiers with provisions which, in effect, limit the licensee to the manufacture or sale of low speed copiers,

h. including in patent licenses provisions having the effect of precluding the licensee from utilizing Xerox patents in the office copier market. . . .

NOTICE OF CONTEMPLATED RELIEF

Should the Commission conclude from the record developed in any adjudicative proceeding in this matter that the respondent, Xerox Corporation, is in violation of Section 5 of the Federal Trade Commission Act, as alleged in the Complaint, the Commission may order such relief as is supported by the record and is necessary and appropriate, including, but not limited to:

1. Mandatory royalty-free unrestricted licensing of all existing patents pertinent to office copiers (including rights resulting from pending patent applications), mandatory unrestricted licensing of patents pertinent to office copiers obtained during the 20 years following the date of the Order, and disclosure to licensees of know-how related to practice of licensed patents.

2. Divestiture of the stock of Rank Xerox, Ltd., and prohibition of any restriction on Rank Xerox from selling or distributing office copiers in the United States.

3. Prohibition of refusal to sell office copiers.

4. Prohibition of acquisition of the stock or assets of any corporation making office copiers or supplies or of entering into any joint venture for the making of office copiers or supplies.

5. Prohibition of the utilization of price plans the terms of which are

based on the fact that the purchaser or lessee of an office copier has purchased or leased, or will purchase or lease, any other office copier, or any supplies, from Xerox.

6. Prohibition of false disparagement of competitors' supply products.

7. Prohibition of requirements that Xerox be the exclusive source of maintenance and repair service for leased Xerox copiers.

8. Any other provisions appropriate to correct or remedy the effects of anticompetitive practices engaged in by respondent.

United States v. *American Telephone and Telegraph Company; Western Electric Company, Inc.; and Bell Telephone Laboratories, Inc.*

United States District Court for the
District of Columbia, 1974
Civil Action No. 74–1698

This is probably the major Section 2 suit to be filed in the 1970s. It challenges a variety of structural forms and restrictive practices in telecommunications, which is dominated by the Bell System. Though much of the sector is "regulated" as a "natural monopoly," many experts now urge that large parts are potentially quite competitive (only local-service switching is universally agreed to be a natural monopoly). The suit aims mainly at Western Electric's monopoly of equipment supply, and at the Long Lines Departments' role. If carried through, it would breed competition both in (1) the supply of equipment to Bell companies and to customers, and in (2) the transmission of bulk message and data traffic among cities. Unless it is settled by compromise, the case is likely to come to trial after 1979 and take perhaps another decade or more to run its full course. It is reproduced in full here as a fine example of a brief complaint which casts a long shadow.

COMPLAINT

The United States of America, plaintiff, by its attorneys, acting under the direction of the Attorney General of the United States, brings this civil action to obtain equitable relief against the defendants named herein, and complains and alleges as follows:

I. Jurisdiction and Venue

1. This complaint is filed and this action is instituted under Section 4 of the Act of Congress of July 2, 1890, as amended (15 U.S.C. § 4), commonly known as the Sherman Act, in order to prevent and restrain the continuing violations by the defendants, as hereinafter alleged, of Section 2 of the Sherman Act (15 U.S.C. § 2).

2. Defendants American Telephone and Telegraph Company and Western Electric Company, Inc., transact business and are found within the District of Columbia.

II. The Defendants

3. American Telephone and Telegraph Company (hereinafter referred to as "AT&T") is made a defendant herein. AT&T is a corporation organized and existing under the laws of the State of New York, with its principal place of business in New York, New York. AT&T, directly and through subsidiaries, is engaged in providing telecommunications service and in the manufacture of telecommunications equipment.

4. Western Electric Company, Inc. (hereinafter referred to as "Western Electric"), is made a defendant herein. Western Electric is a corporation organized and existing under the laws of the State of New York, with its principal place of business in New York, New York. Western Electric is engaged, directly and through subsidiaries, in the manufacture and supply of telecommunications equipment. Western Electric is a wholly-owned subsidiary of AT&T.

5. Bell Telephone Laboratories, Inc. (hereinafter referred to as "Bell Labs"), is made a defendant herein. Bell Labs is a corporation organized and existing under the laws of the State of New York, with its principal place of business in Murray Hill, New Jersey. Bell Labs is engaged in telecommunications research, development and design work. Bell Labs is owned jointly by AT&T and Western Electric.

III. Co-Conspirators

6. Various other persons, firms and corporations not made defendants herein have participated as co-conspirators with the defendants in the violations hereinafter alleged and have performed acts and made statements in furtherance thereof. Said co-conspirators include, but are not limited to, the following telephone companies:

Name of Corporation	Percentage of Voting Shares Owned by AT&T	Area Served
New England Telephone & Telegraph Company	85.4	Maine, Massachusetts, New Hampshire, Rhode Island, Vermont
The Southern New England Telephone Company	17.1	Connecticut
New York Telephone Company	100.0	New York, Connecticut
New Jersey Bell Telephone Company	100.0	New Jersey
The Bell Telephone Company of Pennsylvania	100.0	Pennsylvania
The Diamond State Telephone Company	100.0	Delaware
The Chesapeake and Potomac Telephone Company	100.0	Washington, D.C.
The Chesapeake and Potomac Telephone Company of Maryland	100.0	Maryland
The Chesapeake and Potomac Telephone Company of Virginia	100.0	Virginia
The Chesapeake and Potomac Telephone Company of West Virginia	100.0	West Virginia
Southern Bell Telephone and Telegraph Company	100.0	Florida, Georgia, North Carolina, South Carolina
South Central Bell Telephone Company	100.0	Alabama, Kentucky, Louisiana, Mississippi, Tennessee
The Ohio Bell Telephone Company	100.0	Ohio
Cincinnati Bell Inc.	25.7	Ohio, Kentucky, Indiana
Michigan Bell Telephone Company	100.0	Michigan
Indiana Bell Telephone Company, Incorporated	100.0	Indiana
Wisconsin Telephone Company	100.0	Wisconsin
Illinois Bell Telephone Company	100.0	Illinois, Indiana
Northwestern Bell Telephone Company	100.0	Iowa, Minnesota, Nebraska, North Dakota, South Dakota
Southwestern Bell Telephone Company	100.0	Arkansas, Kansas, Missouri, Oklahoma, Texas, Illinois

Name of Corporation	Percentage of Voting Shares Owned by AT&T	Area Served
The Mountain States Telephone and Telegraph Company	87.8	Arizona, Colorado, Idaho, Montana, New Mexico, Utah, Wyoming, Texas
Pacific Northwest Bell Telephone Company	89.2	Oregon, Washington, Idaho
The Pacific Telephone & Telegraph Company	89.7	California, Nevada

IV. Definitions

7. As used herein:

a. "Bell Operating Companies" shall mean the companies listed in paragraph 6 above, and their subsidiaries.

b. "Bell System" shall mean AT&T and the Bell Operating Companies.

c. "Independent telephone companies" shall mean all telephone operating companies in the United States except the Bell Operating Companies.

V. Trade and Commerce

8. Telecommunications consists of the electronic and electromagnetic transmission of voice, data and other communications by wire, cable, microwave radio and communications satellite.

9. Telephone communication is the most common form of telecommunications service. Telephone service permits voice telephone communication between subscribers, and includes among other services, local exchange service for telephone calls between subscribers located within the same local telephone exchange area and long distance or "message toll service" for telephone calls between subscribers located in different exchange areas.

10. Local exchange service is provided by connecting all subscribers in the same local exchange area through one or more central offices. Typically, wire pairs connect each subscriber to telephone company central office switching facilities in that exchange area.

11. Message toll service is provided by connecting central offices in different local exchange areas. The connection of these local exchange areas, through trunk lines and toll switching offices, permits long distance telephone service throughout the United States. Message toll service typically involves the transmission of telecommunications via microwave radio or

coaxial cable between local telephone exchanges, with central office switching equipment in each local exchange area providing each subscriber access to the long distance toll network. The long distance toll network is a nationwide web of trunk lines and toll offices linking all of the telephone operating companies in the United States.

12. Telephone service in the United States is provided by the Bell System and by approximately 1,705 independent telephone companies. Telephone operating companies typically contract with subscribers for local exchange service, connecting the subscriber with the telephone company central office. Subscribers typically are charged installation fees and a monthly charge for service. The telephone companies retain title to the equipment installed, and retain control over the equipment after service is terminated.

13. The Bell Operating Companies provide local telephone service in the 48 contiguous states. As of December 31, 1973, the Bell Operating Companies served approximately 113.2 million telephones, or approximately 82 percent of the nation's telephones. Approximately 1,705 independent telephone companies account for the remaining 18 percent of the nation's telephones. The AT&T's Long Lines Department provides interstate telephone service. For the year ending December 31, 1973, more than 90 percent of all interstate telephone calls in the United States were routed in whole or in part over Bell System facilities. In 1973 the Bell System's total revenue from telephone service was approximately $22 billion. The Bell System is by far the largest supplier of telephone service in the United States.

14. In addition to telephone service, telecommunications includes the transmission of data, facsimile, audio and video programming and other specialized forms of telecommunications. Transmission of these specialized telecommunications may be accomplished over the same nationwide switched network which accommodates telephone service, or over private lines.

15. Private line service involves the leasing of telecommunications circuits to subscribers with a high volume of communications requirements between specific locations. Private lines may be used for the transmission of voice, data, audio and video programming and other specialized forms of telecommunications. Private line service may simply connect two points or may be switched between and among multiple points. A private line may be connected with the switched telephone network.

16. The Bell System provides intercity private line service for the transmission of voice, data, facsimile, audio and video programming and other telecommunications. Private line services are also provided by Specialized Common Carriers, Miscellaneous Common Carriers and Domestic Satellite Carriers. Specialized Common Carriers, Miscellaneous Common Carriers and Domestic Satellite Carriers compete with the Bell System in providing private line service. Total revenue from private line service in 1973 was

approximately $1.1 billion. In 1973 Bell System revenue from private line service was approximately $1 billion, or approximately 90 percent of total private line revenue. The Bell System is by far the largest supplier of private line service in the United States.

17. Although many organizations with substantial needs for long distance voice and data telecommunications purchase such services on a private line basis, some organizations construct and maintain private systems for the long distance transmission of voice, data and other telecommunications.

18. Land mobile telecommunications consist of paging, dispatch and mobile telephone service provided by radio communication. These services may be interconnected with the nationwide switched telephone system, permitting communication with telephone subscribers on both a local exchange and a message toll basis. Land mobile telecommunications are provided by Radio Common Carriers, independent telephone companies and the Bell Operating Companies.

19. Telecommunications equipment is used to provide telephone service and other telecommunications, and includes terminal equipment, switching equipment and transmission equipment. Terminal equipment is equipment used principally in telecommunications and installed at the premises of the subscriber. Switching equipment is equipment in local exchange central offices and toll offices used to route and switch telecommunications between subscribers. Transmission equipment is used to transmit telecommunications.

20. Until about 1968, telephone operating companies typically prohibited the interconnection of customer provided terminal equipment with telephone company facilities and, with limited exceptions, provided all the terminal equipment located on subscribers' premises. Telephone operating companies were thus the only significant purchasers of telecommunications terminal equipment.

21. Telephone subscribers and other telecommunications customers may provide their own terminal equipment, and need not rely solely on the offerings of telephone operating companies. Customers may obtain terminal equipment from numerous manufacturers and suppliers, known collectively as the "interconnect industry."

22. Western Electric manufactures and supplies telecommunications equipment for the Bell System and is the largest manufacturer of telecommunications equipment in the United States. Western Electric's subsidiary, Teletype Corporation, manufactures teletypewriters and data transmission equipment. A substantial majority of the telecommunications transmission, switching and terminal equipment used by the Bell System is supplied by Western Electric. Although Western Electric also sells telecommunications equipment to government agencies, it typically does not sell equipment to independent telephone companies or other users of telecommuni-

cations equipment. In 1973, Western Electric's sales to the Bell System were $6.2 billion. Western Electric's total sales in 1973 were $7.0 billion. Western Electric is by far the largest supplier, and the Bell System is by far the largest purchaser, of telecommunications equipment in the United States.

23. AT&T provides services to each Bell Operating Company pursuant to agreements known as "License Contracts." Under these agreements AT&T undertakes to maintain arrangements whereby telephones and related equipment may be manufactured under patents owned or controlled by AT&T and may be purchased by each Operating Company for use within a specified territory; to prosecute research in telephony continuously and to make available to the Operating Company benefits derived therefrom; and to furnish advice and assistance with respect to virtually all phases of the Operating Company's business. The License Contracts, or supplementary agreements in the case of four Operating Companies, provide that AT&T will maintain connections between each licensee's telephone system and the systems of the other Bell Operating Companies, and provide for joint use of certain rights-of-way and facilities. Supplementary agreements cover the sharing of revenues derived by AT&T and the Bell Operating Companies from interstate and foreign services.

24. Western Electric manufactures and supplies equipment to AT&T and each Bell Operating Company pursuant to agreements known as "Standard Supply Contracts." Under these agreements, as supplemented, Western Electric agrees, upon the order of each Operating Company and to the extent reasonably required for the latter's business, to manufacture materials or to purchase and inspect materials manufactured by others and to sell these materials to the Operating Company. Western Electric also agrees to maintain stocks at distribution points, to prepare equipment specifications, to perform installations of materials and to repair, sell or otherwise dispose of used materials. Under each agreement Western Electric's prices and terms are to be as low as to its most favored customers for like materials and services under comparable conditions.

25. Bell Labs conducts telecommunications research and development for Western Electric and the Bell System. Owned jointly by AT&T and Western Electric, Bell Labs' 1974 budget for telecommunications research and development exceeded $500 million. Bell Labs maintains its principal laboratories in Murray Hill, Holmdel and Whippany, New Jersey, and Naperville, Illinois, and additional facilities in seven other states. Bell Labs is by far the largest telecommunications research and development facility in the United States.

26. AT&T, directly and through subsidiaries, regularly transmits voice, data and other telecommunications across state lines to customers located throughout the United States. Western Electric, directly and through subsidiaries, manufactures telecommunications equipment at locations in

many states and regularly sells and ships such equipment across state lines to customers located throughout the United States. Bell Labs conducts telecommunications research and development at locations in many states and regularly disseminates the results of such research and development to consumers thereof throughout the United States. AT&T, Western Electric and Bell Labs have been and are engaged in interstate commerce.

VI. Violations Alleged

27. For many years past and continuing up to and including the date of the filing of this complaint, the defendants and co-conspirators have been engaged in an unlawful combination and conspiracy to monopolize, and the defendants have attempted to monopolize and have monopolized, the aforesaid interstate trade and commerce in telecommunications service, and submarkets thereof, and telecommunications equipment, and submarkets thereof, in violation of Section 2 of the Sherman Act. Defendants are continuing and will continue these violations unless the relief hereinafter prayed for is granted.

28. The aforesaid combination and conspiracy to monopolize has consisted of a continuing agreement and concert of action among the defendants and co-conspirators, the substantial terms of which have been and are:

a. That AT&T shall achieve and maintain control over the operations and policies of Western Electric, Bell Labs and the Bell Operating Companies;

b. That the defendants and co-conspirators shall attempt to prevent, restrict and eliminate competition from other telecommunications common carriers;

c. That the defendants and co-conspirators shall attempt to prevent, restrict and eliminate competition from private telecommunications systems;

d. That Western Electric shall supply the telecommunications equipment requirements of the Bell System;

e. That defendants and co-conspirators shall attempt to prevent, restrict and eliminate competition from other manufacturers and suppliers of telecommunications equipment.

29. Pursuant to and in effectuation of the aforesaid combination and conspiracy to monopolize, attempt to monopolize and monopolization, the defendants, among other things, have done the following:

a. Attempted to obstruct and obstructed the interconnection of Specialized Common Carriers with the Bell System.

b. Attempted to obstruct and obstructed the interconnection of Miscellaneous Common Carriers with the Bell System.

  c. Attempted to obstruct and obstructed the interconnection of Radio
     Common Carriers with the Bell System.
  d. Attempted to obstruct and obstructed the interconnection of Domes-
     tic Satellite Carriers with the Bell System.
  e. Attempted to obstruct and obstructed the interconnection of customer
     provided terminal equipment with the Bell System.
  f. Refused to sell terminal equipment to subscribers of Bell System
     telecommunications service.
  g. Caused Western Electric to manufacture substantially all of the tele-
     communications equipment requirements of the Bell System.
  h. Caused the Bell System to purchase substantially all of its telecom-
     munications equipment requirements from Western Electric.

VII. Effects

30. The aforesaid violations have had the following effects, among
others:

  a. Defendants have achieved and maintained a monopoly of telecommunications service, and submarkets thereof, and telecommunications
equipment, and submarkets thereof, in the United States.

  b. Actual and potential competition in telecommunications service,
and submarkets thereof, and telecommunications equipment, and submarkets thereof, has been restrained and eliminated.

  c. Purchasers of telecommunications service and telecommunications
equipment have been denied the benefits of a free and competitive market.

PRAYER

Wherefore, plaintiff prays:

1. That the Court adjudge and decree that defendants have combined
and conspired to monopolize, have attempted to monopolize and have
monopolized interstate trade and commerce in telecommunications service, and submarkets thereof, and telecommunications equipment, and
submarkets thereof, in violation of Section 2 of the Sherman Act.

2. That each of the defendants, their officers, directors, agents, employees and all persons, firms or corporations acting on behalf of defendants or any one of them be perpetually enjoined from continuing to
carry out, directly or indirectly, the aforesaid combination and conspiracy to monopolize, attempt to monopolize and monopolization of the
aforesaid interstate trade and commerce in telecommunications service
and equipment, and that they be perpetually enjoined from engaging in
or participating in practices, contracts, agreements or understandings, or
claiming any rights thereunder, having the purpose or effect of continu-

ing, reviving or renewing any of the aforesaid violations or any violations similar thereto.

3. That defendant AT&T be required to divest all of its capital stock interest in Western Electric.

4. That defendant Western Electric be required to divest manufacturing and other assets sufficient to insure competition in the manufacture and sale of telecommunications equipment.

5. That defendant AT&T be required, through divestiture of capital stock interests or other assets, to separate some or all of the Long Lines Department of AT&T from some or all of the Bell Operating Companies, as may be necessary to insure competition in telecommunications service and telecommunications equipment.

6. That pursuant to Section 5 of the Sherman Act the Court order summons to be issued to Bell Telephone Laboratories, Inc. commanding it to appear and answer the allegations contained in this Complaint, and to abide and perform such orders and decrees as the Court may make in the premises.

7. That the plaintiff have such other and further relief as the nature of the case may require and as the Court may deem just and proper.

8. That the plaintiff recover the costs of this action.

Thomas E. Kauper
    Assistant Attorney General

Earl J. Silbert
    United States Attorney

Baddia J. Rashid
Hugh P. Morrison, Jr.
Samuel Z. Gordon
Philip L. Verveer
Jules M. Fried
Peter E. Halle
Laura F. Rothstein
Thomas A. Mauro
Ruth G. Bell
    Attorneys, Department of Justice

November 1974.

Merger Cases

United States v. E. I. du Pont de Nemours & Co.
Supreme Court of the United States, 1957.
353 U.S. 586, 77 S.Ct. 872, 1 L.Ed.2d 1057.

*This spectacular case involved an old vertical tie be-
tween two very big firms. It foreshadowed the new
stricter policy toward mergers and placed even very
old mergers within possible reach.*

Brennan J. This is a direct appeal . . . from a judgment of the District
Court for the Northern District of Illinois, dismissing the Government's
action brought in 1949 under § 15 of the Clayton Act. The complaint alleged a violation of § 7 of the Act resulting from the purchase by E. I.
du Pont de Nemours and Company in 1917–1919 of a 23 percent stock
interest in General Motors Corporation. This appeal is from the dismissal
of the action as to du Pont, General Motors and the corporate holders of
large amounts of du Pont stock, Christiana Securities Corporation and
Delaware Realty & Investment Company.

The primary issue is whether du Pont's commanding position as General Motors' supplier of automotive finishes and fabrics was achieved on
competitive merit alone or because its acquisition of the General Motors'
stock, and the consequent close intercompany relationship, led to the in-
sulation of most of the General Motors' market from free competition,
with the resultant likelihood, at the time of suit, of the creation of a monopoly of a line of commerce. . . .

We hold that any acquisition by one corporation of all or any part of
the stock of another corporation, competitor or not, is within the reach
of the section whenever the reasonable likelihihood appears that the acquisition will result in a restraint of commerce or in the creation of a
monopoly of any line of commerce. Thus, although du Pont and General
Motors are not competitors, a violation of the section has occurred if, as
a result of the acquisition, there was at the time of suit a reasonable likelihood of a monopoly of any line of commerce.

. . . In 1947 General Motors' total purchases of all products from du

Pont were $26,628,274, of which $18,938,229 (71 percent) represented purchases from du Pont's Finishes Division. Of the latter amount purchases of "Duco" and the thinner used to apply "Duco" totaled $12,224,798 (65 percent), and "Dulux" purchases totaled $3,179,225. Purchases by General Motors of du Pont fabrics in 1948 amounted to $3,700,000, making it the largest account of du Pont's Fabrics Division. Expressed in percentages, du Pont supplied 67 percent of General Motors' requirements for finishes in 1946 and 68 percent in 1947. In fabrics du Pont supplied 52.3 percent of requirements in 1946, and 38.5 percent in 1947. Because General Motors accounts for almost one half of the automobile industry's annual sales, its requirements for automotive finishes and fabrics must represent approximately one half of the relevant market for these materials. Because the record clearly shows that quantitatively and percentagewise du Pont supplies the largest part of General Motors' requirements, we must conclude that du Pont has a substantial share of the relevant market.

The du Pont Company's commanding position as a General Motors supplier was not achieved until shortly after its purchase of a sizeable block of General Motors stock in 1917. At that time its production for the automobile industry and its sales to General Motors were relatively insignificant. General Motors then produced only about 11 percent of the total automobile production and its requirements, while relatively substantial, were far short of the proportions they assumed as it forged ahead to its present place in the industry. . . .

This background of the acquisition, particularly the plain implications of the contemporaneous documents, destroys any basis for a conclusion that the purchase was made "solely for investment." Moreover, immediately after the acquisition, du Pont's influence growing out of it was brought to bear within General Motors to achieve primacy for du Pont as General Motors' supplier of automotive fabrics and finishes. . . .

The fact that sticks out in this voluminous record is that the bulk of du Pont's production has always supplied the largest part of the requirements of the one customer in the automobile industry connected to du Pont by a stock interest. The inference is overwhelming that du Pont's commanding position was promoted by its stock interest and was not gained solely on competitive merit. . . .

Brown Shoe Co., Inc. v. U.S.
370 U.S. 294 (1962)

> Brown Shoe *seemed to involve only marginal effects on competition, in both the vertical and horizontal planes. Yet the Court firmly prohibited the merger, in what is the landmark merger case. Was the Court too strict? Could economies of scale or integration have offset the monopoly effects?*

Mr. Chief Justice Warren.

This suit was initiated in November 1955 when the Government filed a civil action in the United States District Court for the Eastern District of Missouri alleging that a contemplated merger between the G. R. Kinney Company, Inc. (Kinney), and the Brown Shoe Company, Inc. (Brown), through an exchange of Kinney for Brown stock, would violate Section 7 of the Clayton Act. . . .

The Industry

The District Court found that although domestic shoe production was scattered among a large number of manufacturers, a small number of large companies occupied a commanding position. Thus, while the 24 largest manufacturers produced about 35 percent of the Nation's shoes, the top 4—International, Endicott-Johnson, Brown (including Kinney) and General Shoe—alone produced approximately 23 percent of the Nation's shoes or 65 percent of the production of the top 24. . .

The District Court found a "definite trend" among shoe manufacturers to acquire retail outlets. . . . Brown, itself, with no retail outlets of its own prior to 1951, had acquired 845 such outlets by 1956. Moreover, between 1950 and 1956 nine independent shoe store chains, operating 1,114 retail shoe stores, were found to have become subsidiaries of these large firms and to have ceased their independent operations.

And once the manufacturers acquired retail outlets, the District Court found there was a "definite trend" for the parent-manufacturers to supply an ever increasing percentage of the retail outlets' needs, thereby foreclosing other manufacturers from effectively competing for the retail accounts. Manufacturer-dominated stores were found to be "drying up" the available outlets for independent producers. . . .

Brown Shoe

Brown Shoe was found not only to have been a participant, but also a moving factor, in these industry trends. Although Brown had experimented several times with operating its own retail outlets, by 1945 it had disposed of them all. However, in 1951, Brown again began to seek retail outlets by acquiring the Nation's largest operator of leased shoe departments, Wohl Shoe Company (Wohl), which operated 250 shoe departments in department stores throughout the United States. Between 1952 and 1955 Brown made a number of smaller acquisitions. . . . In 1954, Brown made another major acquisition: Regal Shoe Corporation which, at the time, operated one manufacturing plant producing men's shoes and 110 retail outlets.

The acquisition of these corporations was found to lead to increased sales by Brown to the acquired companies. . . .

During the same period of time, Brown also acquired the stock or assets of seven companies engaged solely in shoe manufacturing. As a result, in 1955, Brown was the fourth largest shoe manufacturer in the country, producing about 25.6 million pairs of shoes or about 4 percent of the Nation's total footwear production.

Kinney

Kinney is principally engaged in operating the largest family-style shoe store chain in the United States. At the time of trial, Kinney was found to be operating over 400 such stores in more than 270 cities. These stores were found to make about 1.2 percent of all national retail shoe sales by dollar volume. Moreover, in 1955 the Kinney stores sold approximately 8 million pairs of nonrubber shoes or about 1.6 percent of the national pairage sales of such shoes. . . .

In addition to this extensive retail activity, Kinney owned and operated four plants which manufactured men's, women's, and children's shoes and whose combined output was 0.5 percent of the national shoe production in 1955, making Kinney the twelfth largest shoe manufacturer in the United States.

Kinney stores were found to obtain about 20 percent of their shoes from Kinney's own manufacturing plants. At the time of the merger, Kinney bought no shoes from Brown; however, in line with Brown's conceded reasons for acquiring Kinney, Brown had, by 1957, become the largest outside supplier of Kinney's shoes, supplying 7.9 percent of all Kinney's needs. . . .

THE VERTICAL ASPECTS OF THE MERGER

Economic arrangements between companies standing in a supplier-customer relationship are characterized as "vertical." The primary vice of a vertical merger or other arrangement tying a customer to a supplier is that, by foreclosing the competitors of either party from a segment of the market otherwise open to them, the arrangement may act as a "clog on competition." . . .

The Product Market

The outer boundaries of a product market are determined by the reasonable interchangeability of use or the cross-elasticity of demand between the product itself and substitutes for it. . . .

Applying these considerations to the present case, we conclude that the record supports the District Court's finding that the relevant lines of commerce are men's, women's, and children's shoes. These product lines are recognized by the public; each line is manufactured in separate plants; each has characteristics peculiar to itself rendering it generally noncompetitive with the others; and each is, of course, directed toward a distinct class of customers. . . .

The Geographic Market

We agree with the parties and the District Court that insofar as the vertical aspect of this merger is concerned, the relevant geographic market is the entire Nation. The relationships of product value, bulk, weight and consumer demand enable manufacturers to distribute their shoes on a nationwide basis, as Brown and Kinney, in fact, do. The anti-competitive effects of the merger are to be measured within this range of distribution.

The Probable Effect of the Merger

Once the area of effective competition affected by a vertical arrangement has been defined, an analysis must be made to determine if the effect of the arrangement "may be substantially to lessen competition, or to tend to create a monopoly" in this market.

Since the diminution of the vigor of competition which may stem from a vertical arrangement results primarily from a foreclosure of a share of the market otherwise open to competitors, an important consideration in determining whether the effect of a vertical arrangement "may be substantially to lessen competition, or to tend to create a monopoly" is the size of the share of the market foreclosed. However, this factor will seldom be determinative. . . .

Between these extremes, in cases such as the one before us, in which the foreclosure is neither of monopoly nor *de minimis* proportions, the percentage of the market foreclosed by the vertical arrangement cannot itself be decisive. In such cases, it becomes necessary to undertake an examination of various economic and historical factors in order to determine whether the arrangement under review is of the type Congress sought to proscribe.

The present merger involved neither small companies nor failing companies. In 1955, the date of this merger, Brown was the fourth largest manufacturer in the shoe industry with sales of approximately 25 million pairs of shoes and assets of over $72,000,000 while Kinney had sales of about 8 million pairs of shoes and assets of about $18,000,000. Not only was Brown one of the leading manufacturers of men's, women's, and children's shoes, but Kinney, with over 350 retail outlets, owned and operated the largest independent chain of family shoe stores in the Nation. Thus, in this industry, no merger between a manufacturer and an independent retailer could involve a larger potential market foreclosure. Moreover, it is apparent both from past behavior of Brown and from the testimony of Brown's President, that Brown would use its ownership of Kinney to force Brown shoes into Kinney stores. Thus, in operation this vertical arrangement would be quite analogous to one involving a tying clause.

Another important factor to consider is the trend toward concentration in the industry. It is true, of course, that the statute prohibits a given merger only if the effect of *that* merger may be substantially to lessen competition. But the very wording of Section 7 requires a prognosis of the probable *future* effect of the merger.

The existence of a trend toward vertical integration, which the District Court found, is well substantiated by the record. Moreover, the court found a tendency of the acquiring manufacturers to become increasingly important sources of supply for their acquired outlets. The necessary corollary of these trends is the foreclosure of independent manufacturers from markets otherwise open to them. And because these trends are not the product of accident but are rather the result of deliberate policies of Brown and other leading shoe manufacturers, account must be taken of these facts in order to predict the probable future consequences of this merger. It is against this background of continuing concentration that the present merger must be viewed.

Brown argues, however, that the shoe industry is at present composed of a large number of manufacturers and retailers, and that the industry is dynamically competitive. But remaining vigor cannot immunize a merger if the trend in that industry is toward oligopoly. . . . It is the probable effect of the merger upon the future as well as the present which the Clayton Act commands the courts and the Commission to examine.

Moreover, as we have remarked above, not only must we consider the probable effects of the merger upon the economics of the particular markets affected but also we must consider its probable effects upon the economic way of life sought to be preserved by Congress. Congress was desirous of preventing the formation of further oligopolies with their attendant adverse effects upon local control of industry and upon small business. Where an industry was composed of numerous independent units, Congress appeared anxious to preserve this structure. . . .

THE HORIZONTAL ASPECTS OF THE MERGER

An economic arrangement between companies performing similar functions in the production or sale of comparable goods or services is characterized as "horizontal." The effect on competition of such an arrangement depends, of course, upon its character and scope.

The Product Market

Shoes are sold in the United States in retail shoe stores and in shoe departments of general stores. These outlets sell: (1) men's shoes, (2) women's shoes, (3) women's or children's shoes, or (4) men's, women's or children's shoes. Prior to the merger, both Brown and Kinney sold their shoes in competition with one another through the enumerated kinds of outlets characteristic of the industry. . . .

We therefore agree that the District Court properly defined the relevant geographic markets in which to analyze this merger as those cities with a population exceeding 10,000 and their environs in which both Brown and Kinney retailed shoes through their own outlets. Such markets are large enough to include the downtown shops and suburban shopping centers in areas contiguous to the city, which are the important competitive factors, and yet are small enough to exclude stores beyond the immediate environs of the city, which are of little competitive significance.

The Probable Effect of the Merger

. . . Although Brown objects to some details in the Government's computations used in drafting these exhibits, appellant cannot deny the correctness of the more general picture they reveal. . . . They show, for example, that during 1955 in 32 separate cities, ranging in size and location from Topeka, Kansas, to Batavia, New York, and Hobbs, New Mexico, the combined share of Brown and Kinney sales of women's shoes (by unit volume) exceeded 20 percent. In 31 cities—some the same as those used in measuring the effect of the merger in the women's line—the combined share of children's shoes sales exceeded 20 percent; in 6 cities their share exceeded 40 percent. In Dodge City, Kansas, their combined share of the market for women's shoes was over 57 percent; their share of the children's shoe market in that city was 49 percent. In the 7 cities in which Brown's and Kinney's combined shares of the market for women's shoes were greatest (ranging from 33 percent to 57 percent) each of the parties alone, prior to the merger, had captured substantial portions of those markets (ranging from 13 percent to 34 percent); the merger intensified this existing concentration. In 118 separate cities the combined shares of the market of Brown and Kinney in the sale of one of the relevant lines of commerce exceeded 5 percent. In 47 cities, their share exceeded 5 percent in all three lines.

The market share which companies may control by merging is one of the most important factors to be considered when determining the probable effects of the combination on effective competition in the relevant market. In an industry as fragmented as shoe retailing, the control of substantial shares of the trade in a city may have important effects on competition. If a merger achieving 5 percent control were now approved, we might be required to approve future merger efforts by Brown's competitors seeking similar market shares. The oligopoly Congress sought to avoid would then be furthered and it would be difficult to dissolve the combinations previously approved. Furthermore, in this fragmented industry, even if the combination controls but a small share of a particular market, the fact that this share is held by a large national chain can adversely affect competition. . . .

Of course, some of the results of large integrated or chain operations are beneficial to consumers. Their expansion is not rendered unlawful by the mere fact that small independent stores may be adversely affected. It is competition, not competitors, which the Act protects. But we cannot fail to recognize Congress' desire to promote competition through the protection of viable, small, locally owned businesses. Congress appreciated that occasional higher costs and prices might result from the maintenance of fragmented industries and markets. It resolved these competing considerations in favor of decentralization. We must give effect to that decision.

Other factors to be considered in evaluating the probable effects of a merger in the relevant market lend additional support to the District Court's conclusion that this merger may substantially lessen competition. One such factor is the history of tendency toward concentration in the industry. As we have previously pointed out, the shoe industry has, in recent years, been a prime example of such a trend. . . .

By the merger in this case, the largest single group of retail stores still independent of one of the large manufacturers was absorbed into an already substantial aggregation of more or less controlled retail outlets. As a result of this merger, Brown moved into second place nationally in terms of retail stores directly owned. Including the stores on its franchise plan, the merger placed under Brown's control almost 1,600 shoe outlets, or about 7.2 percent of the Nation's retail "shoe stores" as defined by the Census Bureau, and 2.3 percent of the Nation's total retail shoe outlets.

We cannot avoid the mandate of Congress that tendencies toward concentration in industry are to be curbed in their incipiency, particularly when those tendencies are being accelerated through giant steps striding across a hundred cities at a time. In the light of the trends in this industry we agree with the Government and the court below that this is an appropriate place at which to call a halt.

. . . On the basis of the record before us, we believe the Government sustained its burden of proof. We hold that the District Court was correct in concluding that this merger may tend to lessen competition substantially in the retail sale of men's, women's, and children's shoes in the overwhelming majority of those cities and their environs in which both Brown and Kinney sell through owned or controlled outlets.

The judgment is *Affirmed.*

United States v. Continental Can Co. et al.

378 U.S. 441 (1964)

Here, defining the market was crucial. Who was most correct, the majority or the dissenters? Can any criteria really settle the issue?

Mr. Justice White. In 1956, Continental Can Company, the Nation's second largest producer of metal containers, acquired all of the assets, business and good will of Hazel-Atlas Glass Company, the Nation's third largest producer of glass containers, in exchange for 999,140 shares of Continental's common stock and the assumption by Continental of all of the liabilities of Hazel-Atlas. The Government brought this action seeking a judgment that the acquisition violated Section 7 of the Clayton Act and requesting an appropriate divestiture order. . . .

Continental Can is a New York corporation organized in 1913 to acquire all the assets of three metal container manufacturers. Since 1913 Continental has acquired 21 domestic metal container companies as well as numerous others engaged in the packaging business, including producers of flexible packaging; a manufacturer of polyethylene bottles and similar plastic containers; 14 producers of paper containers and paperboard; four companies making closures for glass containers; and one—Hazel-Atlas—producing glass containers. In 1955, the year prior to the present merger, Continental, with assets of $382 million, was the second largest company in the metal container field, shipping approximately 33 percent of all such containers sold in the United States. It and the largest producer, American Can Company, accounted for approximately 71 percent of all metal container shipments. National Can Company, the third largest, shipped approximately 5 percent, with the remaining 24 percent of the market being divided among 75 to 90 other firms. . . .

Hazel-Atlas was a West Virginia corporation which in 1955 had net sales in excess of $79 million and assets of more than $37 million. Prior to the absorption of Hazel-Atlas into Continental the pattern of dominance among a few firms in the glass container industry was similar to that which prevailed in the metal container field. Hazel-Atlas, with approximately 9.6 percent of the glass container shipments in 1955, was third. Owens-Illinois Glass Company had 34.2 percent and Anchor-Hocking Glass Company 11.6 percent, with the remaining 44.6 percent being divided among at least 39 other firms. . . .

. . . Since the purpose of delineating a line of commerce is to provide an adequate basis for measuring the effects of a given acquisition, its contours must, as nearly as possible, conform to competitive reality. Where the area of effective competition cuts across industry lines, so much the relevant line of commerce; otherwise an adequate determination of the merger's true impact cannot be made.

Based on the evidence thus far revealed by this record we hold that the interindustry competition between glass and metal containers is sufficient to warrant treating as a relevant product market the combined glass and metal container industries and all end uses for which they compete. There may be some end uses for which glass and metal do not and could not compete, but complete interindustry competitive overlap need not be shown. . . .

Continental occupied a dominant position in the metal can industry. It shipped 33 percent of the metal cans shipped by the industry and together with American shipped about 71 percent of the industry total. Continental's share amounted to 13 billion metal containers out of a total of 40 billion and its $433 million gross sales of metal containers amounted to 31.4 percent of the industry's total gross of $1,380,000,000. Continental's total assets were $382 million, its net sales and operating revenues $666 million.

In addition to demonstrating the dominant position of Continental in a highly concentrated industry, the District Court's findings clearly revealed Continental's vigorous efforts all across the competitive front between metal and glass containers. Continental obviously pushed metal containers wherever metal containers could be pushed. Its share of the beer can market ran from 43 percent in 1955 to 46 percent in 1957. Its share of both beer can and beer bottle shipments, disregarding the returnable bottle factor, ran from 36 percent in 1955 to 38 percent in 1957. Although metal cans have so far occupied a relatively small percentage of the soft drink container field, Continental's share of this can market ranged from 36 percent in 1955 to 26 percent in 1957 and its portion of the total shipments of glass and metal soft drink and beverage containers, disregarding the returnable bottle factor, was 7.2 percent in 1955, approximately 5.4 percent in 1956 and approximately 6.2 percent in 1957 (for 1956 and 1957 these figures include Hazel-Atlas' share). In the category covering all nonfood products, Continental's share was approximately 30 percent of the total shipments of metal containers for such uses.

Continental's major position in the relevant product market—the combined metal and glass container industries—prior to the merger is undeniable. Of the 59 billion containers shipped in 1955 by the metal (39¾ billion) and glass (19⅓ billion) industries, Continental shipped 21.9 percent, to a great extent dispersed among all of the end uses for which glass and metal compete. Of the six largest firms in the product market it ranked second.

When Continental acquired Hazel-Atlas it added significantly to its position in the relevant line of commerce. Hazel-Atlas was the third largest glass container manufacturer in an industry in which the three top companies controlled 55.4 percent of the total shipments of glass containers. Hazel-Atlas' share was 9.6 percent, which amounted to 1,857,000,000 glass containers out of a total of 19⅓ billion industrial total. Its annual sales amounted to $79 million, its assets exceeded $37 million and it had 13 plants variously located in the United States. In terms of total containers shipped, Hazel-Atlas ranked sixth in the relevant line of commerce, its almost 2 billion containers being 3.1 percent of the product market total.

The evidence so far presented leads us to conclude that the merger between Continental and Hazel-Atlas is in violation of Section 7. The product market embracing the combined metal and glass container industries was dominated by six firms having a total of 70.1 percent of the business. Continental, with 21.9 percent of the shipments, ranked second within this product market, and Hazel-Atlas, with 3.1 percent, ranked sixth. Thus, of this vast market—amounting at the time of the merger to almost $3 billion in annual sales—a large percentage already belonged to Continental before the merger. By the acquisition of Hazel-Atlas stock Continental not only increased its own share more than 14 percent from 21.9 percent to 25 percent, but also reduced from five to four the most significant competitors who might have threatened its dominant position. The resulting percentage of the combined firms approaches that held presumptively bad in *United States* v. *Philadelphia National Bank*. . . . The case falls squarely within the principle that where there has been a "history of tendency toward concentration in the industry" tendencies toward further concentration "are to be curbed in their incipiency." *Brown Shoe Co.* v. *United States*. . . . Where "concentration is already great, the importance of preventing even slight increases in concentration and so preserving the possibility of eventual de-concentration is correspondingly great." *United States* v. *Philadelphia National Bank.* . . .

We think our holding is consonant with the purpose of Section 7 to arrest anticompetitive arrangements in their incipiency. Some product lines are offered in both metal and glass containers by the same packer. In such areas the interchangeability of use and immediate interindustry sensitivity to price changes would approach that which exists between products of the same industry. In other lines, as where one packer's products move in one type container while his competitor's move in another, there are inherent deterrents to customer diversion of the same type that might occur between brands of cans or bottles. But the possibility of such transfers over the long run acts as a deterrent against attempts by the dominant members of either industry to reap the possible benefits of their position by raising prices above the competitive level or engaging in other comparable practices. And even though certain lines are today regarded as safely within the domain of one or the other of those industries, this pattern may be altered, as it has in the past. From the point of view not only of the static competitive situation but also the dynamic long-run potential, we think that the Government has discharged its burden of proving prima facie anticompetitive effect. Accordingly the judgment is reversed and the case remanded for further proceedings consistent with this opinion.

Reversed.

Justice Harlan, whom Justice Stewart joins, dissenting:

. . . The truth is that "glass and metal containers" form a distinct line of commerce only in the mind of this Court.

The District Court found, and this Court accepts the finding, that this case "deals with three separate and distinct industries manufacturing separate and distinct types of products": metal, glass, and plastic containers. . . .

Only this Court . . . without support in reason or fact, . . . dips into this network of competition and establishes metal and glass containers as a separate "line of commerce," leaving entirely out of account all other kinds of containers: "plastic, paper, foil and any other materials competing for the same business," . . . *Brown Shoe*, . . . on which the Court relies for this travesty of economics, . . . spoke of "*well-defined* submarkets" within a broader market, and said that "the boundaries of such a submarket" were to be determined by "*practical indicia*," . . . (Emphasis added.) Since the Court here provides its own definition of a market, unrelated to any market reality whatsoever, *Brown Shoe* must in this case be regarded as a bootstrap. . . .

United States v. Von's Grocery Co.

Supreme Court of the United States, 1966.
384 U.S. 270, 86 S.Ct. 1478, 16 L.Ed.2d 555.

> Von's *drew the line against horizontal mergers roughly as it stands today: no more than 10 percent combined, if concentration has been rising, even if competition might still be vigorous. The dissent followed the same line as before.*

Black, J.   On March 25, 1960, the United States brought this action charging that the acquisition by Von's Grocery Company of its direct competitor Shopping Bag Food Stores, both large retail grocery companies in Los Angeles, California, violated § 7 of the Clayton Act. . . .

The record shows the following facts relevant to our decision. The market involved here is the retail grocery market in the Los Angeles area. In 1958 Von's retail sales ranked third in the area and Shopping Bag's ranked sixth. In 1960 their sales together were 7.5 percent of the total two and one-half billion dollars of retail groceries sold in the Los Angeles market each year. For many years before the merger both companies had enjoyed great success as rapidly growing companies. From 1948 to 1958 the number of Von's stores in the Los Angeles area practically doubled from 14 to 27, while at the same time the number of Shopping Bag's stores jumped from 15 to 34. During that same decade, Von's sales increased fourfold and its share of the market almost doubled while Shopping Bag's sales multiplied seven times and its share of the market tripled. The merger of these two highly successful, expanding and aggressive competitors created the second largest grocery chain in Los Angeles with sales of almost $172,488,000 annually. In addition the findings of the District Court show that the number of owners operating a single store in the Los Angeles retail grocery market decreased from 5,365 in 1950 to 3,818 in 1961. By 1963, three years after the merger, the number of single-store owners had dropped still further to 3,590. During roughly the same period from 1953 to 1962 the number of chains with two or more grocery stores increased from 96 to 150. While the grocery business was being concentrated into the hands of fewer and fewer owners, the small companies were continually being absorbed by the larger firms through mergers. According to an exhibit prepared by one of the Government's expert witnesses, in the period from 1949 to 1958 nine of the top 20 chains acquired 126 stores from their smaller competitors. Figures of a principal defense witness, set out below, illustrate the many acquisitions and mergers in the Los Angeles grocery industry from 1953 through 1961 including acquisitions made by Food Giant, Alpha Beta, Fox, and Mayfair, all among the 10 leading chains in the area. Moreover, a table prepared by the Federal Trade Commission appearing in the Government's reply brief, but not a part of the record here, shows that acquisitions and mergers in the Los Angeles retail grocery market have continued at a rapid rate since the merger. These facts alone are enough to cause us to conclude contrary to the District Court that the Von's-Shopping Bag merger did violate § 7. Accordingly, we reverse.

. . . By using these terms in § 7 which look not merely to the actual present effect of a merger but instead to its effect upon future competition, Congress sought to preserve competition among many small businesses by arresting a trend toward concentration in its incipiency before that trend developed to the point that a market was left in the grip of a few big companies. Thus, where concentration is gaining momentum in a market, we must be alert to carry out Congress' intent to protect competition against ever increasing concentration through mergers.

The facts of this case present exactly the threatening trend toward concentration which Congress wanted to halt. The number of small grocery companies in the Los Angeles retail grocery market had been declining rapidly before the merger and continued to decline rapidly afterwards. This rapid decline in the number of grocery store owners moved hand in hand with a large number of significant absorptions of the small companies by the larger ones. In the midst of this steadfast trend toward concentration, Von's and Shopping Bag, two of the most successful and largest companies in the area, jointly owning 66 grocery stores merged to become the second largest chain in Los Angeles. This merger cannot be defended on the ground that one of the companies was about to fail or that the two had to merge to save themselves from destruction by some larger and more powerful competitor. What we have on the contrary is simply the case of two already powerful companies merging in a way which makes them even more powerful than they were before. If ever such a merger would not violate § 7, certainly it does when it takes place in a market characterized by a long and continuous trend toward fewer and fewer owner-competitors which is exactly the sort of trend which Congress, with power to do so, declared must be arrested.

Appellees' primary argument is that the merger between Von's and Shopping Bag is not prohibited by § 7 because the Los Angeles grocery market was competitive before the merger, has been since, and may continue to be in the future. Even so, § 7 "requires not merely an appraisal of the immediate impact of the merger upon competition, but a prediction of its impact upon competitive conditions in the future; this is what is meant when it is said that the amended § 7 was intended to arrest anticompetitive tendencies in their 'incipiency.'" United States v. Philadelphia Nat. Bank, 374 U.S. at p. 362, 83 S.Ct., at 1741, 10 L.Ed.2d 915. It is enough for us that

Congress feared that a market marked at the same time by both a continuous decline in the number of small businesses and a large number of mergers would, slowly but inevitably, gravitate from a market of many small competitors to one dominated by one or a few giants, and competition would thereby be destroyed. Congress passed the Celler-Kefauver Act to prevent such a destruction of competition. Our cases since the passage of that Act have faithfully endeavored to enforce this congressional command. We adhere to them now.

Federal Trade Commission v. Procter & Gamble Co.
386 U.S. 568 (1967)

This major case embraced several alternative doctrines for stopping conglomerate mergers. Procter & Gamble was a potential entrant. *It could not acquire the largest firm (Clorox), but a* toehold *acquisition of a smaller bleach firm might have been permitted. Massive* advertising advantages *were involved, and Procter & Gamble was a very* large firm.

Mr. Justice Douglas.

This is a proceeding initiated by the Federal Trade Commission charging that respondent, Procter & Gamble Co., had acquired the assets of Clorox Chemical Co. in violation of § 7 of the Clayton Act, . . . as amended by the Celler-Kefauver Act. . . . The charge was that Procter's acquisition of Clorox might substantially lessen competition or tend to create a monopoly in the production and sale of household liquid bleaches. . . .

At the time of the merger, in 1957, Clorox was the leading manufacturer in the heavily concentrated household liquid bleach industry. It is agreed that household liquid bleach is the relevant line of commerce. The product is used in the home as a germicide and disinfectant, and, more importantly, as a whitening agent in washing clothes and fabrics. It is a distinctive product with no close substitutes. Liquid bleach is a low-price, high-turnover consumer product sold mainly through grocery stores and supermarkets. The relevant geographical market is the Nation and a series of regional markets. Because of high shipping costs and low sales price, it is not feasible to ship the product more than 300 miles from its point of manufacture. Most manufacturers are limited to competition within a single region since they have but one plant. Clorox is the only firm selling nationally; it has 13 plants distributed throughout the Nation. Purex, Clorox's closest competitor in size, does not distribute its bleach in the northeast or mid-Atlantic States; in 1957, Purex's bleach was available in less than 50 percent of the national market.

At the time of the acquisition, Clorox was the leading manufacturer of household liquid bleach, with 48.8 percent of the national sales—annual sales of slightly less than $40,000,000. Its market share had been steadily increasing for the five years prior to the merger. Its nearest rival was Purex, which manufactures a number of products other than household liquid bleaches, including abrasive cleaners, toilet soap, and detergents. Purex accounted for 15.7 percent of the household liquid bleach market.

Since all liquid bleach is chemically identical, advertising and sales promotion are vital. In 1957 Clorox spent almost $3,700,000 on advertising, imprinting the value of its bleach in the mind of the consumer. In addition, it spent $1,700,000 for other promotional activities. The Commission found that these heavy expenditures went far to explain why Clorox maintained so high a market share despite the fact that its brand, though chemically indistinguishable from rival brands, retailed for a price equal to or, in many instances, higher than its competitors.

Procter is a large, diversified manufacturer of low-price, high-turnover household products sold through grocery, drug, and department stores. Prior to its acquisition of Clorox, it did not produce household liquid bleach. Its 1957 sales were in excess of $1,100,000,000 from which it realized profits of more than $67,000,000; its assets were over $500,000,000. Procter has been marked by rapid growth and diversification. It has successfully developed and introduced a number of new products. Its primary activity is in the general area of soaps, detergents, and cleansers; in 1957, of total domestic sales, more than one half (over $500,000,000) were in this field. Procter was the dominant factor in this area. It accounted for 54.4 percent of all packaged detergent sales. The industry is heavily concentrated—Procter and its nearest competitors, Colgate-Palmolive and Lever Brothers, account for 80 percent of the market.

In the marketing of soaps, detergents, and cleansers, as in the marketing of household liquid bleach, advertising and sales promotion are vital. In 1957, Procter was the Nation's largest advertiser, spending more than $80,000,000 on advertising and an additional $47,000,000 on sales promotion. Due to its tremendous volume, Procter receives substantial discounts from the media. As a multiproduct producer Procter enjoys substantial advantages in advertising and sales promotion. Thus, it can and does feature several products in its promotions, reducing the printing, mailing, and other costs for each product. It also purchases network programs on behalf of several products, enabling it to give each product network exposure at a fraction of the cost per product that a firm with only one product to advertise would incur.

Prior to the acquisition, Procter was in the course of diversifying into product lines related to its basic detergent-soap-cleanser business. Liquid bleach was a distinct possibility since packaged detergents—Procter's primary product line—and liquid bleach are used complementarily in washing clothes and fabrics, and in general household cleaning. . . .

The anticompetitive effects with which this product-extension merger is fraught can easily be seen: (1) the substitution of the powerful acquiring firm for the smaller, but already dominant, firm may substantially reduce the competitive structure of the industry by raising entry barriers and by dissuading the smaller firms from aggressively competing; (2) the acquisition eliminates the potential competition of the acquiring firm.

. . . There is every reason to assume that the smaller firms would become more cautious in competing due to their fear of retaliation by Procter. It is probable that Procter would become the price leader and that oligopoly would become more rigid.

The acquisition may also have the tendency of raising the barriers to new entry. The major competitive weapon in the successful marketing of bleach is advertising. Clorox was limited in this area by its relatively small budget and its inability to obtain substantial discounts. By contrast, Procter's budget was much larger; and, although it would not devote its entire budget to advertising Clorox, it could divert a large portion to meet the short-term threat of a new entrant. Procter would be able to use its volume discounts to advantage in advertising Clorox. Thus, a new entrant would be much more reluctant to face the giant Procter than it would have been to face the smaller Clorox.

Possible economies cannot be used as a defense to illegality. Congress was aware that some mergers which lessen competition may also result in economies but it struck the balance in favor of protecting competition. . . .

The Commission also found that the acquisition of Clorox by Procter eliminated Procter as a potential competitor. The Court of Appeals declared that this finding was not supported by evidence because there was no evidence that Procter's management had ever intended to enter the industry independently and that Procter had never attempted to enter. The evidence, however, clearly shows that Procter was the most likely entrant. Procter had recently launched a new abrasive cleaner in an industry similar to the liquid bleach industry, and had wrested leadership from a brand that had enjoyed even a larger market share than had Clorox. Procter was engaged in a vigorous program of diversifying into product lines closely related to its basic products. Liquid bleach was a natural avenue of diversification since it is complementary to Procter's products, is sold to the same customers through the same channels, and is advertised and merchandised in the same manner. Procter had substantial advantages in advertising and sales promotion, which, as we have seen, are vital to the success of liquid bleach. No manufacturer had a patent on the product or its manufacture, necessary information relating to manufacturing methods and processes was readily available, there was no shortage of raw material, and the machinery and equipment required for a plant of efficient capacity were available at reasonable costs. Procter's management was experienced in producing and marketing goods similar to liquid bleach. Procter had considered the possibility of independently entering but decided against it because the acquisition of Clorox would enable Procter to capture a more commanding share of the market. . . .

The judgment of the Court of Appeals is reversed and remanded with instructions to affirm and enforce the Commission's order.

It is so ordered.

Justice Harlan, concurring:

. . . The Commission—in my opinion quite correctly—seemed to accept the idea that economies could be used to defend a merger, noting that "[a] merger that results in increased efficiency of production, distribution or marketing may, in certain cases, increase the vigor of competition in the relevant market." . . . But advertising economies were placed in a different classification since they were said "only to increase the barriers to new entry" and to be "offensive to at least the spirit, if not the letter, of the antitrust laws." . . . Advertising was thought to benefit only the seller by entrenching his market position, and to be of no use to the consumer.

I think the Commission's view overstated and oversimplified. Proper advertising serves a legitimate and important purpose in the market by educating the consumer as to available alternatives. This process contributes to consumer demand being developed to the point at which economies of scale can be realized in production. The advertiser's brand name may also be an assurance of quality, and the value of this benefit is demonstrated by the general willingness of consumers to pay a premium for the advertised brands. Undeniably advertising may sometimes be used to create irrational brand preferences and mislead consumers as to the actual differences between products, but it is very difficult to discover at what point advertising ceases to be an aspect of healthy competition. . . . It is not the Commission's function to decide which lawful elements of the "product" offered the consumer should be considered useful and which should be considered the symptoms of industrial "sickness." It is the consumer who must make that election through the exercise of his purchasing power. In my view, true efficiencies in the use of advertising must be considered in assessing economies in the marketing process, which as has been noted are factors in the sort of § 7 proceeding involved here.

I do not think, however, that on the record presented Procter has shown any true efficiencies in advertising. Procter has merely shown that it is able to command equivalent resources at a lower dollar cost than other bleach producers. No peculiarly efficient marketing techniques have been demonstrated, nor does the record show that a smaller net advertising expenditure could be expected. Economies cannot be premised solely on dollar figures, lest accounting controversies dominate § 7 proceedings. Economies employed in defense of a merger must be shown in what economists label "real" terms, that is in terms of resources applied to the accomplishment of the objective. For this reason, the Commission, I think, was justified in discounting Procter's efficiency defense.

Federal Trade Commission: The Bendix Corp.
Docket No. 8739 (1970), 1970
Trade Cases ¶19, 288

The Bendix-Fram decision extended and clarified the toehold and potential-entrant criteria. But was Bendix really a major potential entrant?

OPINION OF THE COMMISSION

I. Introduction

By Commissioner Elman.   On June 29, 1967, one day before consummation of a merger between Fram Corporation (Fram) and the Bendix Corporation (Bendix), the Commission issued its complaint herein charging that the merger violated Section 7 of the Clayton Act . . . and Section 5 of the Federal Trade Commission Act. . . . Although the merger was thereafter consummated, Fram has been operated as a separate subsidiary of Bendix by agreement between the parties. . . .

There are over 30 manufacturers of automotive filters, including the giant auto makers, General Motors and Ford. Nevertheless, the market is a relatively concentrated one. In 1966, in the broad overall market, the top three companies accounted for 62.9 percent of industry sales, and the top six companies accounted for 79.6 percent. . . .

B. The Respondents

1. *Fram* is a leading United States producer of various kinds of filters, including automotive filters, aerospace filters, and filter water separators. . . . Its sales, earnings, and assets in 1966 were the highest in its history, and it was a financially sound, profitable, and growing company. . . .

Approximately 55 percent of Fram's 1966 sales were in automotive filters. In that field, Fram was not only the third-ranking producer, with 12.4 percent of the market, but a pioneer in technology and promotion. . . . Although Fram sold filters in all the distributional channels in the industry, about 90 percent of Fram's filter sales were in the passenger car filter aftermarket, where Fram ranked third in sales with 17.2 percent of the market.

2. *Bendix* is a diversified manufacturer of components and assemblies for aerospace, automotive, automation, scientific, oceanic, and other uses. . . . Bendix sells, through eight separate divisions, a wide variety of automotive parts: fuel pumps, starter drives, ignition components, brakes, brake drums, power steerings, universal joints, carburetors, radios, speed controls, temperature controls, and filters. While the predominant portion of these automotive sales is made to automobile manufacturers and other original equipment makers, Bendix makes substantial sales to the automotive aftermarket, both as proprietary and private brands. . . . Indeed, in 1961, Bendix formed an Automotive Services Division to facilitate the distribution of all Bendix automotive parts in the aftermarket. . . .

In the automotive filter industry, Bendix focused upon the production and sale of heavy duty oil and fuel filters for original equipment makers. The Bendix Filter Division was one of the company's smallest and in the early 1960s was losing money. . . . The only filter product manufactured by Bendix specifically for passenger car application was an air filter element made in the late 1950s for Ford and American Motors. After losing money on the venture, Bendix in 1960 began subcontracting these filters, until 1963 when its Ford contract was terminated.

Thus, the principal remaining issue in this case is whether the merger may substantially lessen competition by eliminating Bendix as a potential entrant and competitor in the automotive filter market. . . .

B. Bendix as a Likely Entrant and Competitor

The evidence in the record and the hearing examiner's relevant findings overwhelmingly establish that Bendix was likely and able to enter the passenger car filter aftermarket, one way or another. The probability of its entry into this market was clear: the only question was the form that such entry would take.

Bendix was a major participant in the automotive parts business, with 1966 sales well over $200 million. Bendix also made substantial sales in the automotive parts replacement market, with 1966 sales of $40.6 million; and half of these sales were under Bendix's proprietary label. . . .

Furthermore, Bendix was already a minor participant in the automotive filter industry. In 1966, Bendix's automotive filter sales allowed Bendix to control 0.35 percent of the market—a share equal to or larger than almost one third of the firms in that market. . . .

In sum, from the objective evidence only one conclusion is possible: the whole logic of Bendix's corporate development, its size, resources, and direct proximity to the passenger car filter aftermarket, and the unambiguous direction of its business growth, all pointed to expansion into the passenger car filter aftermarket.

The record also establishes that this was recognized by Bendix's management. . . .

. . . [I]t . . . was convinced that Bendix should make a substantial entry into the passenger car filter aftermarket, in an attempt to salvage the current Bendix investment in filters, and to bring greater profits and stability to the corporation as a whole. . . .

Thus, all likely routes for potential entry into the relevant market must be considered in determining the legality of the merger route which was in fact chosen. A potential entrant may enter not only by internal expansion; he may enter the market by acquiring a failing company, or a small company in difficulty, or by making a toehold acquisition of a small member of the industry. These methods of entry, no less than internal expansion, and in some cases perhaps more than entry by internal expansion, may inject a new competitive element of vigor and strength into an otherwise stagnant market. Indeed, where entry into some markets by internal expansion is foreclosed and/or restricted, entry by toehold acquisition may be the most feasible route for developing new competition. Furthermore, in an age of mergers and acquisitions, the threat of a toehold merger by a powerful firm may often serve as a much greater incentive to competitive performance in the affected market than does the prospect of more costly and slower internal, *de novo* expansion.

In short, it is offensive to the merger law to eliminate the potential competition offered by likely entrants at a market's edge that may come into it through a toehold or other procompetitive acquisition, especially where the market is a concentrated one in need of new competition. . . .

The record leaves no doubt that, if Bendix had based its expansion decisions on a correct legal premise, namely, that Section 7 firmly closed the door to entry into the aftermarket by a leading firm acquisition but left the door wide open to a toehold acquisition, Bendix would long ago have entered the market by the latter route.

The evidence as to the likelihood of such an acquisition entry is substantial. . . . [I]n the 1960s, Bendix management decided to diversify into non-government, non-military business. One area seen as not only lucrative but compatible with Bendix's other business was the automotive filter market—particularly the profitable and growing aftermarket.

As a result, between 1961 and 1966, Bendix considered the acquisition of numerous filter makers. . . .

Bendix possessed the resources and size necessary to engage in any prolonged battle against the major filter makers, which included the nation's industrial giants—Ford and General Motors. Bendix also had the experience and necessary technology for making filters. This could be advantageous in expanding a small filter maker that might not have the experience in producing a full line of filters. . . .

If any barrier to entry by this acquisition route existed for Bendix, it was, as respondents contend, due to the mass marketing and promotional techniques necessary to sell filters in the aftermarket. But this was precisely the barrier that Bendix could have surmounted by a toehold acquisition of a firm with substantial promotional facilities. . . .

The only question was the form that new entry would take. Bendix had three choices: (1) to expand internally; (2) to make a toehold acquisition looking toward expansion on that base; and (3) to merge with a leading firm. If Bendix had taken either of the first two routes of entry, it would have become an actual competitor of Fram, and would have provided a beneficial new element in the market. Either of those two routes would have promoted competition; neither violated Section 7; indeed, either was the sort of entry into a new market which Congress intended to encourage. Instead, Bendix chose the third route—acquisition of Fram, a leading firm —and thus the likelihood of substantial competition between these two firms was forever eliminated. By the same token, the competitive input that Bendix could have brought to the entire market, had it entered by a toehold acquisition, was also lost. . . .

The competitively lethargic state of the industry is reflected in the stabilized pricing patterns found by the hearing examiner. Whatever competition there is seems to be in terms of promotion, selling, and distribution. Manufacturers build up sales by brand differentiation, advertising, by large numbers of salesmen and promotional men, and by such promotional gimmicks as bonus stamps, coupons, contests, and prizes. All these various forms of nonprice competition seem to have contributed to a continued dominance by the leaders in the industry, and the comfortable profits prevalent among all sellers. . . .

Cases on Price-Fixing and Other Restraints

United States v. *Addyston Pipe & Steel Co.*

United States Circuit Court of Appeals,
Sixth Circuit, 1898. 85 F. 271, 29 C.C.A. 141,
affirmed 175 U.S. 211, 20 S.Ct. 96,
44 L.Ed. 136 (1899).

*William Howard Taft, then a District Judge, early
set a firm line against price-fixing in* Addyston. *The
Supreme Court affirmed fully.*

* * * * *

The defendants, being manufacturers and vendors of cast-iron pipe, entered into a combination to raise the prices for pipe for all the states west and south of New York, Pennsylvania, and Virginia, constituting considerably more than three quarters of the territory of the United States, and significantly called by the associates "pay territory."

. . . Much evidence is adduced upon affidavit to prove that defendants had no power arbitrarily to fix prices, and that they were always obliged to meet competition. To the extent that they could not impose prices on the public in excess of the cost price of pipe with freight from the Atlantic seaboard added, this is true; but, within that limit, they could fix prices as they chose. The most cogent evidence that they had this power is the fact, everywhere apparent in the record, that they exercised it. . . . The defendants were, by their combination, therefore able to deprive the public in a large territory of the advantages otherwise accruing to them from the proximity of defendants' pipe factories, and, by keeping prices just low enough to prevent competition by Eastern manufacturers, to compel the public to pay an increase over what the price would have been, if fixed by competition between defendants, nearly equal to the advantage in freight rates enjoyed by defendants over Eastern competitors. The defendants acquired this power by voluntarily agreeing to sell only at prices fixed by their committee, and by allowing the highest bidder at the secret "auction pool" to become the lowest bidder of them at the public letting. Now, the restraint thus imposed on themselves was only partial. It did not cover the United States. There was not a complete monopoly. It was tempered by the fear

120

of competition, and it affected only a part of the price. But this certainly does not take the contract of association out of the annulling effect of the rule against monopolies.

It has been earnestly pressed upon us that the prices at which the cast-iron pipe was sold in pay territory were reasonable. A great many affidavits of purchasers of pipe in pay territory, all drawn by the same hand or from the same model, are produced, in which the affiants say that, in their opinion, the prices at which pipe has been sold by defendants have been reasonable. We do not think the issue an important one, because, as already stated, we do not think that at common law there is any question of reasonableness open to the courts with reference to such a contract. Its tendency was certainly to give defendants the power to charge unreasonable prices, had they chosen to do so. But, if it were important, we should unhesitatingly find that the prices charged in the instances which were in evidence were unreasonable. The letters from the manager of the Chattanooga foundry written to the other defendants, and discussing the prices fixed by the association, do not leave the slightest doubt upon this point, and outweigh the perfunctory affidavits produced by the defendants. The cost of producing pipe at Chattanooga, together with a reasonable profit, did not exceed $15 a ton. It could have been delivered at Atlanta at $17 to $18 a ton, and yet the lowest price which that foundry was permitted by the rules of the association to bid was $24.25. The same thing was true all through pay territory to a greater or less degree, and especially at "reserved cities."

✽ ✽ ✽ ✽ ✽

United States v. Trenton Potteries Co.

Supreme Court of the United States, 927.
273 U.S. 392, 47 S.Ct. 377, 71 L.Ed. 700.

A "rule of reason" about price fixing was again rejected by the Court in Trenton Potteries.

Chief Justice Harlan F. Stone.   Respondents, engaged in the manufacture or distribution of 82 percent of the vitreous pottery fixtures produced in the United States for use in bathrooms and lavatories, were members of a trade organization known as the Sanitary Potters' Association. Twelve of the corporate respondents had their factories and chief places of business in New Jersey, one was located in California, and the others were situated in Illinois, Michigan, West Virginia, Indiana, Ohio, and Pennsylvania. Many of them sold and delivered their product within the Southern district of New York, and some maintained sales offices and agents there.

There is no contention here that the verdict was not supported by suffi-

cient evidence that respondents, controlling some 82 percent of the business
of manufacturing and distributing in the United States vitreous pottery of
the type described, combined to fix prices and to limit sales in interstate
commerce to jobbers.

The issues raised here by the government's specification of errors relate
only to the decision of the Circuit Court of Appeals upon its review of certain rulings of the District Court made in the course of the trial. It is urged
that the court below erred in holding in effect that the trial court should
have submitted to the jury the question whether the price agreement complained of constituted an unreasonable restraint of trade.

. . . The question therefore to be considered here is whether the trial
judge correctly withdrew from the jury the consideration of the reasonableness of the particular restraints charged.

That only those restraints upon interstate commerce which are unreasonable are prohibited by the Sherman Law was the rule laid down by
the opinions of this Court in the Standard Oil and Tobacco Cases. But it
does not follow that agreements to fix or maintain prices are reasonable
restraints and therefore permitted by the statute, merely because the prices
themselves are reasonable. Reasonableness is not a concept of definite and
unchanging content. Its meaning necessarily varies in the different fields of
the law, because it is used as a convenient summary of the dominant considerations which control in the application of legal doctrines. Our view
of what is a reasonable restraint of commerce is controlled by the recognized purpose of the Sherman Law itself. Whether this type of restraint is
reasonable or not must be judged in part at least, in the light of its effect on
competition, for whatever difference of opinion there may be among economists as to the social and economic desirability of an unrestrained competitive system, it cannot be doubted that the Sherman Law and the
judicial decisions interpreting it are based upon the assumption that the
public interest is best protected from the evils of monopoly and price control by the maintenance of competition.

The aim and result of every price-fixing agreement, if effective, is the
elimination of one form of competition. The power to fix prices, whether
reasonably exercised or not, involves power to control the market and to
fix arbitrary and unreasonable prices. The reasonable price fixed today may
through economic and business changes become the unreasonable price of
tomorrow. Once established, it may be maintained unchanged because of
the absence of competition secured by the agreement for a price reasonable
when fixed. Agreements which create such potential power may well be
held to be in themselves unreasonable or unlawful restraints, without the
necessity of minute inquiry whether a particular price is reasonable or unreasonable as fixed and without placing on the government in enforcing
the Sherman Law the burden of ascertaining from day to day whether it
has become unreasonable through the mere variation of economic conditions. Moreover, in the absence of express legislation requiring it, we should

hesitate to adopt a construction making the difference between legal and illegal conduct in the field of business relations depend upon so uncertain a test as whether prices are reasonable—a determination which can be satisfactorily made only after a complete survey of our economic organization and a choice between rival philosophies. . . .

United States v. Socony-Vacuum Oil Co., Inc.

Supreme Court of the United States, 1940.
310 U.S. 150, 60 S.Ct. 811, 84 L.Ed. 1129.

In Appalachian Coals in 1933, the Court let by a plan for stabilizing coal prices, under Depression conditions. This slight aberration was closed by Socony-Vacuum, which dealt with an extensive industry system to protect gasoline prices from competition. That price fixing is illegal per se *was flatly reaffirmed.*

* * * * *

Justice Douglas. Therefore the sole remaining question on this phase of the case is the applicability of the rule of the Trenton Potteries case to these facts.

Respondents seek to distinguish the Trenton Potteries case from the instant one. They assert that in that case the parties substituted an agreed-on price for one determined by competition; that the defendants there had the power and purpose to suppress the play of competition in the determination of the market price; and therefore that the controlling factor in that decision was the destruction of market competition, not whether prices were higher or lower, reasonable or unreasonable. Respondents contend that in the instant case there was no elimination in the spot tank car market of competition which prevented the prices in that market from being made by the play of competition in sales between independent refiners and their jobber and consumer customers; that during the buying programs those prices were in fact determined by such competition; that the purchases under those programs were closely related to or dependent on the spot market prices; that there was no evidence that the purchases of distress gasoline under those programs had any effect on the competitive market price beyond that flowing from the removal of a competitive evil; and that if respondents had tried to do more than free competition from the effect of distress gasoline and to set an arbitrary noncompetitive price through their purchases, they would have been without power to do so.

But we do not deem those distinctions material.

In the first place, there was abundant evidence that the combination had the purpose to raise prices. And likewise, there was ample evidence that the buying programs at least contributed to the price rise and the stability of the spot markets, and to increases in the price of gasoline sold in the Mid-Western area during the indictment period. That other factors also may have contributed to that rise and stability of the markets is immaterial. For in any such market movement, forces other than the purchasing power of the buyers normally would contribute to the price rise and the market stability. So far as cause and effect are concerned it is sufficient in this type of case if the buying programs of the combination resulted in a price rise and market stability which but for them would not have happened. For this reason the charge to the jury that the buying programs must have "caused" the price rise and its continuance was more favorable to respondents than they could have required. Proof that there was a conspiracy, that its purpose was to raise prices, and that it caused or contributed to a price rise is proof of the actual consummation or execution of a conspiracy under § 1 of the Sherman Act.

Secondly, the fact that sales on the spot markets were still governed by some competition is of no consequence. For it is indisputable that that competition was restricted through the removal by respondents of a part of the supply which but for the buying programs would have been a factor in determining the going prices on those markets. But the vice of the conspiracy was not merely the restriction of supply of gasoline by removal of a surplus. As we have said, this was a well organized program. The timing and strategic placement of the buying orders for distress gasoline played an important and significant role. Buying orders were carefully placed so as to remove the distress gasoline from weak hands. Purchases were timed. Sellers were assigned to the buyers so that regular outlets for distress gasoline would be available. The whole scheme was carefully planned and executed to the end that distress gasoline would not overhang the markets and depress them at any time. And as a result of the payment of fair going market prices a floor was placed and kept under the spot markets. Prices rose and jobbers and consumers in the Mid-Western area paid more for their gasoline than they would have paid but for the conspiracy. Competition was not eliminated from the markets; but it was clearly curtailed, since restriction of the supply of gasoline, the timing and placement of the purchases under the buying programs, and the placing of a floor under the spot markets obviously reduced the play of the forces of supply and demand.

The elimination of so-called competitive evils is no legal justification for such buying programs. The elimination of such conditions was sought primarily for its effect on the price structures. Fairer competitive prices, it is claimed, resulted when distress gasoline was removed from the market.

But such defense is typical of the protestations usually made in price-fixing cases. Ruinous competition, financial disaster, evils of price cutting, and the like appear throughout our history as ostensible justifications for price-fixing. If the so-called competitive abuses were to be appraised here, the reasonableness of prices would necessarily become an issue in every price-fixing case. In that event the Sherman Act would soon be emasculated; its philosophy would be supplanted by one which is wholly alien to a system of free competition; it would not be the charter of freedom which its framers intended.

The reasonableness of prices has no constancy due to the dynamic quality of the business facts underlying price structures. Those who fixed reasonable prices today would perpetuate unreasonable prices tomorrow, since those prices would not be subject to continuous administrative supervision and readjustment in light of changed conditions. Those who controlled the prices would control or effectively dominate the market. And those who were in that strategic position would have it in their power to destroy or drastically impair the competitive system. But the thrust of the rule is deeper and reaches more than monopoly power. Any combination which tampers with price structures is engaged in an unlawful activity. Even though the members of the price-fixing group were in no position to control the market, to the extent that they raised, lowered, or stabilized prices they would be directly interfering with the free play of market forces. The Act places all such schemes beyond the pale and protects that vital part of our economy against any degree of interference. Congress has not left with us the determination of whether or not particular price-fixing schemes are wise or unwise, healthy or destructive. It has not permitted the age-old cry of ruinous competition and competitive evils to be a defense to price-fixing conspiracies. It has no more allowed genuine or fancied competitive abuses as a legal justification for such schemes than it has the good intentions of the members of the combination. If such a shift is to be made, it must be done by the Congress.

As we have indicated, the machinery employed by a combination for price-fixing is immaterial.

Under the Sherman Act a combination formed for the purpose and with the effect of raising, depressing, fixing, pegging, or stabilizing the price of a commodity in interstate or foreign commerce is illegal per se. Where the machinery for price-fixing is an agreement on the prices to be charged or paid for the commodity in the interstate or foreign channels of trade, the power to fix prices exists if the combination has control of a substantial part of the commerce in that commodity. Where the means for price-fixing are purchases or sales of the commodity in a market operation or, as here, purchases of a part of the supply of the commodity for the purpose of keeping it from having a depressive effect on the markets, such power may be found to exist though the combination does not control a substantial part of the commodity. In such a case that power may be established if, as a result of market conditions, the resources available to the combinations, the timing and the strategic placement of orders and the like, effective means are at hand to accomplish the desired objective. But there may be effective influence over the market though the group in question does not control it. Price-fixing agreements may have utility to members of the group though the power possessed or exerted falls far short of domination and control. Monopoly power . . . is not the only power which the Act strikes down, as we have said. Proof that a combination was formed for the purpose of fixing prices and that it caused them to be fixed or contributed to that result is proof of the completion of a price-fixing conspiracy under § 1 of the Act. The indictment in this case charged that this combination had that purpose and effect. And there was abundant evidence to support it. Hence the existence of power on the part of members of the combination to fix prices was but a conclusion from the finding that the buying programs caused or contributed to the rise and stability of prices.

. . . As we have seen, price-fixing combinations which lack Congressional sanction are illegal per se; they are not evaluated in terms of their purpose, aim, or effect in the elimination of so-called competitive evils. Only in the event that they were, would such considerations have been relevant.

American Tobacco Company v. *United States*
328 U.S. 781 (1946).

Is oligopoly liable to antitrust treatment, even though there is no tangible collusion (Sherman Act, Section 1) nor single dominant firm (Section 2)? This landmark decision said yes. But the legal conclusion was not followed by significant remedy, and so the doctrine has lain dormant ever since.

Mr. Justice Burton.   The petitioners are The American Tobacco Company, Liggett & Myers Tobacco Company, R. J. Reynolds Tobacco Company, American Suppliers, Inc., a subsidiary of American, and certain officials of the respective companies who were convicted by a jury, in the District Court of the United States for the Eastern District of Kentucky, of violating §§ 1 and 2 of the Sherman Anti-trust Act. . . .

The requirement stated to the jury and contained in the statute was only that the offenders shall "monopolize any part of the trade or commerce among the several States, or with foreign nations." This particular conspiracy may well have derived special vitality, in the eyes of the jury, from the fact that its existence was established, not through the presentation of a formal written agreement, but through the evidence of widespread and effective conduct on the part of petitioners in relation to their existing or potential competitors. . . .

First of all, the monopoly found by the jury to exist in the present cases appears to have been completely separable from the old American Tobacco Trust which was dissolved in 1911. The conspiracy to monopolize and the monopolization charged here do not depend upon proof relating to the old tobacco trust but upon a dominance and control by petitioners in recent years over purchases of the raw material and over the sale of the finished product in the form of cigarettes. The fact, however, that the purchases of leaf tobacco and the sales of so many products of the tobacco industry have remained largely within the same general group of business organizations for over a generation, inevitably has contributed to the ease with which control over competition within the industry and the mobilization of power to resist new competition can be exercised. . . . The verdicts indicate that practices of an informal and flexible nature were adopted and that the results were so uniformly beneficial to the petitioners in protecting their common interests as against those of competitors that, entirely from circumstantial evidence, the jury found that a combination or conspiracy existed among the petitioners from 1937 to 1940, with power and intent to exclude competitors to such a substantial extent as to violate the Sherman Act as interpreted by the trial court. . . .

The Government introduced evidence showing . . . that petitioners refused to purchase tobacco on these [auction] markets unless the other petitioners were also represented thereon. There were attempts made by others to open new tobacco markets but none of the petitioners would participate in them unless the other petitioners were present. Consequently, such markets were failures due to the absence of buyers. . . . In this way the new tobacco markets and their locations were determined by the unanimous consent of the petitioners and, in arriving at their determination, the petitioners consulted with each other as to whether or not a community deserved a market.

The Government presented evidence to support its claim that, before the markets opened, the petitioners placed limitations and restrictions on the prices which their buyers were permitted to pay for tobacco. None of the buyers exceeded these price ceilings. Grades of tobacco were formulated in such a way as to result in the absence of competition between the petitioners. There was manipulation of the price of lower grade tobaccos in order to restrict competition from manufacturers of the lower priced cigarettes. Methods used included the practice of the petitioners of calling their respective buyers in, prior to the opening of the annual markets, and giving them instructions as to the prices to be paid for leaf tobacco in each of the markets. These instructions were in terms of top prices or price ranges. The price ceilings thus established for the buyers were the same for each of them. . . .

Where one or two of the petitioners secured their percentage of the crop on a certain market or were not interested in the purchase of certain offerings of tobacco, their buyers, nevertheless, would enter the bidding in order to force the other petitioners to bid up to the maximum price. The petitioners were not so much concerned with the prices they paid for the leaf tobacco as that each should pay the same price for the same grade and that none would secure any advantage in purchasing tobacco. . . .

The verdicts show also that the jury found that the petitioners conspired to fix prices and to exclude undesired competition in the distribution and sale of their principal products. The petitioners sold and distributed their products to jobbers and to selected dealers who bought at list prices, less discounts. . . . The list prices charged and the discounts allowed by petitioners have been practically identical since 1923 and absolutely identical since 1928. Since the latter date, only seven changes have been made by the three companies and those have been identical in amount. The increases were first announced by Reynolds. American and Liggett thereupon increased their list prices in identical amounts.

It is not the form of the combination or the particular means used but the result to be achieved that the statute condemns. It is not of importance whether the means used to accomplish the unlawful objectives are in themselves lawful or unlawful. Acts done to give effect to the conspiracy may be in themselves wholly innocent acts. Yet, if they are part of the sum of the acts which are relied upon to effectuate the conspiracy which the statute forbids, they come within its prohibition. No formal agreement is necessary to constitute an unlawful conspiracy. Often crimes are a matter of inference deduced from the acts of the person accused and done in pursuance of a criminal purpose. Where the conspiracy is proved, as here, from the evidence of the action taken in concert by the parties to it, it is all the more convincing proof of an intent to exercise the power of exclusion acquired through that conspiracy. The essential combination or conspiracy in violation of the Sherman Act may be found in a course of dealing or other circumstances as well as in an exchange of words. . . . Where the circumstances are such as to warrant a jury in finding that the conspirators had a unity of purpose or a common design and understanding, or a meeting of minds in an unlawful arrangement, the conclusion that a conspiracy is established is justified. Neither proof of exertion of the power to exclude nor proof of actual exclusion of existing or potential competitors is essential to sustain a charge of monopolization under the Sherman Act. . . .

In the present cases, the petitioners have been found to have conspired to establish a monopoly and also to have the power and intent to establish and maintain the monopoly. To hold that they do not come within the prohibition of the Sherman Act would destroy the force of that Act. Accordingly, the instructions of the trial court under § 2 of the Act are approved and the judgment of the Circuit Court of Appeals is *Affirmed.*

United States v. Container Corp. of America, et al.
393 U.S. 333 (1969).

This case explored the margin of cooperation among firms in sharing price information. The key: sellers could routinely demand and get each others' latest sale price, but buyers could not do the same. By reducing sellers' uncertainty about competitive offers, it could reduce the likelihood of price cutting, thereby "chilling" competition.

Mr. Justice Douglas. This is a civil antitrust action charging a price-fixing agreement in violation of § 1 of the Sherman Act. . . .

The case as proved is unlike any of other price decisions we have rendered. There was here an exchange of price information but no agreement to adhere to a price schedule as in *Sugar Institute v. United States*, 297 U.S. 553, or *United States v. Socony-Vacuum Oil Co.*, 310 U.S. 150. There was here an exchange of information concerning specific sales to identified customers, not a statistical report on the average cost to all members, without identifying the parties to specific transactions, as in *Maple Flooring Mfrs. Assn. v. United States*, 268 U.S. 563. While there was present here, as in *Cement Mfrs. Protective Assn. v. United States*, 268 U.S. 588, an exchange of prices to specific customers, there was absent the controlling circumstance, *viz.*, that cement manufacturers, to protect themselves from delivering to contractors more cement than was needed for a specific job and thus receiving a lower price, exchanged price information as a means of protecting their legal rights from fraudulent inducements to deliver more cement than needed for a specific job.

Here all that was present was a request by each defendant of its competitor for information as to the most recent price charged or quoted, whenever it needed such information and whenever it was not available from another source. Each defendant on receiving that request usually furnished the data with the expectation that it would be furnished reciprocal information when it wanted it. That concerted action is of course sufficient to establish the combination or conspiracy, the initial ingredient of a violation of § 1 of the Sherman Act.

There was of course freedom to withdraw from the agreement. But the fact remains that when a defendant requested and received price information, it was affirming its willingness to furnish such information in return.

There was to be sure an infrequency and irregularity of price exchanges between the defendants; and often the data were available from the records of the defendants or from the customers themselves. Yet the essence of the agreement was to furnish price information whenever requested.

Moreover, although the most recent price charged or quoted was sometimes fragmentary, each defendant had the manuals with which it could compute the price charged by a competitor on a specific order to a specific customer.

Further, the price quoted was the current price which a customer would need to pay in order to obtain products from the defendant furnishing the data.

The defendants account for about 90 percent of the shipment of corrugated containers from plants in the Southeastern United States. While containers vary as to dimensions, weight, color, and so on, they are substantially identical, no matter who produces them, when made to particular specifications. The prices paid depend on price alternatives. Suppliers when seeking new or additional business or keeping old customers, do not exceed a competitor's price. It is common for purchasers to buy from two or more suppliers concurrently. A defendant supplying a customer with containers would usually quote the same price on additional orders, unless costs had changed. Yet where a competitor was charging a particular price, a defendant would normally quote the same price or even a lower price.

The exchange of price information seemed to have the effect of keeping prices within a fairly narrow ambit. Capacity has exceeded the demand from 1955 to 1963, the period covered by the complaint, and the trend of corrugated container prices has been downward. Yet despite this excess capacity and the downward trend of prices, the industry has expanded in the Southeast from 30 manufacturers with 49 plants to 51 manufacturers with 98 plants. An abundance of raw materials and machinery makes entry into the industry easy with an investment of $50,000 to $75,000.

The result of this reciprocal exchange of prices was to stabilize prices though at a downward level. Knowledge of a competitor's price usually meant matching that price. The continuation of some price competition is not fatal to the Government's case. The limitation or reduction of price competition brings the case within the ban, for as we held in *United States v. Socony-Vacuum Oil Co., supra,* at 224, n. 59, interference with the setting of price by free market forces is unlawful *per se.* Price information exchanged in some markets may have no effect on a truly competitive price. But the corrugated container industry is dominated by relatively few sellers. The product is fungible and the competition for sales is price. The demand is inelastic, as buyers place orders only for immediate, short-run needs. The exchange of price data tends toward price uniformity. For a lower price does not mean a larger share of the available business but a sharing of the existing business at a lower return. Stabilizing prices as well as raising them is within the ban of § 1 of the Sherman Act. . . . The inferences are irresistible that the exchange of price information has had an anticompetitive effect in the industry, chilling the vigor of price competition. . . .

Price is too critical, too sensitive a control to allow it to be used even in an informal manner to restrain competition.

Reversed.

Mr. Justice Marshall, with whom Mr. Justice Harlan and Mr. Justice Stewart join, dissenting.

. . . Complete market knowledge is certainly not an evil in perfectly competitive markets. This is not, however, such a market, and there is admittedly some danger that price information will be used for anticompetitive purposes, particularly the maintenance of prices at a high level. If the danger that price information will be so used is particularly high in a given situation, then perhaps exchange of information should be condemned.

I do not think the danger is sufficiently high in the present case. Defendants are only 18 of the 51 producers of corrugated containers in the Southeastern United States. Together, they do make up 90 percent of the market and the six largest defendants do control 60 percent of the market. But entry is easy; an investment of $50,000 to $75,000 is ordinarily all that is necessary. In fact, the number of sellers has increased from 30 to the present 51 in the eight-year period covered by the complaint. The size of the market has almost doubled because of increased demand for corrugated containers. Nevertheless, some excess capacity is present. The products produced by defendants are undifferentiated. Industry demand is inelastic, so that price changes will not, up to a certain point, affect the total amount purchased. The only effect of price changes will be to reallocate market shares among sellers. . . .

The Government is ultimately forced to fall back on the theoretical argument that prices would have been more unstable and would have fallen faster without price information. As I said earlier, I cannot make this assumption on the basis of the evidence in this record. The findings of the Court below simply do not indicate that the exchange of information had a significant anticompetitive effect; if we rely on these findings, at worst all we can assume is that the exchange was a neutral factor in the market. . . .

United States v. Jerrold Electronics Corporation

187 F.Supp. 545 (E.D. Pa. 1960),
affirmed per curiam 365 U.S. 567 (1961).

Tie-in sales—to get X you must also buy Y—became virtually per se *illegal in the 1950s, as a device for extending market power. This case explores the further edges of the problem: an "infant industry," involving the innovation of complex new technology. The decision carefully limits any possible exemption to just those temporary, unusual conditions.*

Van Dusen, District Judge.   This action was commenced with the filing of a complaint on February 15, 1957, charging Jerrold Electronics Corporation, its president, Milton Jerrold Shapp, and five of its corporate subsidiaries with being parties to a conspiracy and contracts in unreasonable restraint of trade and commerce in community television antenna equipment in violation of Section 1 of the Sherman Act . . . ; with being parties to a conspiracy and attempting to monopolize trade and commerce in community television antenna equipment in violation of Section 2 of the Sherman Act . . . ; and with contracting to sell and making sales upon unlawful conditions in violation of Section 3 of the Clayton Act. . . .

There are four parts to a community television antenna system. The first is the antenna site, referred to in the trade as the "head end." The second is the apparatus which carries the signal from the antenna into the community, known as the "run to town." The third is the "skeleton system" that is constructed through the town to carry the television signals to the extremities of the area to be covered. Finally, there is the "tap-off" from the skeleton system which carries the signal to the home of each subscriber to the service. . . .

By the spring of 1951, the Jerrold people felt they were prepared to start selling equipment for community television antenna purposes. As a result of their work in Lansford and Mahanoy City, they had developed a new line of equipment for community antenna systems designated "W" equipment. After consulting with his engineers and several of Jerrold's commission salesmen who dealt with the distributors, Shapp decided that the W equipment should only be sold with engineering services to insure that the system would function properly. A general policy, therefore, was established of selling electronic equipment to community antenna companies only on a full system basis and in conjunction with a service contract which provided for technical services with respect to the layout, installation, and operation of the system.

> Since we cannot reasonably be required to perform our obligations as enumerated in this letter if the system contains electronic equipment other than that manufactured by Jerrold Electronics Corporation, you agree not to install, as part of the system, any equipment or attachments which, in our opinion, will impair the quality of television reception and signal distribution capabilities of the system, or which might cause damage to, or impair the efficiency of, any of the equipment comprising the System.

The Government contends that Jerrold's policy and practice of selling on a system basis only and of making sales only in conjunction with a service contract constituted unlawful tie-ins in violation of Section 1 of the Sherman Act . . . and Section 3 of the Clayton Act. . . . It also asserts that the provision in the 103 series contracts for the exclusive use of Jerrold equipment for the addition of extra channels to the system, and the provision in all of the contracts not to install unapproved, non-Jerrold equipment, violated these sections of the anti-trust laws.

III–A. Service Contracts

❋   ❋   ❋   ❋   ❋

The Government concedes that Section 3 of the Clayton Act does not apply to . . . tie-ins involving services. The Government asserts, however, that sales upon the condition that the purchaser subscribe to the services of the vendor constitute an unreasonable restraint of trade in violation of Section 1 of the Sherman Act. Jerrold admits that, as to the sale of complete community television antenna systems, it was an undoubted leader up until mid-1954, and more than a majority of the new systems from 1950 to mid-1954 were purchased from it. Indeed, Jerrold consistently advertised throughout this period that at least 75 percent of the community systems in the United States were "Jerrold systems." Economic power over a product can be inferred from sales leadership. . . . Another fact from which economic power can be inferred is the desirability of the tying product to the purchaser. *Northern Pacific Railway Co.* v. *United States, supra* . . . (dissent). Mr. Shapp has stated that Jerrold's highly specialized head end equipment was the only equipment available which was designed to meet all of the varying problems arising at the antenna site. It was thus in great demand by system operators. This placed Jerrold in a strategic position and gave it the leverage necessary to persuade customers to agree to its service contracts. This leverage constitutes "economic power" sufficient to invoke the doctrine of *per se* unreasonableness.

When Jerrold was ready to place its W equipment on the market in May 1950, it was confronted with a rather unique situation. In the first place, while it was convinced that its equipment would work, Jerrold recognized that it was sensitive and unstable. Consequently, modifications were still being made. . . . Secondly, as has already been noted, there were hundreds of people anxious to set up community antenna systems. Most of these people had no technical background at all. . . . Finally, Jerrold had directed most of its resources toward the development of its community equipment. It was of utmost importance to it that its investment prove successful.

Shapp, his engineers and salesmen, envisioned widespread chaos if Jerrold simply sold its community equipment to anyone who wanted it. . . . Therefore, it was desirable that the system be installed under the supervision of men whose ability was known to the utility companies through other dealings. For these reasons, it was decided that community equipment should be sold with engineering services in order to foster the orderly growth of the industry on which the future of Jerrold depended.

The Government does not dispute the reasonableness of the contracts for services but objects to the fact that they were compulsory. The crucial question, therefore, is whether Jerrold could have accomplished the ends it sought without requiring the contracts. . . . If Jerrold's equipment was available without a contract, many impatient operators probably would have attempted to install their systems without assistance. . . . Jerrold's supply of equipment was limited. Unrestricted sales would have resulted in much of this equipment going into systems where prospects of success were at best extremely doubtful. Jerrold's short- and long-term well-being depended on the success of these first systems. It could not afford to permit some of its limited equipment to be used in such a way that it would work against its interests. A wave of system failures at the start would have greatly retarded, if not destroyed, this new industry and would have been disastrous for Jerrold. . . . For these reasons, this court concludes that Jerrold's policy and practice of selling its community equipment only in conjunction with a service contract was reasonable and not in violation of Section 1 of the Sherman Act at the time of its inception. . . .

The court's conclusion is based primarily on the fact that the tie-in was instituted in the launching of a new business with a highly uncertain future. As the industry took root and grew, the reasons for the blanket insistence on a service contract disappeared.

. . . [W]hile Jerrold has satisfied this court that its policy was reasonable at its inception, it has failed to satisfy us that it remained reasonable throughout the period of its use, even allowing it a reasonable time to recognize and adjust its policies to changing conditions. Accordingly, the court concludes that the defendants' refusal to sell Jerrold equipment except in conjunction with a service contract violated Section 1 of the Sherman Act during part of the time this policy was in effect.

III–B. Full System Sales

Jerrold also admits that it was its policy and practice from May 1951 to March 1954 not to sell its various items of equipment designed for community antenna systems separately, but only to sell them as components of a complete system. As a result of this program, individual pieces of Jerrold equipment were unavailable for both new systems and existing non-Jerrold systems. The government contends that this too constitutes an unlawful tie-in because Jerrold is driving competitors from the field by using its market power with respect to some of its equipment to induce the purchase of other equipment it manufactures. . . .

There is a further factor, however, which, in the court's opinion, makes Jerrold's decision to sell only full systems reasonable. There was a sound business reason for Jerrold to adopt this policy. Jerrold's decision was intimately associated with its belief that a service contract was essential. This court has already determined that, in view of the condition of Jerrold, the equipment, and the potential customers, the defendants' policy of insisting on a service contract was reasonable at its inception. Jerrold could not render the service it promised and deemed necessary if the customer could purchase any kind of equipment he desired. The limited knowledge and instability of equipment made specifications an impractical, if not impossible, alternative. Furthermore, Jerrold's policy could not have been carried out if separate items of its equipment were made available to existing systems or any other customer because the demand was so great that this equipment would find its way to a new system. Thus, the court concludes that Jerrold's policy of full system sales was a necessary adjunct to its policy of compulsory service and was reasonably regarded as a product as long as the conditions which dictated the use of the service contract continued to exist. As the circumstances changed and the need for compulsory service contracts disappeared, the economic reasons for exclusively selling complete systems were eliminated. Absent these economic reasons, the court feels that a full system was not an appropriate sales unit. . . .

FINAL JUDGMENT

*   *   *   *   *

The defendants are enjoined and restrained from, directly or indirectly:

(A) Selling or offering to sell equipment on the condition or understanding that the purchaser thereof purchase services from the defendants;

(B) Furnishing or offering to furnish services on the condition or understanding that the recipient thereof purchase any Jerrold equipment;

(C) Selling or offering to sell any item of Jerrold equipment on the condition or understanding that the purchaser thereof buy or use any other Jerrold equipment;

(D) Selling or offering to sell any equipment on the condition or understanding that the purchaser thereof will not purchase or use equipment manufactured or sold by any other person. . . .

White Motors Co. v. United States
372 U.S. 253 (1963).

The Court here took a cautious first look at vertical territorial restrictions (e.g., exclusive dealer franchises). But the minority was trenchantly opposed, and the line soon became more strict (see the next case).

Justice Douglas.   This is the first case involving a territorial restriction in a *vertical* arrangement; and we know too little of the actual impact both of that restriction and the one respecting customers to reach a conclusion on the bare bones of the documentary evidence before us. . . .

Horizontal territorial limitations, like "[g]roup boycotts, or concerted refusals by traders to deal with other traders" . . . are naked restraints of trade with no purpose except stifling of competition. A vertical territorial limitation may or may not have that purpose or effect. We do not know enough of the economic and business stuff out of which these arrangements emerge to be certain. They may be too dangerous to sanction or they may be allowable protections against aggressive competitors or the only practicable means a small company has for breaking into or staying in business . . . and within the "rule of reason." We need to know more than we do about the actual impact of these arrangements on competition to decide whether they have such a "pernicious effect on competition and lack any redeeming virtue" . . . and therefore should be classified as per se violations of the Sherman Act. . . .

We conclude that the summary judgment . . . was improperly employed in this suit. . . . [W]e do not intimate any view on the merits. We only hold that the legality of the territorial . . . limitations should be determined only after a trial.

Reversed.

Mr. Justice Clark, with whom The Chief Justice and Mr. Justice Black join, dissenting.

. . . [This is] one of the most brazen violations of the Sherman Act that I have experienced in a quarter of a century. . . . [U]nder these contracts a person wishing to buy a White truck must deal with only one seller who by virtue of his agreements with dealer competitors has the sole power as to the public to set prices, determine terms, and even to refuse to sell a particular customer. In the latter event the customer could not buy a White truck because a neighboring dealer must reject him under the White Motor contract unless he has "a place of business and/or purchasing headquarters" in the latter's territory. He might buy another brand of truck, it is true, but the existence of interbrand competition has never been a justification for an explicit agreement to eliminate competition. . . .

Moreover, White Motor has admitted that each of its distributors and dealers, numbering some 300, has entered into identical contracts. In its "argument" it says that "it has to" agree to these exclusive territorial arrangements in order to get financially able and capable distributors and dealers. It has nowise denied that it has been required by the distributors or dealers to enter into the contracts. Indeed the clear inference is to the contrary. The motivations of White Motor and its distributors and dealers are inextricably intertwined; the distributors and dealers are each acquainted with the contracts and have readily complied with their requirements, without which the contracts would be of no effect. It is hard for me to draw a distinction on the basis of who initiates such a plan. Indeed, under Interstate Circuit, Inc. v. United States, 306 U.S. 208, 223 (1939), the unanimity of action by some 300 parties here forms the basis of an "understanding that all were to join" and the economics of the situation would certainly require as much. . . .

The Court says that perhaps the reasonableness or the effect of such arrangements might be subject to inquiry. But the rule of reason is inapplicable to agreements made solely for the purpose of eliminating competition. . . . To admit, as does the petitioner, that competition is eliminated under its contracts is, under our cases, to admit a violation of the Sherman Act. No justification, no matter how beneficial, can save it from that interdiction.

Today the Court does a futile act in remanding this case for trial. In my view appellant cannot plead nor prove an issue upon which a successful defense of its contracts can be predicated. Neither time (I note the case is now in its sixth year) nor all of the economic analysts, the statisticians, the experts in marketing or for that matter the ingenuity of lawyers can escape the unalterable fact that these contracts eliminate competition and under our cases are void. . . .

United States v. Arnold, Schwinn & Co.
388 U.S. 365 (1967).

Exclusive franchises were now said to be illegal virtually per se. The issue gained force as franchising spread further (e.g., fast-food chains and motels) after 1967. By 1974, tightly exclusive franchises were presumptively illegal, but there remained some room to defend them. Is this line too tight? or still too loose?

Mr. Justice Fortas. The United States brought this appeal to review the judgment of the District Court in a civil antitrust case alleging violations of § 1 of the Sherman Act. . . . The complaint charged a continuing conspiracy since 1952 between defendants and other alleged co-conspirators involving price fixing, allocation of exclusive territories to wholesalers and jobbers, and confinement of merchandise to franchised dealers. Named as defendants were Arnold, Schwinn & Company ("Schwinn"), the Schwinn Cycle Distributors Association ("SCDA"), and B. F. Goodrich Company ("B. F. Goodrich"). . . .

The challenged marketing program was instituted in 1952. In 1951 Schwinn had the largest single share of the United States bicycle market —22.5 percent. In 1961 Schwinn's share of market had fallen to 12.8 percent although its dollar and unit sales had risen substantially. In the same period, a competitor, Murray Ohio Manufacturing Company, which is now the leading United States bicycle producer, increased its market share from 11.6 percent in 1951 to 22.8 percent in 1961. Murray sells primarily to Sears, Roebuck & Company and other mass merchandisers. By 1962 there were nine bicycle producers in the Nation, operating 11 plants. Imports of bicycles amounted to 29.7 percent of sales in 1961. . . .

Schwinn sells its products primarily to or through 22 wholesale distributors, with sales to the public being made by a large number of retailers. In addition, it sells about 11 percent of its total to B. F. Goodrich for resale in B. F. Goodrich retail or franchised stores. There are about 5,000 to 6,000 retail dealers in the United States which are bicycle specialty shops, generally also providing servicing. About 84 percent of Schwinn's sales are through such specialized dealers. Schwinn sells only under the Schwinn label, never under private label, while about 64 percent of all bicycles are sold under private label. Distributors and retailers handling Schwinn bicycles are not restricted to the handling of that brand. They may and ordinarily do sell a variety of brands.

After World War II, Schwinn had begun studying and revamping its distribution pattern. As of 1951–1952, it had reduced its mailing list from about 15,000 retail outlets to about 5,500. It instituted the practice of franchising approved retail outlets. The franchise did not prevent the retailer from handling other brands, but it did require the retailer to promote Schwinn bicycles and to give them at least equal prominence with competing brands. The number of franchised dealers in any area was limited, and a retailer was franchised only as to a designated location or locations. Each franchised dealer was to purchase only from or through the distributor authorized to serve that particular area. He was authorized to sell only to consumers, and not to unfranchised retailers. . . .

Schwinn assigned specific territories to each of its 22 wholesale cycle distributors. These distributors were instructed to sell only to franchised Schwinn accounts and only in their respective territories which were specifically described and allocated on an exclusive basis. . . .

On this basis, restraints as to territory or customers, vertical or horizontal, are unlawful if they are "ancillary to the price-fixing" *(White Motor Co.* v. *United States)* . . . or if the price fixing is "an integral part of the whole distribution system." . . . In those situations, it is needless to inquire further into competitive effects because it is established doctrine that, unless permitted by statute, the fixing of prices at which others may sell is anticompetitive, and the unlawfulness of the price fixing infects the distribution restrictions. . . . At the other extreme, a manufacturer of a product other and equivalent brands of which are readily available in the market may select his customers, and for this purpose he may "franchise" certain dealers to whom, alone, he will sell his goods. . . . If the restraint stops at that point—if nothing more is involved than vertical "confinement" of the manufacturer's own sales of the merchandise to selected dealers, and if competitive products are readily available to others, the restriction, on these facts alone, would not violate the Sherman Act. It is within these boundary lines that we must analyze the present case. . . .

As the District Court held, where a manufacturer *sells* products to his distributor subject to territorial restrictions upon resale, a *per se* violation of the Sherman Act results. And, as we have held, the same principle applies to restrictions of outlets with which the distributors may deal and to restraints upon retailers to whom the goods are sold. . . . On the other hand, as indicated in *White Motor*, we are not prepared to introduce the inflexibility which a *per se* rule might bring if it were applied to prohibit all vertical restrictions of territory and all franchising, in the sense of designating specified distributors and retailers as the chosen instruments through which the manufacturer, retaining ownership of the goods, will distribute them to the public.

We do not suggest that the unilateral adoption by a single manufacturer of an agency or consignment pattern and the Schwinn type of restrictive distribution system would be justified in any and all circumstances by the presence of the competition of mass merchandisers and by the demonstrated need of the franchise system to meet that competition. But certainly, in such circumstances, the vertically imposed distribution restraints—*absent* price fixing and in the presence of adequate sources of alternative products to meet the needs of the unfranchised—may not be held to be *per se* violations of the Sherman Act. . . .

. . . Critical in this . . . [case] are the facts: (1) that other competitive bicycles are available to distributors and retailers in the marketplace, and there is no showing that they are not in all respects reasonably interchangeable as articles of competitive commerce with the Schwinn product, (2) that Schwinn distributors and retailers handle other brands of bicycles as well as Schwinn's; (3) in the present posture of the case we cannot rule that the vertical restraints are unreasonable because of their intermixture with price fixing; and (4) we cannot disagree with the findings of the trial court that competition made necessary the challenged program; that it was justified by, and went no further than required by, competitive pressures; and that its net effect is to preserve and not to damage competition in the bicycle market. Application of the rule of reason here cannot be confined to intrabrand competition. When we look to the product market as a whole, we cannot conclude that Schwinn's franchise system with respect to products as to which it retains ownership and risk constitutes an unreasonable restraint of trade. . . .

Mr. Justice Stewart, whom Mr. Justice Harlan joins, concurring in part and dissenting in part.

I agree with the Court's basic determination that Schwinn's marketing system is, under the rule of reason, entirely consonant with the antitrust laws. But I cannot understand how that marketing system becomes *per se* unreasonable and illegal in those instances where it is effectuated through sales to wholesalers and dealers. . . .

Despite the Government's concession that the rule of reason applies to all aspects of Schwinn's distribution system, the Court nevertheless reaches out to adopt a potent *per se* rule. No previous antitrust decision of this Court justifies this action. Instead, it completely repudiates the only case in point, *White Motor.* . . . The Court today is unable to give any reasons why, only four years later, this precedent should be overruled. . . . And I am completely at a loss to fathom how the Court can adopt its *per se* rule concerning distributional sales and yet uphold identical restrictions in Schwinn's marketing scheme when distribution takes the form of consignment or Schwinn Plan deliveries. It does not demonstrate that these restrictions are in their actual operation somehow more anticompetitive or less justifiable merely because the contractual relations between Schwinn and its jobbers and dealers bear the label "safe" rather than "agency" or "consignment." Such irrelevant formulae are false guides to sound adjudication in the antitrust field. . . .

Utah Pie Co. v. *Continental Baking Co.*
386 U.S. 685 (1967).

This unusual case further limited the range of permissible price discrimination. It could not now be done by large firms even if the "victim" firm held a dominant market share. This has drawn much criticism from some economists, as well as from Justices Harlan and Stewart.

Mr. Justice White. This suit for treble damages and injunction under §§ 4 and 16 of the Clayton Act . . . was brought by petitioner, Utah Pie Company, against respondents, Continental Baking Company, Carnation Company, and Pet Milk Company. The complaint charged a conspiracy under §§ 1 and 2 of the Sherman Act . . . and violations by each respondent of § 2(a) of the Clayton Act as amended by the Robinson-Patman Act. . . .

The product involved is frozen dessert pies—apple, cherry, boysenberry, peach, pumpkin, and mince. The period covered by the suit comprised the years 1958, 1959, and 1960 and the first eight months of 1961. Petitioner is a Utah corporation which for 30 years has been baking pies in its plant in Salt Lake City and selling them in Utah and surrounding States. It entered the frozen pie business in late 1957. It was immediately successful with its new line and built a new plant in Salt Lake City in 1958. The frozen pie market was a rapidly expanding one: 57,060 dozen frozen pies were sold in the Salt Lake City market in 1958, 111,729 dozen in 1959, 184,569 dozen in 1960, and 266,908 dozen in 1961. Utah Pie's share of this market in those years was 66.5 percent, 34.3 percent, 45.5 percent, and 45.3 percent respectively, its sales volume steadily increasing over the four years. Its financial position also improved. Petitioner is not, however, a large company. . . .

Each of the respondents is a large company and each of them is a major factor in the frozen pie market in one or more regions of the country. Each entered the Salt Lake City frozen pie market before petitioner began freezing dessert pies. None of them had a plant in Utah. . . . The Salt Lake City market was supplied by respondents chiefly from their California operations. They sold primarily on a delivered price basis. . . .

The major competitive weapon in the Utah market was price. The location of petitioner's plant gave it natural advantages in the Salt Lake City marketing area and it entered the market at a price below the then going prices for respondents' comparable pies. For most of the period involved here its prices were the lowest in the Salt Lake City market. It was, however, challenged by each of the respondents at one time or another and for varying periods. There was ample evidence to show that each of the respondents contributed to what proved to be a deteriorating price structure over the period covered by this suit, and each of the respondents in the course of the ongoing price competition sold frozen pies in the Salt Lake market at prices lower than it sold pies of like grade and quality in other markets considerably closer to its plants. Utah Pie, which entered the market at a price of $4.15 per dozen at the beginning of the relevant period, was selling "Utah" and "Frost 'N' Flame" pies for $2.75 per dozen when the instant suit was filed some 44 months later. Pet, which was offering pies at $4.92 per dozen in February 1958, was offering "Pet-Ritz" and "Bel-air" pies at $3.56 and $3.46 per dozen respectively in March and April 1961. Carnation's price in early 1958 was $4.82 per dozen but it was selling at $3.46 per dozen at the conclusion of the period, meanwhile having been down as low as $3.30 per dozen. The price range experienced by Continental during the period covered by this suit ran from a 1958 high of over $5 per dozen to a 1961 low of $2.85 per dozen. . . .

Petitioner's case against Continental is not complicated. Continental was a substantial factor in the market in 1957. But its sales of frozen 22-ounce dessert pies, sold under the "Morton" brand, amounted to only 1.3 percent of the market in 1958, 2.9 percent in 1959, and 1.8 percent in 1960. Its problems were primarily that of cost and in turn that of price, the controlling factor in the market.

. . . In June 1961, it took the steps which are the heart of petitioner's complaint against it. Effective for the last two weeks of June it offered its 22-ounce frozen apple pies in the Utah area at $2.85 per dozen. It was then selling the same pies at substantially higher prices in other markets. The Salt Lake City price was less than its direct cost plus an allocation for overhead. . . . Utah's response was immediate. It reduced its price on all of its apple pies to $2.75 per dozen. . . . Continental's total sales of frozen pies increased from 3,350 dozen in 1960 to 18,800 dozen in 1961. Its market share increased from 1.8 percent in 1960 to 8.3 percent in 1961. . . .

Even if the impact on Utah Pie as a competitor was negligible, there remain the consequences to others in the market who had to compete not only with Continental's 22-ounce pie at $2.85 but with Utah's even lower price of $2.75 per dozen for both its proprietary and controlled labels. . . . The evidence was that there were nine other sellers in 1960 who sold 23,473 dozen pies, 12.7 percent of the total market. In 1961 there were eight other sellers who sold less than the year before—18,565 dozen or 8.2 percent of the total—although the total market had expanded from 184,560 dozen to 226,908 dozen. We think there was sufficient evidence from which the jury could find a violation of § 2(a) by Continental.

. . . After Carnation's temporary setback in 1959 it instituted a new pricing policy to regain business in the Salt Lake City market. The new policy involved a slash in price of 60¢ per dozen pies, which brought Carnation's price to a level admittedly well below its costs, and well below the other prices prevailing in the market. The impact of the move was felt immediately, and the two other major sellers in the market reduced their prices. Carnation's banner year, 1960, in the end involved eight months during which the prices in Salt Lake City were lower than prices charged in other markets. The trend continued during the eight months in 1961 that preceded the filing of the complaint in this case. In each of those months the Salt Lake City prices charged by Carnation were well below prices charged in other markets, and in all but August 1961 the Salt Lake City delivered price was 20¢ to 50¢ lower than the prices charged in distant San Francisco.

. . . Sellers may not sell like goods to different purchasers at different prices if the result may be to injure competition in either the sellers' or the buyers' market unless such discriminations are justified as permitted by the Act. This case concerns the sellers' market. In this context, the Court of Appeals placed heavy emphasis on the fact that Utah Pie constantly increased its sale volume and continued to make a profit. But we disagree with its apparent view that there is no reasonably possible injury to competition as long as the volume of sales in a particular market is expanding and at least some of the competitors in the market continue to operate at a profit. Nor do we think that the Act only comes into play to regulate the conduct of price discriminators when their discriminatory prices consistently undercut other competitors. . . . In this case there was some evidence of predatory intent with respect to each of these respondents. There was also other evidence upon which the jury could rationally find the requisite injury to competition.

Mr. Justice Stewart, with whom Mr. Justice Harlan joins, dissenting.

. . . There is only one issue on this case in its present posture: . . . [D]id the respondents' actions have the anticompetitive effect required by the statute as an element of a cause of action?

The Court's own description of the Salt Lake City frozen pie market from 1958 through 1961, shows that the answer to that question must be no. In 1958 Utah Pie had a quasi-monopolistic 66.5 percent of the market. In 1961—after the alleged predations of the respondents—Utah Pie still had a commanding 45.3 percent, Pet had 29.4 percent, and the remainder of the market was divided almost equally between Continental, Carnation, and other, small local bakers. Unless we disregard the lessons so laboriously learned in scores of Sherman and Clayton Act cases, the 1961 situation has to be considered more competitive than that of 1958. Thus, if we assume that the price discrimination proven against the respondents had any effect on competition, that effect must have been beneficial.

That the Court has fallen into the error of reading the Robinson-Patman Act as protecting competitors, instead of competition, can be seen from its unsuccessful attempt to distinguish cases relied upon by the respondents. Those cases are said to be inapposite because they involved "no general decline in price structure," and no "lasting impact upon prices." But lower prices are the hallmark of intensified competition. . . .

I cannot hold that Utah Pie's monopolistic position was protected by the federal antitrust laws from effective price competition, and I therefore respectfully dissent.

Kenneth G. Elzinga (1941–   )

THE ANTIMERGER LAW: PYRRHIC VICTORIES?*

After the big decisions and formal victories, what happens? Mergers should be particularly open to good practical remedies. But Elzinga shows, with chapter and verse, that the actual correctives fall far short. Can we assume that remedies elsewhere are even less effective?

The relief that has been obtained by the Government in antimerger cases is the object of study in this paper. In short this is an economic study of the "back-side" of the antimerger law—what has happened *after* a merger has been found in violation of the law or the respondents have decided no longer to fight the suit and instead to submit to a consent decree. Its concern will be with the economic effectiveness of relief and the obstacles to the formulation of satisfactory relief. . . .

Whenever an anticompetitive increment in market power is attained by merger, structural relief requires the restoration of the acquired firm through a divestiture order. Only this sort of relief strikes at the very structure of the markets involved. Injunctive relief, that is, some form of order directing the acquiring firm to behave *as if* it did not gain this market power, is clearly unacceptable. Indeed placing such a regulatory role on the government is repugnant to the whole concept of antitrust. . . .

But disgorging the acquired firm from its acquirer is only a necessary, not a sufficient condition, for enacting effective relief. Along with reestablishing the acquired firm, it is also necessary that this "new" firm be made *viable;* a mere shadow of its former self is not acceptable. Indeed, reestablishing "new" firms that are unable to stand on their own would make any relief efforts farcical.

* Kenneth G. Elzinga, "The Antimerger Law: Pyrrhic Victories?" *Journal of Law and Economics,* 1969, excerpted from pp. 43–52. Elzinga was Special Economic Assistant to the Assistant Attorney General for Antitrust during 1970–71 and is now at the University of Virginia.

. . . As long as an anticompetitive acquisition remains consummated, the incremental market power can be used by the acquiring firm. Consequently, effective relief is also a function of the *time* required to reestablish the independent, viable firm. . . .

The Sample

The sample of merger cases to be evaluated is drawn from the universe of all *amended* Section 7 cases filed by the Government since the law's inception through the calendar year 1960, which have been settled either by consent order or decided for the Government by the end of calendar year 1964. The Government had filed eighty-one antimerger cases by 1960. Forty-two of these were either still pending by 1965, were dropped or settled for the defendant, or were eliminated because of data problems or regulatory aspects. Thirty-nine cases, then, constitute the sample.

IV. THE RESULTS

These thirty-nine cases have been placed on two four-category continuums in Table 2. . . .

For a relief case to qualify for the *successful* category, the acquired firm must be reestablished as an independent firm, or the anticompetitive effects of the acquisition must be stopped in their incipiency so that no restoration is necessary. . . .

. . . In the *sufficient* category a true independent center of initiative has not been restored. Instead the unlawfully acquired firm has been divested in one of four ways:

A.   sold to a "small" horizontal competitor
B.   sold as a vertical acquisition but with no foreclosure problems
C.   sold as a market or product extension acquisition with no obvious loss of potential competition
D.   sold as a conglomerate acquisition to a "very large firm."

*   *   *   *   *

[The *deficient*] category essentially includes those cases with one "hole" in the relief decree. The "holes" are:

E.   assets are sold in such manner that an obvious loss of potential competition resulted
F.   structural relief borders on *sufficient* but a complex marketing order, if enforced, leaves a "hole" in the case condemning it to a lower rung
G.   Government secures only a partial divestiture of the unlawfully acquired firm (or firms).

TABLE 2

Successful Relief	Sufficient Relief	Deficient Relief	Unsuccessful Relief
Bethlehem Steel	Gamble-Skogmo	American Radiator†	American Cyanamid†
Std. Oil of Ohio		Anheuser-Busch*	Automatic Canteen
Union Bag &		National Sugar†	Brillo
Paper		Spalding†	Brown Shoe†
			Continental Baking†
			Continental Can†
			Crown Zellerbach†
			Diamond Crystal
			Diebold
			Farm Journal
			General Shoe
			Gulf Oil
			Hertz
			Hilton
			Hooker Chemical
			International Paper
			Jerrold Electronics
			Leslie Salt†
			Lucky Lager
			Maremont
			MMM†
			National Dairy†
			Owens Illinois†
			Reynolds Metal
			Ryder
			Schenley
			Scott Paper
			Scovill
			Simpson Timber
			Union Carbide†
			Vendo

* Case dropped one rank where structural relief took at least three years, but less than five, from the date of acquisition.

† Case dropped two ranks (where possible) when structural relief was enacted five or more years after the date of acquisition.

In short, the *deficient* category is basically for cases where the Government secured structural relief, but where it was either incomplete or the assets fell into less than desirable hands. . . .

The category of *unsuccessful* cases includes the following:

H. no relief whatsoever
I. no structural relief, only a ban on future acquisitions
J. insignificant or *de minimus* divestiture, not striking at the heart of the restraint
K. relief takes the form of a marketing order
L. relief is a combination of J and K
M. divestiture to a significant horizontal competitor

N.   vertical divestiture with foreclosure problems
O.   divestiture of a non-viable firm.

In the *deficient* category, "partial divestiture" was mentioned; in this category the term "*de minimus* divestiture" was used. . . .

A glance at this Table provides no gray area. The first three ranks of the continuum have been decimated, now holding less than one quarter of the cases. The last category is full to the brim. Of the four cases remaining in the *successful-sufficient* categories, three involved acquisitions stopped in their incipiency *before* full consummation so that no divestiture was actually necessary; the other was a stock acquisition. This points to the difficulty of unraveling acquisitions after their consummation.

Average Time Spans

The Federal Trade Commission (FTC) cases in the sample had an average time of 19.0 months from the acquisition to the FTC's complaint. For those FTC cases which ended with some form of divestiture, the average duration from acquisition to divestiture was 67.5 months!

The Antitrust Division of the Department of Justice fared somewhat better. For those cases in the sample, the average time span from the acquisition to the complaint was 10.6 months. Where the Antitrust Division secured some form of divestiture in these cases, the average period from the acquisition to the structural relief was 63.8 months! . . .

To find that the Government has been unable to obtain effective relief in many of its antimerger cases is unlikely to surprise those acquainted with the history of the relief obtained in antimonopoly enforcement. In 1955, Dewey stated that "it is a commonplace in antitrust work that the Government wins the opinions and the defendants win the decrees." This position seems well documented. . . .

Donald J. Dewey (1922–   )

THE ACHIEVEMENTS OF ANTITRUST POLICY*

Antitrust has had little clear effect, but there may have been large indirect influences. Dewey's appraisal is lucid, sophisticated, and still valid. How can the effects be tested further, scientifically? Or is it inescapably a matter of impressions and guesswork?

*   *   *   *   *

1. A Limited Effort

The total amount of money spent to enforce the antitrust laws over sixty-five years would not buy a medium-size naval vessel, and even if one adds to this figure the costs incurred by private parties in antitrust suits, the resulting sum probably would not finance a modern aircraft carrier. But then where the functions of the State are concerned, money outlay is a poor yardstick of a project's effect on economic welfare. Conceivably the economic consequences of antitrust policy have been, for better or worse, greater than the modest budgets of the enforcement agencies would suggest. We may therefore ask without being naive or cynical, Are there any good reasons for supposing that the structure of the American economy would now be perceptibly different had there been no attempt at an antitrust policy?

2. Cartels and Antitrust Policy

In the domain of cartel regulation, the direct impact of the antitrust laws has been slight. Some considerable fraction of the national income—perhaps as much as one-half—originates in firms that are viewed as engaging only in "intrastate commerce" and hence beyond the reach of the federal power. (Not that the Supreme Court has evidenced much concern for States' rights in antitrust matters; the antitrust agencies have never had the funds which would allow them to litigate the boundaries of federal jurisdiction.) The state government effort against cartels has been too cyni-

---

* Donald J. Dewey, "The Achievements of Antitrust Policy," chapter 20 in *Monopoly in Economics and Law* (Chicago: Rand McNally, 1959), excerpted from pp. 302–9. Dewey, one of the most learned and literate scholars of antitrust, is at Columbia University.

cally frivolous to merit our attention. In industries where the federal government undoubtedly has the authority to act, its challenge to cartel monopoly has been praiseworthy but not much more effective. The poverty of the federal antitrust agencies and the poor political returns to be had from the harassment of cartels have meant that fear of prosecution has not discouraged businessmen from viewing collusion as a normal method of conducting business. But then the amount of federal surveillance needed to ensure that *all* businessmen will think twice before co-operating to restrain competition is staggering to contemplate. The total elimination of collusion should probably be written off as a technical impossibility. At any rate the striving for this goal can only commend itself to one who believes that the biggest government is preferable to the smallest private monopoly.

Antitrust policy, however, has achieved two notable successes in the control of cartels. In the handful of industries that the antitrust agencies elect to police with their limited resources, the threat of prosecution has succeeded in discouraging—and sometimes eliminating—overt collusion. Indeed, in industries that have been visited with the expense and publicity of litigation, notably oil, tobacco, steel, meat packing, and automobiles, officials of rival firms often go to humorous lengths to make sure that they do not have dealings with one another without legal counsel present. Strictly speaking, the whole theory of oligopoly or tacit collusion as manifested in price leadership, market sharing, delivered pricing, etc., is a tribute to the occasional effectiveness of antitrust policy, for these roundabout and inefficient ways of restraining competition are unknown within legal frameworks that permit overt collusion. There is, after all, no point in guessing about the future price policy of a competitor when it is possible to ask him outright for such information.

Second, the development of the doctrine that collusion to restrain competition is illegal per se has rendered the restrictive agreement unenforceable and, thus, has largely eliminated the more elaborate—and profitable —types of co-operation, especially the use of the income-pooling agreement. (The decline of income pooling is perhaps the most striking feature of cartel history in the United States over the last sixty years.) ...

The victory of the per se doctrine has not been without its costs. When firms lose the right to have their contracts construed in the light of some reasonableness test, their obvious move is agitation to secure statutory exemption from the antitrust laws. Just as any increase in the rate of income taxation (at any rate in the United States) is accompanied by an increase in the number and types of exemptions, so the increasing effectiveness of antitrust policy has led to special treatment for politically powerful or obviously unfortunate industries. At the federal level, the list of industries virtually exempt from the antitrust laws has come to include railroads, trucking, inland waterways, airlines, banking, pipelines, farmer co-operatives, and shipping. At the state level, there is scarcely an important "intrastate" industry that has not somewhere received back from the legislature the rights of collusion taken away by the court.

We should not make too much of the tie between the rise of the per se doctrine and the spread of special-interest legislation. A statute that confers the State's blessing on collusion is always worth having; the refusal of the courts to enforce contracts restraining competition merely gives interested parties a further incentive to seek this boon. When the balance is struck, however, the rule that the courts, unless directed otherwise by the legislature, will not enforce a private agreement that restricts competition is the supreme achievement of antitrust policy in the United States. It is a sobering thought that this result could have been achieved by a brief, explicitly worded statute that required no enforcement machinery, and that even without such legislation, English courts since 1890 have hardly ever enforced contracts restraining competition.

3. Close Combination and Antitrust Policy

The harassing of cartels by antitrust suits, though it may be a worthy thing, does not stir the imagination. The success of antitrust policy, rightly or wrongly, is commonly measured by its consequences for the world of big business, and the enduring importance of the large corporation is often cited as evidence of the inutility of antitrust policy.

We have seen that, so far as corporate concentration is concerned, the antitrust agencies have set two main tasks for themselves. They have sought to check the further progress of concentration by preventing mergers which threaten a reduction of competition, and they have sought to rectify the mistakes of history by dissolving and divesting established corporations that exercise more control over the market than is needed for efficient operation. The success of antitrust policy is generally taken to have been negligible in both ventures, the only serious differences of opinion relating to the reasons for failure. . . .

Actually the main impact of antitrust policy on the structure of the economy has probably resulted from its influence on two industries—oil and steel. In 1948 the Standard Oil Company of New Jersey had an estimated 7.2 percent of the assets of the hundred largest industrial firms, while four other oil companies created by the 1911 decree had a combined total of 8.7 percent of the assets of the hundred largest. (Not that the oil trust had it been left undisturbed in 1911 would necessarily have grown as rapidly as have the modern Standard Oil companies.) The fear that the absorption of major rivals would provoke litigation certainly accounts for some of the decline in the relative importance of the United States Steel Corporation. This company held 22.3 percent of the assets of the hundred largest firms in 1909 and only 5.2 percent in 1948. In fine, antitrust policy has perceptibly reduced concentration in American industries.

❖   ❖   ❖   ❖   ❖

Some authorities have suggested that the limited success of the Sherman Act can be blamed on the inability of the federal government to match the legal talent that the corporate defendants command; that "the people have been represented, in the main, by men of very meagre legal ability." Undoubtedly private attorneys in antitrust cases get paid more than federal attorneys—and there are more of them. (Is there any branch of public business law where this is not true?) Even so, it is difficult to name an important case that the government lost mainly because its attorneys were outclassed in advocacy by the opposition. Nor, at least in recent years, do government briefs appear to have been seriously marred by hasty preparation.

So far as ingenuity in argument goes, the honors in antitrust cases have gone mainly to the government side, but this is because the federal attorneys have faced a more challenging task. Defense lawyers concentrate on cultivating the apprehension, never far below the level of consciousness in the mind of the court, that dissolution and divestiture *might* jeopardize operating efficiency and technological progress. To checkmate this maneuver the federal attorneys must bear the burden of educating the courts in the intricacies of economic analysis and industrial technology—a task which is often, as in the *Columbia Steel* case, a truly formidable undertaking.

✻   ✻   ✻   ✻   ✻

We may therefore reaffirm the thesis argued in Chapter XVII that the effort at trust busting has had so little success because it seeks a deliberate unsettling of property rights that offends the conservative bias of the courts. Nor, as we have seen, should this failure be taken as evidence that judges have consciously or unconsciously sabotaged Congressional intent. The conservative bias is all-pervasive in any legal system worthy of the name. If the courts have been reluctant to order dissolution and divestiture, the moral is only that judges strive to behave in a judicious manner. The road to trust busting on a grand scale must lie through the Congressional committee and federal bureau, not through the suit in equity. This is tantamount to saying that trust busting probably has little future as an anti-monopoly measure in the United States.

The control of mergers offers a more promising line of action since the courts may reasonably enjoin the consummation of a merger that they would not set aside ten years later. . . . If, as the author believes, technological progress is a centrifugal force making for decentralization, a close check on mergers should ultimately produce lower concentration ratios in important industries.

The tendency of antitrust policy to become a permanent inquisition on the conduct of the country's two or three hundred largest corporations, resulting in endless consent decrees, is understandable given the courts' hostility to dissolution and divestiture. Nevertheless, the tendency is unfortunate. It multiplies uncertainty respecting the law and rests on the doubtful assumption that civil servants are competent to make decisions assessing the welfare consequences of particular business practices, *e.g.*, a patent exchange between two firms. Moreover, it may well be futile. For in the negotiation of a complicated consent decree governing the conduct of a firm, one may presume both that the passage of time will soon make the decree irrelevant and that, since the defendant knows more about his operations than the government, he probably had the best of the compromise in the first place. In any event the ultimate object of policy is not a more detailed surveillance of the business world by the antitrust agencies but rather an economy sufficiently free of monopoly that such surveillance is largely unnecessary.

Eleanor M. Hadley (1916–   )

ANTITRUST IN JAPAN*

The Allied Forces' dismantling of the "zaibatsu" (leading family) industrial conglomerates in Japan after World War II is perhaps the most drastic "antitrust" restructuring ever done. But the program was stopped by U.S. business interests before it touched the key banking units, and a new wave of combinations largely wiped out its effects during the 1950s. A brief sampling of Hadley's thorough review of the "Allied trustbusting" follows.

✻   ✻   ✻   ✻   ✻

There was no difference of opinion among the Allies about the desirability of economic deconcentration in Japan. Differences concerned only what should replace Japan's system of private collectivism. The United States wanted free private competitive enterprise, and under the circum-

---

* Selections from Eleanor M. Hadley, *Antitrust in Japan* (copyright © 1970 by Princeton University Press): pp. 10–11, 68–72, and 164–65. Reprinted by permission of Princeton University Press. Hadley was a key official in the restructuring program and currently is with the International Division of the General Accounting Office. (Corwin Edwards—see above—did key research in 1945–46 to prepare the basis for the program.) A parallel restructuring of part of German industry was also cut short by intervention of U.S. interests anxious that the foreign experiments not set a successful precedent for the U.S.

stances, this policy prevailed. Most broadly put, the United States position, which became the Allied position, called for removal of the *zaibatsu* families from their position of business power and severing the ties—ownership, personnel, credit, contracts—which bound the component corporations into combine structures. Proposed, but essentially abandoned, was an effort to split up certain of the giant operating companies of the combines. This way, the Allies sought to achieve free competitive enterprise in the modern sector of the economy.

. . . In calling for a competitive structure to replace concentrated business in Japan, the Allies were attempting to create a situation in which there would be reasonable opportunity for entry into the markets of the modern sector of the economy and in which ownership of the means of production in that sector would be widespread, rather than concentrated under the control of a handful of business families. They were in no sense proposing to atomize Japanese industry along textbook lines. . . .

At the outset conversations began between Headquarters and the Japanese government with respect to *zaibatsu* dissolution. On November 4, 1945, the Japanese government submitted for approval by MacArthur a proposal incorporating the "Yasuda Plan," under which, in a consent-decree type of action, the holding companies of the Big Four would enter into dissolution procedures and a Holding Company Liquidation Commission would be created to administer the program. . . .

Between September 1946 and September 1947 the HCLC designated 83 holding companies. . . . The Japanese government had undoubtedly hoped to limit the designations to the five companies named in the original designation, the top-holding companies of the Big Four—Mitsui, Mitsubishi, Sumitomo, and Yasuda, plus Fuji Industries, the renamed Nakajima Aircraft Company. Under SCAP pressure, however, there were additional designations. Two additional designations were made in December 1946, adding 40 and 20 companies, respectively. A fourth, made in March 1947, added two, and the fifth and final one in September 1947 added 18. That 83 holding companies were named does not indicate that there were 83 combines. As has been seen, combines numbered about 15 or 20. Rather, the designation of 83 holding companies came about out of the inclusion of major second-level holding companies within the combines—with the signal exception of financial subsidiaries—as well as certain independent operating companies with complexes of subsidiaries and also some minor *zaibatsu*. . . .

The list of designated holding companies contained striking omissions —no bank or other financial institution was included. This occurred in spite of the fact that the Basic Directive specifically called for action in this regard and in spite of the fact that MacArthur had specifically informed the Japanese government it would be expected to dissolve the "private, industrial, commercial, *financial* and agricultural combines in Japan."

Further, this occurred in spite of the key role financial institutions had played in the development of *zaibatsu* power. As has been stated, a real factor in the growth of Japan's pattern of concentrated business power was the partiality with which combine commercial banks extended credit to subsidiaries within their own ranks. The list of designated holding companies not only omitted commercial banks, but all other financial institutions as well—trust banks, property insurance companies, and life insurance companies. In view of the importance of banks and other financial institutions among Japan's combines, the omission of these companies was strange and extremely important. . . .

As observed in Chapter 2, the HCLC, using 10-percent ownership as its definition of *subsidiary*, found the 10 *zaibatsu* to have some 1,200 subsidiaries. Firms on the Schedule of Restricted Concerns at peak likewise numbered some 1,200. . . .

Throughout the combine-dissolution program, financial institutions were consistently treated preferentially. No bank became a designated holding company though banks qualified for such designation a good deal more fully than certain other operating companies named.

The net effect of the foregoing was that the banks came through the wringer of the deconcentration program virtually intact, whereas elsewhere there were numerous changes. Many Japanese have regarded the combine banks as inheriting the mantle of the former top-holding companies. For the reasons set forth in Part II of this study, I do not subscribe to this point of view, but there is no question financial institutions represented the least part of the deconcentration effort.

The contrast in action between trading companies and financial institutions was striking. That the scale of the disparity in treatment was the product of reversing policy makes it no less incongruous, though it does become more understandable.

Senator Philip A. Hart (1906–   )

INDUSTRIAL REORGANIZATION ACT*

*After extensive hearings by his Antitrust and Mo-
nopoly Subcommittee during the 1960s (see Blair,
above, p. 19), Senator Hart finally filed a bill which, if
ever passed, would create agencies and powers to abate
monopoly directly. The gist of his rationale, and of the
bill's key provisions, follows. The bill is unlikely ever to
pass in its original form, but it is widely discussed. It
does crystallize the problems of seeking direct structural change.*

By Mr. Hart:
S. 3832. A bill to supplement the antitrust laws, and to protect trade and
monopoly power, and for other purposes. Referred to the Committee on
the Judiciary.

INDUSTRIAL REORGANIZATION ACT

Mr. Hart: Mr. President, admittedly, with some effort, I shall resist a
flowery and overdone introduction for the bill which I offer today.

It is called the Industrial Reorganization Act. It seeks to bring closer to
reality what this country has pretended to have for years: a competitive
economy. . . .

This bill offers an alternative to Government regulation and control. It is
a difficult choice. It involves changing the life styles of many of our largest
corporations, even to the restructuring of whole industries. It involves positive Government action, not to control but to restore competition and freedom of enterprise in the economy. . . .

---

* Senator Philip A. Hart, "Industrial Reorganization Act," *Congressional Record*,
vol. 118, no. 115 (Washington, D.C.: July 24, 1972), excerpted. The bill actually is
rather mild and far from punitive (note the amnesty on past profits, which *removes*
triple damages). This reflects Senator Hart's cautious and open-minded views. For a
well-known forerunner, see the careful draft proposal by Carl Kaysen and Donald F.
Turner, *Antitrust Policy* (Cambridge: Harvard University Press, 1959).

While I still believe that the antitrust laws could go a long way toward eliminating much of the concentrated economic power, I have given up hope that—absent a new congressional mandate—any attorney general will bring the necessary cases to undo the concentration which has already taken place. . . .

In the past, the enforcement agencies have built a poor record for attacking existing concentration. In a way that is understandable because even if an existing agency could find the time and personnel to present the big case—of which there may have been only 10 in the history of antitrust —they would not likely face a court equipped to handle the case. . . .

In truth, many companies would be treated better under this approach than under existing antitrust law. There are many who feel several companies in the target industries should be sued criminally for monopolization. This statute, however, is not a criminal one—nor would it open up the companies to treble damage claims from customers or competitors.

Just what would happen under the bill? What sort of remedies would be imposed?

Let me start by saying I do not expect any remedy to be as simplistic as one that has constantly come up for years when talk turned to eliminating concentration: break up General Motors into two, three or even eight separate auto companies.

The Commission's remedies should grow out of the sort of sophisticated search which thus far has been conducted by no one. I expect the remedies to reflect this sophistication.

Several types do now come to mind.

A company could spin off subsidiaries—or replace long-term supply contracts with frequently negotiated contracts—or alter its financial backing commitments—or eliminate exclusive dealerships—or alter its advertising expenditures—or license patents and trademarks—or actually divest.

The remedy could be one, several, or all of the above—or many others which the Commission may recommend.

No matter what plan the Commission proposed, it would be subject to full hearings before the Industrial Reorganization Court, which would make the final decision. At the hearings, the company would have a chance not only to attack the Commission's plan but to make its own proposal. . . .

Mr. President, I do not offer this legislation lightly. Certainly, I know the discontent and uncertainness merely discussing it can cause for many. It does propose reformation of a basic—our economic structure. This is nothing to be taken on hastily.

However, the need to move is great. This bill may not be the answer. But it can start us talking responsibly of solutions to a problem that must be solved.

* * * * *

TITLE I—POSSESSION OF MONOPOLY POWER

Sec. 101. (a) It is hereby declared to be unlawful for any corporation or two or more corporations, whether by agreement or not, to possess monopoly power in any line of commerce in any section of the country or with foreign nations.

(b) There shall be a rebuttable presumption that monopoly power is possessed—

(1) by any corporation if the average rate of return on net worth after taxes is in excess of 15 per centum over a period of five consecutive years out of the most recent seven years preceding the filing of the complaint, or

(2) if there has been no substantial price competition among two or more corporations in any line of commerce in any section of the country for a period of three consecutive years out of the most recent five years preceding the filing of the complaint, or

(3) if any four or fewer corporations account for 50 per centum (or more) of sales in any line of commerce in any section of the country in any year out of the most recent three years preceding the filing of the complaint.

In all other instances, the burden shall lie on the Industrial Reorganization Commission established under title II of this Act to prove the possession of monopoly power.

(c) A corporation shall not be required to divest monopoly power if it can show—

(1) such power is due solely to the ownership of valid patents, lawfully acquired and lawfully used, or

(2) such a divestiture would result in a loss of substantial economies.

The burden shall be upon the corporation or corporations to prove that monopoly power should not be divested pursuant to paragraphs (1) and (2) of the above subsection; *Provided however,* That upon a showing of the possession of monopoly power pursuant to paragraph (1), the burden shall be upon the Industrial Reorganization Commission to show the invalidity, unlawful acquisition, or unlawful use of a patent or patents.

TITLE II—INDUSTRIAL REORGANIZATION COMMISSION

❖ ❖ ❖ ❖ ❖

Duties of the Commission

Sec. 203. (a) (1) In order to determine whether or not any corporation, or two or more corporations, are in violation of title I of this Act, and develop a plan of reorganization to make competition more effective within each industry, the Commission shall study the structure, performance, and control of each of the following industries:

(A) chemicals and drugs;

(B) electrical machinery and equipment;

(C) electronic computing and communication equipment;

(D) energy;

(E) iron and steel;

(F) motor vehicles; and

(G) nonferrous metals.

(2) The Commission shall develop a plan of reorganization for each such industry whether or not any corporation is determined to be in violation of title I. In developing a plan of reorganization for any industry, the Commission shall determine for each such industry—

(A) the maximum feasible number of competitors at every level without the loss of substantial economies;

(B) the minimum feasible degree of vertical integration without the loss of substantial economies; and

(C) the maximum feasible degree of ease of entry at every level.

(3) The Commission shall study the collective bargaining practices within each industry named in paragraph (1), and determine the effect of those practices on competition within that industry.

✻   ✻   ✻   ✻   ✻

Chapter 96—INDUSTRIAL REORGANIZATION COURT

✻   ✻   ✻   ✻   ✻

§ 1591. Powers generally.

The Industrial Reorganization Court and each judge thereof shall possess all the powers of a district court of the United States for preserving order, compelling the attendance of witnesses and the production of evidence.

§ 1952 Jurisdiction.

(a) The Industrial Reorganization Court shall have original jurisdiction to hear and determine all complaints and proposed orders of reorganization filed by the Industrial Reorganization Commission under Title I of the Industrial Reorganization Act.

(b) After the Industrial Reorganization Commission has filed a complaint and proposed order of reorganization, the Industrial Reorganization Court shall enter a judgment determining whether a corporation or two or more corporations possess monopoly power in any part of trade or commerce among the several states or with foreign nations.

(c) The Industrial Reorganization Court shall also have original jurisdiction of petitions filed pursuant to section 207 of title II of this Act and of such other proceedings under that Act as the Court shall deem necessary and appropriate to effectuate its purposes.

§ 1593. Restoration of Effective Competition.

(*a*) Any corporation or two or more corporations may, within sixty days from the entry of judgment pursuant to section 1592 (*b*), file an alternative proposed order or orders of reorganization.

(*b*) Prior to the entry of an order or reorganization, the Industrial Reorganization Court shall conduct a proceeding to determine whether or not the proposed order or orders of reorganization would restore effective competition. In making its determination, the court may call witnesses in accordance with the provisions of sections 2652 and 2653 of this title.

(*c*) The court shall enter an order of reorganization appropriate to effectuate the purposes of this Act. The order of reorganization may require a corporation or two or more corporations to take such action as the court shall find necessary to restore effective competition. The order may include—

(1) a requirement that a corporation modify any contract to which it is a party, terminate any agreement with another corporation, or modify its methods of distribution;

(2) a requirement that a corporation grant licenses (with or without provision for the payment of royalties) under any patent, copyright, or trademark owned by that corporation, share technical information with others, or dispose of any such patent, copyright, or trademark;

(3) a requirement that a corporation divest itself of particular assets, including tangible and intangible assets, cash, stock, securities, accounts receivable, and other obligations; and

(4) such other requirements as the court may find necessary to restore effective competition.

II. Questions for Review: Antitrust

"Attempts to apply antitrust are just a misguided application of an extreme theory of perfect competition, which never was valid and certainly has little relation to the real economy now." Is this an accurate statement?

Most markets do not have clear boundaries. Yet the definition of the market is critically important to most structural antitrust decisions. Are optimum policy choices therefore impossible?

Can vertical integration extend monopoly power from one level of production to another? What public policy would you recommend toward vertical integration?

Under what conditions will the extent of vertical integration by existing firms affect the height of the barrier to entry into a market? Explain.

If you encountered a "price squeeze," how would you recognize it?

What is a *per se* rule? Does a *per se* rule on price-fixing fit cost-benefit criteria?

Is the economic rationale for a *per se* prohibition of price-fixing equally valid for internal "price fixing" by firms with large market shares?

Significant attempts at price-fixing among competitors occur usually in industries with *moderate* concentration. Why?

Explain the significance of *two* of the following for the development of antitrust policy toward price fixing: *(a)* Addyston Pipe, *(b)* Trenton Potteries, *(c)* Socony-Vacuum.

In what sense is there a sharp contrast between the American and most European public policies toward collusive business practices?

Explain the basic reason why a high-fixed-cost oligopolist is more likely to cut price deeply in a recession than are his low-fixed-cost rivals.

Identical prices are often observed, both in atomistic industries and in tight oligopolies. Do identical prices therefore reflect effective competition? What if the three bidders differ sharply in size, location, extent of order backlogs, and current profitability?

How would you determine whether pricing behavior in a specific oligopoly market reflected barometric or collusive price leadership?

Can price discrimination ever really reduce competition in the long run?

Name three industries which have large and systematic price discrimination. Taking one of these, is action against such discrimination warranted? Is it being taken?

Why might the common phenomenon of bulk discounts be harmful to competition?

Top Dollar Inc. sells chocolate bananas for $15 to some customers and $12 to others. Is this definitely price discrimination? Is it anti-competitive?

Are dominant firms likely to be imitators rather than innovators?

Outline the alternative market definitions which Judge Learned Hand considered in his Alcoa decision. Which definition did he finally accept? Outline the argument which he employed to support that definition of the relevant market. Is it valid?

Despite the strictness of Section 2 of the Sherman Act, actual enforcement has had little effect on U.S. industrial structure. To test this hypothesis, what main categories of information would you need and how would you analyze it? Illustrate with an actual case.

Is it true that most antitrust activity in recent years has come to focus upon conduct (e.g., price-fixing) rather than structure? Would this be futile, since one may have to change the structure in order to change conduct? Cite specific examples where possible.

Several new cases have recently touched some of the main firms with high market shares: IBM, Xerox, automobiles (fleet sales), cereals, etc. Do these correct the Section 2 "gap" since 1952 in action toward dominant firms?

Under present law, what prospects are there for reducing the market power of the leading instances in the industrial sector? Discuss three of the "leading instances," from among the following: Western Electric, IBM, General Motors, Xerox, Eastman Kodak, General Electric, Procter & Gamble, Campbell Soup, and Kellogg.

Make the best case that you can that there *is* effective competition in either (1) computers, or (2) automobiles.

Horizontal mergers are constrained by antitrust policy to 10 percent of the market and below. Section 2 monopoly restructuring cases are confined to 60 percent and above. The gap between 10 and 60 percent is:
1. a measure of the gross inconsistency in antitrust policy toward structure, or
2. fully consistent with reliable evidence about costs and benefits of policy choices, or
3. _____ (other).
Pick your ground and explain.

"Firms merge only to acquire market power." True?

The Justice Department merger guidelines of 1968 have been criticized for rejecting economies of scale as an element in evaluating mergers. Is there a better strategy for reaching full, neutral evaluations?

"Some conglomerate mergers are purely financial, with few real effects. Others take advantage of genuine economies. Still others are pro-competitive. Therefore the Antitrust Division should promote conglomerate mergers, or at least not stop them." Do you agree?

Are diversified companies more likely to engage in systematic and/or predatory price discrimination than nondiversified companies? In either case, are there serious grounds for antitrust concern?

Do the current policies toward horizontal mergers fit good economic analysis (including the possible trade-offs between economics and monopoly effects)?

A prohibition of leading-firm conglomerate mergers has both benefits and costs. In light of these, what is an optimum treatment for such mergers?

What changes, if any, in the patent laws would be indicated by economic analysis?

An antitrust task force in 1968 proposed a drastic program of restructuring major industries. Another task force in 1969 urged instead that resources be used primarily against price-fixing. You now head another task force. What will you recommend on this issue, and why?

Antitrust is regularly condemned for being ineffective and praised for maintaining a competitive economy. Choose one of these positions and explain what antitrust has done, or has not done, that makes the case.

Problem industries often need joint treatment by two or more public policy tools. Pick such an industry and explain the package of policies you would provisionally recommend for it.

Part III

⁂

THE FINANCIAL
SECTOR

Banking, stock markets, and insurance play special roles in supervising firms and affecting the degree of competition and equity in distribution. They have been bound by certain restrictive policies—some enforced by public agencies—which now seem likely to be unnecessary and harmful. These issues are touched on in these readings.

Almarin Phillips (1925–   )

COMPETITIVE POLICY FOR DEPOSITORY FINANCIAL INSTITUTIONS[*]

It has been apparent to most experts that the banking regulation imposed in the 1930s—reinforcing the naturally clubby behavior of banks—has gone too far in reducing competition. Phillips here summarizes the problem and the reforms needed to restore a balanced degree of competition in banking markets. Bank insurance would avert the dangers of bank "runs" and "crises."

I have expressed the view elsewhere that regulatory reform constitutes the most effective means of increasing competition among commercial banks. This is because, I argued, regulation of the behavior of banks and the structure of banking markets is the principal source of monopoly power among banks. In addition, "private regulation," in the form of accepted patterns of behavior reinforced by the formal and informal associations of bankers, also inhibits the operation of competitive forces. This argument suggests, as I then noted, that efforts at the federal level to improve the performance of banking markets by control of bank mergers and holding companies are but tilting at windmills. That is, the regulatory framework seems to dominate the other determinants of market performance to the extent that policies aimed at maintaining a competitive structure and preventing collusion can have only minor effect, at best. . . .

Market conduct in the mid-twenties was openly collusive. No antitrust case charging conspiracy among financial institutions had ever been suc-

---

[*] Almarin Phillips, "Competitive Policy for Depository Financial Institutions," chapter 10 in A. Phillips, ed., *Promoting Competition in Regulated Markets,* © 1975 by The Brookings Institution, Washington, D.C. Phillips is a foremost specialist on banking regulation, antitrust policy, and industrial behavior. For a more favorable view of banking regulation, see Gerald C. Fischer, *American Banking Structure* (New York: Columbia University Press, 1968).

cessfully brought, and it was generally believed that banks were immune from the Sherman Act because of their regulated character and because their services were not commodities in interstate commerce. In cities where the number of banks was large enough to require them, clearinghouse associations prescribed banking hours, rates of interest on loans and deposits, and rates of exchange and collection charges for check and banknote clearings. In smaller towns, and as a supplement to clearinghouse agreements in the larger cities, private agreements and custom produced similar results. Whatever the structure of markets, privately and collusively determined conduct worked to mitigate substantially any incentives to compete on the basis of price, banking hours, or other nonprice variables that might seriously influence market results for individual firms.

A number of important controls on conduct were instituted in the thirties. The Banking Acts of 1933 and 1935 prohibited interest payments on demand deposits and gave regulatory powers over the maximum rates on time and savings accounts at commercial banks to the Board of Governors and the FDIC. The stated purpose behind these measures was to prevent undue competition among banks. The Glass-Steagall Act of 1932 largely separated the investment banking business from commercial banking by prohibiting national banks from underwriting anything other than direct U.S. government obligations, a few indirect federal government obligations, and general obligations of states and municipalities. Section 21 of the Banking Act of 1933 went further, making it illegal for any firm engaged in the securities business to engage also in the business of receiving deposits. The Securities Exchange Act of 1934 authorized the Board of Governors to set margin requirements for loans made by any bank for the purchase of securities registered on national exchanges. And the supervision by federal agencies of investment portfolios, begun under the McFadden Act in 1927, was generally tightened after 1933, mainly with regard to "investment grade" securities.

By 1935, then, commercial banks were far more regulated, both as to structure and conduct, than they had been in the 1920s. Entry was controlled, branching was controlled, loan portfolios were more restricted and more closely examined, deposit interest rate competition was controlled, and the banks were more isolated from investment banking and security dealing.

✿   ✿   ✿   ✿   ✿

PROPOSALS FOR REGULATORY REFORM

1. *Eliminate laws and regulations that force specialization and restrict competition with and among institutional types.* This measure applies primarily to the thrift institutions. It would, for example, allow savings and loan associations and mutual savings banks to make mortgage loans on all types of property, residential and nonresidential, and to make construc-

tion, consumer, and commercial loans related to real estate activities. It would also allow them to invest in investment grade debt instruments. On the liability side, it would allow them to offer demand deposit services, credit card services, and other forms of third-party payment arrangements. These reforms would include abolition of geographic restrictions on areas in which loans may be made and an extension of the nonfinancial services institutions may provide, subject to the antitrust protestations and civil remedies for damages explained below. The statutory restrictions on real estate loans embodied in the National Banking Act should be removed.

The primary rationale for these changes is that they permit existing institutions to enter new financial and nonfinancial markets. Whether the degree of institutional and geographic specialization would in fact be decreased, monopoly power would certainly be reduced by the increase in potential competition, and cross-supply elasticities would be increased, even if no new competitors actually entered. In addition to the procompetitive rationale, the greater freedom in asset selection that the changes would allow is a necessary predicate to the abolition of interest rate controls and other subsidization techniques now used to protect deposit intermediaries during periods of rising and high rates of interest. . . .

2. *Eliminate interest rate ceilings on time and savings deposits and certificates of deposits.* These regulations were instituted to restrain interest rate competition among banks, and they still have that effect. Now, however, the restraints extend to competition among institutional types and between deposit institutions and the remainder of the money market. The controls have encouraged many varieties of nonprice competition, including locational convenience and the provision of services with no explicit prices attached. Moreover, because the cross-interest rate elasticity of savers between the deposit institutions and the rest of the market is higher for large savers than for small, the regulations have become highly discriminatory. Finally, the regulations have had the effect of increasing the cyclical sensitivity of supplies of credit to certain classes of borrowers. Small mortgage borrowers and small businesses—often with few, if any, alternative sources of credit outside the deposit institutions—find funds unavailable during times of high interest rates.

3. *Eliminate the prohibition of interest payments on demand deposits.* This prohibition was also instituted to restrain competition, and, as with ceilings on time deposits, it has encouraged the development of various forms of nonprice competition. In addition, large customers of commercial banks, often with the cooperation of the banks, have found means to invest transactions balances in interest-bearing assets, the incidental costs of which might be largely eliminated if the prohibition were lifted. Thrift institutions and credit unions have been encouraged to enter limited forms of third-party payment services that provide interest on the savings account balances used for customer payments orders. The innovation and

growth of negotiable orders of withdrawal accounts is illustrative of techniques used to circumvent the prohibition. Further improvements in computerized payments systems should increase the ability of financial institutions other than banks to generalize these payment methods.

4. *Eliminate anticompetitive geographic restrictions on branching and holding companies.* Geographic restrictions on branching operate to protect the markets of individual institutions and, often, to prevent the achievement of scale economies and branching economies except at the expense of greater market concentration. Intermarket branching, both de novo and by merger, shoud be permissible in the absence of anti-competitive effects; and holding companies should be permitted to acquire banks under the same conditions. This would require repeal of the McFadden Act and permission for federally chartered banks, savings and loan associations, and mutual savings banks to branch irrespective of the state laws. Interstate branching would also have to be allowed if full adaptation to the economic characteristics of markets is to be achieved. The Bank Holding Company Act would have to be amended to permit interstate holding company acquisitions. Unless state-chartered institutions are to be severely disadvantaged, parallel changes in state laws would be necessary, and would probably be rapidly forthcoming.

5. *Eliminate anticompetitive restrictions on chartering.* At present, both federal and state chartering provisions make it possible for the authorities to refuse charters even when the applicants have adequate initial capital and all the necessary safeguards for investors have been met. Some test based on "adequacy of existing services" or "convenience and needs of the community" can be invoked as a barrier to entry. However, the desired performance results of competition are impossible to achieve when regulations, such as those affecting chartering, are used to protect the structure of existing institutions. . . . Free entry without regulatory promises of quasimonopolistic returns, however, need not, and should not, result in over-banked financial markets with concommitant high failure rates. Furthermore, deposit insurance has largely dissipated the earlier threat of systemic bank runs.

6. *Provide for risk-related deposit insurance premiums.* Deposit insurance is necessary to prevent systemic collapses in the payments mechanism and to protect individual depositors from losses, the probability of which they are incapable of judging. The current system of uniform premiums regardless of the asset portfolios of the insured institutions discriminates against conservatively managed firms. At the same time, and for related reasons, it encourages the insuring agency to supervise portfolios to minimize the likelihood of claims against the fund.

7. *Eliminate discriminatory reserve requirements and taxes.* Reserve requirements for commercial banks are different for members and non-members of the Federal Reserve System. In addition, state requirements

obtain for nonmembers, and these vary from state to state. Requirements for members vary depending on the type of deposit, the size and location of the bank, and, in terms of marginal and average reserves, the size of the bank's deposits. . . . If reserves are required at all—and it is arguable that formal reserve requirements are unnecessary for monetary policy purposes—a procompetitive policy would have identical requirements for the same type of deposits irrespective of the size, location, or class of the institution. In view of the fading distinction between time and demand deposits, it is probable that a continuation of higher requirements for the latter would serve only to hasten the development of third-party payments from time deposits. High reserves for all classes of deposit institutions would also encourage the use of other institutions for savings purposes and the development of payments mechanisms that minimize the deposit balances required for funds transfers. . . .

8. *Full application of the antitrust laws to financial institutions.* Under current legislation, special laws, involving some degree of regulation by financial regulatory agencies, pertain to bank mergers, bank holding companies, savings and loan holding companies, and interlocking directorates among banks. While the Sherman Act presumably applies in full force to all financial institutions, its use to prevent anticompetitive tying agreements, exclusive dealing contracts, and discriminatory pricing is largely unexplored. A strong antitrust policy would place competitive matters with the Antitrust Division of the Department of Justice, excluding the regulatory agencies and, with them, consideration of the so-called banking factors in individual cases. The special statutes would be rescinded, and mergers and holding companies made subject to the Clayton Act without qualification. Full enforcement of the conspiracy and collusion provisions of section 1 of the Sherman Act should, of course, also prevail.

9. *Clarify by legislation the rules pertaining to the "piercing of the corporate veil" in order to facilitate private actions for damages and to preserve the safety and soundness of deposit institutions. . . .*

What is advocated here is the reverse of the policy actions of the 1930s. Then the aim was to mitigate competitive forces in order to preserve the structure of financial markets; here the aim is to increase competitive forces by deregulation and antitrust policy, letting the structure adapt as efficiency requires. While economies of scale and branching do appear to exist, they are not so extensive as to suggest that structure itself makes competition impossible. But it may be impossible anyway. A pervasive and fundamental reorganization of social institutions is involved. The public at large is unlikely to perceive the possible gains, and the few who do can easily be dismissed as theorists with no real understanding of the practical world.

The industries and the regulators would both perceive a common threat in such drastic changes, and they would undoubtedly prevail in a fight against them. It must be recognized that the strong homeostatic properties built into the institutional response mechanism of the system may indeed make competition impossible.

❀   ❀   ❀   ❀   ❀

William J. Baumol (1922–   )

COMPETITIVE PRICING AND THE CENTRALIZED MARKET PLACE*

Baumol here reads a stiff lecture to the stock exchanges—and the public—about the effects of price-fixing in brokerage services. If such restrictions have been dropped by 1975, as the S.E.C. decreed in 1974, it will be partly because they have been so self-destructive of the exchanges themselves!

Many economists have for some time been vociferous in urging increased freedom of competition upon the securities industry. Until recently this was advocated almost exclusively for the benefit of the general investing public. But it becomes increasingly apparent that such measures have become important and perhaps even critical for the welfare of the securities industry and some of its leading institutions. Paradoxically, the industry is in danger of becoming the most patent victim of the arrangements which many of its constituents have defended so adamantly. . . .

ENTRY IN THE BROKERAGE INDUSTRY AND ENFORCEABILITY OF PRICING RULES

Any particular stock exchange can adopt more or less restrictive rules limiting its membership as severely as it wishes. The history of the ex-

* William J. Baumol, "Competitive Pricing and the Centralized Market Place,' *Eastern Economic Journal,* January 1974, excerpted. Baumol is a major figure in economics since 1950, as well as an expert on finance, industry, and the economics of American (and classical Athenian!) theater. For an extensive empirical analysis of these points, confirming Baumol's views, see Irwin Friend and Marshall E. Blume's study, "The Consequences of Competitive Commissions on the New York Stock Exchange," in Subcommittee on Securities, Senate Committee on Banking, Housing and Urban Affairs, Hearings on *Stock Exchange Commission Rates,* 92d Cong., 2d sess. (Washington, D.C.: U.S. Government Printing Office, 1972), pp. 259–404.

changes is a tale centered about that sort of restriction, and the attempts by those outside the club either to gain entry or to find a *modus vivendi* outside its doors. If entry into the industry could be limited as effectively as entry into an exchange, there might be no difficulty in enforcing pricing rules.

However, persons excluded from dealing directly on one exchange can always adopt alternatives. They can set up new exchanges that will operate in competition with the one from which they have been excluded, or they can avoid the use of organized exchanges altogether, seeking to bring together individual buyers and sellers without benefit of a market on which many traders meet simultaneously.

The history of the stock markets in the United States is a tale of the rise and fall of exchanges organized by those who had been condemned to outer darkness by the established institutions. Today, the regional exchanges and the "third" market serve to provide an outlet for those who are unhappy about doing business on the terms called for by the major exchanges.

Effectively, this has already served to undermine the regulation of brokerage commissions. The institutionalization of "give-ups," and recourse to "reciprocal deals," are ways of maintaining nominal obeissance to the regulations while effectively circumventing them where they hurt most. So far, the large institutions, the mutual funds, the insurance companies, and even government agencies—about which I will say more presently— have proved most effective in finding ways to obtain prices more appropriate to their market power and the lower unit transactions costs permitted by their volume. However, there are signs that innovative firms, themselves not members of the major exchanges, are beginning to find ways to serve the small customer at lower prices. . . .

SUBSTITUTION OF SERVICES FOR PRICE REDUCTIONS

The bundling of services is a well known phenomenon in the brokerage industry. The customer is offered, in addition to the carrying-out of transactions, a variety of services including research and advice based on that research, record keeping, storage of securities, and even the use of the long distance telephone free of charge.

I will not dwell upon the questions that have been raised in recent years by economists and statisticians about the quality of the research and the advice offered by the securities industry, particularly since they have been discussed elsewhere. Rather, the question is whether, regardless of its quality, the customer should be forced to purchase and pay for such research each time he effects a transaction, whether or not he wants the information. Surely, we are not prepared to argue on paternalistic grounds that he ought to be forced to buy information for his own good. Are those who take this view also prepared to require a customer to subscribe to *Consumer Reports* before he is permitted to buy a car or a refrigerator?

ENCOURAGEMENT OF INEFFICIENCY

It is dangerous to make charges of inefficiency without careful study and documentation, and it is my purpose neither to make nor imply such charges. But a few questions can be raised in passing—questions which I do not intend to be considered rhetorical.

For questions have been raised in recent years about the relatively limited or inefficient use of computerization in carrying out and recording transactions in the securities industry. The continued issue of negotiable securities which could largely be replaced by a recorded datum in a computer memory may be justified by the fallibility of computers or by investors' predilection for a tangible embodiment of their holdings, but one wonders whether full price competition might not force some changes in this and in other related matters. The fact that only a few years ago the stock exchange had to be closed at regular intervals to permit offices to catch up with their paper work may perhaps be ascribed partly to the same influence. One wonders, finally, whether the vulnerability of a number of brokerage firms to a relatively small change in the state of the economy, which manifested itself rather dramatically just a few years ago, does not suggest that fixed commissions have retained in the field a number of firms which might otherwise have been forced to "shape up or ship out." I repeat, these are questions which should be asked, but our asking them should not be taken to imply that we think we know the answers.

RESOURCE MISALLOCATION AND FIXED COMMISSIONS

Much of what has already been said indicates how fixed commissions may result in non-optimal use of society's resources. For example, the supply of services to customers whose money equivalent they might otherwise prefer to receive, represents a diversion of resources from the uses in which they might most effectively serve the desires of the community, and that is precisely what we mean by a misallocation of resources.

However, there are other manifestations of this phenomenon which have not been mentioned yet. Artificially high rates encourage participants in the industry to adapt themselves in a number of ways, all of which are likely to introduce inefficiencies of one form or another.

a. They may encourage, as already implied, an excessively large number of firms, i.e., a number of brokerage houses greater than that which would be sufficient to transact the nation's investment business at minimum cost to the community. One suspects that this has happened, though it probably cannot be proved.

b. It has led financial institutions to seek entry into the brokerage business, a diversion of resources and a diversification of functions which might otherwise not have proved attractive to them.

c. More generally, high fees have encouraged a combination of brokerage and money management functions which may not be in the public interest. . . .

A second major category of resulting resource misallocation revolves about the creation and survival of a considerable number of exchanges and the growth of the third market. To the extent that these exchanges' existence or volume is to be ascribed simply to the desire to escape the brokerage commission regulations, a variety of significant types of waste are introduced by these pricing policies:

a. The cost of operation and administration of exchanges that would otherwise be superfluous is obviously wasteful;

b. More important, it means fragmentation of the market, reducing its efficiency as an instrument for the bringing together of buyers and sellers, and decreasing its depth and stability. In sum, fixed commission rates become a prime instrument making for fragmentation of the financial market, and thereby threatening to undermine its effectiveness as an instrument for the effective conduct of the nation's security transactions and the allocation of its financial capital.

This development is more than a little ironic, because preservation of the depth and stability of the money markets is one of the grounds on which fixed commission rates have been defended. . . .

THE THREAT TO THE MAJOR EXCHANGES

So much for the costs of price fixing to society as a whole—where it requires the customer to pay more than he otherwise would, and gives him in exchange a less efficient allocation of resources. However, it should be clear by now that this same set of consequences contains within it a serious threat to the major exchanges themselves. For, by definition, every diversion of business means a corresponding loss in their own volume of transactions.

With many stocks that are listed on the New York and the American Stock Exchanges now traded on regional exchanges and on the third market, with the progress of information technology making generally available information on at least some of the securities traded on the major markets, the temptation to go elsewhere to seek savings in their operations becomes overwhelming. This is encouraged further by a number of court decisions which have held, in effect, that it is the obligation of mu-

tual funds, and perhaps of others in a fiduciary capacity, to avail themselves of all proper means to recover commissions for their customers.

Private organizations such as mutual funds, insurance companies, and
private pension funds have not been the only ones to respond in this manner. Thus, the State of Connecticut has recently been accepted as a member of the PBW exchange, and several other state and city governments
have recently expressed interest in seats in order to save on commissions.
One of the dangers is that business lost in this way will never be regained.
Thus, time may not be on the side of the major exchanges. The longer
they resist full and unhampered competitive processes the harder they
may find it to retrieve what they have lost.

Paul L. Joskow (1947–   )

CARTELS, COMPETITION AND REGULATION IN THE PROPERTY-LIABILITY INSURANCE INDUSTRY*

*In this long empirical paper, Joskow shows that this
industry is naturally competitive. Regulation impairs
performance and should, he says, be replaced by an
antitrust treatment.*

The property and liability insurance industry had assets of $68 billion
and premiums of $35 billion in 1971. The products sold by this industry, in
the form of contingent claims against accidental property loss and liability
judgments, are purchased in one form or another by virtually all economic agents in the U.S. economy. Despite the size and importance of
the property insurance industry in the U.S. economy, the literature in the
area of industrial organization has all but ignored it. . . .

Conclusions: Why Regulate Insurance Rates? In light of the foregoing analysis we may conclude that the property-liability insurance industry under prior approval rate regulation has the following features:

* Copyright 1974, American Telephone and Telegraph Company, 195 Broadway,
New York, New York 10007. Reprinted with permission from *The Bell Journal of Economics and Management Science.* Paul L. Joskow, "Cartels, Competition and Regulation in the Property-Liability Insurance Industry." An MIT faculty member, Joskow
has also applied econometric analysis to regulatory commissions' behavior.

1. A competitive market structure with a large number of firms and low levels of concentration;

2. Constant returns to scale in production;

3. Low to moderate barriers to entry for agency companies; moderate to high barriers to entry for direct writers;

4. A combination of rate making in concert and regulation which makes true price competition difficult;

5. An inefficient sales technique, probably costing consumers hundreds of millions of dollars per year, which is being eroded, but only slowly;

6. Supply shortages induced by the inability or the resistance of regulatory authorities to establish truly homogeneous risk classifications; and

7. Insurance premiums which are probably too high and effective capacity which is probably too large.

Faced with this picture, one wonders why insurance rates and rating classifications should be regulated at all. There are no natural monopoly characteristics which would indicate that open competition would be unstable and eventually lead to monopoly. Rather, the argument has been that rate making in concert through rating bureaus is a necessity to insure the public and the industry against "destructive" competition and large numbers of bankruptcies. There does not seem to be any reason why this industry should be more unstable than others as long as fraudulent practices are guarded against and proper consumer information is provided for. . . .

On the basis of this analysis, the experience in California, and the experience in New York since the no-filing statute was enacted in 1970, the following general public policy recommendations are made with regard to the property-liability insurance industry.

1. Prior approval rate regulation should be eliminated and replaced with a no-filing system allowing insurance prices to be determined competitively. State Insurance Departments should be retained to perform certain consumer protection functions to be outlined below. Insurance companies should file rate schedules with the insurance department as a source of general information. Companies should be free, however, to set any level of rates which they please.

2. All anticompetitive aspects of rating bureaus should be eliminated. The rating bureaus should become strictly service organizations, collecting and processing loss and expense data for their customers. Any information provided to one company should be provided to all at appropriate fees.

3. Flexibility in establishing truly homogeneous rating classifications should be encouraged. While a great deal of uniformity among companies is probably desirable with regard to the establishment of risk classifications so as to facilitate the collection of consistent loss data, no company

should be forced to adhere to any established structure if it believes rate variability is justified. . . .

4. The Insurance Department should play a consumer information and consumer protection role. The greatest possible amount of price information should be put into the hands of consumers. . . .

5. All insurance companies should be required to carry complete insurance against bankruptcy. Insurance rates should not be uniform for each company nor should a state insurance fund be made available to pay off for bankrupt companies. Neither of these schemes would give companies additional incentives to evaluate the premium-capital ratio they are carrying in terms of the true risk adjusted opportunity cost of capital. Rather, bankruptcy insurance rates should be geared to the insolvency risk of the companies themselves as determined by semiannual audits of their operations. . . .

6. Attempts should be made to speed up the transition from agency production of customers to direct writing wherever possible. The social costs of current laws forbidding agency companies from writing existing customers should be more thoroughly studied and an equitable scheme for phasing out independent agents devised. Trade associations of insurance agents should be strictly enjoined from taking any concerted action against a company which attempts to switch to direct writing region by region. Other barriers to entry of direct writers should be isolated and efforts made to lower them.

7. Assigned risk pools will, by necessity, have to be continued as long as supply shortages continue to exist. Hopefully competition in rates and rating classification and extended consumer information will eventually cause the shortage problem to disappear. The practice of subsidizing high risk drivers in the assigned risk plans should be carefully reevaluated.

8. Attempts by some states to go toward more price regulation rather than less should be vigorously discouraged. . . .

. . . Regulators attempting to apply public utility ratemaking procedures to individual insurance firms or for the industry as a whole will be applying these techniques to an industry which has every single characteristic of historical regulatory disasters.

United States v. Philadelphia National Bank
374 U.S. 321 (1963)

*After a wave of major bank mergers, the Court finally
drew the line in this landmark case. Though some banking markets are national, the Court held that the local
banking market is real and important enough to govern
the decision. After this case, banking mergers came under much the same limits as others (see* Von's *above).*

Mr. Justice Brennan.   The United States, appellant here, brought this
civil action . . . to enjoin a proposed merger of The Philadelphia National
Bank (PNB) and Girard Trust Corn Exchange Bank (Girard), appellees
here. The complaint charged violations of Section 1 of the Sherman Act,
. . . and Section 7 of the Clayton Act. . . . From a judgment for appellees
after trial . . . the United States appealed to this Court. . . . We reverse
the judgment of the District Court. We hold that the merger of appellees
is forbidden by Section 7 of the Clayton Act and so must be enjoined; we
need not, and therefore do not, reach the further question of alleged violation of Section 1 of the Sherman Act. . . .

The Proposed Merger of PNB and Girard

The Philadelphia National Bank and Girard Trust Corn Exchange
Bank are, respectively, the second and third largest of the 42 commercial
banks with head offices in the Philadelphia metropolitan area, which consists of the City of Philadelphia and its three contiguous counties in Pennsylvania. The home county of both banks is the city itself; Pennsylvania
law, however, permits branching into the counties contiguous to the home
county, . . . and both banks have offices throughout the four-county area.
PNB, a national bank, has assets of over $1,000,000,000, making it (as of
1959) the twenty-first largest bank in the Nation. Girard, a state bank, is
a member of the FRS and is insured by the FDIC; it has assets of about
$750,000,000. Were the proposed merger to be consummated, the result-
ing bank would be the largest in the four-county area, with (approxi-

mately) 36 percent of the area banks' total assets, 36 percent of deposits, and 34 percent of net loans. It and the second largest (First Pennsylvania Bank and Trust Company, now the largest) would have between them 59 percent of the total assets, 58 percent of deposits, and 58 percent of the net loans, while after the merger the four largest banks in the area would have 78 percent of total assets, 77 percent of deposits, and 78 percent of net loans.

The present size of both PNB and Girard is in part the result of mergers. Indeed, the trend toward concentration is noticeable in the Philadelphia area generally, in which the number of commercial banks has declined from 108 in 1947 to the present 42. Since 1950, PNB has acquired nine formerly independent banks and Girard six; and these acquisitions have accounted for 59 percent and 85 percent of the respective banks' asset growth during the period, 63 percent and 91 percent of their deposit growth, and 12 percent and 37 percent of their loan growth. During this period, the seven largest banks in the area increased their combined share of the area's total commercial bank resources from about 61 percent to about 90 percent. . . .

THE LAWFULNESS OF THE PROPOSED MERGER
UNDER SECTION 7

. . . We agree with the District Court that the cluster of products (various kinds of credit) and services (such as checking accounts and trust administration) denoted by the term "commercial banking," . . . composes a distinct line of commerce. Some commercial banking products or services are so distinctive that they are entirely free of effective competition from products or services of other financial institutions; the checking account is in this category. Others enjoy such cost advantages as to be insulated within a broad range from substitutes furnished by other institutions. For example, commercial banks compete with small-loan companies in the personal-loan market; but the small-loan companies' rates are invariably much higher than the banks', in part, it seems, because the companies' working capital consists in substantial part of bank loans. Finally, there are banking facilities which, although in terms of cost and price they are freely competitive with the facilities provided by other financial institutions, nevertheless enjoy a settled consumer preference, insulating them, to a marked degree, from competition; this seems to be the case with savings deposits. In sum, it is clear that commercial banking is a market "sufficiently inclusive to be meaningful in terms of trade realities." *Crown Zellerbach Corp.* v. *Federal Trade Comm'n*, 296 F. 2d 800, 811 (C.A. 9th Cir. 1961).

We part company with the District Court on the determination of the appropriate "section of the country." The proper question to be asked in this case is not where the parties to the merger do business or even where they compete, but where, within the area of competitive overlap, the effect of the merger on competition will be direct and immediate. See Bock, *Mergers and Markets* (1960), 42. This depends upon "the geographic structure of supplier-consumer relations." Kaysen and Turner, *Antitrust Policy* (1959), 102. In banking, as in most service industries, convenience of location is essential to effective competition. Individuals and corporations typically confer the bulk of their patronage on banks in their local community; they find it impractical to conduct their banking business at a distance. . . . The factor of inconvenience localizes banking competition as effectively as high transportation costs in other industries. . . . Therefore, since, as we recently said in a related context, the "area of effective competition in the known line of commerce must be charted by careful selection of the market area in which the seller operates, *and to which the purchaser can practicably turn for supplies*," *Tampa Elec. Co. v. Nashville Coal Co.*, 365 U.S. 320, 327 (emphasis supplied); see *Standard Oil Co. v. United States*, 337 U.S. 293, 299 and 300, n. 5, the four-county area in which appellees' offices are located would seem to be the relevant geographical market. Cf. *Brown Shoe Co., supra*, at 338–339. In fact, the vast bulk of appellees' business originates in the four-county area. Theoretically, we should be concerned with the possibility that bank offices on the perimeter of the area may be in effective competition with bank offices within; actually, this seems to be a factor of little significance.

We recognize that the area in which appellees have their offices does not delineate with perfect accuracy an appropriate "section of the country" in which to appraise the effect of the merger upon competition. Large borrowers and large depositors, the record shows, may find it practical to do a large part of their banking business outside their home community; very small borrowers and depositors may, as a practical matter, be confined to bank offices in their immediate neighborhood; and customers of intermediate size, it would appear, deal with banks within an area intermediate between these extremes. . . . So also, some banking services are evidently more local in nature than others. But that in banking the relevant geographical market is a function of each separate customer's economic scale means simply that a workable compromise must be found: some fair intermediate delineation which avoids the indefensible extremes of drawing the market either so expansively as to make the effect of the merger upon competition seem insignificant, because only the very largest bank customers are taken into account in defining the market, or so narrowly as to place appellees in different markets, because only the smallest customers are considered. We think that the four-county Philadelphia metropolitan area, which state law apparently recognizes as a meaningful banking community in allowing Philadelphia banks to branch within it, and which would seem roughly to delineate the area in which bank customers that are neither very large nor very small find it practical to do their banking business, is a more appropriate "section of the country" in which to appraise the instant merger than any larger or smaller or different area. We are helped to this conclusion by the fact that the three federal banking agencies regard the area in which banks have their offices as an "area of effective competition." . . .

. . . There is no reason to think that concentration is less inimical to the free play of competition in banking than in other service industries. On the contrary, it is in all probability more inimical. For example, banks compete to fill the credit needs of businessmen. Small businessmen especially are, as a practical matter, confined to their locality for the satisfaction of their credit needs. . . . If the number of banks in the locality is reduced, the vigor of competition for filling the marginal small business borrower's needs is likely to diminish. At the same time, his concomitantly greater difficulty in obtaining credit is likely to put him at a disadvantage *vis-à-vis* larger businesses with which he competes. In this fashion, concentration in banking accelerates concentration generally.

. . . Section 7 does not mandate cutthroat competition in the banking industry, and does not exclude defenses based on dangers to liquidity or solvency, if to avert them a merger is necessary. It does require, however, that the forces of competition be allowed to operate within the broad framework of governmental regulation of the industry. The fact that banking is a highly regulated industry critical to the Nation's welfare makes the play of competition not less important but more so. At the price of some repetition, we note that if the businessman is denied credit because his banking alternatives have been eliminated by mergers, the whole edifice of an entrepreneurial system is threatened; if the costs of banking services and credit are allowed to become excessive by the absence of competitive pressures, virtually all costs, in our credit economy, will be affected; and unless competition is allowed to fulfill its role as an economic regulator in the banking industry, the result may well be even more governmental regulation. . . .

The judgment of the District Court is reversed and the case remanded with direction to enter judgment enjoining the proposed merger.

It is so ordered.

Thill Securities Corporation v. The New York Stock Exchange

433 F. 2d 264 (1970),
cert. denied, 401 U.S. 994 (1971)

In Thill, *antitrust was first extended to limit "self-regulation" and restrictions on the stock exchanges. Later changes have moved gradually to reduce these restrictions further.*

Campbell, District Judge.   The basic question presented here is whether stock-brokers who are members of the New York Stock Exchange should continue to enjoy their self-acquired freedom from competition by stock-brokers who are not members. Using the vehicle of Stock Exchange rules, members seem effectively to have negated the congressionally mandated principle of competition as it would otherwise apply to them.

The New York Stock Exchange ("Exchange") is the largest organized securities market in the United States. Its dominance of the securities industry is a well known and commonly accepted commercial and historical fact. It transacts well over 70 percent of the dollar value of all stock transactions on exchanges in the United States. . . . Its policies and practices have an ever increasing effect on our economy.

By the Exchange's Constitution, its membership is limited to 1,366 members. . . .

In many respects the Exchange has been delegated governmental authority. Its counsel describes it as a "unique self regulator." Under the Securities Exchange Act of 1934 (15 U.S.C. § 78a . . .) it may adopt its own constitution and rules, and discipline violations thereof. The Securities Exchange Commission ("SEC") has the power, however, to order changes in Exchange rules respecting a number of subjects, set forth in section 19(b) of the Act. 15 U.S.C. § 78s(b). Except for the limited review authority of the SEC, the Exchange's economic power in the securities field appears complete and absolute.

Plaintiff Thill Securities Corporation ("Thill") is a licensed securities dealer-broker, registered with the Securities and Exchange Commission, and a member in good standing of the National Association of Securities Dealers, Inc., but is not a member of the New York Stock Exchange. . . . In its complaint Thill charges the Exchange with substantial anti-competitive conduct in violation of the antitrust laws of the United States. Sherman Antitrust Act, § 1 and § 2 . . . and Clayton Act, § 4. . . . Specifically, Thill charges that the Exchange has engaged in an unlawful and unreasonable combination and conspiracy in restraint of interstate trade and commerce and has unlawfully and unreasonably monopolized the securities market in the United States by among other things adopting, subscribing, and adhering to a rule which prohibits any member of the Exchange from sharing any commission earned from the purchase or sale of securities with a non-member, even though the non-member may have furnished the order; and by discriminately discouraging customers and prospective customers of Thill and other non-members from doing business with non-members.

Thill alleges that as a proximate result of the unlawful and monopolistic rules and practices of the Exchange, it and other non-members of the Exchange are totally deprived of commissions or other fair compensation on transactions which they have initiated and serviced. It further alleges that the intended, necessary, and actual effect of this unlawful conduct is to restrain trade by preventing any competition by and between members of the Exchange and non-member securities dealers and brokers. Thill alleges to have suffered damages in the amount of seven million dollars, for which it seeks treble damages ($21,000,000) under the antitrust laws. It also seeks a declaratory judgment that the Exchange's prohibition against sharing of commissions constitutes a violation of the antitrust laws; and an injunction prohibiting the Exchange from enforcing the prohibition. Subsequent to the filing of this action, Thill Securities Corporation went out of business.

The defendant Exchange does not contest the anti-competitive effects of its rule prohibiting the sharing of commissions—sometimes referred to as the antirebate rule. At oral argument its counsel admitted, as is obvious, that the conduct complained of would constitute a violation of the antitrust laws, were those statutes applicable to the activities of the Exchange in this case. Its position is that the Sherman Act does not apply to the rule of the Exchange prohibiting the sharing of commissions by members with non-members. It contends that this broad immunity is enjoyed by virtue of the Securities Exchange Act of 1934 . . . which authorizes registered national securities exchanges to adopt rules in respect to the "fixing of reasonable rates of commission" subject to review and revision by the Securities Exchange Commission under section 19(b) of the Act. . . . It also contends that the SEC has and is exercising exclusive review jurisdiction over such rules of the Exchange, and that its conduct is thus immune from antitrust liability. This immunity, in its view, extends beyond the "fixing of reasonable rates of commission" and includes rules relating to the "sharing" of commissions, because the prohibition against sharing of commissions with non-member broker dealers is an integral part of the "fixing of reasonable rates." . . .

In our consideration of the issues presented in this appeal we must begin with the teachings of the Supreme Court in *Silver* v. *New York Stock Exchange,* 373 U.S. 341 . . . (1963). . . . [T]he Supreme Court soundly rejected any notion that the Exchange enjoyed blanket immunity from the enforcement of the antitrust laws simply because its activities were to a certain extent subject to the regulatory provisions of the Securities Exchange Act. On the contrary, the Court concluded that the proper approach is an *analysis* which reconciles the operation of both statutory schemes (the antitrust laws and the Securities Exchange Act) with one another rather than holding one completely ousted. In undertaking the analysis to attempt to reconcile the two statutes, courts were admonished that repeal or ouster of antitrust laws is not favored. . . .

Despite these admonitions the Exchange argues, as the court below concluded, that the antitrust court's analysis ends once it is determined that the conduct complained of, here the antirebate rule, is subject to potential review by the SEC under section 19(b).

. . . We disagree. . . . In our view, *Silver* teaches that a reconciliation of the two statutory schemes is not foreclosed simply because the Securities Act and the review jurisdiction of the SEC may touch upon the activity challenged under the antitrust laws. As the Court in *Silver* pointed out, the New York Stock Exchange's constitution and rules are permeated with instances of regulation of member relationships with non-members. . . . That general power to adopt rules relating to the relations of its members with non-members, however, does not in and of itself place the application of such rules outside the reach of the antitrust laws. Rather it is at this point that the analysis of reconciliation really begins.

Before the investing public of the United States may be deprived of the benefit of competition through the vehicle of Exchange rules, it must be established that the Exchange's exemption from the antitrust laws is necessary to discharge its responsibilities under the Securities Exchange Act. . . .

In the record before us there is no evidence, save for the allegations of plaintiff, as to the effects of the anti-competitive conduct complained of; there is no evidence as to the extent to which the challenged rule is subject to actual review by the SEC; there is no evidence as to what in the regulatory scheme "performs the antitrust function"; and, most notably, there is no evidence as to why the antirebate rule must be preserved as "necessary to make the Securities Exchange Act work." In sum, this record falls woefully short of the meticulous analysis called for in *Silver*. . . .

As we observed above, there is no evidence in the record that the SEC is exercising actual and adequate review jurisdiction under the Act. Furthermore, even the fact that the SEC may be exercising its proper supervisory power over the rules of the Exchange does not in and of itself cloak the Exchange with antitrust immunity for its conduct relating to those rules. . . .

In our view the facts here are much stronger in favor of application of the antitrust laws than were those in the *Philadelphia Bank* case. In reviewing the rules of the Exchange the SEC is not required to consider their effect upon competition. On the contrary, its history in reviewing rules adopted by the Exchange indicates a reluctance to do so. It has been suggested that the SEC has never, "forcibly altered an Exchange's commission rate structure, and there is little to indicate that it has even thoroughly investigated proposed rate revisions." Note: Monopolies—Immunity From Antitrust Liability—Minimum Commission Rates Of Stock Exchanges, 19 *Case Wes. Res. L. Rev.* 167, 173 (1967). . . . [T]he underlying data used by the SEC in reviewing each of the five rate increases since 1934 have been essentially those supplied by the Exchange, and have been very limited in scope and content. . . .

Parenthetically, and by way of expressing our agreement with the Supreme Court's policy of strictly limiting all antitrust exemptions in deference to regulatory bodies, we also note that the history of United States regulatory agencies in general seems usually to record an ever growing absence of the spirit required for vigorous enforcement of the antitrust laws. Rather, it seems to demonstrate that shortly following the establishment of administrative procedures the regulatory agency usually becomes dominated by the industry which it was created to regulate.

III. Questions for Review: Finance

How may the structure of financial markets affect market power in other markets?

"Large firms generally borrow at interest rates lower than for small firms. This proves that (1) financial markets are imperfect and (2) large firms generally have unfair advantages over their smaller competitors." Do you agree?

Is the case for competition in banking as complete as Phillips suggests?

Policies toward market power (antitrust, regulation) usually ignore possible relations between industrial firms and their financial sources. On reflection, how might *either* antitrust *or* regulation be altered if financial ties were important and were explicitly included in policy treatments?

Do the Justice Department Merger Guidelines on horizontal mergers apply to banking mergers?

"To be fair and efficient, the Antitrust Division should now seek to take apart many of the 1950s bank mergers which created large market shares." How far should it try to go?

Is banking concentration justified by economies of scale?

Should banks be limited to banking and closely related activities?

"Banking regulation simply carries out the interests of the established bank interests." Is this true? What effects has bank regulation had? How should it be revised?

What is the "insider" problem? Does it undermine the performance of the stock market?

Summarize and appraise the arguments for and against free competition in stock exchange activities versus fixed minimum rates and entry controls.

"The SEC only averts the worst excesses. It doesn't prevent the main stream of stock-market abuses or provide for a really fair market." Do you agree?

"Insurance is vital and financially powerful. So it should be regulated." Is this logical? What regulation is needed?

Part IV

REGULATION

Regulation is a distinctively American experiment, which has had some real content for 20–50 years in various sectors. Ideally, "natural monopolies"—"utilities"—are put under strict, thorough control, which keeps prices close to minimum costs and sets an efficient and fair price structure.

Practice has worked out differently, as these readings explore. Agencies have modest funds, unsure powers, and heavy tasks. Issues grow complex and confusing. The agency first promotes, then negotiates with, then defends its utilities. The 1960s brought new skepticism about regulation, plus after 1965 a convergence of intense new problems: ecology problems, inflationary pressures, high interest rates, in general the end of the age of utility abundance. Calls for abolition or drastic changes in regulation have become frequent and more plausible.

Because regulation has been only partly tried, under diverse conditions, no one can sort out its effects and lessons precisely. These readings do pose the main issues about control, induced waste, and social yields. They also face the thorny problems of permitting the "optimal" degree of competition against utility firms who have only a core of "natural monopoly" operations but are keen to monopolize adjacent markets too. With these issues in hand, the student can perhaps begin devising a more effective and adjustable regulatory approach.

Roger C. Cramton (1929–   )

THE EFFECTIVENESS OF ECONOMIC REGULATION: A LEGAL VIEW*

Cramton poses the simplest and most important question about regulation: What are its effects?

Some time ago I came across a quotation which ever since has been weighing on my mind. It is reported to have been spoken by an aged West Coast Indian, sitting on a rock and looking out to sea, under circumstances which I do not know. It reads as follows: "Lighthouse, him no good for fog. Lighthouse, him whistle, him blow, him ring bell, him flash light, him raise hell; but fog come in just the same." . . .

The most basic question one can ask about economic regulation is whether it makes a difference in the behavior of the regulated industry. . . . The net effect of the busy humming of the regulatory machinery may be only to irritate entrepreneurs and to enrich their lawyers, without effecting a fundamental alteration in the state of affairs that would have existed in the absence of regulation.

A moment's thought will indicate why the economic effect of regulation is essentially independent of the content of formal regulation. The regulation may prohibit conduct which no one desires to engage in or it may encourage conduct which will take place anyway. Even if the regulation deals with conduct that would take a different course in the absence of regulation, it is always possible that the objective so devoutly desired by the regulators will not be achieved. The regulatory machinery may be too cumbersome or the ingenuity of circumvention too great. In order to determine whether the observed economic behavior in a particular industry is due to the existence of regulation, the possible effect of regulation must be isolated from other factors influencing behavior.

---

* Roger C. Cramton, "The Effectiveness of Economic Regulation: A Legal View," *American Economic Review*, May 1963, excerpted from pp. 182–89. Cramton is now Dean of the Cornell Law School.

The significance of individual regulatory actions cannot be judged by the number of lawyers or regulators engaged in the fray, the heat of the battle, or the length of the struggle. These external indicia have little relationship to the economic significance of the proceeding. It is a safe generalization that many of the most time-consuming and expensive controversies in regulatory annals have had little economic or social significance—other than as tribal rites which lend legitimacy to conduct that otherwise might be viewed as antisocial behavior. On the other hand, some regulatory actions, which may or may not be accompanied by formal proceedings, elaborate trappings, and controversial publicity, are of great economic importance.

There are inherent limitations on the effectiveness of economic regulation even where public policy is fairly clear and the regulatory task, relatively speaking, is confined and manageable. The simpler case of economic regulation—the determination of maximum rates of a conventional public utility—has not been performed with obvious success. I do not assert that public utility regulation has been a failure. I do maintain, however, that unqualified assertions of its effectiveness would be unwarranted. The lesson of a half-century of experience is that the environment generates enduring problems which limit the potential effectiveness of rate regulation.

The regulation of interstate telephone rates by the Federal Communications Commission during the period 1953 through 1962 illustrates the general proposition. The objectives are clear and limited; and the methods are traditional and well established. Yet a detailed look at the methods and mechanics of regulation suggests strong doubts concerning its effectiveness: disputed issues have been compromised by the Commission after private negotiation with the Bell System; standards for determining allowable expense, items includible in investment, and cost of capital have never been determined; and a relatively high rate of return of 7.5 percent over an extended period has encouraged investors to treat A. T. & T. stock as a growth rather than as an income security. The FCC has never even explained or attempted to justify this state of affairs.

I do not offer this as a demonstration of the ineffectiveness of federal telephone regulation. My thesis is that this pattern is typical, that doubts of similar dimension could be raised concerning the performance of nearly all regulatory schemes. Why is this so? What are the limiting conditions on the effectiveness of economic regulation that emerge from the task itself or that are imposed by the environment in which it operates?

I have spoken of the relative simplicity of conventional public utility regulation in that its purposes are fairly clear and its methods well established. . . . Even so, the complexity of the regulatory task is staggering. The treatment of joint costs in the telephone industry or the explanation of the toll rate disparity between interstate and intrastate rates are problems that tax the abilities of able economists. It is easy to under-estimate the difficulty of the problems if one is not responsible for the results nor embarrassed by an overabundance of information.

Inadequacies of personnel and appropriations constitute a second lim-iting factor that seems to be endemic. A handful of poorly paid employees are asked to perform complex tasks of regulation requiring zeal and imagi-nation. Before long nearly all of the available manpower is tied down in the processing or review of routine matters. Once the immediate needs which produced regulation have been assuaged, the public loses interest and the agency falls into a routine in which day-to-day accommodations are made with those subject to the regulation.

After the first years of regulation, when the initial enthusiasm has been replaced by a convenient reliance on routine solutions, the vague mandate —expressed in terms of some undefined "public interest"—is likely to produce a timid and unimaginative approach. Agency members, who are readily identifiable and exposed to attack, are reluctant to assume tasks of national planning which they or others may feel are beyond their com-petence or commission. Lack of a clear legislative mandate stultifies ad-ministration.

The so-called "independence" of the regulatory agency is a source of weakness when the agency is not implementing policies that find strong support in a democratic consensus. Isolated from the sources of political power, forced to evolve working arrangements with those it regulates, dependent on Congress for funds and on the President for reappointment, and harassed by an unending succession of congressional investigations and industry pressures, the agency withdraws from committing itself on decisive issues of policy. It drifts along, responding to the most urgent pressures as they arise and perpetuating, for the most part, regulatory patterns which were created in the past to meet different problems. In short, the agency becomes passive, backward-looking, and resistant to change.

An important implication of these general tendencies is that the more passive functions of protectionism are more effectively implemented than the affirmative functions of planning, development, and coordination.

Alfred E. Kahn (1917–   )

THE ECONOMICS OF
REGULATION*

Kahn here treats marginal-cost pricing and then argues that the Averch-Johnson "rate-base effect" (see below) is probably a good thing, not a cause of waste.

* * * * *

THE CENTRAL ECONOMIC PRINCIPLE:
MARGINAL COST PRICING

The central policy prescription of microeconomics is the equation of price and marginal cost. If economic theory is to have any relevance to public utility pricing, that is the point at which the inquiry must begin.

As almost any student of elementary economics will recall, marginal cost is the cost of producing one more unit; it can equally be envisaged as the cost that would be saved by producing one less unit. Looked at the first way, it may be termed incremental cost—the added cost of (a small amount of) incremental output. Observed in the second way, it is synonymous with avoidable cost—the cost that would be saved by (slightly) reducing output. . . .

If consumers are to make the choices that will yield them the greatest possible satisfaction from society's limited aggregate productive capacity, the prices that they pay for the various goods and services available to them must accurately reflect their respective opportunity costs; only then will buyers be judging, in deciding what to buy and what not, whether the satisfaction they get from the purchase of any particular product is worth the sacrifice of other goods and services that its production entails. If their judgments are correctly informed in this way, they will, by their independent purchase decisions, guide our scarce resources into those lines of production that yield more satisfaction than all available alternatives—which means that total satisfaction will be maximized.

* Excerpted from *The Economics of Regulation*, Alfred E. Kahn, Vol. I, pp. 65–66, 75, 83–85, 95, 98–100, and Vol. II, pp. 106–7. Copyright © 1971 John Wiley & Sons, Inc. Reprinted by permission of John Wiley & Sons, Inc. Something of a universal force in the field, Kahn has written widely on antitrust, patents, the oil industry, and even the British economy, as well as producing this major text. He has also been Dean of the Cornell University faculty and, since 1974, Chairman of the New York Public Service Commission.

. . . The economic principles are clear-cut. They are two. First, the essential criterion of what belongs in marginal cost and what not, and of which marginal costs should be reflected in price, is causal responsibility. All the purchasers of any commodity or service should be made to bear such additional costs—*only* such, but also *all* such—as are imposed on the economy by the provision of one additional unit. And second, it is short-run marginal cost to which price should at any given time—*hence always*—be equated, because it is short-run marginal cost that reflects the social opportunity cost of providing the additional unit that buyers are at any given time trying to decide whether to buy.

Specifying the Incremental Block of Output

The level of incremental cost per unit depends, also, on the size of the increment. Consider the passenger airplane flight already scheduled, with the plane on the runway, fueled up and ready to depart, but with its seats not completely filled. The incremental unit of service in this case might be defined as the carrying of an extra passenger on that flight—in which case, the marginal cost would be practically zero. It was just such a marginal cost calculation, involving the smallest possible number of additional units and the shortest-possible run, that underlay the introduction of standby youth-fares by some American airlines in 1966—half-price for young people willing to come out to the airport and take their chances of finding an empty seat on their flight ten minutes before departure time.

Or is the incremental unit in question the particular scheduled flight, taken as a whole, involving the carrying of 50 or 100 passengers between a particular pair of cities at a particular time? If the plane must fly anyhow, as long as the flight is scheduled, the additional cost of taking on all the passengers is still practically zero. But schedules can be changed in the comparatively short run, in which event the relevant marginal costs of a particular flight include all the costs of flying the plane as compared with not flying it. Or is the incremental unit of sales the provision of regular service between a pair of cities, involving an entire schedule of flights? In this case, still more costs enter into the marginal calculation —airport rentals, ticket offices, the cost of advertising in local newspapers, indeed the cost of the planes themselves, which need not be acquired or can be used in other service. The larger the incremental unit of service under consideration, the more costs become variable. . . .

TEMPERING PRINCIPLE WITH PRACTICALITY— OR ONE PRINCIPLE WITH ANOTHER

The outcome of this entire discussion about the problems of defining (as contrasted with actually measuring and applying) marginal cost is that neither the choice between short- and long-run, nor the problem of defining the incremental unit of sale, nor the prevalence of common and joint costs, raises any difficulties in principle about the economically efficient price. It is set at the short-run marginal cost of the smallest possible additional unit of sale. Common costs do not preclude separable marginal production costs, and joint products have separate marginal opportunity costs.

But, as we have already suggested, short-run marginal costs (SRMC) are the place to begin. There are situations in which it is both efficient and practical to base rates on them, as we shall see. Typically, this is not the case; principle must be compromised in various ways in the interest of practicality, for a number of interrelated reasons:

1. It is often infeasible, or prohibitively expensive, for businesses to make the necessary fine calculations of marginal cost for each of their numerous categories of service.

2. Marginal costs will vary from one moment to the next, in a world of perpetually changing demand, as firms operate at perpetually changing points on their SRMC functions (unless marginal costs happen to be constant, that is, horizontal), and between far wider extremes than either average variable or average total costs. [They] will vary also because cost functions themselves are constantly shifting. Thus, it would be prohibitively costly to the seller to put into effect the highly refined and constantly changing pricing schedules, reflecting in minute detail the different short-run marginal costs of different sales. It would also be highly vexatious to buyers, who would be quick to find discrimination in departures from uniform prices, who would be put to great expense to be informed about prices that were constantly changing, and whose ability to make rational choices and plan intelligently for the future would be seriously impaired.

3. For these reasons the practically-achievable version of SRMC pricing is often likely to be pricing at *average* variable costs (AVC), themselves averaged over some period of time in the past and assumed to remain constant over some period in the future—until there occurs some clear, discrete shift caused by an event such as a change in wage rates. But since short-term AVC (in contrast with SRMC) are never as large as average total costs, . . . universal adoption of this type of pricing is infeasible if sellers are to cover total costs, including (as always) a minimum required return on investment. This in turn produces a strong tendency in industry to price on a "full cost" basis—usually computed at AVC (really *average* AVC over some period of time) plus some percentage mark-up judged sufficient to cover total costs on the average over some time period—a far cry, indeed, from marginal cost pricing.

4. SRMC can be above or below ATC, as we have seen; but whether it is above often enough for businesses pricing on that basis to cover total costs on the average depends on the average relationship over time between demand and production capacity. As J. M. Clark has often pointed out, excess capacity is the typical condition of modern industry, and we would probably want this to be the case in public utilities, which we tend to insist be perpetually in a position to supply whatever demands are placed on them. In these circumstances, firms could far more often be operating at the point where SRMC is less than ATC than the reverse, and if they based their prices exclusively on the former they would have to find some other means of making up the difference. Partly for this reason, and partly because of the infeasibility of permitting prices to fluctuate widely along the SRMC function, depending on the immediate relation of demand to capacity, the practically achievable benchmark for efficient pricing is more likely to be a type of average long-run incremental cost, computed for a large, expected incremental block of sales, instead of SRMC, estimated for a single additional sale. This long-run incremental cost (which we shall loosely refer to as long-run marginal cost as well) would be based on (1) the average incremental variable costs of those added sales and (2) estimated additional capital costs per unit, for the additional capacity that will have to be constructed if sales at that price are expected to continue over time or to grow. Both of these components would be estimated as averages over some period of years extending into the future.

5. The prevalence of common costs has similar implications. Service A bears a causal responsibility for a share of common costs only if there is an economically realistic alternative use of the capacity now used to provide it, or if production of A requires the building of additional capacity. The marginal opportunity cost of serving A depends on how much the alternative users would be willing to pay for devoting the capacity to serving them instead. The sum of the separable marginal costs will therefore cover the common costs only if at separate prices less than this the claims on the capacity exceed the available supply.

6. Long-run marginal costs are likely to be the preferred criterion also in competitive situations. Permitting rate reductions to a lower level of SRMC, which would prove to be unremunerative if the business thus attracted were to continue over time, might constitute predatory competition—driving out of business rivals whose *long-run* costs of production might well be lower than those of the price-cutter. . . .

Public utility companies do employ peak-responsibility pricing to some degree. The telephone companies charge lower rates for night than for daytime long-distance calls; electric companies frequently have low night rates for hot-water heating; both they and natural gas companies—local distributors and interstate pipelines alike—offer at lower rates service that the customer will agree may be interrupted if capacity is being taxed by other users and try to promote off-peak sales in numerous ways; railroads charge lower rates for return-hauls of freight, when the greater flow is in the opposite direction; airlines offer special discount fares—family plans, youth fares, and so forth—for travel on unfilled planes or in slack seasons or days of the week.

Although most public utility executives and regulators recognize that peak responsibility pricing has some validity, probably most would also vigorously resist its wholehearted acceptance. William G. Shepherd's survey disclosed that the majority of American electric utilities practice little or no explicit marginal cost pricing, and among those that do, the main emphasis is on raising off-peak sales, by charging them something less than average capacity costs, instead of purposefully imposing all the capacity charges on the peak users.[1] He found, moreover, that publicly-owned companies, if anything, follow marginalist and peak responsibility principles even less than private; and that electric utilities in states with "tough" regulatory commissions, such as New York and California, similarly incorporate little marginalism in their rate structures.

An outstanding illustration of the resistance of strong regulatory commissions is provided by the Federal Power Commission's formula for natural gas pipeline rate-making specified in its famous *Atlantic Seaboard* decision of 1952. The distinctive feature of the Atlantic Seaboard formula is that it requires that capacity costs be distributed 50–50 between the demand and commodity charges instead of incorporated exclusively in the former. Since the demand costs are distributed among customers in proportion to their shares in the volume of sales at the system's (three-day) peak, while the commodity costs are borne in proportion to their annual volume of purchases, the consequence of the 50–50 formula is to shift a large proportion of capacity costs to off-peak users. This produces an uneconomic encouragement to sales at the peak (whose price falls short of the true marginal costs of peak service) and an uneconomic discouragement of off-peak. (In fairness, it should be pointed out that the FPC has permitted departures from this strict formula when it appeared that the pipelines would suffer large losses of interruptible, off-peak sales at the inflated commodity charges it produced—permitting them instead to "tilt" the rate schedule downward on the commodity side of the balance. Among other alleged harmful consequences of *Atlantic Seaboard* has been a tendency to discourage distribution companies from installing storage capacity: demand and commodity charges more fully reflecting the true respective marginal costs of peak and off-peak purchases would have increased their incentive to "shave" their purchases at the former by installing storage, which they could fill by low-cost purchases off-peak and draw on at the peak.

---

[1] "Marginal Cost Pricing in American Utilities," *Southern Economic Journal,* July 1966, pp. 58–70.

We present two last examples of the pervasive uneconomic departure from peak responsibility pricing. First, commutation books and other such devices that give commuters quantity discounts on passenger trains and toll bridges have the consequence that occasional travelers, who usually travel off-peak, pay a higher rate than commuters, who concentrate their traveling in the rush hours. Second, airplane landing fees do not reflect the enormous variations in airport congestion, from one time of day, day of the week, or one airport to another. These variations themselves doubtless tend to induce air travelers and airplane companies to rearrange their traveling plans and schedules to avoid peak hours and locations and make fuller use of off-peak time; equivalently varying landing fees could make a further contribution. . . .

[The Averch-Johnson (A–J–W) Effect]

If regulation were instantaneously effective, it would eliminate this restrictive effect of monopoly; and that is precisely what it is supposed to do. The economic purpose of holding price to average total cost, including only a competitive return on investment, is to produce the competitive level of investment and output. . . .

But the fact is, as we have seen, that regulation is not instantaneously effective. Public utility companies therefore do have some opportunity to choose between higher and lower rates of profit, at correspondingly lower and higher respective rates of output. . . .

As an offset to monopoly, the A–J–W distortion probably does more good than harm. It encourages risk-taking and output-expanding investment. We have earlier suggested that one possible manifestation of the A–J–W effect is some reluctance of public utilities to adopt thoroughgoing peak-responsibility pricing: if peak users can be charged less than the full capacity costs for which they are (marginally) responsible, this "justifies" a greater capacity and a larger rate base, the costs of which can then be recouped partially from off-peak users. But it is precisely with respect to such investments that monopoly has heretofore been accused of producing excessive conservatism.

Harvey A. Averch and
Leland L. Johnson (1930–   )

BEHAVIOR OF THE FIRM UNDER REGULATORY CONSTRAINT*

The "Averch-Johnson Effect" sprang full-grown from this landmark article in 1962. There are really two effects: regulation may induce the firm (1) to waste capital and (2) to capture adjacent markets by pricing for low or even negative profitability ("cut-throat" pricing). Despite utility-sponsored efforts to refute or dilute these points, they stand largely intact. The second effect, though neglected, may be the more important.

The purpose here is *(a)* to develop a theory of the monopoly firm seeking to maximize profit but subject to such a constraint on its rate of return, and *(b)* to apply the model to one particular regulated industry—the domestic telephone and telegraph industry. We conclude in the theoretical analysis that a "regulatory bias" operates in the following manner: (1) The firm does not equate marginal rates of factor substitution to the ratio of factor costs; therefore the firm operates inefficiently in the sense that (social) cost is not minimized at the output it selects. (2) The firm has an incentive to expand into other regulated markets, even if it operates at a (long-run) loss in these markets; therefore, it may drive out other firms, or discourage their entry into these other markets, even though the competing firms may be lower-cost producers. Applying the theoretical analysis to the telephone and telegraph industry, we find that the model does raise issues relevant to evaluating market behavior.

I. THE SINGLE-MARKET MODEL

First we shall consider a geometrical and a mathematical framework showing the effect of the regulatory constraint on the cost curves of the

---

* Harvey A. Averch and Leland L. Johnson, "Behavior of the Firm under Regulatory Constraint," *American Economic Review,* December 1962, excerpted from pp. 1052–59 and 1068. A brief retrospect by Johnson is also included: "A Reassessment," *American Economic Review,* May 1973, excerpted from pp. 91 and 95–96. A RAND staff member, Johnson is a leading expert on the economics of telecommunications, including satellites and cable TV as well as more traditional issues. Averch has also done research on economic development.

firm employing two factors. The essential characteristic to be demonstrated is: if the rate of return allowed by the regulatory agency is greater than the cost of capital but is less than the rate of return that would be enjoyed by the firm were it free to maximize profit without regulatory constraint, then the firm will substitute capital for the other factor of production and operate at an output where cost is not minimized.

FIGURE 1.

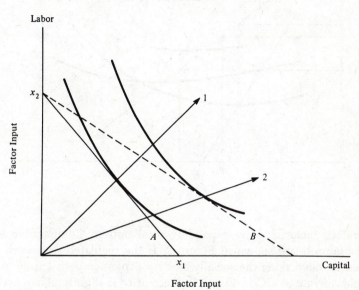

Figure 1 denotes the firm's production where capital x_1 is plotted on the horizontal axis and labor x_2 on the vertical axis. The market or "social" cost of capital and labor generates the isocost curve A and the *unregulated* firm would move along expansion path 1 where market cost is minimized for any given output. With regulation, however, the cost of capital to the firm—the "private" cost—is no longer equal to market cost. For each additional unit of capital input, the firm is permitted to earn a profit (equal to the difference between the market cost of capital and rate of return allowed by the regulatory agency) that it otherwise would have to forego. Therefore, private cost is less than market cost by an amount equal to this difference. The effect of regulation is analogous to that of changing the relative prices of capital x_1 and labor x_2: isocost curve B becomes relevant and the firm moves along expansion path 2—a path along which market cost is not minimized for any given output. The firm finds path 2 advantageous simply because it is along that path that the firm is able to maximize total profit given the constraint on its rate of return. . . .

The firm adjusts to the constraint, then, by substituting capital for the

FIGURE 2.

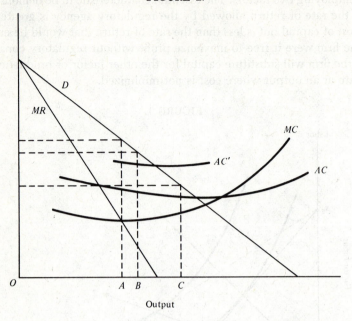

Output

cooperating factor and by expanding total output. Comparative equilibrium outputs are shown in Figure 2. If the regulated firm were constrained to move along the socially efficient expansion path 1 in Figure 1, it would operate at OC in Figure 2. Here price is slightly above average cost AC to reflect the fact that $s_1 > r_1$ (profit is not entirely eliminated). Since the regulated firm moves along path 2, the social cost curve rises from AC to AC', and the regulatory constraint is satisfied at the lower output OB. The effect of regulation is to force the firm to expand output from the unregulated position OA, but output does not expand to C because a portion of what would otherwise be profit is absorbed by cost. The extent to which regulation affects output depends upon the nature of the production function.

II. THE MULTIMARKET CASE

Suppose that in addition to operating in a single market, the firm can also enter other regulated markets, and that the regulatory agency bases its "fair rate of return" criterion on the firm's over-all value of plant and equipment for all markets taken together rather than computing a separate rate of return for each market. In this case the firm may have an incentive (that it would not have in the absence of regulation) to enter these other markets, even if the cost of so doing exceeds the additional revenues. Expanding into other markets may enable the firm to inflate its rate base to satisfy the constraint and permit it to earn a greater total constrained profit than would have been possible in the absence of second markets.

A noteworthy implication is that the firm operating in oligopolistic second markets may have an advantage over competing firms. The regulated firm can "afford" to take (long-run) losses in these second markets while competing firms cannot. Under these circumstances, it is conceivable that the firm could drive out lower-cost producers—the loss it willingly takes in second markets could exceed the difference between its costs and the lower costs of other firms. It may succeed, therefore, in either driving lower cost firms out of these markets or of discouraging their entry into them. This is unlike the textbook case of "predatory price-cutting" where the regulated monopolist may temporarily cut prices in outside competitive markets to drive out rivals and subsequently raise prices to monopoly levels. The monopolist would ordinarily engage in such a practice only if he had the expectation that in the long run he would make a positive profit in these additional markets; but here even in the case of a long-run loss the regulated firm may find operations in such markets to be advantageous as long as the firm is permitted to include its capital input in these markets in its rate base.

. . . While the unregulated firm would be indifferent about operating in market 2, the regulated firm in this example finds market 2 attractive because it can add capital to the rate base at "no loss"; i.e., for any capital input in market 2 the output generates revenues just equal to factor cost. Since in market 2 the actual cost of capital is below the allowed rate of return, the firm can apply the difference in satisfying the constraint in market 1 and thereby enjoy additional profit equal to $s_1 - r_1$ for each unit of capital in market 2.

This analysis suggests that even if the firm suffers a loss in market 2 (measured in terms of social costs r_1 and r_2) it may still operate there provided the value of $x_{12} (s_1 - r_1)$ exceeds this level of loss. If it suffers a loss it would no longer operate in market 1 at the profit-maximizing output OA in Figure 1; seeking to equate the marginal value product of capital in both markets, it would move toward OB.

III. THE TELEPHONE AND TELEGRAPH INDUSTRY

Turning to the domestic telephone and telegraph industry, we find that the market structure and the regulatory setting are consistent with those described in the model. And the implications drawn from the model, concerning relative factor inputs and incentives to operate in some markets even at a loss, raise issues relevant to assessing market behavior of firms in the industry. . . .

IV. CONCLUSIONS

The preceding analysis discloses that a misallocation of economic resources may result from the use by regulatory agencies of the rate-of-return
constraint for price control. The firm has an incentive to substitute between
factors in an uneconomic fashion that is difficult for the regulatory agency
to detect. Moreover, if a large element of common costs exists for the
firm's outputs in the various markets, the widely used "fully allocated"
cost basis for rate-of-return computation is likely to prove satisfactory in
determining whether the firm is operating at a loss in any given market, or
whether its activities in some markets tend to restrict competition in an
undesirable manner. At the same time, regulatory practices that provide an
incentive for the firm to operate in some markets even at a loss may constitute a convenient mechanism through which certain activities of the firm
judged to be in the "public interest" can be subsidized.

* * * * *

[From Johnson, "A Reassessment" (1973)]

In light of the extensive discussion over the past decade, it seems fair to
say that the Averch-Johnson analysis, given its assumptions, remains valid
on theoretical grounds. But the question remains about the importance
of overcapitalization and cross-subsidization in reality. Are the Averch-
Johnson effects merely an intellectual curiosity, or do they describe serious distortions in the behavior of regulated firms? Unfortunately the
answer is not clear. It is not enough to compare the behavior of regulated
and unregulated firms because, as mentioned above, the capital-labor ratio
of the regulated firm is not necessarily greater than that of the unregulated
monopolist. The search for goldplating and obviously wasteful use of
capital is likely to prove fruitless since, within the regulatory constraint,
the firm does seek to use capital in a manner that produces additional
revenue.

To the extent that Averch-Johnson effects operate, they do so subtly:
the firm can engage in activities for a number of reasons that seem plausible; to separate the real from the merely plausible reasons is not easy. . . .

With respect to regulatory lags, as [Elizabeth] Bailey and Roger Cole-
man point out, the longer the firm must wait for an increase in rates to
bring the allowable rate of return to a point above the market cost of
capital, the less incentive the firm has to add to rate base in the interim;
for during the time lag it suffers a loss that only eventually will be
compensated.

However, it is useful to distinguish between two kinds of regulatory
lags. The first I shall call Type I to describe the situation in which the firm
is caught in a general inflationary spiral leading eventually to rate increases. It is this kind of lag that would dampen incentives to overcapi-

talize, and it is this kind of lag with which so many utilities are faced today as a consequence of the strong inflationary forces that have persisted since the mid-1960s. Under a second kind of lag, which I shall call Type II, the firm is able to enjoy technological advances of such magnitude and/or such large economies of scale in the face of growing demand that its unit costs fall in spite of inflationary forces. This situation leads eventually to rate decreases rather than increases. It is under Type II lags that one would expect overcapitalization to emerge most clearly. In the extreme case, by sufficient overcapitalization, the firm could remain within the range of a fair rate of return and postpone indefinitely pressures by the regulatory agency to reduce rates.

The differences in the cases in which firms seek or avoid capital investment are, I would conjecture, traceable in part to whether Type I or Type II lags are at work. Today, Type I lags are far more evident than they were a decade ago. Hence the potential for overcapitalization is probably less than it was in 1962 when the Averch-Johnson model was formulated.

E. E. Zajac (1926–   )

A GEOMETRIC TREATMENT OF AVERCH-JOHNSON'S BEHAVIOR OF THE FIRM MODEL*

Zajac here restates and redraws the rate-base analysis.

To clarify issues, a simple geometric analysis of the AJ model is given which uses no advanced mathematics. It is hoped that it will help show precisely what the model does and does not imply....

I. THE AVERCH-JOHNSON MODEL AND ITS GEOMETRIC SOLUTION

Consider a firm producing a single good, q, with two factor inputs, K (capital) and L (labor). Its output q is given by a production function,

---

* E. E. Zajac, "A Geometric Treatment of Averch-Johnson's Behavior of the Firm Model," *American Economic Review*, March 1970, excerpted from pp. 117–20. Zajac is at Bell Telephone Laboratories, Inc. The balance of the article attempts to reduce the scope and validity of the rate-base effect.

$q = q(K, L)$ with the price of q given by the inverse demand function, $p = p(q)$. The firm's per unit costs of capital and labor are given by i and w so that its total costs are $iK + wL$ and its profit, π, is

$$(1) \qquad \pi = pq - (iK + wL).$$

Since p and q depend on K and L, the profit, π, also depends only on K and L. In a K, L, π coordinate system, the function $\pi = \pi(K, L)$ can be visualized as a surface, the "profit hill," spanning the K, L plane (Figure 1). It is

FIGURE 1.
Profit Hill and Constraint Plane

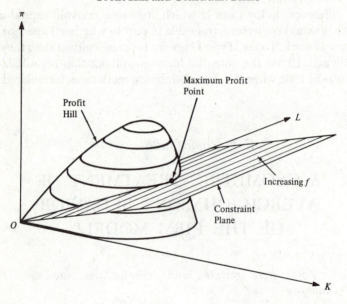

assumed that for each K, L there is a single value of π, that the profit hill has a single peak, and that the surface continually falls away from the peak, so that the peak is the only point which is tangent to a horizontal plane.

Regulation may limit the firm so that it cannot operate at the very top of the profit hill. To model regulation, Averch and Johnson neglect depreciation and take K, the amount of capital the firm uses, to be its rate base. The money earned to be applied to the rental of capital is revenue minus labor expense: $pq - wL$. This divided by the rate base gives the rate of return to capital. Regulation requires that this rate be no greater than a fair rate of return, f. Thus, symbolically, the AJ model of the regulatory constraint is

$$(2) \qquad \frac{pq - wL}{K} \leq f.$$

It is more convenient to rearrange (2) by multiplying by K and to use equation (1) to get

$$(3) \qquad \pi \leq (f - i)K.$$

Averch and Johnson assume that the allowed rate of return f is greater than the average cost of capital i. The regulated firm is then allowed a positive (excess) profit, but by the constraint (3) this must be no greater than the product of the excess rate of return, $(f - i)$, and the rate base K.

The constraint $\pi \leq (f - i)K$ requires that the firm operate below or on the plane $\pi = (f - i)K$ in the K, L, π coordinate system. This plane can be visualized as a door hinged on the L-axis and swung upward from the K, L plane. The greater the value of the fair rate of return f, the higher the constraint plane is swung above the K, L plane (Figure 1).

In the case of interest, the constraint plane slices a prohibited bump off the top of the profit hill. The facts of demand and production put the firm on the profit hill but, except for uninterestingly high f's, the constraint plane keeps the firm from attaining the hill's top. At the same time, the point of highest profit on or below the constraint plane is obvious. Because the constraint plane is hinged on the L-axis, *maximum profit occurs at the point of maximum K along the intersection of the constraint plane and the profit hill* (Figure 1).

To complete the analysis of the AJ model, it remains to be shown that at the K_{max} point, the firm will operate inefficiently with overintensive capital utilization. For a fixed output (along an isoquant), efficient operation occurs at that allocation of capital and labor resources which results in minimum cost of production. Likewise, since revenue is fixed along an isoquant, the efficient point represents maximum profit to the firm along that isoquant. The π_{max} point at the top of the profit hill (Figure 1) is the maximum of all fixed-output profit maxima, and hence lies on the locus of efficient points (expansion path). Furthermore, in the simple case considered here of a profit hill which has a single peak and which is nowhere tangent to a horizontal plane, the fixed-output profit maxima continually decrease as one moves away from π_{max} in either direction along the locus of efficient points.

Consider then the projection onto the K, L plane of the intersection of the constraint plane and the profit hill (Figure 2). This will be called the *constraint curve*. It encloses the region beneath the prohibited bump (shown shaded in Figure 2). If the firm operates within the shaded region, it violates the regulatory constraint, while operation at the K_{max} point results in maximum profit under regulation. The isoquant through K_{max} cannot intersect the locus of efficient points *outside* of the constraint curve, as at point P in Figure 2(a). For then, since π_{max} is *inside* the constraint curve, the point P' at the intersection of the locus of efficient points and the constraint curve would lie between π_{max} and P (Figure 2(a)). Inasmuch as

FIGURE 2.

(a) **Impossible Location, Outside the Constraint Curve, of the Efficient Point *P* for the Isoquant Through K_{max}**

(b) **Only Possible Location of *P*, Inside the Constraint Curve**

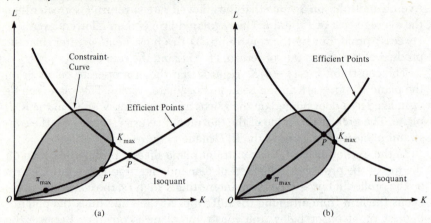

profit continuously decreases along the efficient point locus away from π_{max}, profit at *P'* would be greater than at *P*, and hence still greater than at K_{max}. But this would contradict the fact that K_{max} is the maximum profit point along the constraint curve. Likewise, coincidence of the K_{max} and efficient points can also be ruled out. Profit is a maximum at K_{max} as one traverses the constraint curve and at the efficient point as one traverses an isoquant. Hence, if the two coincide, profit is a maximum along two directions through the point of coincidence. This implies that the coincident point is tangent to a horizontal plane, which by the original assumption occurs only at the profit hill's peak. In other terms, K_{max} will also be an efficient point only when the constraint plane slices through the top of the profit hill.

Hence, the efficient point for the output curve passing through K_{max} must be inside the constraint curve as in Figure 2(b). To maximize profit under regulation, the firm should operate at point K_{max} in Figure 2(b). But the same amount of output could be obtained at lower cost if the firm were to move to efficient point *P* in Figure 2(b). Since a higher-than-necessary cost to the firm means the inefficient use of resources, society is the loser (so is the firm because it could increase its profits by moving to *P*). Fair rate of return regulation thus would appear to drive the profit-maximizing firm to an operating point which is undesirable to society. This, then, is the oft-quoted AJ result, obtained originally by the application of the Kuhn-Tucker theorem rather than by the geometric arguments given here.

Nicholas Johnson (1934–   ) and
John J. Dystel

A DAY IN THE LIFE: THE
FEDERAL COMMUNICATIONS
COMMISSION*

The flood of issues, large and small, which the FCC must "decide" is graphically portrayed here, and the dubious results are bluntly appraised. Johnson was an outstanding, maverick FCC commissioner during 1966– 73, alert to the economic issues and to the political forces beating upon—and within—the agency. These excerpts give only a small part of the whole. Other commissions have much the same experience: struggling to cope.

"I read the news today, oh boy!"—The Beatles, "A Day in the Life"

For seven years I have struggled with the FCC in an effort to inject some rationality into its decision-making process and to reveal its workings to the public. There is reason enough to assert that everything the FCC does is wrong.[1] But, like contributions to the literature detailing disasters in given areas of Commission responsibility, such assertions are almost universally dismissed as exaggerations.

And so it is that I have come to try to describe the agency one more time, but from a unique perspective: "A day in the life" of the Federal Communi-

---

* Nicholas Johnson and John J. Dystal, "A Day in the Life: The Federal Communications Commission." Reprinted by permission of The Yale Law Journal Company and Fred B. Rothman & Company from *The Yale Law Journal*, vol. 82, pp. 1575–79, 1582, 1586–89, 1595, 1626, 1633–34. Johnson was bounced over to his seat on the FCC after attempting to shake up the Federal Maritime Commission as Commissioner during 1965–66. He is now in political oblivion but active in policy groups.

[1] There are many who have bemoaned what may aptly be described as the FCC's analytical void. For example, Newton Minow, a former FCC Chairman, complained upon leaving the Commission that the FCC is "a quixotic world of undefined terms, private pressures and tools unsuited to the work." Drew, *Is the FCC Dead? Atlantic*, July 1967, at 29. For a somewhat different view, however, see Cox, *Does the FCC Really Do Anything?* 11 *Broadcasting* 97 (1967).

cations Commission.[2] The day—Wednesday, December 13, 1972—was selected from the Commission's meeting days in 1972. It is neither better nor worse than any other day during the past seven years. It is typical. This article is an effort to describe what the FCC did on that typical Wednesday.

Professors and students of administrative law tend to concentrate on a particular agency decision—usually one that has gone to the appellate courts. But a look at one day's events may well be more instructive than a close examination of a single event in determining why an agency is failing at its job or why it acts in a consistently unprincipled manner.[3]

The seven FCC Commissioners meet weekly, on Wednesdays,[4] to vote on the items brought to their attention by the Commission's various bureaus.[5] It is not clear who decides what matters will be considered. The agenda is the product of industry pressures, staff idiosyncrasies, and political judgments. If he chooses, however, the Chairman is in a position to control the flow of items to the Commission.

Most matters are not handled at FCC meetings but are delegated by the Commission to the staff for action. In theory these items are in areas of settled Commission policy but, in fact, the Commission has not so limited the scope of its delegations. During my term the majority has been unwilling to examine its delegation orders or to enunciate what standards control the delegation of decision-making authority.

Those issues which do reach the Commissioners each week often take them by surprise. Opening a new agenda (the stack of mimeographed staff memos and accompanying recommended opinions for a Wednesday meet-

---

[2] Numerous books, articles, and government reports have been written about the FCC. *See* H. Friendly, *The Federal Administrative Agencies* (1962); J. Landis, *Report on Regulatory Agencies to the President-Elect*, Senate Comm. on the Judiciary, 86th Cong., 2d Sess. (1960); Drew, *supra* note 1; Kalven, *Broadcasting, Public Policy and the First Amedment*, 10 *J. Law & Econ.* 15 (1967); Zeidenberg, *Is the FCC Obsolete?* *Television*, October 1966, at 27, 51.

[3] There are some shortcomings in this expository device. Considerable background material must be included in order to analyze the Commission's actions. Moreover, although one day does include a range of Commission activities, such concentration runs the risk inherent in any evaluation based on a random sample.

[4] Most Commission meetings last for a day or less. If several important matters must be resolved, however, the meetings may last as long as two days. The meeting which constitutes the subject matter of this article began on Wednesday, December 13, and ended the following day. These meetings are closed to the public.

[5] The FCC has a number of major regulatory responsibilities including regulation of broadcast and cable television (CATV), allocation of the nongovernmental portion of the radio spectrum, regulation of interstate telephone, telegraph, miscellaneous radio common carriers, *e.g.*, land mobile radio users, domestic satellites and international communications services.

To deal with these primary areas of concern, the Commission is divided into four substantive bureaus: the Broadcast Bureau, the Cable Bureau, the Safety and Special Radio Services Bureau, and the Common Carrier Bureau. The Chief Engineer's Office and General Counsel's Office are comparable to bureaus. Each bureau, in turn, has various divisions to which I shall refer throughout this article.

ing) is like Christmas morning. All too often the agenda includes a long, detailed staff document dealing with a controversial and complicated matter in which: (1) numerous alternatives are presented (or excluded) after extensive staff work, (2) the proposed resolution is endorsed by all of the Commission's bureau chiefs, (3) an immediate decision is required, and (4) any alteration in the proposed resolution will mean considerably more staff work and costly delay. As a result, rational decision-making suffers.

On December 13, 1972, the Commission was presented with fifty-nine items.[6] In each case the staff made a recommendation to the Commissioners. If a majority votes to approve the staff's recommendation, it adopts the proposed Commission opinion as well. If one of the Commissioners questions a particular item, there is a discussion with the staff prior to a vote. On December 13, twenty-eight of the fifty-nine items were discussed.[7]

Each week's agenda is divided into thirteen substantive categories: Hearing, General, Safety and Special, Common Carrier, Personnel, Classified, CATV, Assignment and Transfer, Renewals, Aural, Television, Broadcast, and Complaints and Compliance—in that order.[8]

Briefing for Commissioners

In recent months the Commissioners have scheduled briefings during regular agenda meetings by each Bureau and Office on its work, resources, and problems. Such briefings often consist of a superficial review of an organizational chart or may deteriorate into a discussion of a pending case. They seldom involve consideration of any innovative changes and amount to little more than the Commissioners' collective nod toward fulfillment of their management responsibilities.

---

[6] Fifty-seven of these items had been distributed to each Commissioner's office at the close of the preceding week. Two, however, did not reach the Commissioners until just prior to the meeting. These latter items are called "walk-in items," and because they are rushed to the Commission for resolution, the Commission's analysis is often extremely superficial.

[7] Twenty-four of the remaining items were adopted without discussion in what is called the "consent agenda." On December 13, the consent agenda lasted one half hour. The remaining seven items were simply passed over for future consideration. Of the twenty-eight items which the Commissioners discussed eleven were deferred for future resolution.

[8] There is a final category of agenda materials which can be called information items. Some are copies of previous agenda items which were acted upon before a regular distribution of materials could be completed. Others are matters acted upon by circulation: The item is passed from one Commissioner's office to the next for the recording of votes. Some are staff memos (or occasionally Commissioner memos) that contain important information—among them staff papers on major policy proceedings underway at the Commission, reports on meetings attended by staff, or reports on work underway in the Commission.

Measured by past briefings the Cable Bureau's December 13 briefing was excellent. It focused on the growth and geographic distribution of the CATV industry, developments in the industry's ownership structure, bureau backlog problems, reports filed with the Commission but as yet unprocessed, and bureau organization.

The Cable Bureau's Chief noted, "The trouble we are in now will only deepen." Backlogs were growing, the toughest certification cases were yet to come, and time lost due to inadequate staff could not be recouped. The Commissioners were advised that there was no staff to process and analyze the annual reports from CATV systems.

The discussion turned to mergers within the Cable industry. The Cable Bureau saw no harmful effects from growing concentration of control within the industry and attempted to rationalize recent mergers by analogy to companies in other communications industries which serve more subscribers than the largest cable corporation. No rule yet governs multiple ownership of cable systems by a single corporation and adoption of such a rule now would probably be too late.

The Bureau presented no written recommendations on any of these issues and the Commission gave no orders, designated no one to study the problems further, and scheduled no future meetings; nothing, in short, has been done. Some of these matters will come before the Commission again only if the briefings continue and the Bureau Chief thinks it worthwhile to mention them.

Finally, the Bureau Chief and the Commissioners discussed some consulting work on Bureau resource needs performed by Harbridge House, Inc. It is common practice to pay consultants to "recommend" that an agency do what it wants to do anyway, the report being used only to convince the budgeting authority. Based on a draft report and the Cable Bureau's recommendation, the Commission proposed large increases in the Cable Bureau Budget for Fiscal Year 1974. . . .

The General Agenda

The General Agenda consists of matters not contained in other substantive agenda categories. On December 13, the Commissioners considered twelve such matters. Resolution of at least one required a level of expertise which the Commissioners lack. On other matters, the majority, presumably capable of comprehending the issues, reached bizarre conclusions or no conclusions at all. . . .

An item involving common carrier issues appeared on the General rather than Common Carrier Agenda because more than one bureau was involved. For years the FCC has struggled with the problem of whether a customer has the right to attach his own accessory equipment to the common carriers' communications networks. Customers prefer to use their own equipment and independent equipment manufacturers are happy to supply it, but common carriers, particularly if they own very profitable equipment manufacturers, oppose such arrangements.

The FCC has furthered the carriers' interests in this controversy by delay and selective approval of the carriers' tariffs. Tariffs describe the rates and practices which govern the services offered by the carrier. In 1968 the Commission struck down AT&T's tariffs on the ground that they were an unreasonable barrier to the connection of customer equipment.[55] Bell then filed new tariffs and the lengthy review process began again. The Commission has still not resolved this matter, though the tariffs have gone into effect. Delay has obviously worked to the carriers' benefit.[56]

The Commission has also delayed taking affirmative action to assist customers in the exercise of their right to connect personally owned equipment. The Chief Engineer's report on that subject (recommending a program for customer-interconnection) was considered by the Commission at the December 13 meeting. The majority, obviously sympathetic to AT&T's interests, temporized, assuring those of us concerned about further delay that the Chief Engineer's proposals would receive consideration within thirty days. Four months later, when the Commission issued a further notice, no action had been taken, and it seems clear that final resolution of this question will take several more years. . . .

The Commissioners' deliberations in this proceeding illustrate the problems inherent in FCC policy formulation. The Commission lacks data, makes no independent analysis, relies heavily on information provided by interested parties, considers broad questions piecemeal, defers to industry interests, postpones difficult decisions, hopes for compromises that the agency can ratify, and fails to anticipate major problems before they arise. Had the FCC been more prescient, it might have been prepared to handle the massive "hotelvision" problem that presented itself on December 13. Instead, the Commission simply drifted.

---

[55] Carterfone, 13 F.C.C.2d 420 (1968).

[56] The FCC can reject a carrier's tariff as unlawful (47 C.F.R. § 61.69 (1972)) or take no action and let the tariff go into effect. In between these extremes there are two other possibilities. First, the tariff can be suspended for up to ninety days and a hearing on its lawfulness ordered. The implementation of the tariff is thus merely delayed ninety days since there is almost no possibility that the Commission can complete hearings in that period. Second, the Commission can require carriers to ask permission to file additional tariff changes which could affect existing proceedings that have been underway for a long period of time. This permission may be withheld if the tariff filing would disrupt the Commission's deliberations. A.T.&T., 33 F.C.C.2d 522, *aff'd*, 36 F.C.C.2d 484 (1972). My own view is that the Commission has the authority to suspend tariffs for as long as is necessary to litigate major issues raised by them. A.T.&T., 37 F.C.C.2d 754, 761 (1972). On rare occasions a carrier will "voluntarily" postpone a tariff at the Commission's request. Usually, however, a new carrier tariff goes into effect ninety days after the carrier scheduled it to become effective.

The Cable Television Agenda

Cable television, a new industry, could have an impact upon the American people rivaling that of the telephone or the automobile. The Commission, however, very solicitous of the interests of the commercial broadcasting industry, and hence, of that industry's fear of cable television, has for years been antagonistic toward Cable. Such bureaucratic intransigence cannot last forever—especially in view of the broadcast industry's rush to buy cable systems. In February 1972, the Commission "opened up" the cable industry by promulgating a set of complex rules which, while allowing cable to begin operating on a national scale, nevertheless prevented the industry from fully developing. . . .

Television Station License Renewals

❖   ❖   ❖   ❖   ❖

On December 13, after a seemingly routine investigation had uncovered a multitude of violations, the FCC designated the renewal application of WHBI, a medium-size operation, for hearing on fifteen issues. Thus another blow was struck on behalf of what a former Commission General Counsel calls the "three outhouses policy of broadcast regulation—any broadcaster with three outhouses or fewer will be far more likely to bear the full brunt of Commission regulatory fervor than his larger broadcast colleagues.

It is ironically in the case-by-case and unsystematic atmosphere of the Complaints and Compliance Agenda that the Commissioners engage in their most sensitive and best known form of regulation, *i.e.*, regulation of programming content. It is therefore at the end of a grueling day that the Commissioners are confronted with questions requiring the most difficult balancing of competing interests. The FCC's regulation of programming content has long been of greatest concern to broadcast licensees. While the broadcaster communicates the same ideas as publishers or private speakers, he finds himself clothed in a different set of First Amendment obligations. He alone must deal with the rights of listeners and speakers who have no financial or corporate interest in his venture.

❖   ❖   ❖   ❖   ❖

Several conclusions emerge.

First, it seems evident that the FCC deals each week with an incredibly broad range of communications matters. On December 13, the FCC considered everything from personnel decisions to significant issues of international consequence. The Commission delved into areas surely beyond its expertise and into issues simply beyond its ken.

Second, as the Hearing Agenda reveals, the Commission, burdened with so much work and having so few resources, takes years to resolve important cases.

Third, as both the Cable and Aural Agendas illustrate, the FCC is manipulated daily by the industries it is supposed to regulate and by its own staff. As a result the Commissioners often make precedents which return to haunt them.

Fourth, if the FCC no longer approves of its own rules and precedents, it simply ignores them—either by waiving them to death or otherwise evading them. In short, the concept of principled decision-making does not exist at the FCC.

Fifth, the FCC not only disdains its own administrative principles, but it also ignores those established by the judiciary. Thus, on December 13 the FCC simply turned its back on numerous decisions construing the National Environmental Policy Act and relied on a construction of a recent case involving programming "format changes" not justified by the language of that case.

Sixth, as the General and Common Carrier Agendas show especially well, the Commissioners often decide cases they do not understand.

Finally, the Commission has not developed rational communications policies for governing its day-to-day decisions.

Perhaps it is easier to understand the Commission's sloppy work, its serious gaffs, when one sees an individual decision in the context of the burdensome "day in the life" on which it was voted. Yet much of the burden is of the Commission's own making. It is neither necessary nor advisable to divide up the FCC's workload between a "Broadcasting Commission" and a "Communications Common Carrier Commission." First semester business school principles would suggest that the Commission should formulate *some* statements of national communication policy for the benefit of itself, its staff, the business community, the Congress, the press, and the public. Having done this, it should prepare precise delegation orders to its staff, allow the staff to handle individual cases as they come up, and create a management information reporting system whereby the Commission is able to follow the processing of cases, modifying policy and delegation orders as warranted.

Another purpose of this piece is to offer the public some information concerning the operation of one of its administrative agencies, one which has struggled to keep its activities secret. The FCC is a *public* agency, receiving public funds for the purpose of regulating, "in the public interest," communications industries whose services are crucial to the continued vitality of a democratic society. Ironically, though the agency keeps the public in the dark, the communications interests learn all the details of Commission actions through information services provided by lawyers, lobbyists, and the trade press.

Neither the Commission majority nor its staff is troubled by the agency's treatment of the public. Whether because they adhere to notions of "laissez faire" economics or because they sympathize with communications industry interests, a majority of the staff at the FCC exploit the lack of public representation day after day.

Stephen Breyer (1938–   ) and
Paul W. MacAvoy (1934–   )

ENERGY REGULATION BY THE FEDERAL POWER COMMISSION*

> *This careful attempt, by skeptics, to appraise the results of FPC regulation finds scant benefits for the public. It is a good example of the post-1960 efforts to find regulation's real effects.*

✻   ✻   ✻   ✻   ✻

MAJOR EFFORTS

The commission's major efforts went into regulating the profits and prices of natural gas pipeline companies, setting the field price of natural gas, and promoting coordinated planning among firms engaged in interstate electric power transmission. On the average, 25 percent of the FPC's annual budget had to do with pipelines, and about 20 percent had to do with gas producers. The share of FPC budget allotted to electric power planning was relatively small. The activity, nevertheless, was important, for it was the commission's most serious and sustained effort to foster increased production efficiency. . . .

RESULTS

From the account given of the commission's work in each of the stipulated areas, it is possible to show approximately the total direct expense of regulation during a typical year in the late 1960s. Table 1 sets forth a single

---

* Stephen Breyer and Paul W. MacAvoy, *Energy Regulation by the Federal Power Commission.* © 1974 by The Brookings Institution, Washington, D.C., excerpted from pp. 4, 3–15, 122–23 and 132–34. Breyer teaches at Harvard Law School and was legal assistant to the Antitrust Division chief during 1965–67. MacAvoy has analysed regulation from many angles, with books on natural gas and railroad regulation (both concluding that regulation has been superfluous and/or harmful). He has also done a major study of breeder reactors and is the editor of the *Bell Journal of Economics and Management Science.*

TABLE 1

Estimated Expenses for FPC Regulation during a Typical Year in the 1960s (millions of dollars)

Activity	Federal Power Commission	Expenditures Companies		Combined	Benefits from Regulation for Consumers	
		Estimate	Range		Direct	Indirect or Long-Term Benefits
Gas pipeline price and systems regulation	3.5	2.5	2.0 to 3.0	6.0	1–10	Insignificant
Gas field price regulation	3.1	18.0*	18.0 to 76.0	21.1	Negative	Negative
Electric power						
Price regulation	1.6	1.6	0.2 to 3.1	3.2 ⎫	Insignificant	Insignificant
Systems evaluation	1.3	1.9	1.4 to 2.4	3.2 ⎬		
General FPC administration	1.1	—	—	1.1		
Total	10.6	24.0	21.6 to 84.5	34.6		

* Area rate proceedings only; excludes certification expenses and individual price cases.

Sources: Col. 1 derived from data in *The Budget of the United States Government—Appendix*, various issues; cols. 2 and 3 estimated on the basis of information discussed in the text.

column for FPC expenditures, derived from budget information. Two columns are offered for company expenditures. One lists a "most probable" figure in each category of activity; the other shows the range within which the precise amount could fall. Some record-keeping and reporting expenses are routinely imposed on the companies by FPC regulations. Other administrative expenses are "initiated" by the companies on the supposition that the decisions obtained thereby may benefit them. Both forms of company expense count as costs of regulation in Table 1. . . .

The combined agency and private expenditures set the minimum value of the benefits that regulatory activities must "buy" if the game is to be worth the price of admission. From the public's standpoint, regulation is not worthwhile unless it produces benefits greater than the total regulatory expense. . . .

Unfortunately the reader *cannot* take the utility of the Federal Power Commission for granted or assume that the remaining chapters merely cover technicalities and fine points. On the contrary, economic analysis reveals that in the late 1960s, with the commission operating at full steam, results were dismal: prices collected by the pipeline companies were not perceptibly lower than they would have been without regulation; setting field prices for natural gas did the residential consumer more harm than good by affecting the market so as inadvertently to bring on a gas shortage; and with federally regulated sales constituting only a minor portion of electricity sales, manifold opportunities to shift costs tended to render federal pricing ineffective. Commission planning efforts faltered. . . .

Three conclusions emerge from this study. First, commission activity benefited the consumer very little if at all. The administrative costs of operating the commission, including the costs to litigants, ranged between $31 million and $95 million per year and probably averaged approximately $35 million. Although this expenditure is small when compared with gas and electricity revenues, it did not buy much. Measures of the effectiveness of gas pipeline price regulation indicate that pipeline prices were not lower than they would have been without regulation. Gas producer price regulation, which accounted for the largest portion of the administrative expense attributable to commission operation, caused more harm than good. Ceiling prices at the wellhead were set too low, creating a reserve shortage and a production shortage. In all probability, the gas shortage hurt residential consumers more than lower prices helped them. Efforts to plan for increased efficiency in electricity production achieved a few minor successes but did not gain for the consumer the considerable benefits that increased coordination might have provided. The full array of these calculations is shown in Table 1. Perhaps the commission's secondary activities—gathering statistics, reviewing construction plans, providing a forum for complaints—justified the administrative expenses shown there. But certainly FPC regulation did not achieve direct gains to consumers.

Second, the study adds support to the growing suspicion that regulation by commission is at best a clumsy tool for achieving economic goals. In each instance, the FPC responded slowly and inefficiently to changing conditions. . . .

Third, the study shows the serious risks that flow from an agency's single-minded pursuit of lower prices. . . .

STEPS TOWARD REFORM

The behavior of the Federal Power Commission indicates the immediate desirability of three specific changes in regulatory policy. First, efforts to regulate the prices charged by natural gas producers should be abandoned. Deregulation in all likelihood would end the gas shortage, while competition among producers probably would keep prices near market-clearing levels. Competition prices would be higher than recent ceiling prices, by several cents per Mcf. The government should consider changes in tax policy, such as abolition of the depletion allowance, rather than rely upon regulatory policy to capture any inordinately high producer rents that might follow from the price increases.

Second, the commission should consider relaxing, rather than tightening, its supervision of pipeline prices and profits. Our findings suggest that the pipelines face a certain amount of competition in many of their regulated markets. Such competition limits the extent to which they can raise prices above costs. That fact, together with the near impossibility of regulating prices in such a way as to eliminate monopoly profit, makes it most unlikely that regulation provides benefits worth its administrative cost. The commission should consider abandoning the cost-of-service price setting method and instead investigate the extent to which various pipeline markets are competitive. Where competition exists—where there are more than two gas pipelines and there are close substitute sources of energy—it could de-regulate. Where effective competition does not exist, it could set prices based upon costs and prices in the more competitive markets. Such a "comparative" price-setting technique, though approximate, is likely to be as effective as present rate-setting methods and to require less extensive supervision. The commission should begin to explore the details of such an alternative.

Third, energy policy planners, who are now groping with the problems posed by the need for economy, reliability, and environmental protection, ought not to look to traditional regulation for solutions. The need for coordination in planning and operating electricity systems is great. Electric power should be provided through unified systems that each serve several states and include several companies. Yet, the Federal Power Commission's history suggests that it cannot be relied upon to bring about any major change in industry structure, and chapter 4 suggests that the reasons lie in the nature of the regulatory process itself. Policymakers should begin to study the desirability of injecting the government more directly into the planning process. Such governmental involvement might take a variety of forms, ranging from the creation of special task forces with power to order the building of particular lines and plants to the creation of industry/ government regional power authorities with direct planning and operating responsibilities. Our study does not indicate to what extent such systems are preferable to the status quo; it indicates only that the status quo, and similar forms of regulation, will not solve the coordination problem. Thus policymakers must begin the study of very different institutional alternatives.

These three changes do not constitute a detailed program. Our basic objective here has been to assess the effectiveness of past commission action. That assessment indicates that it is expecting too much to ask a commission to undertake profit regulation or complex planning. As A. E. Kahn notes in *The Economics of Regulation,* some critics of the regulatory agencies suggests that "the present institution embodies the worst of both possible worlds—monopoly without effective control, private enterprise without effective incentive or stimulus, governmental supervision without the possibility of effective initiative in the public interest." The performance of the FPC adds support to this view.

Leonard W. Weiss (1925–   )

AN EVALUATION OF ANTITRUST IN THE ELECTRIC POWER INDUSTRY*

Can bulk electric power be converted—at least in part—to an effectively competitive industry? Weiss maintains that it can and should, if the rigidities which regulation now embodies could be relaxed. The conditions and the needed policy changes are fairly complex, but their main features are given here.

Electric power is often pictured as a "natural monopoly." Yet some competition exists in the industry today, and the possibility of more competition

* Leonard W. Weiss, "An Evaluation of Antitrust in the Electric Power Industry," Chapter 5 in A. Phillips, *Competition and the Regulation of Industry* © 1975 by The

might well be enhanced if the structure of the industry were changed. In recent years, the Antitrust Division of the Department of Justice has adopted an active policy toward the industry. This chapter evaluates the possibilities both for more competition and for various types of antitrust action.

THE POTENTIAL ROLE OF COMPETITION

The electric power industry is conventionally subdivided into generation, transmission, and distribution components. Generation accounts for about 53 percent of the total costs of the industry, transmission about 12 percent, and distribution about 35 percent. The possibilities for competition vary among the three sectors.

Generation

Most important regions could support enough generating plants to permit extensive competition if the plants were under separate ownership and had equal access to transmission and distribution. The physical limits on the size of the market are set by transmission costs, which vary approximately in proportion to distance and inversely with the square of transmission voltages. As the power load has grown, extra-high-voltage transmission (currently 230 to 765 kilovolts) has become profitable, thus greatly reducing the impediment to long-distance transmission. One result has been such spectacular developments as the 850-mile, 750-kilovolt Pacific Northwest–Pacific Southwest intertie, connecting the Columbia River with Los Angeles, and the 600-mile, 500-kilovolt line running from the Four Corners site in New Mexico to Los Angeles. In the more populous parts of the country, the possibility of high-voltage networks makes it technologically feasible for plants anywhere in a wide region to supply any consuming center connected with the network, though costs will still vary with the supplier's location. Much of the new capacity intended to supply the largest load centers is, in fact, being constructed at points more than 100 miles away in order to use local fuel supplies and to reduce air pollution in the more congested areas.

Table 1 gives estimates of concentration among bulk-power producers within 100 or 200 miles of ten of the thirteen largest load centers.[1] Although there are at least two bulk-power producers within 100 miles, and several

Brookings Institution. A tireless and perceptive researcher, Weiss has treated a wide range of industrial and policy issues. His textbooks are also well known. During 1969–70 he was Special Economic Assistant to the Assistant Attorney General for Antitrust, U.S. Department of Justice.

[1] Seattle-Tacoma, Portland, Oregon, and Knoxville–Oak Ridge are excluded because the predominance of federal power in those areas makes concentration measures unrepresentative.

TABLE 1

Estimated Concentration in Electric Generating Capacity
within 100 and 200 Miles of Ten Major Load Centers, 1968[a]

	Within 100 Miles			Within 200 Miles		
Load Center	Number of Firms with Greater Than 100-Megawatt Capacity	Share of Largest Firm (Percent)	Share of Four Largest Firms (Percent)	Number of Firms with Greater Than 100-Megawatt Capacity	Share of Largest Firm (Percent)	Share of Four Largest Firms (Percent)
New York	12	29	75	18	21	57
Chicago	7	61	93	17	43	67
Los Angeles	6	67	97	8	55	93
San Francisco	2	97	100	8	76	89
Detroit[b]	8	48	90	13	30	75
Philadelphia	9	29	79	19	21	57
Houston	2	79	100	7	44	81
St. Louis	5	52	94	15	24	59
Washington	8	38	79	11	16	57
Boston	6	26	79	14	32	65

[a] All members of a holding company are treated as a single firm, but members of pools are treated as separate firms. Where data are available, joint ventures are allocated among owners within the specific market in the proportions reported; on an equal-shares basis otherwise. The portion of joint ventures within a market owned by firms otherwise outside the market is considered a single firm. All federal capacity and individual municipals in a market are also treated as owned by a single firm.

[b] Includes Hydro-Electric Power Commission of Ontario.

Sources: For firms that operate entirely within the market, specified total capacity is from Federal Power Commission, *Statistics of Privately Owned Electric Utilities in the United States, 1968: Classes A and B Companies* (1969), and FPC, *Statistics of Publicly Owned Electric Utilities in the United States* (1969). Where only part of a firm's capacity is within the market only the capacities reported in FPC, *Steam-Electric Plant Construction Cost and Annual Production Expenses, Twenty-First Annual Supplement—1968* (1969), and FPC, *Hydroelectric Plant Construction Cost and Annual Production Expenses, Twelfth Annual Supplement, 1968* (1970), are included. Ontario capacities are from Hydro-Electric Power Commission of Ontario, *Annual Report, 1968.*

within 200 miles, of each of these cities, the markets are highly concentrated. Their oligopolistic character is reinforced by the present regulatory blockade to entry by large, private bulk-power producers.

Some features of bulk-power transactions, however, tend to make tacit collusion difficult. Sales among bulk-power producers or to distribution utilities or large industrial users (that is, customers that can receive power at high voltage) are often for large blocks of power over long periods of time, and the transactions are very diverse in character. They include long-term sales of blocks of capacity from particular units; long-term sales of blocks of firm power from the supplying system as a whole; sales of interruptible energy; spot sales of "economy" energy arising from the allocation of a region's load among units on the basis of short-run marginal costs; exchanges of "diversity" power to take advantage of different peaks; and sales or exchanges of emergency assistance, with varying limits on the seller's commitments. Marginal costs vary among the types of transactions, among producers for any given type of transaction, and even within a firm according to the size, timing, and duration of the transaction. Since these sales are large (some in the hundreds of megawatts) and individually negotiated, substantial price competition seems possible in many of the load centers shown in Table 1, where regulatory and ownership conditions permit.

In practice, competition among generating companies is impeded by the ownership of transmission and distribution systems by individual generating firms. Transactions involving "wheeling" do occur, but they are voluntary and of minor importance at present.[2] If the owners of transmission lines or systems were treated as common carriers, the generating firms of a region could compete for the loads of independent distribution systems and, conceivably, large industrial users throughout the region. Where generation costs and environmental considerations are similar throughout a region, plants would still tend to supply neighboring load centers, but generating companies would have only limited local monopoly because of potential competition from more distant plants whose costs would exceed theirs by only the extra transmission expense. . . .

Other Effects of Competition

Increased competition would have a mixed effect on the extent of rate discrimination. More competition for industrial load would presumably lead to lower industrial rates relative to residential rates; this could mean higher, lower, or unchanged residential rates, depending on whether long-run marginal generation and transmission costs are respectively increasing, decreasing, or constant. If residential rates were limited by regulation, the Averch-Johnson argument would imply higher residential rates as industrial demand became more elastic. However, if, as Moore suggests residential rates are set at approximately profit-maximizing levels already, any further Averch-Johnson effect would be nil. In any event, since competition for large industrial load is already intense, further reductions in industrial rates relative to residential rates would be limited. The major effect of pro-competitive policy on discrimination is thus likely to be simply to preserve the opportunities for competition that already exist.

---

[2] Wheeling refers to transmission by one firm of energy generated by another firm and delivered to a third party—that is, the generating company inputs energy into the transmission system of the intermediate utility, which delivers the same amount of energy to the third firm. The generating company is paid by the customer for the power, and the intermediate firm receives a wheeling charge for the use of its transmission lines. Wheeling differs from a sale of power to and resale by the intermediate firm in that it is the generating company that controls the price. Although the FPC requires voluntary wheeling agreements to be filed with it, it has never regulated wheeling charges. In 1968, privately owned utilities generated 1,022 billion kilowatt-hours, sold 175 billion for resale, and wheeled 33 billion (*Statistics of Privately Owned Utilities, 1968*, p. XLIII).

Intermodal competition would lead to discrimination in favor of uses of electricity that compete closely with gas. While such discrimination at the residential level could cause Averch-Johnson rate increases on the inelastic elements of demand, the main effects of intermodal competition would be to make large segments of residential demand more elastic, thus reducing the opportunity to discriminate between industrial and residential customers, and to make discrimination between gas and electric customers impossible.

Increased competition for the load of distribution utilities might result in some uneconomic geographic rate differences, but the main effect would be to reduce residential rates generally.

There could be conflict between the effects of increased competition and the goals of environmental protection. Intermodal competition and competition for industrial load encourage the increased use of energy, while some environmentalists have proposed flat or even inverted rate structures to discourage it. There would be no conflict between flat or inverted rates and competition among generation companies for the loads of distribution utilities, however, and a system of effluent charges would be fully consistent with all forms of competition in the power industry. The shift of generating facilities away from densely populated areas for environmental reasons would, in fact, increase the possibilities for competition.

If the separation of generation and distribution functions caused widespread bilateral monopoly, the result could conceivably be wholesale rates above the internal marginal generating and transmission costs of an integrated company, with higher retail rates as the ultimate effect.[3] A competitive wholesale market would prevent such a development. For vertical disintegration to be unequivocally beneficial to consumers, it should be accompanied by free access to interconnection and wheeling and by the absence of mergers that greatly increase regional concentration.

The classic concern about "cream skimming" is given little attention today in the electric power industry, but it might well become a problem if regionwide competition for industrial and retail utilities' loads should develop. It could be argued that the capture of large industrial loads by more distant bulk-power suppliers would result in high costs and hence higher residential rates in the service area of the original supplier. But, because of the transmission costs involved, such a result is likely only where the distant utility has a large cost advantage. In that case, the high-cost utility could reduce costs by buying power to supply its own load, an option that would be available to it in a competitive market. If generation and distribution utilities were separate, the high-cost generating company would also be forced into some such adjustment. Even with no vertical divestiture, the

<hr>

[3] See Fritz Machlup and Martha Taber, "Bilateral Monopoly, Successive Monopoly, and Vertical Integration," *Economica*, U.S. (May 1960), pp. 101–19.

generator would still be under pressure to adjust because of the threatened loss of bulk-power customers and the conceivable loss of retail business caused by the formation of new municipals. Cream skimming would therefore seem to be a minor problem at worst, and might even have beneficial effects in encouraging vertical disintegration and a more rational geographic rate pattern.

Summary

The question posed at the beginning of this section—what would be the net effects of increased competition?—can now be tentatively answered. The economies of gas and electric combination are probably small. Those of vertical integration have not been investigated thoroughly but are also likely to be small. Any net losses from increased competition due to the advantages won by municipals and REA cooperatives, to discrimination, successive monopoly, or cream skimming are problematical. The net effects of these changes might, in fact, be socially useful in and of themselves. The main concern about the effect of competition on the power industry's performance must thus be the conventional one—the industry's ability to attain economies of scale. The crucial question is whether pools or contracts among independent firms can achieve such economies as efficiently as the multiunit firm. Experience with pooling or bilateral contracting where there is extensive high-voltage interconnection among independent firms has been too brief and incomplete, however, to warrant a final assessment at present of the desirability of large-scale horizontal mergers. . . .

AN EVALUATION OF COMPETITIVE POLICY ALTERNATIVES

Given the costs and consequences of increased competition explored above, and the implications of various antitrust positions toward the industry, what ought public policy toward the electric power industry to be?

Maximum Competition

Maximum competition consistent with low costs, though possibly an unattainable ideal, would require a restructuring of the power industry to include: (1) the separation of generation-transmission companies from distribution companies; (2) the dissolution of combination utilities; (3) the elimination of public and private territorial restrictions on sales to distributors or large industrial customers; (4) a general requirement of interconnection and wheeling at reasonable charges; (5) the elimination of preferential access to federal power and preferential tax and capital-cost treatment for municipals and cooperatives; (6) the elimination of legal restrictions on entry into bulk power; and (7) the limitation of horizontal

mergers among generation-transmission companies to cases where the
partners are too small to negotiate effectively with other bulk-power producers of a region. The last of these stipulations is the least certain. As
more information accumulates, large-scale mergers may be needed to
attain reasonable economies of scale. On the other hand, in a more competitive setting bilateral contracts by unaffiliated firms or less restrictive
pooling agreements may offer the same economies as either large single-
owner systems or closely coordinated pools.

Modified Competition

Such a thorough restructuring of the industry may not be practically
or politically possible in the foreseeable future. A more limited set of policy goals may be more nearly attainable [and] would involve (1) the elimination of private and public territorial restrictions on sales for resale, and
possibly private restrictions on sales to large industrial customers, as well;
(2) a general requirement of interconnection and wheeling; (3) control
of horizontal and vertical mergers; and (4) at least some divestiture of
gas properties in connection with further mergers. These changes would
effect further reduction in vertical integration because of the increased
access of municipals and cooperatives to power at competitive prices and
the increased competitive pressure on small utilities that are presently
integrated. If such policies resulted in a large-scale expansion of municipals, political circumstances might allow the elimination of some of their
special advantages, as well. A more general dissolution of combination
utilities, under the structures of the Sherman Act, may also be within the
range of possibility; the country has once, after all, accepted such a change
for a large part of the industry.

Under these second-best policies, the public could still benefit from
increased wholesale competition and, to the extent that combination utilities could be dissolved, intermodal competition. The increase in wholesale
competition might be substantial or minor, depending on whether economies of scale are attainable short of large-scale merger, or, even better,
short of closely coordinated pooling. Since complete elimination of the
special advantages of municipals and cooperatives seems unlikely, industry reorganization might lead to some uneconomic expansion by such
utilities, and probably would bring about a redistribution in favor of their
customers. On the other hand, municipals and cooperatives would probably be less prone to invest in suboptimal capacity than they are now. . . .

The Role of Regulation

Even with the most thorough reorganization of the industry, regulation
would still have a role. Transmission would continue to be a monopoly,

so the requirement of interconnection and wheeling and the regulation of wheeling charges would be essential. The determination of reasonable wheeling charges could be a difficult problem because the decreasing costs of transmission result in marginal costs that are below average costs. How effective regulation of these charges would be is not certain, but it is to be hoped that the FPC could at least prevent charges that were designed to be prohibitive.

Retail distribution would also remain monopolistic, except perhaps for large industrial loads and under intermodal competition, so conventional state regulation of retail rates would still be in order. Such regulation might well be more effective than it is now because pure distribution utilities would be less complex and thus easier to regulate, and because intermodal competition and competition for industrial load would reinforce regulatory controls in important areas.

If territorial and wheeling restrictions were removed, vertical integration disbanded, and substantial numbers of firms maintained at the generation level, much of the need for regulation at wholesale would be obviated. Since this falls under FPC jurisdiction, a national policy of partial deregulation would seem appropriate. Controls over interconnections and wheeling charges would still be necessary, and the industry would still be subject to public actions with respect to environmental matters, but entry and rate questions could be left to the marketplace. If regulation were retained (as might happen if large mergers are permitted), the increased competition should serve to reinforce rather than weaken its impact.

The continuation of widespread integration between retail and generation utilities seems likely under present policies. If so, competition will continue to have only a peripheral effect on a large part of bulk-power supply, and widespread regulation at both retail and wholesale levels will still be necessary. Even under those conditions, however, a procompetitive policy would probably help to offset some of the manifest imperfections in regulation.

John W. Wilson (1943–   )

COMPETITION AND REGULATION
IN NATURAL GAS*

> *Many experts (recall Breyer and MacAvoy) and oth-
> ers urge de-regulating natural gas production, because
> it has "effectively competitive" conditions. Wilson ar-
> gues, instead, that natural gas is highly monopolistic
> and needs tight public controls. How competitive
> would the industry be if it were de-regulated?*

I would like to thank the Chairman and Members of this Subcommittee for once again inviting me to appear before you to present testimony
on a most important national economic policy matter. . . .

CONCENTRATION

. . . Initially, it should be observed that when we address the "natural
gas producing industry" we are really discussing the "petroleum industry."
The dominant firms are the same, and these firms have fully integrated
gas and oil producing and marketing operations which can not be analyzed intelligently in isolation. As shown in Table 1, the top 14 natural
gas producers in 1970 were also among the top 15 oil and liquids producers and among the top 17 petroleum refiners. These 14 leading gas
producers were also among the 17 largest sellers of gasoline and other
refined petroleum products and among the 17 largest sellers of natural gas
to interstate pipelines.

Perhaps a better impression of actual concentration can be obtained
from Table 2. The four-firm and eight-firm ratios shown there are based
on an actual survey by the FPC of available uncommitted gas supplies as
of December 31, 1971, and June 30, 1972. These ratios are extremely high,
and they tend to be rather stable from one period to the other. . . .

Also, . . . concentration appears to be quite high even in a prospective
sense. Over 80 percent of the federal offshore leases acquired (weighted
by bonus dollars paid) in each of three recent lease sales were accounted

---

* John W. Wilson, "Competition and Regulation in Natural Gas," Testimony be-
fore the Senate Subcommittee on Antitrust and Monopoly, *Hearings on the Industrial
Reorganization Act,* June 27, 1973 (Washington, D.C.: U.S. Government Printing
Office), excerpted. Wilson is an expert on energy markets and policy; in 1973 he was
Chief of the Division of Economic Studies at the FPC.

TABLE 1
Rankings of Largest Firms in the Petroleum Industry (1970)

	Natural Gas Producers	Oil and Gas Liquids Producers	Petroleum Refining	U.S. Refined Product Sales	Natural Gas Sales to Interstate Pipelines
1.	Exxon	1	1	1	1
2.	Texaco	2	2	2	7
3.	Amoco	6	6	4	4
4.	Gulf	3	5	7	2
5.	Phillips	12	11	9	5
6.	Mobil	8	3	6	6
7.	Shell	4	7	3	3
8.	Atlantic-Richfield	7	8	8	8
9.	Sun	11	9	10	12
10.	Chevron	5	4	5	11
11.	Union Oil	9	10	11	9
12.	Getty	10	15	17	17
13.	Continental	13	14	14	10
14.	Cities Service	15	17	13	14

TABLE 2
Concentration of the Available New Gas Supplies as of 12/31/71 and 6/30/72* (percentage of reported uncommitted reserves controlled by 4 and 8 largest producers)†

	12/31/71		6/30/72	
Producing Area	Four Largest	Eight Largest	Four Largest	Eight Largest
Permian Basin	63.6%	86.4%	80.6%	94.2%
Hugoton Anadarko	76.6	94.5	62.6	83.3
Other Southwest	93.3	98.6	94.4	99.3
South Louisiana				
Onshore	96.9	99.6	92.3	98.4
Offshore (federal)	57.0	83.3	49.6	74.9
Offshore (state)	84.5	100.0	94.9	100.0
Texas Gulf Coast				
Onshore	89.4	96.7	84.4	92.4
Offshore (federal)	98.5	100.0	100.0	100.0
Offshore (state)	100.0	100.0	100.0	100.0
Rocky Mountain	63.4	82.9	70.4	86.0
Appalachian	99.6	100.0	100.0	100.0
Unclassified				
Michigan	100.0	100.0	—	—
California	95.4	100.0	94.3	100.0
Miscellaneous	87.7	99.9	98.0	100.0
Alaska‡	93.9	99.9	93.9	99.9
Total U.S.‡	51.4	75.9	51.0	73.9

  * Concentration ratios are based on individual company reserve reports. To the extent that two or more companies report pro rata ownership shares of jointly held leases for which there is a single operation, the concentration ratios tend to underestimate the actual degree of seller concentration.

  † Reports were obtained from 79 large producers. These producers provide most of the gas sold to interstate pipelines (e.g., in 1971 the top 22 supplied over 70 percent of all interstate gas). Nevertheless, to the extent that nonreporting small producers may have had significant volumes, the ratios reported here tend to slightly overstate actual market concentration.

  ‡ Does not include certain North Slope reserves reported in the aggregate for all companies by one producer.

for by the top eight bidders and their bidding partners. In all three sales combined, the top eight accounted for 70 percent of the successful bids. As shown below, these bidding partnerships generally become producing partnerships, and consequently future prospects, for our offshore areas at any rate, are for continued high levels of supply concentration.

JOINT VENTURES, INTERTIES, AND INTERLOCKS

There is substantial direct evidence of mutual interdependence between virtually all of the major firms in the petroleum industry. This interdependence includes joint ventures, interlocks, and institutional interties in the following general areas of activity:

1. Joint lease acquisition (bidding combines).
2. Banking interlocks (directorates and common stock ownership).
3. Joint ownership of pipelines and gathering systems.
4. Joint ownership and production from oil and gas leases.
5. International joint ventures.
6. Vertical relationships between the producing, transporting, processing, and marketing sectors of the industry.

Bidding Combines

In any given sale, it is obvious that when four firms such as the CATC group, each able to bid independently, combine to submit a single bid, three interested, potential bidders have been eliminated; i.e., the combination has restrained trade. This situation does not differ materially from one of explicit collusion in which four firms meet in advance of a given sale and decide who among them should bid (which three should refrain from bidding) for specific leases and, instead of competing among themselves, attempt to rotate the winning bids. The principal difference is that explicit collusion is illegal.[1]

The logic of this observation is unexceptionable, and though it was made some six years ago, the situation which it describes has grown substantially since then so that today bidding combines tend to dominate even the acquisition of federal offshore leases. Table 3 lists the major bidding combines which participated in federal offshore lease sales in 1970 and 1972. Because various majors belonged to two or more of these combines, the web of interdependence is far more pervasive than the membership of any single combine would suggest. . . .

My own view is that the offshore leasing program, as currently admin-

[1] Walter Mead, "The Competitive Significance of Joint Ventures," *Antitrust Bulletin*, Fall 1967, p. 839; quoted in the Federal Power Commission Staff's Reply Brief in Belco Petroleum Corporation, *et al.*, Docket No. CI73-293, et al., April 20, 1973.

TABLE 3

**Major Bidding Combines Which Participated in
Recent Federal Offshore Lease Sales**

1. Tenneco*, Texaco
2. Cities Service, Tenneco*, Continental
3. Atlantic Richfield, Cities Service*, Continental, Getty
4. Phillips, Skelly (Getty), Allied Chemical, American Petrofina
5. Getty, Placid, Superior
6. Superior, Placid, Hunt, Transocean*, Ashland
7. Superior, Chevron, Murphy, Pelto, General American
8. Chevron, Mobil, Pennzoil*
9. Chevron, Mesa, Burmah
10. Mobil, Gulf, Pennzoil*
11. Mobil, Gulf, Chevron
12. Ashland, Mesa, Pennzoil*
13. Mobil, Burmah, Mesa, Pennzoil*
14. General American, Burmah, CNG*
15. Burmah, General American
16. Amoco, CNG*, Shell, Transco*
17. Amoco, Union, Texas Eastern*
18. Amoco, Southern Natural*, Champlin
19. Texas Gas*, Union, Florida Gas*
20. Signal, La. Land, Amerada, Marathon, Texas Eastern*
21. Shell, Florida Gas*

* An affiliate of a major interstate gas pipeline company.

istered by the Interior Department, has become one of the most onerous anticompetitive cartelization devices at work in our domestic gas producing industry. Not only is it a vehicle for further joint ventures and the integration of intercorporate interests, it has also become an effective entry blockade for all but the very largest firms in the industry. As the president of an established oil company with annual revenues of over $100 million recently testified in an FPC hearing, it would now take a consortium of 15 or more firms like his to surmount the offshore entry barriers which have been erected under Interior's watchful eye. Consequently, his company and others like it have been effectively precluded from entering these producing areas except by obtaining limited farmouts of unwanted acreage from the dominant majors or perhaps by joining one of the established combines as a junior partner. Neither is likely to have much of a procompetitive effect, and that is most critical because our Federal domain contains a large portion of our nation's remaining oil and gas reserves.

*   *   *   *   *

Banking Interlocks

A listing of certain interlocking directorates in the petroleum industry by major banks, as of 1968, is provided in Table 4. This situation is a

TABLE 4

**Bank Director Interlocks between Major Firms
in the Petroleum Industry (1968)**

La. Land and Exploration Co. Belco Petroleum Corp. Texas Gulf Sulphur* Continental Oil Cities Service Co. Atlantic Richfield Columbia Gas System	Morgan Guaranty Trust Co.
Allied Chemical Monsanto Co. W. R. Grace Co. Standard Oil of N.J. Mobil Oil Sinclair Oil	First National City Bank
Standard Oil of N.J. Standard Oil of Ind.	Chase Manhattan
Diamond Alkali Texaco, Inc. Marathon Oil Standard Oil of Ohio* Consolidated Natural Gas	National City Bank (Cleveland)
General Crude Oil Co. Texas Gulf Sulphur Union Carbide W. R. Grace Co.	Manufacturers Hanover Trust
Amerada Petroleum Freeport Sulphur Co. Texaco, Inc. Cities Service Co. Texas Gas Transmission Co.	Chemical Bank

* The bank specified also owns a substantial equity interest in this oil company.

Source: *Commercial Banks and their Trust Activities,* Staff Report for the Subcommittee on Domestic Finance, Committee on Banking and Currency, House of Representatives, 90th Congress, 2d Session, July 8, 1968.

threat to effective competition among these petroleum companies not only because the interlocks create a commonality between their boards, but even more so because of the critical role of the financial community in providing the capital which will be needed to expand energy production to meet future needs. . . .

Joint Ownership of Oil Pipelines

Virtually all of the major integrated petroleum companies hold joint interest with others in the transportation network that moves crude oil and products from producing regions to refineries and markets. . . . Whereas early in this century Standard's control of the pipeline network gave it a distinct upper hand over all of its rivals, today's joint venture arrangements, which dominate the oil pipeline industry, draw ostensibly independent firms together into the common pursuit of a mutual purpose. Moreover, these jointly owned transportation links between producing, refining, and marketing operations (about three fourths of all crude and one fourth of refined products move through pipelines) require that producing and processing operations of the various partners be coordinated with each other so that the whole vertically integrated system functions smoothly. . . .

Joint Production

Only 4 of the 16 largest majors with interests in Federal offshore producing leases own 50 percent or more of their leases independently. Conversely, 10 of the 16 own 80 percent or more of their offshore properties

TABLE 5
Four Joint Ventures in the Oil Pipeline Industry

Pipeline Company	Co-Owners and Percent Held by Each	
Dixie Pipeline Co.	Amoco	12.1
(Assets—$ 46.4 million)	Atlantic-Richfield	7.4
	Cities Service	5.0
	Continental	4.1
	Exxon	11.1
	Mobil	5.0
	Phillips	14.5
	Shell	5.5
	Texaco	5.0
	Gulf	18.2
	Transco	3.6
	Allied Chemical	8.6
Laurel Pipeline Co.	Gulf	49.1
(Assets—$ 35.9 million)	Texaco	33.9
	Sohio	17.0
Colonial Pipeline Co.	Amoco	14.3
(Assets—$480.2 million)	Atlantic-Richfield	1.6
	Cities Service	14.0
	Continental	7.5
	Phillips	7.1
	Texaco	14.3
	Gulf	16.8
	Sohio	9.0
	Mobil	11.5
	Union Oil	4.0
Plantation Pipeline Co.	Exxon	48.8
(Assets—$176.1 million)	Shell	24.0
	Refiners Oil Corp.	27.1

TABLE 6

Joint Production in the Permian Basin (Texas) (matrix shows number of joint unitization agreements)

	1 Amerada	2 Atlantic	3 Cities	4 Continental	5 Getty	6 Gulf	7 Marathon	8 Mobil	9 Phillips	10 Shell	11 Amoco	12 Exxon	13 Sohio	14 Sun	15 Texaco	16 Union
Amerada 1																
Atlantic 2	16															
Cities 3	14	32														
Continental 4	8	18	15													
Getty (Skelly) 5	17	32	19	9												
Gulf 6	5	3	12	8	17											
Marathon 7	7	10	6	4	8	6										
Mobil 8	9	25	14	10	20	12	8									
Phillips 9	13	33	20	15	20	12	6	13								
Shell 10	9	28	15	11	17	11	8	10	16							
Stand. of Ind. (Amoco) 11	18	36	30	20	29	21	9	24	29	25						
Stand. of N.J. (Exxon) 12	12	29	14	13	18	20	6	18	17	15	29					
Stand. of Ohio (Sohio) 13	4	10	4	6	6	5	2	6	6	2	8	8				
Sun 14	12	29	20	13	23	15	5	14	21	15	33	17	6			
Texaco 15	12	42	23	19	25	23	8	19	22	18	30	22	10	23		
Union 16	5	18	12	5	13	13	4	13	11	5	21	12	7	17	11	

jointly with each other. In addition, very few companies outside of the top 16 have any independent holdings at all. In addition to the top 16, 23 medium- to large-size producers were surveyed. Of these, only 2 held as much as 25 percent of their leases independently and 17 had no independently owned leases at all. . . .

In addition to these studies of the ownership of Federal offshore producing leases and State of Louisiana leases, a study has also been made of producing units in the Permian Basin in West Texas. Again, what emerges is a picture of extensive intercorporate interties. As shown in the following matrix, Table 6, literally every one of the sixteen large major oil companies studied had a significant number of joint producing arrangements with every other major. . . .

International Joint Ventures

In addition to the interrelated domestic operations of the major American petroleum companies, we should not lose sight of the fact that it is largely these same corporate entities or their affiliates which make up the international oil cartel. . . .

Other Interties

The evidence presented above was obtained entirely from public sources. In addition, American Petroleum Institute records indicate that there are substantial crude oil exchange agreements among the majors, ranging from more than 50 percent of their total domestic liquid hydrocarbon production for some companies down to only a few percentage points for others. . . .

POLICY PROPOSALS

As shown above, market control in the petroleum industry, including the natural gas producing sector, is held by a closely knit consortium comprised of the large, fully integrated oil companies and their jointly interlocked affiliates. These firms, working in cooperation with each other, have the ability to control petroleum supplies and, in so doing, to maneuver for monopolistic market price levels.

Federal regulation of the field price of natural gas was supposedly designed to deal with this problem. Apparently, it is not working well. As in the case of fuel oil and gasoline, natural gas supplies are short and prices are rising rapidly. No one can deny that policy changes are needed. The prescription offered by the petroleum industry and its various spokesmen is for unrestrained "market freedom"—a situation wherein the industry (not the public) would be "free"; free, that is, to extract the maximum possible price that the market will bear. Unless capitulation to the monopoly power of private economic interests is now viewed as a national policy alternative, this prescription makes no sense. Certainly, from the consuming public's view, it cannot be described as a rational stratagem.

Clay T. Whitehead (1938–   )

COMPETITION IN TELECOMMUNICATIONS*

> *Whitehead assesses the extent of "natural monopoly" in the communications sector and how policy should treat the margin of competition.*

It is important to emphasize that up until about the 1940s common carrier communications services consisted exclusively of telephone and telegraph, both of which were characterized by natural monopoly features. But the advent of new technologies—new developments in radio communications, microwave transmissions, solid state circuitry, and so on —began to provide us new methods of communication. It became possible to send a message electronically from one point to another without having to go through the switched telephone network; and it became possible to use the telephone lines for a variety of new communications purposes. These new services, made possible by advances in electronics technology, do not have natural monopoly characteristics, and it became apparent that there was no need for all communications services and equipment to be provided by a single supplier such as the telephone company. . . .

We have traditionally viewed monopoly as an exception to the general rule of competitive free enterprise, and the Supreme Court and the Congress have repeatedly stressed the broad public interest benefits of anti-monopoly policies. Monopolistic industry structure has been sanctioned

---

* Clay T. Whitehead, Statement on "Competition in Telecommunications," before the Senate Subcommittee on Antitrust and Monopoly, *Hearings on the Industrial Reorganization Act,* July 9, 1974 (Washington, D.C.: U.S. Government Printing Office), excerpted. This is the Hart Subcommittee (recall the Blair reading above). As the young director of White House policy on telecommunications during 1969–74, Whitehead dealt with strong political forces and developed several new policy lines (especially on satellites, public television, and cable television). He is now at MIT.

historically only in key public services where necessary and where justi-fied by the presence of natural monopoly characteristics. In short, the burden has been on the monopolist to justify his monopoly status, and regulation has been directed at protecting customers and other businesses from the monopoly.

But a curious and perverse twist has occurred in the communications industry. The Communications Act vested the FCC with regulatory juris-diction over all interstate electronic communications. This was perfectly acceptable in 1934 when communications meant telegraph and switched telephone services, both of which were and are characterized by condi-tions that justify a monopolistic industry structure and, hence, extensive economic regulation. But with all communications services by statute under a regulatory umbrella, affirmative authorization is required before any new service can be offered—to a few desirous customers or to the general public—by a new entrant.

The FCC has thus been placed in the posture of "permitting competi-tion," a posture that is entirely antithetical to our basic traditions. The burden and the benefit of regulation have shifted: the would-be provider of a new communications service, rather than the monopolist, is now required to justify his existence, and the monopolist, rather than the would-be customer of that new service, receives the protection of the reg-ulatory machinery. . . .

What, then, should be the fundamental principles upon which our fu-ture communications policy should be based? I believe there are four basic principles that should apply:

1. *The public-utility monopoly in conventional telephone service is still appropriate today.* The natural monopoly conditions that originally dictated this industry structure remain unchanged, and no one suggests that basic local telephone service be provided on anything but a monop-oly basis. Indeed, thanks to the Bell System and to the regulatory policies of the past, the United States has universal, low-cost telephone service that is unparalleled throughout the world.

2. *The monopoly concept should not be extended to other communi-cations services.* As I have indicated, we have traditionally viewed mo-nopoly as the exception, not the rule, and unless the would-be monopolist or the public can demonstrate special public policy considerations that justify monopoly, it should not be permitted. Communications was once a homogeneous service that could properly be viewed as a public utility. But this is no longer the case. Most everyone wants or needs a telephone; but not everyone wants a private branch exchange, or access to data processing equipment, or a private line between two cities, or an auto-matic answering device, or a phone in his car, or any of the special capa-bilities which electronic technology can make available to particular users,

packaged to meet their particular needs. At present there does not appear to be any service other than the local public telephone service where monopoly rather than competition would best serve the public interest.

3. *Any new entrant should be free to offer any service except conventional public telephone service.* In the absence of a showing of need to protect the monopolist from competition, there is no public policy basis for prohibiting customers and suppliers from doing business with one another. Indeed, industry innovation to meet a wide variety of customer needs and interests will take place only if the customer is free to seek out whichever company offers him the service best suited to his needs and means.

4. *Any telephone customer should be allowed to buy and use any communications device over the telephone lines.* The natural monopoly features inherent in local switched telephone service relate to the installation of transmission lines and switching facilities; they are not present in the production and sale of terminal equipment. There are no technical or economic considerations which dictate that a consumer be prohibited from acquiring terminal equipment from whatever source he chooses to use with his telephone line to suit his particular needs. The consumer should pay for his access to the line and for the demands he places on the switching and transmission facilities of the telephone company. But what he does with the communications capability he pays for is his business— just as what he does with his water, his electricity, and his gas is his business.

*   *   *   *   *

The inescapable conclusion, Mr. Chairman, is that competition and monopoly must coexist in our communications industry. In such an environment, the major policy issues are: (1) which nonmonopoly services should the telephone companies be allowed to offer, and on what basis; and (2) what are the responsibilities of monopoly telephone companies in facilitating the use of their lines?

Donald C. Beelar (1903–   )

CABLES IN THE SKY AND THE STRUGGLE FOR THEIR CONTROL*

Utility markets often embrace both "natural monopoly" parts and competitive activities. A key instance is microwave transmission, which the Bell System has controlled since 1950. Since 1965, the gradual opening of the microwave market has involved small but ambitious entrants, strenuous Bell resistance, and landmark FCC decisions. The initial closure during 1948–50, as analysed by Beelar, is typical of utility moves into many other markets which have long-lasting effects.

The struggle for control of microwave which began more than twenty years ago was in every way as hard fought as that now involving satellites. And the similar potentialities of microwave and domestic satellites —each in its own time—indicate why. Microwave in the 1940s emerged as a competitive threat to the wire line and cable transmission modes; domestic satellites in the 1960s pose a new threat to both wire line and cable and microwave systems. Both developments in turn have raised broad policy issues, namely (a) monopoly or competition between common carriers, or between different modes of transmission; (b) private system competition; (c) captive or free enterprise manufacturing markets; (d) interconnection restraints and (e) the permissible common carrier rate base for the lower cost new communication mode.

These are the issues which, with respect to microwave, remain largely unresolved and which, as to domestic satellites, should be decided before authorization of any initial system. A consideration of these issues in the context of the domestic satellite technology may provide an opportunity to review and complete the unfinished business of microwave regulation. The microwave story, heretofore untold, is the subject of this article.

* Donald C. Beelar, "Cables in the Sky and the Struggle for Their Control," *Federal Communications Bar Journal,* January 1967, excerpted from pp. 26–33, and 40–41. Beelar is an attorney.

ROUND ONE: CHECKMATE IN MICROWAVE

The struggle for control of the new microwave industry in the late 1940s, as seen from the perspective of the 1960s, may be likened to a chess game. Not one between two players, but one in which multiple opponents were taken on by one master, AT&T. The contestants in that encounter were the leading electronic manufacturers and the communications carriers; the trophy at stake was the emerging television network market and the franchise for a nation-wide microwave system of unprecedented broad-band channel capacity, not necessarily a part of the wire line public telephone network.

The Contestants

1. *Philco* was the first in the field with an operational video relay system, applied for in the fall of 1944 and put into operation between Washington, D.C., and Philadelphia, Pennsylvania, in the spring of 1945. The inauguration of this system, as well as the events which forced it out of business three years later, is described later.

2. *Raytheon*'s was far and away the most ambitious and imaginative proposal, and it was the most active challenger throughout the 1944–1948 period. In early 1945, Raytheon announced its intention to construct and operate a transcontinental microwave relay system for television, broadcasting, aviation, weather, press, and other business uses. By 1947, it had license authorizations for a microwave system from Boston to New York to Chicago paralleling that of AT&T. A year later Raytheon withdrew from the scene.

3. *Western Union* placed a microwave system in operation between New York and Philadelphia in 1945. It had ideas about constructing a transcontinental microwave system and getting into the video network business. It got as far west as Pittsburgh, Pennsylvania, in the 1940s where it came to a 10-year halt. Western Union's dream of owning a transcontinental microwave system was not realized until the 1960s.

4. *General Electric* joined with *IBM* in obtaining experimental licenses in November, 1944, for a microwave system from Schenectady to New York to Philadelphia to Washington. Their proposal emphasized a system for the transmission of modern business machine data. This system was expressly restricted to experimentation.

5. *AT&T*, as of the end of World War II, was a wire-line and cable company and wire-line minded, but in June, 1944, it did obtain experimental licenses for a microwave system between New York and Boston which became operational November 11, 1947. AT&T proposed to use

microwave relay stations for television, facsimile, sound programs, and multiplex telephony, eventually over nationwide networks.

6. *DuMont*, one of the pioneers in television broadcasting, was the last entry in the contest for inter-city microwave relay facilities. Its proposal, a five-station relay system between New York and Washington, D.C., filed in June, 1947, was in a large measure a protest against what it considered excessively high AT&T rates for video transmission service ($5.15 per hour per station for 28 hours a week).

So much for the principal contestants and their proposals. The scene is now set for the play-by-play account of the microwave chess game which shaped the destiny of this new industry during its first decade.

Move One

In the beginning the wire line common carriers, AT&T and Western Union, were outnumbered 5 to 2. The opening gambit was deceptively innocent. In the FCC's landmark 1945 frequency allocation proceeding, which made 8 bands of frequencies available for microwave relay systems, AT&T took the position that it was undesirable for frequencies used by public relay telephone systems to be shared with other services. AT&T's request was initially rejected on the ground that all microwave assignments at that time were on an experimental basis. A bit later, however, the position sponsored by AT&T was adopted by the FCC and this became the cornerstone of the microwave regulatory structure. The effect of setting aside bands of microwave frequencies for use only by a "common carrier" operated, in fact, as a reservation of frequencies for the exclusive use of the Bell System. This in turn put the free enterprise sector of the infant microwave industry into a captive market situation.

Move Two

The second move further solidified control over the microwave market in the wire-line common carriers. When IBM and General Electric filed applications for a Schenectady-New York-Washington microwave system, Western Union protested on the ground that the experimental authorization should be limited to experimental purposes and precluded from handling any commercial operations. The FCC agreed and imposed a condition on these licenses expressly prohibiting any commercial use of the system, either as a common carrier or otherwise. The effect of this action was to strictly limit the five non-wire-line companies to experimental operations, in the strict sense of that term, and to make it impossible for these operations to ripen into any form of commercial service without further FCC authority. At this early stage of the contest, therefore, the battle lines appeared to be drawn between the established wire-line common carriers, AT&T and Western Union, and the would-be newcomers to the microwave field. In reality, as made apparent by subsequent events, the contest was one between AT&T and the rest of the field.

Interlude: The significance of the next move is highlighted by reference to intervening events in the market place. Philco's 6-station system between Washington and Philadelphia was dedicated at a banquet in the Statler Hotel in Washington on the night of Tuesday, April 16, 1945. On that occasion, the image and speech of then FCC Chairman Paul Porter and Dr. Karl Compton, President of MIT, were transmitted over the Philco microwave system from Washington to Philadelphia and there broadcast over TV station WPTZ, with excellent technical quality, it was reported. Chairman Porter observed that this event marked "a historic milestone in our progress towards a nation-wide system of television" and "this demonstration is a harbinger of exciting things to come." These remarks were indeed prophetic, except that Philco, an active pioneer in the microwave field, was soon to lose out as a contender for the TV video market. By 1947, the microwave capability for video program transmission, which required a very wide band carrier channel of four megacycles, or the equivalent of 1,000 voice transmissions, was confined to the northeast sector of the United States and the facilities of AT&T, Western Union, Raytheon, Philco, IBM, and General Electric.

Move Three

In 1948, AT&T revealed its intention to be the sole supplier of video network program service. It proceeded to challenge all comers, both in proceedings before the FCC and in the market place. On March 29, 1948, AT&T filed a video transmission tariff, to be effective May 1, 1948.* Western Union joined in the proceeding a day later by filing a similar tariff for program transmission service, also effective May 1, 1948, between New York and Philadelphia. These tariffs were formally challenged by the Television Broadcasters Association (TBA), which raised various issues, including the validity of the provision in AT&T's tariff precluding interconnection with the facilities of any other company. An investigation was ordered April 28, 1948.

While this hearing before the FCC was under way, AT&T administered a mortal blow to the Philco system. On September 9, 1948, AT&T refused to transmit an NBC-TV program from New York to Boston over its facilities which originated in Philadelphia and was carried over the Philco microwave system. On another occasion, AT&T refused to carry an NBC tele-

---

* The fact that AT&T's microwave station licenses were still experimental did not preclude it from launching a commercial service by a public tariff offering, in contrast to the FCC restraints imposed on G.E. and IBM. See "Move Two," supra.

cast of an Army football game from West Point to New York City which NBC proposed to transmit from New York City to Philadelphia via the Philco microwave system. Philco went to court to enjoin AT&T, but this proved unsuccessful. Thereafter Philco's vice president of engineering, in testimony before the FCC, announced Philco's withdrawal from the inter-city microwave relay service because of interconnection refusal. AT&T's victory over Philco showed AT&T's willingness to take on any and all would-be newcomers to the microwave market, and signaled the retreat or surrender of all the original contestants, except Western Union.

Move Four

Television broadcasters appeared unexpectedly as a late challenger to AT&T's position as the sole source of TV network service. In the late 1940s, many television broadcasters could not get video network channels from AT&T for network television programs, a serious handicap to a rapidly expanding TV industry. Accordingly, several television broadcasters undertook to construct microwave facilities to other cities where physical connection could be made with common carrier facilities. AT&T, however, had by tariff precluded the interconnection of private microwave systems with its own facilities. In its December 23, 1949, decision in the tariff investigation in Docket No. 8963, the FCC required AT&T, over its objection, to interconnect with TV broadcasters' private microwave facilities. Otherwise, it was pointed out, the Commission's grant of license to TV broadcasters for the operation of interim microwave video program transmission facilities would be rendered a nullity.

While the broadcasters had won the battle, it was AT&T which had nonetheless won the war. For previously, on February 20, 1948, the FCC had rather casually made a policy determination that frequencies for video network facilities would be only for service furnished by common carrier facilities, and that broadcasters operating interim private microwave stations would be required to abandon such systems whenever service became available from a common carrier, i.e. AT&T. Hence, while the broadcasters were accorded interim interconnection rights, the long term result was to give AT&T the green light to displace private microwave systems of broadcasters whenever it was ready, willing, and able to do so. This eliminated the threat to AT&T of the broadcasting sector. Thus, AT&T entered the 1950s with only one remaining opponent of those originally seeking entry into the microwave field 5 years earlier—Western Union.

Move Five and Checkmate

In the spring of 1950, hearings were commenced in Docket No. 9539 on Western Union's effort to require AT&T to interconnect with the former's microwave system between New York and Philadelphia. Previously, Western Union found itself in the middle between the TV broadcasters and AT&T on interconnection, and it was promised a separate proceeding on that issue. Two and one half years later AT&T emerged as the victor in this controversy in a split decision, the majority holding that Western Union had failed to make out a sufficient showing warranting compulsory interconnection on the facts of that case. The real significance of this decision was made apparent in the opening paragraph of the dissenting opinion of two Commssioners, Rosel H. Hyde, now Chairman of the FCC, and Frieda B. Hennock, which stated:

> The decision of the majority, while it states in its conclusions that "it is not intended to support any claim which the Bell System may have made to a monopoly in the field of intercity video transmission," effectively does grant such a monopoly to Bell. Moreover, this de facto monopoly is granted without specific recognition by the Commission of such effect and without a finding that such a result would be in the public interest.

With the defeat or elimination of Philco, GE, IBM, Raytheon, and DuMont, and the containment of Western Union to the New York-Philadelphia-Pittsburgh route without interconnection arrangements, the infant microwave industry was completely under AT&T's control by 1950. . . .

On these basic issues the Commission's approach to date has either been negative, passive, or piecemeal. Without ever having conducted a general investigation on interconnection or rendering a decision on that issue, the Commission has permitted AT&T to use interconnection to defeat common carrier competition and to restrict private microwave competition, thereby limiting the utility and services of competing microwave systems. Without specifying the issue, conducting a hearing, or rendering a decision, the FCC permitted AT&T to convert from a privately owned cable and wire plant to a public domain radio spectrum resource without providing that the investment in the lower unit cost microwave system would be the rate base for its use. Without specifying the issue, conducting a hearing, or rendering a decision, the Commission allowed the noncompetitive public telephone network to impose the traditional noncompetitive characteristics on an otherwise potentially competitive private line market. Without specifying the issue, conducting a hearing, or rendering a decision, the Commission has allowed Western Union's high capacity, east-west transcontinental and north-south, western, central, and eastern microwave plant to remain largely unused and unavailable for low cost video and other bulk private line services by reason of restrictive pricing policies controlled by the rate base of the wire line telephone network.

Peter O. Steiner (1922–   )

MONOPOLY AND COMPETITION IN TELEVISION: SOME POLICY ISSUES*

What conditions foster "good" television broadcasting? How many channels? Private or public ownership? Fees, taxes, or advertising funds? Steiner lays out some of the main issues in these policy choices.

The new debate upon public policy toward television has centered on the award of broadcasting rights for a third channel. Should it go to the BBC, to a new public corporation, to a new or existing commercial organization, or to toll television? More is at stake than the nature of the new channel since the additional service may fundamentally alter the behavior and performance of the existing services and thus affect the pattern of development of the whole broadcasting system. This is one of those rare moments when the public has a real opportunity to choose among alternatives; the purpose of this paper is to explore them. . . .

THE CHARACTER OF AMERICAN TELEVISION

Three national network organizations (NBC, CBS, ABC) dominate American television. Each offers its affiliated stations about twice as many hours of programs per week as BBC television. Some of these programs are sponsored, some not; of the former some are network produced, some produced by advertising agencies or independent producers. While the networks own a few key stations, most stations are independent, private, commercial organizations that have voluntarily affiliated with the networks, yielding to the networks options on a significant portion of their time, the major share of the revenue from the sale of their time, the major share of the revenue from the sale of their time to network advertisers, and much of their jurisdiction over programming. In return they are provided with the cable interconnection that makes simultaneous national broad-

---

* Peter O. Steiner, "Monopoly and Competition in Television: Some Policy Issues," *Manchester School of Economic and Social Studies,* May 1961, excerpted. Steiner's research also includes basic work on cost-benefit analysis and the economics of mergers.

casting possible, with a stream of programs of all types, and with the minor share of the revenue from the sale of their time as part of the network. The two biggest networks are enormously profitable by any standard; ABC is less profitable, but is above the average of American corporations of its size. Stations typically enjoy moderate profits and are clearly better off with network affiliation than without it.

Stations, rather than networks, are licensed by the Federal Communications Commission and renewal, while subject to standards of overall performance, is virtually automatic. Stations receive additional revenue from spot commercial announcements and from sale of their time for local or non-network "national spot" broadcasting. Non-network sources account for perhaps a quarter of the total time of stations and more than half of their revenue. These fractions should not lead one to underestimate the importance of network programming for two reasons: firstly, virtually all of the high budget programs, entertainment and public service alike, are network and their drawing power creates the audience at which both spot commercial announcements and the adjacent programs aim; secondly, with only two or three stations in the typical market area, virtually all stations are affiliated to one of the networks and rely heavily on their network programs for the "quality" programming with which they justify themselves to the FCC.

COMPETITION, MONOPOLY, AND THE PUBLIC INTEREST: PROTOTYPES COMPARED

1. An Ample, Unbiased Source of News and an Open Forum for Commentary and Public Discussion. The arguments against monopoly power in these areas need no rehearsing here. Nor is it the fear of outrageous abuse of freedom of thought or expression that motivates opposition to a benevolent and public spirited monopoly like that of the BBC in sound broadcasting. It is, rather, that the centralization of authority over the selection and presentation of public issues imposes an awesome responsibility for a benevolent monopoly; it must be prudent and it must be studiously impartial. This responsibility leads, apparently inevitably, to paternalism. At best, and the BBC frequently achieves this best, it produces the broadcasting equivalent of a superbly balanced book. But this is not the equivalent of a balanced library. The brilliance of individual items may obscure the fact that there is no appeal from the decision *not to cover* a particular story, or to give it merely routine coverage. This can, of course, occur under any system, but is less likely if there are several independent decision units than if there is one. This is a major objection to monopoly in broadcasting.

How does American experience compare? With respect to news reporting it is by usage free from advertisers' preview or editing. Both unsponsored and sponsored broadcasts are common, at both the station and network level; selection and production decisions reside with the broadcasters in all cases. The frequency of such news broadcasts is great, and because of the diversity of the selection, the number of stories reported in a given day is substantially larger than on the BBC. News commentary is also frequent and exhibits substantial range of opinion—from the extreme right to the middle left. While punditry far outweighs polemic, both are present. In the field of public discussion, panel interviews and documentary coverage in depth are frequent—once in a while in bad taste, typically informative, and occasionally superb.

2. *Existence of a Sufficient Number of Independent Sources of Employment.* The market for television performers, directors, producers, and technical personnel is necessarily discontinuous and imperfect. The advantages of having even two or three potential employers rather than one are obvious. They are particularly compelling where artistic judgments are involved. Blacklisting, favoritism, and discrimination may occur, but they may also be imagined if there is no real alternative source of employment. Pluralism of decision making provides an essential element of protection.

Because skills are specialized and markets are imperfect, appropriate levels of compensation are difficult to determine. It is clear that introduction of independent television in Britain has led to a significant increase in the pay scales of the BBC as a response to the loss of personnel to its competitor. This suggests that monopoly, public or private, exercises significant monopsony power as well.

If one accepts the view that these considerations are important, it is clear that competition—even competition limited to a few competitors—has a major advantage over monopoly.

3. *Public Service Responsibility.* A semipublic monopoly has one enormous asset: it is free to undertake a wholehearted commitment to public service. Freed from any crass scratching for revenue, freed from competition for listeners, and insulated from pressure groups; it may consciously and conscientiously pursue its image of the public interest. The BBC's worldwide reputation and its many programming triumphs attest to the public benefits that can be achieved.

These benefits are not without costs. The image served is that of the monopoly. That it may be paternalistic, that it may identify too closely with the Establishment, that it may resist changes in itself and become impervious to changes in the public climate, are real rather than phantom dangers. They are the hazards of power wherever it is found. Complete lack of power, the characteristic of atomistic competition, while avoiding the dangers, negates the benefits as well in cases where public service is not identical with private interest. The challenge is to find the mixture of monopoly and competition that gives the best balance.

The American mixture does not. Not that the conscious pursuit of public service is absent; the networks do have such an image and it is reflected in news and documentary programs, and elsewhere as well. But even networks can afford to be "uneconomic" in some areas only if they attend to the business of collecting revenue most of the time. If one makes a rough distinction between entertainment and other programming it is only slightly unfair to say that networks abdicate public service responsibility in the former and embrace it in the latter. As to entertainment, the creed is to "give them (the listeners and/or the advertisers) what they want." (How well they do this is discussed below.) For the other they can be magnificent.

But these activities are inversely related to competition. ABC has gained both listeners and profits by leaving prestige programming to its rivals and developing "adult" Westerns. National spot programming eschews it entirely, and individual stations frequently reject unsponsored network prestige programs in favor of national spot or locally sponsored film series if they have an option. Subjecting the networks to fiercer and more compelling competition, a goal frequently advocated and fruitlessly pursued by the FCC, would work against, rather than for, public service responsibility.

The successes of the networks should not detract from the question of whether enough of the networks' time is devoted to programs of this sort. This is the problem of the program mix.

4. The Provision of a Rich and Varied Program. Here the disadvantages of limited competition are most pronounced. This fact, and the reasons for it, are very important but only dimly appreciated. It is convenient to consider the problem in stages.

Consider first a situation in which there are three channels operating concurrently for a single period (say thirty minutes) broadcasting to a population of potential listeners whose tastes vary in the following very simple way; out of every one hundred potential listeners, eighty want a program of type A (e.g., Western), eighteen want a program of type B (e.g., dramatic show), and the remaining two want a program of type C (e.g., discussion of current events). Further assume to start with that a listener will turn on his set only if a program of the type he wants is broadcast.

A monopoly interested in maximizing the number of listeners (which in this case is the same as satisfying the largest number of people) will clearly produce one program of each type, one on each channel, and both capture and satisfy the whole audience. Three competing firms, each trying to get as many listeners *for itself* as it can, will probably *all* produce a program of type A for the simple reason that each one's share of the mass audience will be larger than the whole of the potential audience for programs of types B or C. If we assume that two or more stations producing the same program type will share the audience equally, it is easily seen that a fourth channel will also produce type A (20 percent of the audience) rather than type B (18 percent). Indeed, one would need five stations before one could expect type B to be produced, and at least forty-eight channels before type C would appear attractive. Duplication is a consequence of competition for listeners, and if choices are varied and the number of channels limited, duplication will leave some listeners unnecessarily dissatisfied. While each of the duplicating program producers can claim that "we give people what they want," this is not so in the aggregate.

If viewers will accept (if grudgingly) less-preferred programs rather than none at all, the tendencies for duplication under competition are increased. To see this quickly, suppose 70 percent of the audience prefer type A and 30 percent type B, but will listen to either. If there are only two channels, both will produce type A and each will get 50 percent of the audience. A third channel has a choice of producing type B and getting 30 percent of the listeners, or duplicating type A and getting one-third of the total. If it aims strictly at maximizing its audience it will choose type A. (If viewers had not been shiftable, it would have chosen type B.)

When attention is directed to variation over time rather than to a single period, there are clearly substantial opportunities for increased variety. But there are major forces tending toward duplication as well, and a clear over-representation of the most popular program types. This can be shown theoretically, but the argument is somewhat complex, even tedious, and it will be omitted.[1] Empirically, duplication of program types by channels at the same time, and also over time, are perhaps the most clearly visible features of the American system. The near-saturation of prime evening hours on all networks with Westerns, "private eye" shows, and situation comedies has been noted by many critics. The cost is less coverage of minority tastes than their place in the reference pattern of the population warrants.

So far, then, as satisfying as many listeners as is possible is a sensible objective, and so far as choice is only between program types, it is clear that complete monopoly is, in principle, a more effective instrument than maximum competition when there are binding limits on the number of competitors possible. Monopoly, even private monopoly, is motivated to avoid duplication; competitors are not. . . .

Viewers select specific programs as well as program types. A choice between two Western (or two religious programs, or two variety shows) is, after all, better than no choice. Not only do tastes vary within program types but competition between programs imposes standards of competence

---

[1] For extended theoretical treatment of this and other complications, see P. O. Steiner, "Programme Patterns and Preferences and the Workability of Competition in Radio Broadcasting," *Quarterly Journal of Economics*, vol. 76 (May 1952), pp. 194–223.

on program producers. But such choice is expensive if it precludes the wider alternatives. Further, the same forces that tend toward duplication of program type lead to imitative programming where competition for listeners is the spur. . . .

In summary, the comparison between the prototypes—public monopoly and private, commercial, limited competition—shows:

1. The advantages of pluralism in providing an open forum for news and discussion and in providing alternative sources of employment give competition a decisive edge.

2. Public service responsibility flows from two sources: power and motivation. The public monopoly has both, and has the advantage. But the form of limited competition considered leaves substantial monopolistic power in the hands of the competitors who can (and do) choose to compete for public esteem as well as for audience. In either case the existence of a protected position provides the opportunity for conscious public service.

3. Monopoly is inherently motivated to provide the complementary programming that leads to maximum variety; competitors are not so motivated and a significant restriction on choice owing to both duplication and imitation is to be expected.

4. Competition, if it generates substantial additional resources for programming, can do some things better than a (relatively) underfinanced public monopoly, and (while it should not be overstressed) the need to compete for audiences may have a beneficial effect on the particular programs of the kinds most heavily demanded.

If choice is limited to one or the other of these prototypes, judgment as to a "balance of advantage" is required. The challenge is to find a mixture that can tap the advantages of both. . . .

CASES

Munn v. Illinois
94 U.S. 113 (1877)

This was the first assertion of the public's right to regulate private business "which is affected with a public interest."

Mr. Chief Justice Waite. The question to be determined in this case is whether the general assembly of Illinois can, under the limitations upon the legislative power of the States imposed by the Constitution of the United States, fix by law the maximum of charges for the storage of grain in warehouses at Chicago and other places in the State having not less than one hundred thousand inhabitants, "in which grain is stored in bulk, and in which the grain of different owners is mixed together, or in which grain is stored in such a manner that the identity of different lots or parcels cannot be accurately preserved."

It is claimed that such a law is repugnant.

This brings us to inquire as to the principles upon which this power of regulation rests, in order that we may determine what is within and what is without its operative effect. Looking, then, to the common law, from whence came the right which the Constitution protects, we find that when private property is "affected with a public interest, it ceases to be *juris privati* only."

. . . Property does become clothed with a public interest when used in a manner to make it a public consequence, and affect the community at large. When, therefore, one devotes his property to a use in which the public has an interest, he, in effect, grants to the public an interest in that use, and must submit to be controlled by the public for the common good, to the extent of the interest he has thus created. He may withdraw his grant by discontinuing the use; but, so long as he maintains the use, he must submit to the control. . . .

251

Nebbia v. *New York*
291 U.S. 502 (1934)

> Nebbia *affirmed the public's right to regulate virtually anything which the Legislature chose to regulate. Any other narrow criteria (e.g., a "utility") were not binding.*

Mr. Justice Roberts. The Legislature of New York established, by Chapter 158 of the Laws of 1933, a Milk Control Board with power, among other things, to "fix minimum and maximum . . . retail prices to be charged by . . . stores to consumers for consumption off the premises. . . ." The Board fixed nine cents as the price to be charged by a store for a quart of milk. Nebbia, the proprietor of a grocery store in Rochester, sold two quarts and a five cent loaf of bread for eighteen cents; and was convicted for violating the Board's order. At his trial he asserted the statute and order contravene the equal protection clause and the due process clause of the Fourteenth Amendment, and renewed the contention in successive appeals to the county court and the Court of Appeals. Both overruled his claim and affirmed the conviction.

The question for decision is whether the Federal Constitution prohibits a state from so fixing the selling price of milk.

The Fifth Amendment, in the field of federal activity, and the Fourteenth, as respects state action, do not prohibit governmental regulation for the public welfare. They merely condition the exertion of the admitted power, by securing that the end shall be accomplished by methods consistent with due process. . . .

But we are told that because the law essays to control prices it denies due process. . . . The argument runs that the public control of rates or prices is *per se* unreasonable and unconstitutional, save as applied to businesses affected with a public interest; that a business so affected is one in which property undertakes, or one whose owner relies on a public grant or franchise for the right to conduct the business, or in which he is bound to serve all who apply; in short, such as is commonly called a public utility; or a business in its nature a monopoly. The milk industry, it is said, possesses none of these characteristics, and, therefore, not being affected with a public interest, its charges may not be controlled by the state. Upon the soundness of this contention the appellant's case against the statute depends.

The statement that one has dedicated his property to a public use is, therefore, merely another way of saying that if one embarks in a business which public interest demands shall be regulated, he must know regulation will ensue.

In the same volume the court sustained regulation of railroad rates. After referring to the fact that railroads are carriers for hire, are incorporated as such, and given extraordinary powers in order that they may better serve the public, it was said that they are engaged in employment "affecting the public interest," and therefore, under the doctrine of the Munn case, subject to legislative control as to rates. And in another of the group of railroad cases then heard it is said that the property of railroads is "clothed with a public interest" which permits legislative limitation of the charges for its use. Plainly the activities of railroads, their charges and practices, so nearly touch the vital economic interests of society that the police power may be invoked to regulate their charges, and no additional formula of affection or clothing with a public interest is needed to justify the regulation. And this is evidently true of all business units supplying transportation, light, heat, power and water to communities, irrespective of how they obtain their powers.

The touchstone of public interest in any business, its practices and charges, clearly is not the enjoyment of any franchise from the state. . . .

Many other decisions show that the private character of a business does not necessarily remove it from the realm of regulation of charges or prices. The usury laws fix the price which may be exacted for the use of money, although no business more essentially private in character can be imagined than that of loaning one's personal funds. . . . Insurance agents' compensation may be regulated, though their contracts are private, because the business of insurance is considered one properly subject to public control. . . . Statutes prescribing in the public interest the amounts to be charged by attorneys for prosecuting certain claims, a matter ordinarily one of personal and private nature, are not a deprivation of due process. . . . A stockyards corporation, "while not a common carrier, nor engaged in any distinctively public employment, is doing a work in which the public has an interest," and its charges may be controlled. . . . Private contract carriers, who do not operate under a franchise, and have no monopoly of the carriage of goods or passengers, may, since they use the highways to compete with railroads, be compelled to charge rates not lower than those of public carriers for corresponding services, if the state, in pursuance of a public policy to protect the latter, so determines.

So far as the requirement of due process is concerned, and in the absence of other constitutional restriction, a state is free to adopt whatever economic policy may reasonably be deemed to promote public welfare, and to enforce that policy by legislation adapted to its purpose. The courts are without authority either to declare such policy, or, when it is declared by the legislature, to override it. If the laws passed are seen to have a reasonable relation to a proper legislative purpose, and are neither arbitrary nor discriminatory, the requirements of due process are satisfied, and judicial determination to that effect renders a court functus officio. "Whether the free operation of the normal laws of competition is a wise and wholesome rule for trade and commerce is an economic question which this court need not consider or determine." *Northern Securities Co.* v. *United States,* 193 U.S. 197, 337–8. And it is equally clear that if the legislative policy be to curb unrestrained and harmful competition by measures which are not arbitrary or discriminatory it does not lie with the courts to determine that the rule is unwise. With the wisdom of the policy adopted, with the adequacy or practicability of the law enacted to forward it, the courts are both incompetent and unauthorized to deal. The course of decision in this court exhibits a firm adherence to these principles.

Tested by these considerations we find no basis in the due process clause of the Fourteenth Amendment for condemning the provisions of the Agriculture and Markets Law here drawn into question.

Smyth v. *Ames*
169 U.S. 466 (1898)

The criteria for regulation were here garbled and confused so much that regulation was virtually stalled for several decades. Which criteria listed here are (1) inappropriate on economic grounds, (2) unworkable, and/ or (3) mutually conflicting?

. . . We hold, however, that the basis of all calculations as to the reasonableness of rates must be the fair value of the property being used by it for the convenience of the public. And in order to ascertain that value, the original cost of construction, the amount expended in permanent improvements, the amount and market value of its bonds and stock, the present as compared with the original cost of construction, the probable earning capacity of the property under particular rates prescribed by statute, and the sum required to meet operating expenses, are all matters for consideration, and are to be given such weight as may be just and right in each case. We do not say that there may not be other matters to be regarded in estimating the value of the property. What the company is entitled to ask is a fair return upon the value of that which it employs for the public convenience. On the other hand, what the public is entitled to demand is that no more be exacted from it for the use of a public highway than the services rendered by it are reasonably worth. . . .

Federal Power Commission et al. v. Hope Natural Gas Co.

320 U.S. 591 (1944)

Here the Court cut through the confusion to give commissions power to regulate on any clear and reasonable criteria.

Mr. Justice Douglas.   The primary issue in these cases concerns the validity under the Natural Gas Act of 1938 (52 Stat. 821, 15 U.S.C., 717) of a rate order issued by the Federal Power Commission reducing the rates chargeable by Hope Natural Gas Co., 44 P.U.R. (N.S.) 1. . . .

Hope is a West Virginia corporation organized in 1898. It is a wholly owned subsidiary of Standard Oil Co. (N.J.). Since the date of its organization, it has been in the business of producing, purchasing and marketing natural gas in that state. It sells some of that gas to local consumers in West Virginia. But the great bulk of it goes to five customer companies which receive it at the West Virginia line and distribute it in Ohio and in Pennsylvania. In July 1938 the cities of Cleveland and Akron filed complaints with the Commission charging that the rates collected by Hope from East Ohio Gas Co. (an affiliate of Hope which distributes gas in Ohio) were excessive and unreasonable. Later in 1938 the Commission on its own motion instituted an investigation to determine the reasonableness of all of Hope's interstate rates.

On May 26, 1942, the Commission entered its order and made its findings. Its order required Hope to decrease its future interstate rates so as to reflect a reduction, on an annual basis, of not less than $3,609,857 in operating revenues. And it established "just and reasonable" average rates per million cubic feet for each of the five customer companies.

Hope contended that it should be allowed a return of not less than 8 percent. The Commission found that an 8 percent return would be unreasonable but that 6½ percent was a fair rate of return. That rate of return, applied to the rate base of $33,712,526, would produce $2,191,314 annually, as compared with the present income of not less than $5,801,171.

The Circuit Court of Appeals set aside the order of the Commission for the following reasons. (1) It held that the rate base should reflect the "present fair value" of the property, that the Commission in determining the "value" should have considered reproduction cost and trended original cost, and that "actual legitimate cost" (prudent investment) was not the proper measure of "fair value" where price levels had changed since the investment. (2) It concluded that the well-drilling costs and overhead items in the amount of some $17,000,000 should have been included in the rate base. (3) It held that accrued depletion and depreciation and the annual allowance for that expense should be computed on the basis of "present fair value" of the property, not on the basis of "actual legitimate cost."

We held in Federal Power Commission v. Natural Gas Pipeline Co., supra, that the Commission was not bound to the use of any single formula or combination of formulae in determining rates. Its rate-making function, moreover, involves the making of "pragmatic adjustments." And when the Commission's order is challenged in the courts, the question is whether that order "viewed in its entirety" meets the requirements of the Act. . . . Under the statutory standard of "just and reasonable" it is the result reached not the method employed which is controlling. . . . It is not theory but the impact of the rate order which counts. If the total effect of the rate order cannot be said to be unjust and unreasonable, judicial inquiry under the Act is at an end. The fact that the method employed to reach that result may contain infirmities is not then important. Moreover, the Commission's order does not become suspect by reason of the fact that it is challenged. It is the product of expert judgment which carries a presumption of validity. And he who would upset the rate order under the Act carries the heavy burden of making a convincing showing that it is invalid because it is unjust and unreasonable in its consequences. . . .

The rate-making process under the Act, i.e., the fixing of "just and reasonable" rates, involves a balancing of the investor and the consumer interests. Thus we stated in the Natural Gas Pipeline Co. case that "regulation does not insure that the business shall produce net revenues." But such considerations aside, the investor interest has a legitimate concern with the financial integrity of the company whose rates are being regulated. From the investor or company point of view it is important that there be enough revenue not only for operating expenses but also for the capital costs of the business. These include service on the debt and dividends on the stock. . . . By that standard the return to the equity owner should be commensurate with returns on investments in other enterprises having corresponding risks. That return, moreover, should be sufficient to assure confidence in the financial integrity of the enterprise, so as to maintain its credit and to attract capital. The conditions under which more or less might be allowed are not important here. Nor is it important to this case to determine the various permissible ways in which any rate base on which the return is computed might be arrived at. For we are of the view that the end result in this case cannot be condemned under the Act as unjust and unreasonable from the investor or company viewpoint.

In view of these various considerations we cannot say that an annual return of $2,191,314 is not "just and reasonable" within the meaning of the Act. Rates which enable the company to operate successfully, to maintain its financial integrity, to attract capital, and to compensate its investors for the risks assumed certainly cannot be condemned as invalid, even though they might produce only a meager return on the so-called "fair value" rate base. In that connection it will be recalled that Hope contended for a rate base of $66,000,000 computed on reproduction cost new. The Commission points out that if that rate base were accepted, Hope's average rate of return for the four-year period from 1937–1940 would amount to 3.27 percent. During that period Hope earned an annual average return of about 9 percent on the average investment. It asked for no rate increases. Its properties were well maintained and operated. As the Commission says, such a modest rate of 3.27 percent suggests an "inflation of the base on which the rate has been computed." . . . The incongruity between the actual operations and the return computed on the basis of reproduction cost suggests that the Commission was wholly justified in rejecting the latter as the measure of the rate base.

In the Matters of

Atlantic Seaboard Corporation and Virginia Gas Transmission Corporation

11 F.P.C. 43 (1952)

Despite its rather obscure wording, this is a leading decision grappling with cost allocations and price structure. Its allocations of cost are generally agreed to understate true peak costs relative to off-peak costs, thereby accentuating the rate-base effect (see Kahn, and Averch and Johnson, etc.). Is this criticism valid?

These matters are before the Commission on appeal from the decision, 11 F.P.C. 486, and accompanying order filed herein by the presiding examiner on November 7, 1951. In such decision and order the presiding examiner found, among other things, that the rates contained in the presently effective tariffs of Atlantic Seaboard Corp. (Seaboard) and Virginia Gas Transmission Corp. (Virginia Gas) are, each of them, unjust, unreasonable, and unduly discriminatory. And, after finding that which was conceived by him to be the just and reasonable rates and charges, "coupled with a proper heat content adjustment provision," the presiding examiner ordered Seaboard and Virginia Gas to file new schedules setting forth the rates and charges so found proper.

Prior to 1950, applicants owned and operated a natural-gas transmission pipeline system consisting principally of high-pressure, 20-inch continuous pipeline some 420 miles in length extending from Seaboard's Boldman (Kentucky) compressor station, through West Virginia, Virginia, and Maryland, to a point of connection with the facilities of the Manufacturers Light and Heat Co. (Manufacturers) at a point on the Maryland-Pennsylvania boundary. On January 7, 1950, applicants commenced the operation of a newly constructed 26-inch pipeline some 268 miles in length extending from the vicinity of the Cobb (West Virginia) compressor station of United Fuel Gas Co. (United Fuel) through Virginia to Rockville, Md., where it is interconnected with the 20-inch line. . . .

In this, as in most of our natural gas rate proceedings, we are confronted with a cost allocation problem. Applicants, the staff, and Washington each introduced evidence showing that which they conceived to be the proper method of allocation. The examiner in his intermediate decision did not agree with any of them in respect to all items.

Because this question of proper allocation of costs is of such great importance in practically all rate proceedings before us—and usually, as here, is one of the most controversial of issues—we consider it appropriate to set out at some length our views as to proper methods of cost allocation so that all may be informed and guided in situations which may be substantially similar to the conditions here present.

The controversy generally engendered in rate proceedings as to the proper method for allocation of costs stems largely from the fact that the relative importance of the demand (capacity) and commodity (volume) functions cannot be measured with scientific accuracy. In the final analysis the allocations of cost to these respective functions are and must be largely dictated by informed judgment.

The three witnesses who testified on this subject in this proceeding generally divided costs between demand and commodity factors or elements. Demand costs were characterized as those which are associated with capacity of the facilities, whereas commodity costs are deemed associated with the volume or quantity of gas delivered.

A natural-gas transmission facility performs both a capacity and a volumetric function. In this sense, it is a joint facility, which thus presents the problem, always difficult, of allocating joint costs.

In this present case, applicants, generally speaking, allocated fixed costs or expenses, except return on investment and related income taxes, to the capacity, or demand, function. Return and income taxes were allocated equally between the demand and volume. Variable costs were assigned to the volumetric or commodity function. The staff, on the other hand, apportioned all fixed costs or expenses equally between demand and volume, but, like applicants' witness, assigned variable expenses to commodity. . . .

We are unable, however, to accept the premise that merely because certain costs do not vary with use they automatically become *in toto* demand or capacity costs. A pipeline would not normally be built to supply peak service, that is to say, service on the peak days only. We know from our administration of section 7 of the Natural Gas Act, which involves the issuance of certificates of public convenience and necessity, the pipelines are built to supply service not only on the few peak days but on all days throughout the year. In proving the economic feasibility of the project in certificate proceedings, reliance is placed upon the annual as well as the peak deliveries. Stated another way, the capital outlay for the pipeline facility is made—and justified—not only for service on the peak days but for service throughout the year. Both capacity and annual use are important considerations in the conception of the project and in the issuance of certificates of public convenience and necessity. Both capacity and volume, therefore, are what are known as cost factors or incidences in respect to the capital outlay for a pipeline project. It follows that reasonably accurate results can be achieved only by allocating the fixed expenses flowing from the capital outlay to both operating functions, viz., capacity and volume. . . .

The determination of how much of the fixed costs is assignable to each function, demand or volume, involves judgment. It can only be done by judgment inasmuch as the facts upon which the determination must be made are not susceptible to mathematical computation. We know that both functions are very significant. This is not a case where one form of joint use greatly predominates. It is our opinion that these significant cost factors should be weighted equally, that is to say, 50 percent should be assigned to demand and 50 percent to commodity. In this manner all gas transported by the pipeline will share in all of the various kinds of expenses incurred to transport the gas. Gas which is associated with delivery on the peak day or a group of peak days will share in the total expenses including the total of the fixed charges. That gas which is not associated with deliveries on the peak day or group of peak days will not share in 50 percent of the fixed costs. This solution recognizes the principle that costs associated with peak service are higher than those which are associated with interruptible or off-peak service. In our opinion it reasonably assigns these heavier costs to the service associated with peak deliveries. By the same token, while relieving off-peak service from sharing in 50 percent of the fixed expenses, it, nevertheless, assigns to that service some or all of the costs incurred to construct and operate the pipeline. As stated previously, the equal weighting assigned to the two cost factors of demand and commodity for the purpose of allocating fixed cost or expenses is a judgment determination. It can never be otherwise, for the allocation of joint costs is not and cannot be an exact science.

United States v. El Paso Natural Gas Co.
376 U.S. 651 (1964)

El Paso is a classic "big case": a massive cumulation of facts and litigation, and a remarkable series of delaying actions. It also is a landmark extension of antitrust into a "regulated" sector. More than 16 years have passed as re-appeals and remands have proliferated.

Justice William O. Douglas. This is a civil suit charging a violation of Section 7 of the Clayton Act, by reason of the acquisition of the stock and assets of Pacific Northwest Pipeline Corp. (Pacific Northwest) by El Paso Natural Gas Co. (El Paso). The District Court dismissed the complaint after trial, making findings of fact and conclusions of law, but not writing an opinion. The case is here on direct appeal. . . .

The ultimate issue revolves around the question whether the acquisition substantially lessened competition in the sale of natural gas in California— a market of which El Paso was the sole out-of-state supplier at the time of the acquisition.

In 1954, Pacific Northwest received the approval of the Federal Power Commission to construct and operate a pipeline from the San Juan Basin, New Mexico, to the State of Washington, to supply gas to the then unserved Pacific Northwest area. Later it was authorized to receive large quantities of Canadian gas and to enlarge its system for that purpose. In addition, Pacific Northwest acquired Rocky Mountain reservoirs along its route. . . . By 1958 one half of its natural gas sales were of gas from Canada.

In 1954 Pacific Northwest entered into two gas exchange contracts with El Paso. . . .

El Paso, however, could not get Commission approval to build the pipeline. . . . Consequently, a new agreement on that aspect was negotiated in 1955. . . . Pacific Northwest, still obligated to take 300 million cubic feet per day from Westcoast, disposed of the balance in its own market areas.

Prior to these 1954 and 1955 agreements Pacific Northwest had tried to enter the rapidly expanding California market. It prepared plans regarding the transportation of Canadian gas to California, where it was to be distributed by Pacific Gas & Electric (PGE). That effort—suspended when the 1954 agreements were made—was renewed when the new agreement with El Paso was made in 1955; and the negotiation of the 1955 contract with El Paso was conceived by Pacific Northwest as the occasion for "lifting of all restrictions on the growth of Pacific." In 1956 it indeed engaged in negotiations for the sale of natural gas to Southern California Edison Co. (Edison). The latter, largest industrial user of natural gas in Southern

California, used El Paso gas, purchased through a distributor. It had, however, a low priority from that distributor, being on an "interruptible" basis, *i.e.*, subject to interruption during periods of peak demand for domestic uses. Edison wanted a firm contract and, upon being advised that it was El Paso's policy to sell only to distributors, started negotiations with Pacific Northwest in May 1956. The idea was for Pacific Northwest to deliver to Edison at a point on the California-Oregon border 300 million cubic feet of Canadian gas a day. In July 1956 they reached a tentative agreement. Edison thereupon tried to develop within California an integrated system for distributing Canadian gas supplied by Pacific Northwest to itself and others. El Paso decided to fight the plan to the last ditch, and succeeded in getting (through a distributor) a contract for Edison's needs. Edison's tentative agreement with Pacific Northwest was terminated. Before Edison terminated that agreement with Pacific Northwest, Edison had reached an agreement with El Paso for firm deliveries of gas; and while the original El Paso offer was 40¢ per Mcf, the price dropped to 38¢ per Mcf, then to 34¢ and finally to 30¢. Thereafter, and while the merger negotiations were pending, Pacific Northwest renewed its efforts to get its gas into California.

El Paso had been interested in acquiring Pacific Northwest since 1954. The first offer from El Paso was in December 1955—an offer Pacific Northwest rejected. Negotiations were resumed by El Paso in the summer of 1956, while Pacific Northwest was trying to obtain a California outlet. The exchange of El Paso shares for Pacific shares was accepted by Pacific Northwest's directors in November 1956, and by May 1957 El Paso had acquired 99.8 percent of Pacific Northwest's outstanding stock. In July 1957 the Department of Justice filed its suit charging that the acquisition violated Section 7 of the Clayton Act. In August 1957 El Paso applied to the Federal Power Commission for permission to acquire the assets of Pacific Northwest. On December 23, 1959, the Commission approved and the merger was effected on December 31, 1959. In 1962 we set aside the Commission's order, holding that it should not have acted until the District Court has passed on the Clayton Act issues. . . . Meanwhile (in October 1960) the United States amended its complaint so as to include the asset acquisition in the charged violation of the Clayton Act.

. . . On review of the record—which is composed largely of undisputed evidence—we conclude that "the effect of such acquisition may be substantially to lessen competition" within the meaning of Section 7 of the Clayton Act.

There can be no doubt that the production, transportation, and sale of natural gas is a "line of commerce" within the meaning of Section 7. There can also be no doubt that California is a "section of the country" as that phrase is used in Section 7. The sole question, therefore, is whether on undisputed facts the acquisition had a sufficient tendency to lessen competition or is saved by the findings that Pacific Northwest, as an independent entity, could not have obtained a contract from the California distributors, could not have received the gas supplies or financing for a pipeline project to California, or could not have put together a project acceptable to the regulatory agencies. Those findings are irrelevant. . . .

Pacific Northwest, though it had no pipeline into California, is shown by this record to have been a substantial factor in the California market at the time it was acquired by El Paso. At that time El Paso was the only actual supplier of out-of-state gas to the vast California market, *a market that expands at an estimated annual rate of 200 million cubic feet per day.* At that time Pacific Northwest was the only other important interstate pipeline west of the Rocky Mountains. Though young, it was prospering and appeared strong enough to warrant a "treaty" with El Paso that protected El Paso's California markets.

Edison's search for a firm supply of natural gas in California, when it had El Paso gas only on an "interruptible" basis, illustrates what effect Pacific Northwest had merely as a potential competitor in the California market. Edison took its problem to Pacific Northwest and, as we have seen, a tentative agreement was reached for Edison to obtain Pacific Northwest gas. El Paso responded, offering Edison a firm supply of gas and substantial price concessions. We would have to wear blinders not to see that the mere efforts of Pacific Northwest to get into the California market, though unsuccessful, had a powerful influence on El Paso's business attitudes within the State.

This is not a field where merchants are in a continuous daily struggle to hold old customers and to win new ones over from their rivals. In this regulated industry a natural gas company (unless it has excess capacity) must compete for, enter into, and then obtain Commission approval of sale contracts in advance of constructing the pipeline facilities. In the natural gas industry pipelines are very expensive; and to be justified they need long-term contracts for sale of the gas that will travel them. Those transactions with distributors are few in number. For example, in California there are only two significant wholesale purchasers—Pacific Gas & Electric in the north and the Southern Companies in the south. Once the Commission grants authorization to construct facilities or to transport gas in interstate commerce, once the distributing contracts are made, a particular market is withdrawn from competition. *The competition then is for the new increments of demand that may emerge with an expanding population and with an expanding industrial or household use of gas.*

The effect on competition in a particular market through acquisition of another company is determined by the nature or extent of that market and by the nearness of the absorbed company to it, that company's eagerness to enter that market, its resourcefulness, and so on. Pacific Northwest's position as a competitive factor in California was not disproved by the fact that it had never sold gas there. Nor is it conclusive that Pacific Northwest's attempt to sell to Edison failed. That might be weighty if a market presently saturated showed signs of petering out. But it is irrelevant in a market like California, where incremental needs are booming.

... Had Pacific Northwest remained independent, there can be no doubt it would have sought to exploit its formidable geographical position *vis-à-vis* California. No one knows what success it would have had. We do know, however, that two interstate pipelines in addition to El Paso now serve California—one of the newcomers being Pacific Gas Transmission Co., bringing down Canadian gas. So we know that opportunities would have existed for Pacific Northwest had it remained independent.

Unsuccessful bidders are no less competitors than the successful one. The presence of two or more suppliers gives buyers a choice. Pacific Northwest was no feeble, failing company, nor was it inexperienced and lacking in resourcefulness. It was one of two major interstate pipelines serving the trans-Rocky Mountain States; it had raised $250 million for its pipeline that extended 2,500 miles through rugged terrain. It had adequate reserves and managerial skill. It was so strong and militant that it was viewed with concern, and coveted, by El Paso. If El Paso can absorb Pacific Northwest without violating Section 7 of the Clayton Act, that section has no meaning in the natural gas field. For normally there is no competition—once the lines are built and the long-term contracts negotiated—except as respects the incremental needs.

Since appellees have been on notice of the antitrust charge from almost the beginning—indeed before El Paso sought Commission approval of the merger—we not only reverse the judgment below but direct the District Court to order divestiture without delay.

Reversed.

American Commercial Lines, Inc., et al. v. Louisville & Nashville Railroad Co. et al.

392 U.S. 571 (1968)
(The "Ingot Molds" Case)

Ingot Molds was a leading effort to inject "efficient" —marginal cost—pricing so that railroads could compete more effectively. Yet the Court chose instead to stress "inherent advantages," much to the criticism of most economists. Who is right?

Justice Marshall.

The basic issue in these cases is . . . the action of the Interstate Commerce Commission in disallowing a rate reduction proposed by the appellee railroads, [in 1965] Section 15a (3) of the Interstate Commerce Act, 49 U.S.C. Section 15a (3), added by 72 Stat. 572 (1958), which governs ratemaking in situations involving intermodal competition. . . .

Since 1953, the movement of ingot molds from Neville Island and Pittsburgh, Pennsylvania, to Steelton, Kentucky, has been almost exclusively by combination barge-truck service and since 1960, the overall charge for this service has been $5.11 per ton. In 1963, the Pennsylvania Railroad and the Louisville & Nashville Railroad lowered their joint rate for this same traffic from $11.86 to $5.11 per ton. The competing barge lines, joined by intervening trucking interests, protested to the ICC that the new railroad rate violated Section 15a (3) of the Interstate Commerce Act because it impaired or destroyed the "inherent advantage" then enjoyed by the barge-truck service. The Commission thereupon undertook an investigation of the rate reduction.

In the course of the administrative proceedings that followed, the ICC made the following factual findings about which there is no real dispute among the parties. The fully distributed cost[1] to the railroads of this service was $7.59 per ton, and the "long term out-of-pocket costs"[2] were $4.69 per ton. The fully distributed cost to the barge-truck service was $5.19 per ton. The out-of-pocket cost[3] of the barge-truck service was not separately computed, but was estimated without contradiction, to be approximately the same as the fully distributed cost and higher, in any event, than the out-of-pocket cost of the railroads. The uncontroverted shipper testimony was to the effect that price was virtually the sole determinant of which service would be utilized, but that, were the rates charged by the railroads and the barge-truck combination the same, all the traffic would go to the railroads.

The railroads contended that they should be permitted to maintain the $5.11 rate, once it was shown to exceed the out-of-pocket cost attributable to the service, on the ground that any rate so set would enable them to make a profit on the traffic. The railroads further contended that the fact that the

---

[1] Fully distributed costs are defined broadly by the ICC as the "out-of-pocket costs plus a revenue-ton and revenue ton-mile distribution of the constant cost, including deficits, [which] indicate the revenue necessary to a fair return on the traffic, disregarding ability to pay." *New Automobiles in Interstate Commerce*, 259 I.C.C. 475, 513 (1945).

[2] The long-term out-of-pocket costs were computed under an ICC-sponsored formula which generally holds that 80 percent of rail operating expenses, rents and taxes are out-of-pocket in that they will vary with traffic. To this is added a return element of 4 percent on a portion of the investment (all the equipment and 50 percent of the road property), which is apportioned to all traffic on a proportional basis.

[3] Out-of-pocket costs have been regarded generally in these cases as equivalent to what economists refer to as "incremental" or "marginal" costs. Accordingly we shall equate the terms likewise, although we have no intention of vouching for the accuracy of that equation as a matter of pure economics. . . . Such costs are defined generally as the costs specifically incurred by the addition of each new unit of output and do not include any allocation to that unit of pre-existing overhead expenses.

rate was substantially below their fully distributed cost for the service was irrelevant, since that cost in no way reflected the profitability of the traffic to them. The barge-truck interests, on the other hand, took the position that Section 15a (3) required the Commission to look to the railroads' fully distributed costs in order to ascertain which of the competing modes had the inherent cost advantage on the traffic at issue. They argued that the fact that the railroads' rate would be profitable was merely the minimum requirement under the statute. The railroads in response contended that inherent advantage should be determined by a comparison of out-of-pocket rather than fully distributed costs, and they produced several economists to testify that, from the standpoint of economic theory, the comparison of out-of-pocket, or incremental, costs was the only rational way of regulating competitive rates.

The ICC rejected the railroads' contention that out-of-pocket costs should be the basis on which inherent advantage should be determined. The Commission observed that it had in the past regularly viewed fully distributed costs as the appropriate basis for determining which of two competing modes was the lower cost mode as regards particular traffic. It further indicated that the legislative history of Section 15a (3) revealed that Congress had in mind a comparison of fully distributed costs when it inserted the reference to the National Transportation Policy into that section in place of language sought by the railroads.

Having decided to utilize a comparison between fully distributed costs to determine inherent advantage, the Commission then concluded that the rate set by the railroads would undercut the barge-truck combination's ability to exploit its inherent advantage because the rate would force the competing carriers to go well below their own fully distributed costs to recapture the traffic from the railroads. Moreover, since the result sought by the railroads was general permission to set rates on an out-of-pocket basis, the Commission concluded that eventually the railroads could take all the traffic away from the barge-truck combination because the out-of-pocket costs of the former were lower than those of the latter and, therefore, in any rate war the railroads would be able to outlast their competitors. Accordingly, the Commission ordered that the railroads' rate be canceled.

The District Court read the statute and its accompanying legislative history to reflect a congressional judgment that inherent advantage should be determined in most cases by a comparison of out-of-pocket costs and that, therefore, railroads should generally be permitted to set any individual rate they choose as long as that rate is compensatory.[4] The court also

---

[4] A rate is compensatory in the sense used by the District Court any time it is greater than the out-of-pocket cost of the service for which the rate is set. The term fully compensatory is sometimes used to describe a rate in excess of fully distributed costs.

held that the Commission had failed adequately to articulate its reasons for deciding that the proper way of determining which mode of transportation was the more efficient was by comparison of fully distributed costs rather than out-of-pocket costs.

II.

This court has previously had occasion to consider the meaning and legislative history of Section 15a (3) of the Interstate Commerce Act. . . . So far as relevant here, Section 15a (3) provides that:

> [r]ates of a carrier shall not be held up to a particular level to protect the traffic of any other mode of transportation, giving due consideration to the objectives of the national transportation policy declared in this Act.

The National Transportation Policy, states that it is the intention of the Congress:

> to provide for fair and impartial regulation of all modes of transportation subject to the provisions of this act, so administered as to recognize and preserve the inherent advantages of each. . . .

The District Court apparently believed that the Commission was required to exercise its judgment in the direction of using out-of-pocket costs as the rate floor because that would encourage "hard" competition. We do not deny that the competition that would result from such a decision would probably be "hard." Indeed, from the admittedly scanty evidence in this record, one might well conclude that the competition resulting from out-of-pocket rate-making by the railroads would be so hard as to run a considerable number of presently existing barge and truck lines out of business.

We disagree, however, with the District Court's reading of congressional intent. The language contained in Section 15a (3) was the product of a bitter struggle between the railroads and their competitors. One of the specific fears of those competitors that prompted the change from the original language used in the bill was that the bill as it then read would permit essentially unregulated competition between all the various transportation modes. It was argued with considerable force that permitting the railroads to price on an out-of-pocket basis to meet competition would result in the eventual complete triumph of the railroads in intermodal competition because of their ability to impose all their constant costs on traffic for which there was no competition.

The economists who testified for the railroads in this case all stated that such an unequal allocation of constant costs among shippers on the basis of demand for railroad service, i.e., on the existence of competition for particular traffic, was economically sound and desirable.

The simple fact is that Section 15a (3) was not enacted, as the railroads claim, to enable them to price their services in such a way as to obtain the maximum revenue therefrom. The very words of the statute speak of "preserv[ing]" the inherent advantages of each mode of transportation. If all that was meant by the statute was to prevent wholly noncompensatory pricing by regulated carriers, language that was a good deal clearer could easily have been used. And, as we have shown here, at least one version of such clear language was proposed by the railroads and rejected by the Congress. If the theories advanced by the economists who testified in this case are as compelling as they seem to feel they are, Congress is the body to whom they should be addressed. The courts are ill-qualified indeed to make the kind of basic judgments about economic policy sought by the railroads here. And it would be particularly inappropriate for a court to award a carrier, on economic grounds, relief denied it by the legislature. . . .

The Commission stated here that it intended to exercise its informed judgment by considering the issues presented here in the context of a rule-making proceeding where it could evaluate the alternatives on the basis of a consideration of the effects of a departure from a fully distributed cost standard on the transportation industry as a whole. Until that evaluation was completed, the Commission took the position that it would continue to follow the practice it had observed in the past of dealing with individual rate reductions on a fully distributed cost basis.

. . . In any event, regardless of the label used, it seems self-evident that a carrier's "inherent advantage" of being the low cost mode on a fully distributed cost basis is impaired when a competitor sets a rate that forces the carrier to lower its own rate below its fully distributed costs in order to retain the traffic. In addition, when a rate war would be likely to eventually result in pushing rates to a level at which the rates set would no longer provide a fair profit, the Commission has traditionally, and properly, taken the position that such a rate struggle should be prevented from commencing in the first place. Certainly there is no suggestion here that the rate charged by the barge-truck combination was excessive and in need of being driven down by competitive pressure. We conclude, therefore, that the Commission adequately articulated its reasons for determining that the railroads' rate would impair the inherent advantage enjoyed by the barge-truck service.

The judgment of the District Court is reversed and the cases are remanded to that court with directions to enter a judgment affirming the Commission's order.

It is so ordered.

In the Matter of

Use of the Carterfone Device in Message Toll Telephone Service

13 F.C.C. 420 (1968)

Carterfone and MCI (see below) reversed the FCC's long acquiescence in Bell System policies excluding competition from its various markets. A rapid growth in terminal equipment followed, with improved variety and little adverse effect on the whole system's performance.

By Commissioner Nicholas Johnson for the Commission:

This proceeding involves the application of American Telephone and Telegraph Co. tariffs to the use by telephone subscribers of the Carterfone.

The Carterfone is designed to be connected to a two-way radio at the base station serving a mobile radio system. When callers on the radio and on the telephone are both in contact with the base station operation, the handset of the operator's telephone is placed on a cradle in the Carterfone device. A voice control circuit in the Carterfone automatically switches on the radio transmitter when the telephone caller is speaking; when he stops speaking, the radio returns to a receiving condition. A separate speaker is attached to the Carterfone to allow the base station operator to monitor the conversation, adjust the voice volume, and hang up his telephone when the conversation has ended.

The Carterfone device, invented by Thomas F. Carter, has been produced and marketed by the Carter Electronics Corp., of which Mr. Carter is president, since 1959. From 1959 through 1966, approximately 4,500 Carterfones were produced and 3,500 sold to dealers and distributors throughout the United States and in foreign countries.

The defendant telephone companies, acting in accordance with their interpretation of tariff FCC No. 132, filed April 16, 1957, by American Telephone and Telegraph Co., advised their subscribers that the Carterfone, when used in conjunction with the subscriber's telephone, is a prohibited interconnecting device, the use of which would subject the user to the penalties provided in the tariff. The tariff provides that:

> No equipment, apparatus, circuit or device not furnished by the telephone company shall be attached to or connected with the facilities furnished by the telephone company, whether physically, by induction or otherwise.

❀   ❀   ❀   ❀   ❀

We agree with and adopt the examiner's findings that the Carterfone fills a need and that it does not adversely affect the telephone system. They are fully supported by the record. We also agree that the tariff broadly prohibits the use of interconnection devices, including the Carterfone. Its provisions are clear as to this. Finally, in view of the above findings, we hold, as did the examiner, that application of the tariff to bar the Carterfone in the future would be unreasonable and unduly discriminatory. However, for the reasons to be given, we also conclude that the tariff has been unreasonable, discriminatory, and unlawful in the past, and that the provisions prohibiting the use of customer-provided interconnecting devices should accordingly be stricken.

. . . [O]ur conclusion here is that a customer desiring to use an interconnecting device to improve the utility to him of both the telephone system and a private radio system should be able to do so, so long as the interconnection does not adversely affect the telephone company's operations or the telephone system's utility for others. A tariff which prevents this is unreasonable; it is also unduly discriminatory when, as here, the telephone company's own interconnecting equipment is approved for use. The vice of the present tariff, here as in Hush-A-Phone, is that it prohibits the use of harmless as well as harmful devices.

A.T.&T. has urged that since the telephone companies have the responsibility to establish, operate and improve the telephone system, they must have absolute control over the quality, installation and maintenance of all parts of the system in order effectively to carry out that responsibility. Installation of unauthorized equipment, according to the telephone companies, would have at least two negative results. First, it would divide the responsibility for assuring that each part of the system is able to function effectively and second, it would retard development of the system since the independent equipment supplier would tend to resist changes which would render his equipment obsolete.

There has been no adequate showing that nonharmful interconnection must be prohibited in order to permit the telephone company to carry out its system responsibilities. The risk feared by the examiner has not been demonstrated to be substantial, and no reason presents itself why it should be. No one entity need provide all interconnection equipment for our telephone system any more than a single source is needed to supply the parts for a space probe. We are not holding that the telephone companies may not prevent the use of devices which actually cause harm, or that they may not set up reasonable standards to be met by interconnection devices. These remedies are appropriate; we believe they are also adequate to fully protect the system.

Nor can we assume that the telephone companies would be hindered in improving telephone service by any tendency of the manufacturers and users of interconnection devices to resist change. The telephone companies would remain free to make improvements to the telephone system and could reflect any such improvements in reasonable revised standards for nontelephone company provided devices used in connection with the system. Manufacturers and sellers of such devices would then have the responsibility of offering for sale or use only such equipment as would be in compliance with such revised standards. An owner or user of a device which failed to meet reasonable revised standards for such devices, would either have to have the device rebuilt to comply with the revised standards or discontinue its use. Such is the risk inherent in the private ownership of any equipment to be used in connection with the telephone system. . . .

In view of the unlawfulness of the tariff there would be no point in merely declaring it invalid as applied to the Carterfone and permitting it to continue in operation as to other interconnection devices. This would also put a clearly improper burden upon the manufacturers and users of other devices. The appropriate remedy is to strike the tariff and permit the carriers, if they so desire, to propose new tariff provisions in accordance with this opinion. We make no rulings as to damages since that relief has not been requested. As noted above, the carriers may submit new tariffs which will protect the telephone system against harmful devices, and may specify technical standards if they wish.

Accordingly, we find that tariff FCC 263, paragraphs 2.6.1 and 2.6.9 are, and have since their inception been, unreasonable, unlawful and unreasonably discriminatory under sections 201(b) and 202(a) of the Communications Act of 1934, as amended.

In Re Applications of
Microwave Communications, Inc.
18 F.C.C. 953 (1969)

New entry into bulk transmission in the main routes is regarded as especially threatening by Bell System officials, who assert that such "cream-skimming" undermines the financing of the entire network. Despite this landmark FCC decision, rehearings and further tactics have yielded only slow compliance.

Commissioner Bartley for the Commission:

This proceeding involves applications filed by Microwave Communications, Inc. (MCI), for construction permits for new facilities in the

Domestic Public Point-to-Point Radio Service at Chicago, Ill., St. Louis, Mo., and nine intermediate points. MCI proposed to offer its subscribers a limited common carrier microwave radio service, designed to meet the interoffice and interplant communications needs of small business. . . . MCI, however, does not plan to provide its subscribers with a complete microwave service. The proposed service would be limited to transmissions between MCI's microwave sites, making it incumbent upon each subscriber to supply his own communications link between MCI's sites and his place of business (loop service).

MCI contends that it will offer its subscribers substantially lower rates than those charged for similar services by the established carriers and that subscribers with less than full-time communication needs will be able to achieve additional savings through the channel sharing and half-time use provisions of its proposed tariff. Up to five subscribers will be permitted to share each channel on a party-line basis with a pro-rata reduction in rates. . . . MCI further asserts that its proposed tariff contains fewer restrictions than those of the existing common carriers, so that greater flexibility of use will be possible, particularly with respect to channel bandwidth, splitting channels for voice and data transmissions, and in the attachment of customer equipment.

MCI's applications are opposed by Western Union Telegraph Co. (Western Union), General Telephone Co. of Illinois (General), and the Associated Bell System Cos., American Telephone and Telegraph Co., Illinois Bell Telephone Co., and Southwestern Bell Telephone Co. (Bell), which presently provide microwave services to the geographical area which MCI proposed to serve. In a memorandum opinion and order, on February 11, 1966, we designated the MCI applications for hearing on issues to determine inter alia: *(a)* whether the established common carriers offer services meeting the needs which MCI proposes to meet in the area which MCI proposes to serve; *(b)* whether the grant of MCI's applications would result in wasteful duplication of facilities; *(c)* whether MCI is financially qualified to construct and operate its proposed facilities; *(d)* whether there is need for MCI's proposal; and *(e)* whether operation of MCI's proposed system would result in interference to existing common carrier services.

The evidentiary hearings commenced on February 13, 1967, and were concluded on April 19, 1967. In an initial decision, Hearing Examiner Herbert Sharfman recommended the grant of MCI's applications. The examiner found that the proposed MCI system would not generate harmful electrical interference to the receivers of the existing carriers or receive harmful interference from their stations. Although he indicated that serious questions exist concerning the reliability of MCI's proposal, the examiner nevertheless found no reason to believe that the system would not work, and he concluded that MCI had established that it is technically qualified. The examiner also found that MCI is financially qualified and that it would offer its subscribers a more economical rate structure, additional savings through the utilization of the shared and half-time use provisions of its tariff, and greater flexibility of use which would permit MIC's subscribers to adapt the system to their particular needs. The examiner noted that the proposed Chicago-St. Louis route is served by a wide range of common carrier services, that there is a duplication of facilities, and that the MCI proposal would result in additional duplication. However, he concluded that MCI's lower rates and more flexible use would enable it to serve a market whose needs are unfulfilled by the available common carrier services; that consequently there would be no unnecessary or wasteful duplication; and that the public interest would be served by authorizing MCI's proposed microwave system.

Upon release of the initial decision, we recognized that the questions raised at the hearing involved important policy considerations respecting the entry of new licenses into the communications common carrier field. . . . We have considered the initial decision in light of the record, pleadings, and oral argument. Except as modified below and in the attached appendix, we adopt the hearing examiner's findings and conclusions.

❋   ❋   ❋   ❋   ❋

NEED FOR MCI'S PROPOSALS

This is not a rate proceeding . . . and we are not called upon to make specific findings concerning the reasonableness of MCI's proposed rates or whether they are compensatory. . . .

The significant fact remains that the existing carriers do not offer a 2-kc. voice channel and MCI will; so that a subscriber may achieve a substantial savings in his communications costs by utilizing MCI's services. Further savings may be effected by the sharing and part-time provision of MCI's proposal. . . .

Additional advantages to MCI's subscribers are afforded by the flexibility of its system. In contrast to the protesting carriers which will lease no less than a nominal 4-kc. channel for voice use, MCI will lease and subdivide its channel into bandwidths in increments of 2-kc. and permit multiple terminations of channels. Furthermore, MCI imposes fewer restrictions on the nature of the subscribers' terminal equipment and on the use of its channels. The absence of restrictions gives each MCI subscriber the same flexibility to vary its stations' capability and use as if it were its own private system. Thus, each subscriber may adapt the system to its particular needs and equipment, lease shelter and tower space from MCI, and use the MCI trunk system for the carriage of voice, facsimile, and high speed or lower speed data transmissions, or a combination thereof in a manner which best suits its business requirements. No comparable degree of flexibility is offered by the existing carriers. . . .

The carriers argue that even if lower rates for MCI communications services have been shown, that factor may not properly be considered in resolving the issue of need. They assert that they are required by the Commission to serve both high-density high-profit and low-density low-profit areas and in order to maintain rates which are relatively uniform, all rates are based on a cost averaging principle. Claiming that MCI is "cream skimming," i.e., proposing to operate solely on high density routes where lower fixed costs per channel permit lower rates with higher profits, the carriers state that in order to compete with MCI they will be forced to abandon their cost averaging policies with a resultant increase in rates for subscribers on lightly used routes.

MCI is offering a service intended primarily for interplant and inter-office communications with unique and specialized characteristics. In these circumstances we cannot perceive how a grant of the authorizations requested would pose any serious threat to the established carriers' price averaging policies. Lower rates for the service offered is not the sole basis for our determination that MCI has demonstrated a need for the proposed facilities, but the flexibility available to subscribers, and the sharing and the part-time features of the proposal have been considered to be significant factors as well. . . . It may be, as the telephone companies and Western Union argue, that some business will be diverted from the existing carriers upon the grant of MCI's applications, but that fact provides no sufficient basis for depriving a segment of the public of the benefits of a new and different service.

Moreover, if we were to follow the carriers' reasoning and specify as a prerequisite to the establishment of a new common carrier service that it be so widespread as to permit cost averaging, we would in effect restrict the entry of new licensees into the common carrier field to a few large companies which are capable of serving the entire Nation. Such an approach is both unrealistic and inconsistent with the public interest. Innovations in the types and character of communications services offered or economies in operation which could not at once be instituted on a nationwide basis would be precluded from ever being introduced. In the circumstances of this case, we find the cream skimming argument to be without merit. . . .

RELIABILITY OF SERVICE

No specific standards have been enunciated by the Commission as to what constitutes a minimum degree of reliability which is acceptable for a common carrier communications service, and we believe it would be inconsistent with the public interest, in view of the need for the proposed service and the valuable information to be obtained from the operation of the system, to defer action in this proceeding until such standards are adopted. On the basis of the evidence before us, however, we find that the MCI proposal may reasonably be expected to achieve a degree of reliability which, while not matching the high degree of reliability claimed by the major carriers, will provide an acceptable and a marketable common carrier service. . . .

EFFICIENT UTILIZATION OF THE FREQUENCY SPECTRUM

We recognize, as the carriers argue, that MCI will not make the fullest possible use of the frequencies which it seeks. . . . We have found that by reason of its low-cost, sharing and part-time use provisions, MCI can reasonably be expected to furnish an economical microwave communications service to a segment of the public which presently cannot avail itself of such a service; and that its flexibility features will enable potential users to make more efficient use of their business equipment. These are substantial benefits which, in our view, outweigh the fact that MCI will not make the fullest possible use of its frequencies. When frequencies are used to meet a significant unfulfilled communications need, we do not believe that such use may be considered as "inefficient."

THE FEASIBILITY OF LOOP SERVICE

The testimony of MCI's public witnesses and the findings of the Spindletop survey show that, in general, MCI's potential subscribers have no interest in providing their own communications link between their facilities and MCI's transmitter sites. Therefore, MCI's ability to market its services will be dependent on the ability of its subscribers to secure loop service from the other common carriers serving the service area.

What seems a more likely obstacle in interconnection is, as the hearing examiner indicated, the "carriers' intransigence, manifested in this case. . . ." In these circumstances, the carriers are not in a position to argue that consideration of the interconnection question is premature. Since they have indicated that they will not voluntarily provide loop service we shall retain jurisdiction of this proceeding in order to enable MCI to obtain from the Commission a prompt determination on the matter of interconnection. Thus, at such time as MCI has customers and the facts and details of the customers' requirements are known, MCI may come directly to the Commission with a request for an order of interconnection. We have already concluded that a grant of MCI's proposal is in the public interest.

We likewise conclude that, absent a significant showing that interconnection is not technically feasible, the issuance of an order requiring the existing carriers to provide loop service is in the public interest. . . .

SUMMARY

This is a very close case and one which presents exceptionally difficult questions. We have found MCI to be financially qualified but we realize that any unforeseen circumstances requiring a sizable expenditure may impair the applicant's financial capacity. We have found, based on the weight of the evidence, that there is a substantial likelihood that the communications of its subscribers will arrive promptly, in accurate form, and without extended interruptions due to failures in the system. We wish to make clear, therefore, that the findings and conclusions reached herein, apply only to the frequencies specified, and for the areas described, in the applications now pending before us. Should MCI seek to obtain additional frequencies or to extend its microwave service to new areas, our action on its application will be based on a close scrutiny of its operations, the rules then governing the grant of applications for common carrier microwave frequencies and all other applicable policy considerations. Likewise, in connection with an application for renewal of license, we may deny the application if circumstances so warrant or grant renewal on such conditions as we deem essential to insure that MCI's subscribers receive a reliable transmission service of acceptable quality. However, it would be inconsistent with the public interest to deny MCI's applications and thus deprive the applicant of an opportunity to demonstrate that its proposed microwave facilities will bring to its subscribers the substantial benefits which it predicts and which we have found to be supported by the evidence in this proceeding. We conclude, on the basis of the record as a whole, that the public interest will be served by a grant of MCI's application.

Dissenting Statement of Chairman Rosel H. Hyde:

The decision of the majority is diametrically opposed to sound economics and regulatory principles. It likewise is designed to cost the average American ratepayer money to the immediate benefit of a few with special interests. . . .

Why does the majority condone this obviously grossly inefficient use of the spectrum. Because, they say, of the low cost and flexibility of the facilities proposed by applicants. It should be noted that the so-called flexibility cited by the majority is here, as it was in the TELPAK case, a mere euphemism connoting lower rates. But how is it that applicant is able to propose lower rates than the existing common carriers for private-line service? For no other reason than that it is proposing a typical "cream-skimming" operation. Thus, it has selected a major route, Chicago to St. Louis, with heavy traffic density characteristics and the concomitant lower unit costs. The existing common carriers, on the other hand have been encouraged by the Commission, primarily for social reasons, to base their rates both for message toll and private-line services on nationwide average costs. Thus the small users in the hinterlands are afforded the same rates as the large users in the major cities. The evidence in this record tends to show, and there is no basis in our experience to believe otherwise, that A.T.&T. and Western Union could offer lower rates for private-line service between Chicago and St. Louis than those proposed by MCI, were they to base such rates on their costs for that route alone.

The chances are, and the record so indicates, that A.T.&T. and Western Union will be constrained to lower their private-line rates to meet the competition of MCI. This, however, means that other users, either the small private-line users who are not so fortunate as to live in large cities, or message toll users, or both, will have to make up the difference if total revenue requirements are to be met. . . .

Separate Statement of Commissioner Nicholas Johnson:

What do the proponents of regulation fear about this radical experiment with competition? "Cream-skimming." Once an honorable enough agricultural undertaking, the expression is now used as an economic pejorative. The suggestion is that if competition were ever to be extended to such a sensitive area as pricing, then the correct prices might not be charged. The services for which costs are low might be priced lower than those for which costs are high. The currently exorbitantly high profits from the low-cost services would be "skimmed" by a company that would fail to provide the higher cost services as well. . . .

An additional problem with a cream skimming argument at this time is that it is a little too late. To make the argument is to suggest that any deviation from present pricing policies is somehow immoral, illegal, and unprecedented, and will result in higher prices to all consumers. It is none of the above. The telephone rate system is riddled with subsidies. In the first place, the telephone company itself deals in cream skimming. The really high-cost low-revenue subscribers—those who live in rural America—would never have had telephone service had they waited for Bell to ring. They had to get government assistance through the Rural Electrification Administration, their own cooperative telephone services, and non-Bell microwave carriers. In the second place, Bell has notoriously undercharged for those services in which it is engaged in competition—making up the differences by soaking those subscribers over whom it has a monopoly. . . . Finally, Congress has just given its approval to the principle of free or reduced cost service to educational radio and television interconnection—over the protests of the telephone company. . . .

IV. Questions for Review: Regulation

How can we tell whether an industry is a "public utility" and therefore should be regulated?

The goal of regulation is often thought to be "to simulate the patterns of competition." What problems is such an approach likely to run into?

Public utility regulation has been compared to the cost-plus method for buying military supplies. In both cases, it is said, public policies remove incentives for efficiency. Is this a fair appraisal?

Is a "comparable earnings" criterion appropriate for setting regulatory profit-rate ceilings?

A. "Value-of-service pricing has two great virtues. It charges users according to their ability to pay. And it encourages the maximum use (and growth) of the service. Therefore value of service pricing promotes both equity and efficiency."

B. "Value of service is simply a euphemism to cloak a system of charging what the traffic will bear. It also encourages too much expansion by the utility. Therefore value of service pricing violates both equity and efficiency."

Who's right, A or B? Or are they both wrong?

Under what conditions do "marginal-cost pricing" and "value-of-service pricing" prescribe the same rate structure? Use a diagram, if you think it helpful.

Give a practical example of a conflict between an *efficient* price and an *equitable* (fair) price.

Can an economist determine if a particular utility price is "just and reasonable"? Explain.

Would a utility usually prefer that its yearly depreciation allowance be large or small? Explain.

Outline the reasons why public utility regulation may induce too large a share of resources into the public utility industries.

How does the Averch-Johnson hypothesis now stand, in point of (1) logic and (2) quantitative importance?

You have been assigned to test for the presence of the Averch-Johnson "rate base effect" in regulated utilities. What criteria will guide your selection of possible cases? That is, under what conditions is the A–J effect likely to be strong and observable?

Reconcile the purported "Averch-Johnson effect," according to which utilities should overinvest in capital, with the existence of electricity shortages in many areas.

Define these and indicate their importance for regulation (5 minutes each):
Efficient allocation. Replacement cost depreciation. Fair value. Second-best.

"The cost of capital is simply a weighted average based on the company's
capital structure. The commission can measure this cost."

"The cost of capital is the minimum the utility must offer to attract new
capital funds, and this depends on the rate of return permitted by the commission. The commission cannot measure this cost; it is *making* it."

Which one is right? Explain.

Is regulatory lag really a good way to achieve "incentive regulation?" Explain.

Name two of the "tougher" state regulatory commissions. How can one judge
this?

What is marginal-cost pricing, and why may it be important? In what circumstances is it *not* important? Give a practical example of marginal-cost
pricing.

For what two main reasons might electric companies set lower prices to industrial users than to households?

"Businesses are charged *more* for phone service than are households; e.g.,
$12 per month compared to $4.25. But businesses pay *less* for electricity than
households are charged; e.g., 1¢ per kilowatt hour compared to 2¢." What *economic* factors affecting price discrimination may explain this strange apparent
contrast in price differentials?

Why might utility regulation cause inefficiency? *Does* it? You have been
commissioned to do a comprehensive study evaluating the performance of the
privately owned, regulated part of the electric power industry. *(a)* What performance standards would you use? *(b)* What do you expect your general conclusions would eventually be (excellent, poor, mediocre, etc., on specific standards)? *(c)* Why are performance appraisals such as these usually difficult to
make?

Have Bell System earnings been "comparable" in recent years to those elsewhere? Explain the criteria you use in reaching an answer.

What main effects has regulation had in telecommunications, electric power,
railroads *or* airlines (choose only one)? Distinguish between *structural* (or strategic) regulation and controls on *behavior*. In the case you discuss, what main
changes, if any, would you recommend in regulation?

"Competition between gas and electric utilities is intense." Does this mean
that regulation is no longer necessary?

What is the key difference between price regulation by (1) the CAB, on
the one hand, and (2) the FCC and FPC, on the other?

There are several areas (such as natural gas production) where the proper coverage of regulation is in question. Note *three* of these areas (excluding natural gas production). Appraise the issues and give your recommendation.

The possibility of "destructive competition" has been used to justify the "regulation" of such sectors as air transport, stock trading, and commercial banking. Summarize the theory of destructive competition. Evaluate whether the possibility of destructive competition justifies actual policies now in being.

Part V

PUBLIC ENTERPRISE

The literature on public enterprise is sparse, for several reasons. American ideology has been adverse (cultivated in part by private interests). Research support on the topic is scanty. Experience has been limited. Many economic issues arising under public enterprise—including competition, motivation, and utility pricing—are "covered" elsewhere in a private-ownership context.

The readings here touch on several of the issues, trying to show the diversity of issues and of the public enterprises themselves.

John Kenneth Galbraith (1908–   )

ECONOMICS AND THE PUBLIC PURPOSE*

*Galbraith offers reasons for extending public owner-
ship in both the "planning system" (major industries
dominated by large firms) and the "market system" (the
remainder: small-scale competitive industries)—and in
the weapons sector.*

*   *   *   *   *

In its mature form the corporation can be thought of as an instrument
principally for perpetuating inequality. The stockholders, as we have
seen, have no function. They do not contribute to capital or to management; they are the passive recipients of dividends and capital gains. As
these increase from year to year, so, and effortlessly, do their income and
wealth. And the tradition of privacy accords the technostructure autonomy in setting its own compensation and in continuing and enlarging the
differentials.

A solution would be to convert the fully mature corporations—those
that have completed the euthanasia of stockholder power—into fully
public corporations. Assuming the undesirability of expropriation this
would mean public purchase of the stock with fixed interest-bearing securities. This would perpetuate inequality, but it would no longer increase
adventitiously with further increases in dividends and capital gains. In
time, inheritance, inheritance taxes, philanthropy, profligacy, alimony and
inflation would act to disperse this wealth. Meanwhile the allowable differentials in compensation could be established by the state in accordance
with what is deemed necessary and just.

In principle there would be no effect on management from such a

---

* John Kenneth Galbraith, *Economics and the Public Purpose* (Boston: Houghton
Mifflin, 1973), pp. 271–72 and 277–85. Copyright by John Kenneth Galbraith. Reprinted by permission of Houghton Mifflin Company. Galbraith needs little introduction here, except perhaps to note (1) that he had close experience with industrial
behavior as a chief World War II price-control official and on *Fortune*'s editorial
board before joining the Harvard faculty; and (2) that the gist of his ideas about
large-scale industry has gained increasing acceptance.

change. The stockholder disappears, but the stockholder was previously powerless. Men of talent, even at the lower levels of compensation, would prefer the executive offices to the shop floor. And, in fact, there are numerous such public corporations—Renault, Volkswagen in its best days, the Tennessee Valley Authority, many publicly owned utilities—which are indistinguishable in their operations from so-called private corporations. In any case we are dealing here with the part of the economy which is characterized by relative overdevelopment. In consequence the social claims of efficiency are secondary to those of equality.

. . . The modern corporate enterprise, as we have sufficiently seen, is highly organized—highly bureaucratic. So is, or will be, the publicly owned firm. When the choice was between private monopoly power and public bureaucracy, the case for the latter could seem strong. The public bureaucracy might not be responsive, but it was not exploitative and thus malign. The choice between a private bureaucracy and a public bureaucracy is a good deal less clear. A very great difference in substance has been reduced, seemingly at least, to a much smaller difference in form. Added to this has been the discovery that the larger and more technical of the public bureaucracies—the Air Force, Navy, Atomic Energy Commission —have purposes of their own which can be quite as intransigently pursued as those of General Motors or Exxon. Private bureaucracies rule in their own interest. But so do public bureaucracies. Why exchange one bureaucracy for another? As elsewhere noted, the declining appeal of the Soviet Union to the modern radical is here also explained. Why exchange one bureaucratic society for another? China and Cuba seem much more appealing models. Some of their appeal, alas, is the result of their lower level of development with, and for this reason, less elaborate organization —a defect they are strenuously anxious to correct. . . .

The compelling circumstance, as the reader will have suspected, is the retarded development of the market system. There are industries here which require technical competence, related organization and market power and related command over resource use if they are to render minimally adequate service. Being and remaining in the market system, these they do not have. So they stay in a limbo of nondevelopment or primitive development, and, as development goes forward elsewhere, their contrasting backwardness becomes increasingly dramatic.

Adding forcefully to the drama (and the distress of those who would resist all thought of socialism) is the fact that certain of the retarded industries are of peculiar importance not alone for comfort, well-being, tranquillity and happiness but also for continued existence. They provide shelter, health services and local transportation of people. Housing in a cold climate, medical attention when one is sick and the ability to reach one's place of employment are remarkably unfrivolous needs. One can readily detect the hand of a perverse Providence in the selection of the retarded industries. He is clearly bent on bothering the truly pious free-enterpriser.

The failure of these industries to pass into the planning system has diverse causes. Housing construction and medical services are geographically dispersed. As with all services this militates against the development of a comprehensive organization and specialization at any particular point. Such division of labor as may be possible is accomplished with manifest inefficiency. The time of carpenters, plumbers and electricians or, in the case of medical services, specialized surgical practitioners, physicians or technicians cannot be so scheduled as to avoid long intervals of ineffective use or idleness.

Unions have also played a retarding role. They are not uniquely strong in these industries. But employers have been uniquely weak as in the case of the construction industry, compliant as in the case of the transportation industry or members of the union itself as in the case of the American Medical Association. Thus the unions have had a free hand in regulating or prohibiting technical innovation or (as in the case of the AMA for a long time) organization that would have allowed of more effective economic development. Finally, in construction and transportation, public regulation, often inspired by employees or unions, has acted to inhibit technical innovation and the associated organization.

. . . There is only one solution. These industries cannot function in the market system. They do not develop in the planning system. They are indispensable as people now view their need for means to move about and for protection from disease and the weather. . . .

The only answer for these industries is full organization under public ownership. This is the new socialism which searches not for the positions of power in the economy but for the positions of weakness. And again we remark that most reliable of tendencies—and the best of tests of the validity of social diagnosis—which is that circumstance is forcing the pace. In all the developed countries governments have been forced to concern themselves extensively with housing, health and transportation. Everywhere they are already, in large measure, socialized. This is true in the United States as elsewhere. Local and commuter transportation has passed extensively into public ownership. So, with the arrival of Amtrak, has intercity rail travel. In the United States the old, who combine exceptional medical need with inferior ability to pay—for whom, in other words, the market operates with peculiar inadequacy—are provided with medical and hospital care. There is a bewildering variety of public medical assistance to other individuals and groups. In the housing industry there is an even more intricate complex of publicly sponsored construction, publicly aided construction, publicly financed construction, public subsidies to private occupancy and public control of rents. These functions, in turn, are divided among federal, state and local levels of government in such fashion that it is doubtful if any single official in any major American city knows all of the public sources of support to housing in his community.

This is, however, a highly unsatisfactory form of socialism. The term itself is scrupulously avoided. And the resulting action is not undertaken affirmatively and proudly with the requisite means, the best available organization and with a view to the full accomplishment of the needed task. Rather it is viewed as exceptional and aberrant. It requires apology. The most desirable organization is never that which is best but that which seems least to interfere with private enterprise; the test of result is not the full accomplishment of the task but what is sufficient to get by.

Only as socialism is seen as a necessary and wholly *normal* feature of the system will this situation change. Then there will be public demand for high performance, and there will be public pride in the action. This is not vacuous and untested optimism; proof is to be found in Europe and Japan. There, as noted, the word socialism is evocative, not pejorative. And while socialists in other developed countries are attracted theologically by the positions of power, they are not repelled by the need for public action elsewhere in the economy. This means that they can act pridefully in the market system. This has produced a radically superior result in the areas of weakness where socialism is compelled. Although there is much variation as between countries, urban land has been taken extensively into public ownership; a large part of all urban housing has been built under full public auspices and continued with full public ownership and management. Similarly hospitals are full public enterprises; doctors and other medical attendants are well-paid employees of the state. And it is, of course, taken for granted that public corporations will run the railroads and urban transportation. The performance of all of these industries in Britain, Scandinavia, Germany and Holland is categorically superior to that in the United States. In other countries—France, Italy, Japan, Switzerland—the enterprises that have been fully socialized, notably rail and urban transport, are superior. Only those that have not been socialized are deficient. The difference between Americans and Europeans is not that Americans have a peculiar ineptitude for operating public enterprises. The difference is that Americans have been guided by a doctrine that accords a second-rate and apologetic status to such effort.

In the past the case for public ownership was conceded where, because of the importance of the service, as in the case of education or the national defense, or the difficulty in pricing it to a particular user, as in the case of road building or street cleaning, it could not be left to the market. Or public ownership was pressed where, as in the case of public utilities, there was an inevitable monopoly and thus a danger of public exploitation. With the rise of the market and the planning systems, and the consequent inequality in development, the case for public ownership becomes much more general. It is not that the market, though generally satisfactory, fails in particular cases. It is rather that the market system is generally deficient in relation to the planning system. Accordingly there is a presumption in favor of public intervention anywhere in the market system. . . .

But the story is not yet complete. The case for socialism is imperative in the weakest areas of the economy. It is also paradoxically compelling in the parts of exceptional strength. It is here the answer, or part of the answer, to the power of the planning system that derives from bureaucratic symbiosis.

Where the technostructure of the corporation is in peculiarly close relationship with the public bureaucracy, each, we have seen, draws power from its support by the other. The large weapons firms—Lockheed, General Dynamics, Grumman, the aerospace subsidiaries of Textron and Ling-Temco-Vought—propose to the Pentagon the weapons systems they would find it advantageous to develop and build. The Department of Defense proposes to them the systems the Services would like to have. The resulting decisions are then justified either by the need to keep up with the Soviets or the need to remain ahead of the Soviets. One or the other of these justifications is bound to succeed. As previously noted, not even the most devout defender of orthodox models risks his reputation for minimal percipience by arguing that the resulting output is in response to public will as expressed through the Congress.

Two bureaucracies, one public and one nominally private, are stronger than one. The public bureaucracy, in citing the need for new weapons, can seem to be speaking out of a disinterested concern for the public security. Its control over intelligence allows it, as necessary, to exploit public and congressional fears as to what the Soviets are doing or might be doing. Commonplace procedure requires that any proposed new weapon be preceded by a flood of alarming information on what the Russians are up to. The private bureaucracy has freedom and financial resources not available to the public bureaucracy for making strategic political contributions, for mobilizing union and community support, for lobbying, for advertising and for public and press relations.

The combined power of the two bureaucracies would be usefully reduced by converting the large specialized weapons firms into full public corporations along lines mentioned in the last chapter. The government would acquire their stock at recently prevailing stock market valuation. Thereafter the boards of directors and senior management would be appointed by the Federal Government. Salaries and other emoluments would henceforth be regulated by the government in general relation to public levels; profits would accrue to the government; so also would losses as is now the case. Political activity, lobbying and community persuasion would be subject to such constraints as a public bureaucracy must abide.

This change is one of form rather than substance. For the large, specialized weapons firms the cloak of private enterprise is already perilously, and even indecently, thin. General Dynamics and Lockheed, the two largest specialized defense contractors, do virtually all of their business with the government. Their working capital is supplied, by means of progress payments on their contracts, by the government. A not inconsiderable portion of their plant and equipment is owned by the government. Losses are absorbed by the government, and the firms are subject to financial rescue in the event of misfortune. Their technostructures are the upward extension of the hierarchy of the public bureaucracy; generals, admirals, subordinate officers and civil servants, on completing their careers in the public bureaucracy, proceed automatically and at higher pay to the corporate bureaucracy. The corporate bureaucracy, in return, lends its personnel to the upper civilian levels of the Department of Defense. The large weapons firms are already socialized except in name; what is here proposed only affirms the reality. As a rough rule a corporation (or conglomerate subsidiary) doing more than half of its business with the government should be converted into a full public corporation as here proposed.

* * * * *

Gurney Breckenfeld

NOBODY POURS IT LIKE
FANNIE MAE*

The Federal National Mortgage Association (FNMA: "Fannie Mae") is now a large, active quasi-public firm, as this report attests. It plays a key role in housing finance, and it is fully as entrepreneurial as most private firms. But, like most public firms in the U.S., it is little noticed. Note how it mingles commercial and social objectives.

Even people who ought to know better sometimes mistake Fannie Mae, the world's largest mortgage bank (assets at the end of 1971: $18.6 billion), for Fannie May, the Chicago-based candy manufacturer. . . .

---

* Gurney Breckenfeld, "Nobody Pours It Like Fannie Mae," *Fortune* magazine, June 1972, excerpted from pp. 86–89 and 136, 140, and 145. © 1972 Time Inc. Breckenfeld is a staff writer at *Fortune*.

Anyone who is confused about Fannie Mae has some pretty good excuses. The company is, first of all, neither a purely private enterprise nor a purely government agency, but, rather, a curious combination of the two. It is ultimately controlled by the President of the United States (who, in fact, appointed Hunter after firing his predecessor) and it is charged with major responsibilities in implementing U.S. housing policies; but it is also supposed to seek profits for its stockholders (who have, in fact, done rather well in recent years). It has been renamed once and restructured three times, and its mission has been redefined twice.

FNMA's principal mission these days is to provide lenders and builders with mortgage money for housing when such funds are difficult to obtain from traditional private sources: the savings and loan associations, banks, and insurance companies. During 1970, the most recent year in which mortgage money was in short supply, Fannie Mae financed nearly a quarter of the nation's new housing. By doing so, the association minimized the decline in housing starts, thus tempering the severity of the last recession.

Fannie Mae wields enormous influence over the housing industry and, indeed, over the whole U.S. economy. Her decisions about how and where to pump money into housing finance can diminish or multiply the fortunes of thousands of entrepreneurs in building and allied fields. To a lesser but still interesting degree, the association's policies also affect the interest rate on money that many consumers borrow to buy or build homes.

RESHAPING A $70-BILLION BUSINESS

During most of her lifetime, Fannie Mae has limited her financing to government-backed mortgages. But last February she took a portentous step: the association began dealing in conventional mortgages—those not insured by the Federal Housing Administration or guaranteed by the Veterans Administration. In entering this new field, Fannie Mae is confronting some lively competition. The Federal Home Loan Mortgage Corporation, a new arm of the Federal Home Loan Bank Board, has entered the same field, and in March the wholly private MGIC Investment Corp. started a similar enterprise. . . . All three rivals aim to reshape the $70-billion-a-year residential-mortgage business by creating an enormous trading market in conventional loans, which account for three quarters of the total. One result of this competition should be a marked increase in the availability of 95 percent mortgage loans, of as much as $40,000, for buyers of both new and existing houses.

Fannie Mae has risen to her present preeminence among mortgage lenders because she managed, at least in some respects, to escape from federal captivity. As a government agency, created in 1938, FNMA natu-

rally found it easy to borrow money in the private market to make mortgage loans. But the borrowed funds went on the Treasury's books in red
ink, increasing the federal deficit. In order to keep those funds out of the
deficit, and to free her from the restraints imposed by the government's
debt limit, the 1968 Housing Act transformed Fannie Mae from a government agency into a private corporation. In May, 1970, control of the company's board of directors moved into the hands of 7,300 (now 14,880)
private stockholders.

The stockholders elect ten of the association's directors, but the President of the United States appoints the other five and he may remove any
of the fifteen from office "for good cause shown." The congressional charter also grants . . . [the] Secretary of Housing and Urban Development,
"general regulatory powers" over FNMA affairs; decisions involving dividends, stock issues, total debt, and borrowing must have [his] explicit
approval. In addition, the Secretary of the Treasury must approve the
timing, maturity, and amount of all debt securities that the company sells.

The government's stranglehold over Fannie Mae's finances has not yet
interfered with her operations, but the potential is there because the company runs almost entirely on borrowed money. The allowable ratio of
debt to equity, . . . raised to twenty-five to one, far exceeds that of any
other major financial company in the U.S.; Fannie Mae has roughly one
third as much capital, in relation to liabilities, as a typical commercial
bank. Last year the company floated $13 billion of loans, including refi-
nancing—a volume second only to that of the Treasury.

A PRIVILEGED BORROWER

The financial controls are intended, as Congress made clear in the Senate and House Committee reports accompanying the 1968 legislation, to
ensure that Fannie Mae operates in the public interest. Specifically, she
is supposed to promote an increased flow of mortgage credit and to help
finance housing for low- and moderate-income families. And because of
Fannie Mae's public purpose, Congress let her retain the privileged borrowing status of a government agency—which means lower interest charges
and a broader market for her debentures and notes. To further enhance
her credit standing, the lawmakers also gave Fannie Mae the power, in
an emergency, to borrow up to $2.25 billion from the U.S. Treasury.

Thus enjoying the benefits of federal sponsorship, Fannie Mae has become a gigantic money-transfer machine, using her government credit
rating to borrow billions on Wall Street, and relending the funds at higher
interest rates to finance homes and apartments. During the past four years
the company has more than tripled in size; its $18.6 billion of assets at the
end of 1971 made it, by that measure, the eighth-largest company in the
U.S., just behind Jersey Standard and just ahead of General Motors.

(A.T.&T., with $54.5 billion of assets, is the largest company of all.) Over the same four-year span, Fannie Mae's mortgage holdings rose from $5.5 billion to $17.8 billion and her debt increased even faster, from almost $5 billion to $17.7 billion. Profits climbed 686 percent, from $7,779,000 to $61,181,000, and per-share earnings (adjusted for two stock splits) more than trebled, from 41 cents to $1.43. . . .

In the long search for alternative methods to bring a larger, more reliable flow of money into housing, attention gradually turned toward the vast pool of capital in the nation's bond and money markets. To be sure, a small link between housing and the securities market had been forged a generation ago by Fannie Mae herself and the privately owned, government-run Home Loan Bank System (which supervises the nation's s. and l.'s and lends them money raised on Wall Street in much the same way as FNMA). But until the last half of the Sixties, their operations remained so small, compared with the total volume of residential lending, as to have only a minor impact. . . .

Many large investors consider mortgages to be a cumbersome and undesirable outlet for their money, and the legislation that turned Fannie Mae private also made an effort to attract more of this money into mortgages. Congress created a new agency, the Government National Mortgage Association, nicknamed Ginnie Mae, which took over Fannie Mae's job of making mortgage loans with Treasury money for HUD's galaxy of subsidized housing programs. The law provided Ginnie with an entirely new device to snare capital for both subsidized and unsubsidized FHA and VA loans. Ginnie stamps her guarantee, pledging the full faith and credit of the government to pay both principal and interest, upon "mortgage-backed securities." These represent pools of FHA and VA loans (minimum amount: $2 million) that are, of course, already insured or guaranteed by the government.

Fannie Mae by herself has, of course, far more impact on housing and the U.S. economy than Ginnie Mae and Freddie Mac combined. Yet the company remains almost invisible to most Americans because it deals with the public entirely through 1,500 middlemen, principally mortagage bankers. These companies make loans to builders and home buyers, resell the loans to FNMA, and thereafter collect the monthly payments, forwarding to the association the principal and interest, minus a fee (currently ⅜ of 1 percent).

To sell loans on one- to four-family homes to Fannie Mae, they must submit bids at the company's weekly auctions. What Fannie Mae auctions off at these remarkable events is in effect a four-month "put." Each bidder names the dollar amount he would like to sell, and the interest yield he will accept, on mortgages to be delivered within four months.

The auctions take place on Mondays, normally alternating between FHA and VA loans one week and conventional loans the next. Bidders telephone their offers to a battery of sixteen skilled clerks at Fannie Mae head-quarters in Washington. From the opening at 10:00 A.M. to the closing at 3:00 P.M., the auction staff feverishly jots down the amount and price of each bid, reads the figures back for verification, and simultaneously tape-records each message to permit a subsequent double check. Only after all the bids are in and computers have analyzed the offerings do Fannie Mae's top officers decide which ones to accept. Fannie Mae calls this procedure a "free-market system auction; however, many mortgage bankers argue with the characterization, complaining that the agency can rig the average yield of accepted bids (i.e., by rejecting those they consider too low).

Each winner receives a contractual commitment that the agency will buy all, or a stated part, of its offering if it is delivered to the agency within four months; in exchange for this commitment the winner must pay a non-refundable fee of ¼ of 1 percent of the amount of the loan. A winner is not required to go through with the sale; he may dispose of the loan else-where, and is apt to do so if interest rates fall (and the value of his mort-gage rises) during the four-month period. The rules are different for loans on multifamily dwellings. Fannie Mae buys only FHA-insured mortgages, offers two-year commitments at fixed prices, and requires delivery of the loans.

The auctions attract an enormous amount of business. Last year the company received $10.4 billion in auction offers, rejected $6.8 billion, and accepted $3.6 billion. This year Hunter expects Fannie Mae to issue $7 billion in commitments, mostly through the weekly auctions, and to pur-chase $5 billion of loans, enough to finance 270,000 homes and apartment units.

NEW LIFE IN A PLODDING BUREAUCRACY

The auction was devised by mortgage banker Raymond H. Lapin, an aggressive innovator who, in two and a half years as Fannie Mae president, transformed the organization from a plodding civil-service bureaucracy into a major force in the mortgage market. . . .

Perhaps the largest management problem facing any Fannie Mae chief executive is the recurrent conflict between the company's need to earn profits and its obligation to support housing. For example, when mortgage money grew scarce three years ago, the company borrowed heavily at high and rising interest rates in order to expand its loans and prop up housing starts. As a result, for the sixteen months from May, 1969, to February, 1971, FNMA earned less from its loan portfolio than it spent for borrowed funds. In February, 1970, the month that Hunter calls "the blackest period of our cost-price crisis," the company paid an average of 7.59 percent on $11.7 billion of debt and collected only 6.59 percent on $12.1 billion of mortgages. Only a sharp increase in income from commitment fees kept the company from slipping into the red. Even so, net income fell from $16,400,000 in 1969 to $6,700,000 in 1970, or from 63 cents to 19 cents per share. . . .

There is no clear-cut answer to the perennial question about whether Fannie Mae should place more emphasis on profits or on helping the mortgage market. The company's congressional charter admonishes it to be self-supporting, which means that profits must be adequate to attract private capital; but the law also says that support of the residential mortgage market is the company's prime aim, and this may require it to run in the red at times. "FNMA is nothing but one big conflict of interest," says Director Robert Pease, a prominent Chicago mortgage banker.

Gilbert Burck

A SOCIALIST ENTERPRISE THAT ACTS LIKE A FIERCE CAPITALIST COMPETITOR*

The Yugoslav firm named "Energoinvest" is a remarkable industrial hybrid that is (1) large, (2) a conglomerate, (3) publicly owned, (4) worker-managed (in part), (5) competitive and (6) successful. In Yugoslavia and other countries (including the U.S.), there are other hybrids, mixing these and other features in different ways.

Most Americans who know anything about Sarajevo think of it as the Balkan town where Archduke Franz Ferdinand's assassination touched off World War I. Few would imagine it as a modern industrial center. But that's what it is. Among other things, Sarajevo is the headquarters city for an industrial enterprise called Energoinvest, which may be described without undue exaggeration as one of the most ambitious, arresting, edifying, and important conglomerates the business world has ever sprouted. Founded twenty-one years ago by an entrepreneurial genius named Emerik Blum, Energoinvest has recently been expanding at more than 20 percent

* Gilbert Burck, "A Socialist Enterprise That Acts Like a Fierce Capitalist Competitor," *Fortune* magazine, January 1972, excerpted from pp. 82–86, 126, and 130–132. © 1972 Time, Inc. Burck is a staff writer at *Fortune*.

per annum. It now encompasses forty-one units turning out a wide range of products dominated by electrical and processing equipment such as heat exchangers, and it plans to become a major aluminum producer. It employs some 22,000 people, maintains sales offices in thirty-two countries, grosses about $160 million, and spends $5 million to $6 million a year on research, development, and scholarships. As a conglomerate, it is a rare if not unique phenomenon: because its affiliates can always secede from the group if they choose, the company's very existence depends on doing better for each affiliate than the affiliate can do by itself.

. . . Yugoslavia's Communism is nothing if not flexible, and it practices a kind of market socialism that compels "social" enterprises to operate like private enterprises.

Energoinvest certainly does just that. One of the most enterprising of Yugoslav enterprises, it scours the world for ideas, pays stiff fees to American management consultants, and exists not merely to make things but to sell them in competitive markets. Along with some other successful Yugoslav firms, Energoinvest has shown that the best way to make socialism work is to subject it to the discipline of the market and put it under good management. It provides an excellent example of a truth now being grasped throughout the whole industrial world: no matter what the political and social bent of a country, the art and science of producing and distributing goods and services efficiently are governed by essentially the same economic laws. . . .

The comrade consumers in the East are just as coy and elusive as the freewheeling buyers in the West. Inflation follows an inordinate expansion of the money supply just as inevitably in a totalitarian state as in representative democracies. . . . Whether socialized or private, production and trade flourish under good management and languish under bad.

THE BIGGER THE PROFITS, THE HIGHER THE WAGE

The key to the Yugoslav economic system is that it recognizes these facts. The system is not as strange and paradoxical as it sounds, nor is it something really new. A brilliant job of improvisation, it resembles very closely the private enterprise system, and it needs good management for the same reason the private system does. The basic difference between the two is that the Yugoslav system is based on so-called self-management *(samoupravljanje)*, which does away with private ownership and invests ownership in "the people," and expects workers and their councils to act as trustees for the people. Self-management is not universal in Yugoslavia; most of the country's farms and hundreds of thousands of small enterprises are privately owned. But the great bulk of the nonagricultural labor force works in "social" enterprises run by worker-elected councils. These workers are the "bosses." Technically they can fire their managers and pull their factories out of a complex like Energoinvest; and they make the final decisions on wages and investment. Their pay depends directly on profits, whereas pay in a private enterprise depends indirectly on them. But the profitability of a Yugoslav firm depends, as it does for enterprises at all times and everywhere, on management. . . .

The Yugoslavs concluded that their own economy had to be decentralized, for true socialism had to be based on motivation, not on command. The obvious way to decentralize without restoring private ownership was to turn to the well-known device of workers' councils—to set up councils in the enterprises and transfer most and eventually perhaps all of the state's economic power to them. But that, of course, meant allowing the enterprises to act freely, subject mainly to the discipline of the market. Without self-government, Yugoslav economists agreed, socialism was impossible. Without free enterprise, by the same token, workers' self-government was impossible.

HIRED HANDS TO BOSS THE BOSSES

The independence of the councils has been intermittently strengthened since 1950, when the era of self-management legally began, and today they are beholden to no one, at least in theory. In every firm with more than five jobs, the workers elect a council by secret ballot. Most councils number anywhere from 15 to 120 members, depending on the size of the enterprise, and they serve for two years. Since the councils generally meet only every month or two, they often choose a managing board, which includes the enterprise's director or chief executive, to keep the councils in frequent touch with the company's affairs. Each plant boasts at least one council, and large companies with several plants or divisions elect a central council that generally handles broad policy matters. Thus each of the forty-one affiliates of Energoinvest elects a council, often supplemented at lower levels by informal discussion groups. And a central council of about a hundred, elected by all the workers, assembles periodically in Sarajevo.

Legally, the director has a very ambiguous job. As chief executive officer, he is the chief hired hand, and implements the council's decisions. Appointed by the council from candidates selected by a committee, he must be re-elected by the council every four years; and the council can sack him if the case against him is strong enough. At the same time, he is charged with seeing to it that the enterprise does nothing contrary to the public interest.

As the Yugoslavs cheerfully explain, they are experimenting and learning from experience. In practice, the original statutes or charters of most enterprises have been rewritten to specify managerial prerogatives and authority. Energoinvest's statute, for instance, has been amended several times. It now empowers the managing director to coordinate the activities of the units or affiliates in the interests of the whole enterprise, to annul decisions made by his executives, to ask the councils to annul acts by their management boards if he considers them unwise, to sign agreements on behalf of the enterprise, and so on. He is also allowed to choose his own collegium or advisory body, composed largely of his chief executives and technical specialists. . . .

JOIN US AND MAKE MONEY

Just to keep itself together, therefore, Energoinvest has had to make each affiliate much better off in the federation than it would be on its own. So it built up an organization that offers prospective affiliates advantages they could get nowhere else. As early as the middle 1950s, Blum decided to develop export markets. The Yugoslav market was too small to allow economies of scale, and was still without a really competitive price structure. Blum realized what the Soviet Union and some other East European countries have still to recognize: modern industrial management in a closed society is a contradiction in terms. The only way to become an economic organization was to fight for business in world markets.

The group's first customers were Czechoslovakia and East Germany. Then, as Yugoslavia developed relations with "nonaligned" countries like itself, the company began to develop markets in the Middle East, the Far East, Africa, Pakistan, and eventually even in Europe and North America. Last year it sold cranes to Krupp and refinery equipment to a U.S. supply house, and, competing against the Japanese, it won a $1,500,000 contract to build a penstock for British Columbia Hydro & Power Authority. Exports in 1970 came to nearly 40 percent of revenues; the company's goal is 50 percent.

Energoinvest has also built up staff service departments unmatched anywhere in its part of the world. It maintains four research-and-development centers, including a new high-voltage laboratory; together these centers cost between $4 million and $5 million a year. Other services are provided by a large modern computer center, five designing departments, central export and purchasing departments, and a central financial department complete with a bank that handles all the group's money and financial transactions. And the company has ensured a steady supply of young executive talent, probably the scarcest industrial resource in Yugoslavia, by financing more than 3,100 scholarships at Sarajevo and a few other universities.

So the company's pitch to prospective affiliates can be summed up this way: "We ask you to adhere to our basic program, and charge you 4 to 6 percent of your gross, depending on the kinds of products you make. We have access to money, support all kinds of expertise, and can help you export in a way that nobody else can. If we cannot boost your profits in a couple of years, you are free to withdraw from our group."

. . . Yugoslav workers and directors often find themselves taking very different views of what is good for the business. Unlike a capitalist enterprise, which tends primarily to maximize the earnings on investment, the self-managed enterprise tends to maximize profit *per worker*. Therefore councils are reluctant to hire people for research, market analysis, or other "unproductive" jobs because these outlays reduce, at least temporarily, profits and hence wages per worker. Thus the council tends to take the short-term point of view, while the conscientious director takes the longer view. Blum has estimated that wages could be raised across the board by as much as 15 percent if his "investments" in research and other long-term intangibles were abolished. But this means, as Yugoslavs say, the workers would "eat up their future."

* * * * *

What is more, Blum argues that the workers' management system facilitates rather than hinders his job. Speaking before a symposium in Amsterdam two years ago, he declared flatly that it is easier for a Yugoslav director to function efficiently than it is for managers in the West, who face the incessant and arbitrary opposition of trade unions, or managers in the Soviet Union, who are "subject to the assessments and wills of government bureaucrats." . . .

The Yugoslav economic press has begun to decry the growing power of "big business" and the banks, which supply nearly all industrial capital, and to profess alarm about the growing concentration of the country's resources. Blum's agreement in effect anticipated more of this kind of talk by clarifying, sometimes in great detail, just how the affiliates retain their autonomy. For example, the central organization will handle all financial matters—raise money, pay it out, establish lines of credit at home and abroad. Each affiliate, however, will make its own decisions, within a broad framework of guidelines, about working capital, investment, and the size and disposition of special funds, such as those for housing.

Clyde H. Farnsworth

FRANCE'S SPECIAL KIND OF BANKING GIANT*

*The three largest French banks, nationalized in 1946,
are led by the Banque Nationale de Paris, which is the
fourth largest bank in the world. Its status, objectives,
and diverse interests are portrayed in this news story.
How "public" is this public bank?*

In the heart of the Paris show business district on the Boulevard des Italiens sits the headquarters of the biggest bank in the world outside the United States.

It is called the Banque Nationale de Paris, a $20 billion (in assets) giant. Its chairman is a flamboyant French internationalist named Pierre Ledoux. . . .

In the last 10 years there has been a quiet industrial revolution in France. The fastest growth rate in Europe has converted France's economic base from something akin to cottage industries to the large multinational units (the Pechiney-Ugine-Kuhlmanns, the Saint Gobain-Pont-a-Moussons, the Renaults) that are poking ahead for profits all over the globe.

Such a transformation could not have taken place without the revolution in banking that the Banque Nationale de Paris represents today with its 2,000 branches in France, its 250 branches in 62 foreign countries, its 45,000 employes, its deposit base of more than $20 billion and its fresh ideas.

Mr. Ledoux is a little like an impresario as he describes the bank's ventures into investment banking, Arab banking, Far East banking, student lending, sale-and-leaseback financing, tanker financing, mutual funds, mortgages and the general marketing of banking services. . . .

"When we move," Mr. Ledoux says, gesticulating in his handsome office across the street from the Opéra Comique, "it has a very big impact."

The B.N.P. formed what probably was the first of the multinational banking consortiums in 1967. Today the group comprises eight banks,

---

* Clyde H. Farnsworth, "France's Special Kind of Banking Giant," *New York Times,* December 2, 1973, excerpted. © 1973 by The New York Company. Reprinted by permission. Farnsworth is a reporter.

known as the Sociéte Financière Européene, representing combined assets of $140 billion. . . .

The Banque Nationale de Paris was the first French bank to create and sell mutual funds. Today its *SICAVS*, as the funds are known in France, represent some $5 billion under management.

The bank invented the Eurco, a unit of the nine Common Market currencies that could generate momentum for a common European money if the Europeans ever make further advances toward political union. International bonds are now quoted in Eurcos.

The B.N.P. is the only foreign bank with a branch network in Australia. And it is the lead correspondent bank for the Bank of China in Peking, where Mr. Ledoux was a young French treasury attaché back in 1945–46.

His bank opened up the real estate credit market in France. It adopted some American venture capital ideas by providing money and management services for small companies and then taking an equity interest in them.

It is deeply involved in the financing of the French nuclear power industry. It operates perhaps the most potent Arab banking consortium. And it is heavily engaged in the United States.

Its French American Banking Corporation, with assets of about $400 million, finances imports and exports and is involved increasingly in other types of lending activity for not only European but also American companies. . . .

A B.N.P. agency in California has just opened the French Bank of California with offices in San Francisco and a branch in Los Angeles.

The B.N.P. is the biggest of the three French nationalized banks, which together dominate 60 percent of the French commercial banking industry. The two others are the Société Générale de Paris and the Crédit Lyonnais.

They were nationalized in 1946. Speaking for the Banque Nationale de Paris, Mr. Ledoux says proudly, "We have never had to ask the Government for money."

The French nationalized banks are a special breed of institution. They were taken over by the state in the immediate postwar administration of Charles de Gaulle for two principal reasons: There was a need to mobilize banking resources quickly by the Government for France's postwar reconstruction, and there was a desire to keep the banks independent of private interests.

"We are a business enterprise just like any other, perhaps more than any other," says Mr. Ledoux. In 1972 his bank had a trading profit of 140 million francs, the equivalent of $30 million at the rates of exchange then prevailing. The profit was up 25 percent from 1971. This year, says Mr. Ledoux, it will be higher yet.

"Your money interests me," says the bank to the public in its advertising, and with this money it has brought many of the innovations that have helped the French economy grow.

It is sometimes said that France's three state-owned banks are a private club or even a state cartel, but this isn't really true. They are rather competitive institutions with differing management philosophies.

Crédit Lyonnais and Société Générale de Paris, both of which control deposits of more than $17 billion, are more Europe-oriented than the B.N.P. Both have much closer institutional links with other European banks. . . .

Each of the three state-owned banks has organized its own rival Middle East consortium, another indication of their competitiveness. The three banks feel no compunction about prodding the private sector—or prodding the Government. . . .

It's convenient in managing the French economy for the Government to be able to assemble the chairmen of three banks wtih vast nationwide networks and discuss the making or the carrying out of policy.

When the French Government intensified its exchange controls to defend the franc in 1968, it didn't have to worry about getting the thousands of skilled clerks needed to enforce the measures. It already had them in the state banks. All that was necessary was to make a few telephone calls—"to the gang," as Mr. Gavoty puts it.

The nationalized banks have an advisory function. Through their lending and other activities and their breadth of coverage, they hold the economic pulse of all France.

It's not at all the same in the United States, where banking is organized according to states. The Chase Manhattan Bank has its finger on the pulse of New York City and New York State, but it doesn't know too much about what's happening in California.

When Finance Minister Valéry Giscard d'Estaing is considering new measures, he calls the state bankers together for their views. . . .

The consultation procedures are formal as well as informal. The chiefs of the three state-owned banks have permanent seats on the National Council of Credit. This is a deliberative body, headed by the governor of the Bank of France, that influences credit policy. . . .

In 1950 Mr. Ledoux resigned from the foreign service to become an officer in the Banque Nationale pour le Commerce et l'Industrie. He rose with this bank (spending seven years as its director general for Africa in Algiers) until the merger in 1966 with the Comptoir National Descompte.

The fusion of these two state-owned banks led to the creation of the Banque Nationale de Paris. Five years after the merger, Mr. Ledoux became chairman.

The merger shook up French banking and industry as nothing else in recent history. With the stroke of a pen, a much larger deposit base and wider diversification of services were possible.

The Government took the occasion to open up the mortgage field to commercial banks for the first time and to erase the distinction between commercial and investment banks in moves that stimulated competition on a broad front.

Out of this ferment came the restructuring of French industry and the "greening" of the economy.

Strengthened by its bigger base in France, the B.N.P. continued expanding overseas. It has more foreign branches today than any other bank except First National City.

With activities in Hong Kong, Singapore, Tokyo, South Vietnam, New Caledonia, Australia, India, Jakarta and San Francisco, the B.N.P.'s penetration of the Pacific basin is greater than any other European bank. . . .

James R. Nelson (1915–   )

PRACTICAL APPLICATIONS OF MARGINAL COST PRICING IN THE PUBLIC UTILITY FIELD*

Marginal cost pricing is equally appropriate under public and private ownership, but public firms in France and Britain have done it most thoroughly. Nelson here outlines the French "green tariff," which carefully fits marginal costs rather than price discrimination. With more recent refinements, French and British electricity pricing has become much more efficient than American pricing. This has eased their problems of capacity shortages, ecological impacts, and national energy policy.

The word "Applications" in my title has shrunk all the way from plural to singular. For, so far as I know, the only public utility enterprise in the world to proceed from the theory of marginal cost pricing to both a schedule of rates and a series of rules for investment policy is Electricité

* James R. Nelson, "Practical Applications of Marginal Cost Pricing in the Public Utility Field," *American Economic Review*, May 1963, excerpted from pp. 474–81. A brilliant analyst, Nelson, has written about nearly all economic aspects of utilities, private and public, in the U.S., western Europe, and Latin America. Compare his summary with W. G. Shepherd, "Marginal Cost Pricing in American Utilities," *Southern Economic Journal*, July 1966, pp. 58–70, showing the neglect of marginal cost pricing in the U.S.

de France or E.D.F., hereafter)—a public corporation which is the dominant factor in the generation, transmission, and distribution of electricity in France. . . .

What are the marginal cost principles which have already been mentioned so often? In brief:

1. The first step in the short-run cost analysis proceeds from the fact that Paris is the heaviest center of electricity consumption—and at a great distance from major sources of hydro supply. Therefore, at any given hour of any day, the short-run marginal cost of electricity delivered in the Paris area is the cost of fuel for an extra unit of output from the least efficient thermal plant which must be in service to enable the total demand at that hour to be met. A price which covers the marginal cost of this least efficient plant will, of course, produce a surplus over the fuel cost of all other plants in service.

2. The exception to this general rule that the marginal price should just cover marginal fuel cost occurs at the peak. The peak kilowatt-hour is responsible for the installation of new generating capacity. Here we begin to pass from short-run to long-run marginal cost analysis. But note that the long-run marginal cost is not the total cost of a new base-load generating plant. It is the lesser of two costs, neither of which is as high as the base-load cost: The unit cost of a plant specially designed for peak loads, or the net cost of the base-load plant after subtracting fuel economies because installation of the new baseload plant permits a reduction of the output required from older, less efficient plants.

3. These thermal conclusions must be modified in two ways to allow for French hydro production:

a. Since Paris is the residual deficit market, always ready to soak up hydro production when it is available, Paris is the key to the geographical price structure appropriate for the industry. Consuming areas closer to hydro surpluses than Paris should enjoy a price equal to marginal thermal cost at Paris minus transmission cost. In the limit, the value of the electricity at the site of the hydro plant itself is determined by the cost of a kilowatt-hour from the marginal thermal source at Paris minus transmission costs from the hydro site to the capital.

b. Since hydro supplies depend on variable water conditions, they involve more uncertainty than thermal supplies. Moreover, since hydro supplies reach their peak in France in the summertime, eking out the uncertain winter supply requires substantial investment in reservoir capacity. Thus the familiar problem of supplying peak use is complicated by the further problem of assuring winter supplies of electricity.

E.D.F. has assembled these theoretical ingredients into a new tariff for larger industrial users, the *tarif vert*, which was introduced during 1957.

The structure of the *tarif vert* in a mainly hydro area may be illustrated by actual rates charged in the departments of the lower Rhone valley. The original annual fixed charge was 4,000 francs per kilowatt, or the equivalent of just under $10 at the exchange rate then prevailing.

The price per kilowatt-hour was varied through five standard periods: peak hours in winter, heavy-use hours in winter, slack hours in winter, heavy-use hours in summer, and slack hours in summer. The kilowatt-hour price from the 150-kilovolt transmission system ranged from 7.50 francs, or just under 2 cents, at the winter peak, down to 2.13 francs, or less than 4/10ths of a cent, in the slack hours of summer. If the slack-hour rate in summer is arbitrarily equated to 100, then the other four rates, three winter and one summer, are: 352, 253, 130, and 157. For the smallest customer eligible for the *tarif vert*—one supplied by the 5-kilovolt distribution system—the range of kilowatt-hour rates was from 13.41 franc to 2.31 francs. With the lowest rate as 100, the other rates were 581, 323, 129, and 160. The 5-kilovolt consumer was asked to pay only 15 percent more than the 120-kilovolt consumer in summer, and only 7½ percent more in the slack hours of winter; but the smaller user had to pay 70 percent more in the heavy-use hours in winter and almost 80 percent more at the winter peak.

E.D.F. has estimated that improvement in load factors due to the *tarif vert* permitted an initial saving in capacity equal to six months' investment program. . . .

The French system has adopted the only possible economic rule for marginal cost pricing: in an industry in which costs decrease in any dimension, the economic case for making any sales at less than marginal cost is especially weak. The consistent emphasis in the E.D.F. analysis on at least covering marginal cost provides not only a powerful reason for knowing the exact magnitude of these costs but also a long-run protection against certain types of political pressure. . . .

Although the French electrical rate structure is a product of a special relationship between hydro and thermal resources, the idea of combining peak costs and relatively high rates on the plateau of heavy winter use is doubly useful; it provides partial safeguards against future demand shifts and it establishes principles on which the rate structure itself may be altered if need be. The *tarif vert* might still be hovering in the wings if it had not been for the unsatisfactory rate level and structure produced by the interplay of specific freezes and general inflation. But, once on the scene, it offers more prospect for flexibility than the familiar rigid "on peak-off peak" structure of rates. . . .

William S. Vickrey (1914–   )

PRICING IN URBAN AND
SUBURBAN TRANSPORT*

> *Long a leading advocate of marginal cost pricing,*
> *Vickrey outlines what could be done in pricing city*
> *transport services rationally. Instead, he notes, actual*
> *practices are often sharply—even hilariously—ineffi-*
> *cient, with severe social costs. Though his examples are*
> *from New York City, they are lamentably fitting for*
> *most cities everywhere. Is improvement possible?*

I will begin with the proposition that in no other major area are pricing practices so irrational, so out of date, and so conducive to waste as in urban transportation. Two aspects are particularly deficient: the absence of adequate peak-off differentials and the gross underpricing of some modes relative to others.

In nearly all other operations characterized by peak load problems, at least some attempt is made to differentiate between the rates charged for peak and for off-peak service. Where competition exists, this pattern is enforced by competition: resort hotels have off-season rates; theaters charge more on weekends and less for matinees. Telephone calls are cheaper at night, though I suspect not sufficiently so to promote a fully efficient utilization of the plant. Power rates are varied to a considerable extent according to the measured or the imputed load factor of the consumer, and in some cases, usually for special-purpose uses such as water heating, according to the time of use. . . . But in transportation, such differentiation as exists is usually perverse. Off-peak concessions are virtually unknown in transit. Such concessions as are made in suburban service for "shoppers tickets" and the like are usually relatively small, indeed are often no greater than those available in multitrip tickets not restricted to off-peak riding, and usually result in fares still far above those enjoyed by regular commuters who are predominantly peak-hour passengers.

*   *   *   *   *

* William S. Vickrey, "Pricing in Urban and Suburban Transport," *American Economic Review*, May 1963, excerpted from pp. 452–58. A Columbia professor, Vickrey has also written extensively on microeconomic theory.

But while suburban and transit fare structures are seriously deficient, the pricing of the use of urban streets is all but nonexistent. Superficially, it is often thought that since reported highway expenditures by the state and federal government are roughly balanced by highway tax and license revenues, the motorist is on the whole paying his way. But what is true on the average is far from true of users of the more congested urban streets. Much of the expenditure on such streets is borne by city budgets supported slightly if at all by explicit contributions from highway sources, in most states. More important, much of the real economic cost of providing the space for city streets and highways does not appear in the accounts at all, being concealed by the fact that this space has usually been "dedicated" to the public use at some time in the past. It is extremely difficult to make close evaluations from the scanty and scattered data available, but very roughly it appears to me that if we take the burden of all the gasoline and other vehicular taxes borne by motorists by reason of their use of city streets, this amounts to only about a third of the real economic cost of the facilities they use. In current terms, the high marginal cost of increased street space becomes painfully apparent whenever a street widening scheme is evaluated. Even in terms of long-range planning, urban expressways cost many times as much as expressways in rural areas built to comparable specifications, and while the flow of traffic may be greater, this is not enough to come anywhere near amortizing the cost out of the taxes paid by the traffic flowing over the urban expressways. Even when tolls are charged in conjunction with special features such as bridges or tunnels, these seldom cover the cost of the connecting expressways and city streets. And except where the street layout is exceptionally favorable, such tolls usually have an unfavorable effect on the routing of traffic.

The perversity of present pricing practices is at its height, perhaps, for the East River crossings to Long Island and Brooklyn. Here the peculiar political logic is that the older bridges are in some sense "paid for," and hence must be free, while tolls must be charged on the newer facilities. The result is that considerable traffic is diverted from the newer facilities that have relatively adequate and less congested approaches to the older bridges such as the Manhattan and the Queensboro bridges, which dump their traffic right in the middle of some of the worst congestion in New York. The construction of the proposed expressway across lower Manhattan from the Holland Tunnel to the Manhattan and Williamsburgh bridges would be at least less urgent, if not actually unwarranted, in view of its enormous cost, if, as would seem possible, traffic could be diverted from the Manhattan Bridge to the Brooklyn-Battery tunnel by imposing tolls on the Manhattan and other East River bridges and reducing or removing the toll on the tunnel. The delusion still persists that the primary role of pricing should always be that of financing the service rather than that of promoting economy in its use. In practice there are many alternative ways of financing; but no device can function quite as effectively and smoothly as a properly designed price structure in controlling use and providing a guide to the efficient deployment of capital.

The underpricing of highway services is even more strongly pronounced during peak hours. Even if urban motorists on the average paid the full cost of the urban facilities, rush hour use would still be seriously underpriced; moreover, this underpricing would be relatively more severe than for transit or commutation service. This is because off-peak traffic on the highways and streets is a much larger percentage of the total than is the case for either transit or commutation traffic; and therefore in the process of averaging out the costs, much more of the costs properly attributable to the peak can be shifted to the shoulders of the off-peak traffic than can be thus shifted in the case of transit or commutation service. The effect of this is that while the commutation fare problem is chiefly one of the overpricing of off-peak travel, and to a minor extent if at all one of underpricing of peak travel, the problem of the pricing of automobile travel is chiefly that of remedying the underpricing of peak travel, and to a relatively minor extent if at all of the overpricing of off-peak travel. These two relationships combine to give the result that even if motor traffic and commuter train traffic each on the whole fully paid their way on the basis of a uniform charge per trip, the proportion by which the peak-hour motorist would be subsidized by the off-peak motorists would be far greater than the proportion by which the peak-hour commuter is subsidized by the off-peak commuter.

A quantitative indication of the seriousness of the problem of peak-hour automobile traffic is derivable from some projections made for Washington, D.C. Two alternative programs were developed for taking care of traffic predicted under two alternative conditions, differing chiefly as to the extent to which express transit service would be provided. The additional traffic lanes required for the larger of the two volumes of traffic would be needed almost solely to provide for this added rush hour traffic, the less extensive road system being adequate for the off-peak traffic even at the higher overall traffic level. Dividing the extra cost by the extra rush hour traffic, it turned out that for each additional car making a daily trip that contributes to the dominant flow, during the peak hour, an additional investment of $23,000 was projected. In other words, a man who bought a $3,000 car for the purpose of driving downtown to work every day would be asking the community, in effect, to match his $3,000 investment with $23,000 from general highway funds. Or if the wage earners in a development were all to drive downtown to work, the investment in highways that this development would require would be of the same order of magnitude as the entire investment in a moderate-sized house for each family. It may be that the affluent society will be able to shoulder such a cost, but even if it could there would seem to be many much more profitable and urgent uses to which sums of this magnitude could be put. And even if we assume that staggering of working hours could spread the peak traffic more or less evenly over three hours, this would still mean $8,000 per daily trip, even though achievement of such staggering would represent an achievement second only to the highway construction itself. At 250 round trips per year, allowing 10 percent as the gross return which a comparable investment in the private sector would have to earn to cover interest, amortization, and property and corporate income taxes, this amounts to over $3.00 per round trip, or, on a one-hour peak basis, to $9.00 per round trip, if staggering is ruled out. This is over and above costs of maintenance or of provision for parking. When costs threaten to reach such levels, it is high time to think seriously about controlling the use through pricing. . . .

But talk of direct and specific charges for roadway use conjures up visions of a clutter of toll booths, an army of toll collectors, and traffic endlessly tangled up in queues. Conventional methods of toll collection are, to be sure, costly in manpower, space, and interference with the smooth flow of traffic. Furthermore, unless the street configuration is exceptionally favorable, tolls often contribute to congestion over parallel routes. However, with a little ingenuity, it is possible to devise methods of charging for the use of the city streets that are relatively inexpensive, produce no interference with the free flow of traffic, and are capable of adjusting the charge in close conformity with variations in costs and traffic conditions. My own fairly elaborate scheme involves equipping all cars with an electronic identifier which hopefully can be produced on a large-scale basis for about $20 each. These blocks would be scanned by roadside equipment at a fairly dense network of cordon points, making a record of the identity of the car; these records would then be taken to a central processing plant once a month and the records assembled on electronic digital computers and bills sent out. Preliminary estimates indicate a total cost of the equipment on a moderately large scale of about $35 per vehicle, including the identifier; the operating cost would be approximately that involved in sending out telephone bills. Bills could be itemized to whatever extent is desired to furnish the owner with a record that would guide him in the further use of his car. In addition, roadside signals could be installed to indicate the current level of charge and enable drivers to shift to less costly routes where these are available.

❋   ❋   ❋   ❋   ❋

V. Questions for Review: Public Enterprise

"Public enterprise is a substitute for *private ownership,* not for antitrust or regulation." Explain this.

Under what conditions is public ownership and management the best treatment for all or part of an industry? Illustrate with real cases, if you can.

Public ownership of utilities is common abroad, while private ownership, under regulation, is common in this country. Are there objective standards for deciding, in specific cases, whether public ownership or regulated private ownership is best? If so, what are these standards?

Have public power systems, like TVA, provided a useful "benchmark" or "yardstick" for evaluating the prices and performance of private power companies? Explain.

What criteria are appropriate for pricing and investment decisions in public enterprises? Give instances where these (1) have and (2) have not been followed in actual public enterprises.

Are public firms more effective in achieving rational pricing than regulated private firms? Explain.

You are chairman of a new Task Force on Public Enterprise. What main changes in the scope of public enterprises in this country would *you* make? Give specific examples of the worst and best instances of public enterprises.

"Public enterprises are a costly failure." "Public enterprise is an efficient, flexible policy tool." Which one is correct? Use the practical cases in your explanation.

Choose a public enterprise, assess its performance and specify two main changes in policy or structure which would improve that performance.

"Public enterprise has never been properly tried." "Public enterprise is fine in theory but defective in practice." Explain both of these points of view. Are they correct?

What advantages do public investment banks offer, compared to the older style of public firms in utility sectors?

In what ways might marginal-cost pricing actually be applied to different parts of the urban transportation system?

"Each car crossing the George Washington bridge causes 5¢ of wear to the pavement. A flat toll of 5¢ should therefore be charged, to equate price with marginal cost." Is this pricing rule correct and complete?

"The classic public corporation, in a utility sector, is only one of many possible forms of public enterprise." What other forms are there?

Public firms need not be monopolies. Find five examples of public enterprises that are under competitive pressure.

Identify three public enterprises operating in your present locale.

Is public ownership merely a last resort, suitable only when all other policies fail?

Identify three public enterprises with excellent performance; and three with poor performance. Can you explain why the difference has occurred?

Should the U.S. Postal Service be subjected to more competition? On which parts of its business; or all parts; or none?

Does uniting city transit operations in one public enterprise help achieve social efficiency? Give pro and con.

If you are at a public college or university, how should its pricing policies be improved? Who is benefiting from, and who is paying for, your education?

Are there clear criteria to prescribe the profit and pricing behavior of "social enterprises"?

Should museums and public libraries charge admission or other fees?

Part *VI*

※

SPECIAL CASES

All cases are "special," but some are marked off for special treatment (or non-treatment). These are often pathological cases ingrained with deep social problems. Often the policies are sharply antisocial in effect. In a few cases, the policies are close to optimal.

The small sample here includes health care, drugs, sports, and weapons.

Kenneth J. Arrow (1921–   )

UNCERTAINTY AND THE WELFARE ECONOMICS OF MEDICAL CARE*

Health care is often said to be a special case, needing special treatment (fixing of fees; strict credentials; prohibitions on advertising; or a national health program, etc.). How special is it, and in which ways? Arrow here summarizes several features, focusing on uncertainty and the need for "trust." What special policies do these and other distinctive traits of health care really call for?

This paper is an exploratory and tentative study of the specific differentia of medical care as the object of normative economics. It is contended here, on the basis of comparison of obvious characteristics of the medical-care industry with the norms of welfare economics, that the special economic problems of medical care can be explained as adaptations to the existence of uncertainty in the incidence of disease and in the efficacy of treatment.

. . . The relevance of risk-bearing to medical care seems obvious; illness is to a considerable extent an unpredictable phenomenon. The ability to shift the risks of illness to others is worth a price which many are willing to pay. Because of pooling and of superior willingness and ability, others are willing to bear the risks. Nevertheless, as we shall see in greater detail, a great many risks are not covered, and indeed the markets for the services of risk-coverage are poorly developed or nonexistent. . . .

That risk and uncertainty are, in fact, significant elements in medical care hardly needs argument. I will hold that virtually all the special features of this industry, in fact, stem from the prevalence of uncertainty.

---

* Kenneth J. Arrow, "Uncertainty and the Welfare Economics of Medical Care," *American Economic Review*, December 1963, excerpted from pp. 945–46 and 948–54. A wide-ranging theorist and Nobel laureate in economics, Arrow has also analyzed a variety of specific sectors.

SPECIAL CHARACTERISTICS OF THE MEDICAL-CARE MARKET

This section will list selectively some characteristics of medical care which distinguish it from the usual commodity of economics textbooks. The list is not exhaustive, and it is not claimed that the characteristics listed are individually unique to this market. But, taken together, they do establish a special place for medical care in economic analysis.

A. The Nature of Demand

The most obvious distinguishing characteristics of an individual's demand for medical services is that it is not steady in origin as, for example, for food or clothing, but irregular and unpredictable. Medical services, apart from preventive services, afford satisfaction only in the event of illness, a departure from the normal state of affairs. . . .

In addition, the demand for medical services is associated, with a considerable probability, with an assault on personal integrity. There is some risk of death and a more considerable risk of impairment of full functioning. In particular, there is a major potential for loss or reduction of earning ability.

B. Expected Behavior of the Physician

It is clear from everyday observation that the behavior expected of sellers of medical care is different from that of business men in general. These expectations are relevant because medical care belongs to the category of commodities for which the product and the activity of production are identical. In all such cases, the customer cannot test the product before consuming it, and there is an element of trust in the relation. But the ethically understood restrictions on the activities of a physician are much more severe than on those of, say, a barber. His behavior is supposed to be governed by a concern for the customer's welfare which would not be expected of a salesman. . . .

A few illustrations will indicate the degree of difference between the behavior expected of physicians and that expected of the typical businessman. (1) Advertising and overt price competition are virtually eliminated among physicians. (2) Advice given by physicians as to further treatment by himself or others is supposed to be completely divorced from self-interest. (3) It is at least claimed that treatment is dictated by the objective needs of the case and not limited by financial considerations. While the ethical compulsion is surely not as absolute in fact as it is in theory, we can hardly suppose that it has no influence over resource allocation in this area. Charity treatment in one form or another does exist because of this tradition about human rights to adequate medical care. (4) The physician is relied on as an expert in certifying to the existence of illnesses and injuries for various legal and other purposes. It is socially expected that his concern for the correct conveying of information will, when appropriate, outweigh his desire to please his customers.

Departure from the profit motive is strikingly manifested by the overwhelming predominance of nonprofit over proprietary hospitals. The hospital per se offers services not too different from those of a hotel, and it is certainly not obvious that the profit motive will not lead to a more efficient supply. The explanation may lie either on the supply side or on that of demand. The simplest explanation is that public and private subsidies decrease the cost to the patient in nonprofit hospitals. A second possibility is that the association of profit-making with the supply of medical services arouses suspicion and antagonism on the part of patients and referring physicians, so they do prefer nonprofit institutions. Either explanation implies a preference on the part of some group, whether donors or patients, against the profit motive in the supply of hospital services.

Conformity to collectivity-oriented behavior is especially important since it is a commonplace that the physician-patient relation affects the quality of the medical care product. A pure cash nexus would be inadequate; if nothing else, the patient expects that the same physician will normally treat him on successive occasions. This expectation is strong enough to persist even in the Soviet Union, where medical care is nominally removed from the market place. . . .

C. Product Uncertainty

Uncertainty as to the quality of the product is perhaps more intense here than in any other important commodity. Recovery from disease is as unpredictable as is its incidence. In most commodities, the possibilty of learning from one's own experience or that of others is strong because there is an adequate number of trials. In the case of severe illness, that is, in general, not true; the uncertainty due to inexperience is added to the intrinsic difficulty of prediction. Further, the amount of uncertainty, measured in terms of utility variability, is certainly much greater for medical care in severe cases than for, say, houses or automobiles, even though these are also expenditures sufficiently infrequent so that there may be considerable residual uncertainty.

Further, there is a special quality to the uncertainty; it is very different on the two sides of the transaction. Because medical knowledge is so complicated, the information possessed by the physician as to the consequences and possibilities of treatment is necessarily very much greater than that of the patient, or at least so it is believed by both parties. Further, both parties are aware of this informational inequality, and their relation is colored by this knowledge. . . .

D. Supply Conditions

In competitive theory, the supply of a commodity is governed by the net return from its production compared with the return derivable from the use of the same resources elsewhere. There are several significant departures from this theory in the case of medical care.

Most obviously, entry to the profession is restricted by licensing. Licensing, of course, restricts supply and therefore increases the cost of medical care. It is defended as guaranteeing a minimum of quality. Restriction of entry by licensing occurs in most professions, including barbering and undertaking.

A second feature is perhaps even more remarkable. The cost of medical education today is high and, according to the usual figures, is borne only to a minor extent by the student. Thus, the private benefits to the entering student considerably exceed the costs. (It is, however, possible that research costs, not properly chargeable to education, swell the apparent difference.) This subsidy should, in principle, cause a fall in the price of medical services, which, however, is offset by rationing through limited entry to schools and through elimination of students during the medical-school career. These restrictions basically render superfluous the licensing, except in regard to graduates of foreign schools.

The high cost of medical education in the United States is itself a reflection of the quality standards imposed by the American Medical Association since the Flexner Report, and it is, I believe, only since then that the subsidy element in medical educaton has become significant. Previously, many medical schools paid their way or even yielded a profit. . . .

One striking consequence of the control of quality is the restriction on the range offered. If many qualities of a commodity are possible, it would usually happen in a competitive market that many qualities will be offered on the market, at suitably varying prices, to appeal to different tastes and incomes. Both the licensing laws and the standards of medical-school training have limited the possibilities of alternative qualities of medical care. The declining ratio of physicians to total employees in the medical-care industry shows that substitution of less trained personnel, technicians, and the like, is not prevented completely, but the central role of the highly trained physician is not affected at all.

E. Pricing Practices

The unusual pricing practices and attitudes of the medical profession are well known: extensive price discrimination by income (with an extreme of zero prices for sufficiently indigent patients) and, formerly, a strong insistence on fee for services as against such alternatives as prepayment.

The opposition to prepayment is closely related to an even stronger opposition to closed-panel practice (contractual arrangements which bind the patient to a particular group of physicians). Again these attitudes seem to differentiate professions from business. Prepayment and closed-panel plans are virtually nonexistent in the legal profession. In ordinary business, on the other hand, there exists a wide variety of exclusive service contracts involving sharing of risks; it is assumed that competition will select those which satisfy needs best.

The problems of implicit and explicit price-fixing should also be mentioned. Price competition is frowned on. Arrangements of this type are not uncommon in service industries, and they have not been subjected to antitrust action. How important this is is hard to assess.

Karen Davis (1942–   )

LESSONS OF MEDICARE AND MEDICAID FOR NATIONAL HEALTH INSURANCE*

Many regard Medicare and Medicaid (started in 1965) as trial versions for a comprehensive national health program in this country. These two programs have had quite special features, which a larger program need not copy. Davis assesses their lessons and gives some clear warnings about structure, pricing policy, and financing.

Thank you, Mr. Chairman, for this opportunity to testify on lessons that can be drawn from the Medicare and Medicaid experience in designing national health insurance. These two programs, which have been in operation for eight years, will spend $22 billion on medical care for the poor and the elderly in 1974. Before undertaking new initiatives in medical care fi-

---

* Karen Davis, "Lessons of Medicare and Medicaid for National Health Insurance," House Subcommittee on Public Health and Environment, Hearings on *National Health Insurance—Implications*, 93d Cong., 2d sess. (Washington, D.C.: U.S. Government Printing Office, 1974), excerpted from pp. 206–12. Davis is a leading specialist on health care economics, and is at the Brookings Institution and Harvard.

nancing, it is extremely instructive to reflect on the wealth of experience we have gained with these two major financing programs.

Before the introduction of Medicare and Medicaid, the two groups with the most severe health problems—the poor and the elderly—were also the groups least adequately covered by private health insurance. As a consequence, those most in need of medical care and least able to afford it either did not receive adequate care, had to rely on charity, or incurred heavy financial burdens. The two basic objectives of Medicare and Medicaid, therefore, were: (1) assuring that those covered by the programs received adequate medical care, and (2) eliminating the financial burden of medical care expenses for covered persons.

Today, medical costs and remaining gaps in coverage of private health insurance and public programs have led to pressures for new initiatives in the financing of medical care services. Plans to expand the federal role in financing medical care services are concerned with assuring that all persons—regardless of age or welfare status—have adequate access to medical care and that no one is forced to endure financial hardship as a consequence of high medical bills. In addition, however, there is heightened concern that further expansion of medical care financing be designed in such a way as to slow the rate of inflation in medical care costs.

Although there are many lessons that can be drawn from the Medicare and Medicaid experience, there are at least five which bear centrally on national health insurance plans designed to meet these objectives:

Equality in financing is not sufficient to guarantee equal access to medical care. Even in Medicare with uniform benefits for all covered persons, higher income persons, whites, and persons residing outside the South receive far more benefits than other elderly persons.

All insurance, whether public programs such as Medicare and Medicaid or private insurance, contributes to inflation in medical care costs.

Insurance which does not place a ceiling on the patient's financial responsibility, provides inadequate protection against the financial burden of medical expenditures. Unless the family is guaranteed that its share of medical care bills will never exceed some reasonable fraction of income, the goal of preventing financial burdens can not be achieved.

Programs covering only poor persons must be carefully designed to avoid adverse incentives and inequities resulting when some people receive substantial assistance while equally needy people are unaided.

Any time the states have a major role in setting eligibility and benefit levels, inequities across geographical boundaries are likely to occur.

I would like to elaborate upon each of these points in turn, and suggest how experience with Medicare and Medicaid might be useful in designing future medical care financing plans.

EQUAL TREATMENT AND UNEQUAL BENEFITS:
THE MEDICARE PROGRAM

Medicare is a uniform, federal program providing medical care benefits to all elderly persons covered by the social security retirement program. Even though the same set of benefits are available to all covered persons regardless of income, race, or geographical location, wide differences exist in the use of services and receipt of payments on the basis of each of these factors.

It was originally hoped that the removal of financial barriers to medical care would enable all elderly persons to receive medical care services largely on the basis of medical need. Yet, those elderly population groups with the poorest health are the lowest utilizers of medical care services under the program—the poor, blacks, and residents of the South.

INCOME

Benefits are particularly unequally distributed among income classes. In spite of the better health condition of higher income elderly persons, they receive more medical services and a more expensive mix of services. Furthermore, these differences are not attributable solely to certain advantages which most higher income persons in the United States possess —such as more education or living in areas with a greater concentration of specialized medical resources. Instead, available evidence suggests that the structure of the Medicare program through its reliance on uniform cost-sharing provisions for all elderly persons may be largely responsible for the greater use of medical services by higher income persons.

> The average reimbursement per physician visit for higher income persons is 50 percent higher than for lower income persons. This difference in average price level is not purely a monetary difference, but reflects at least in part the tendency of higher income persons to receive higher quality and more specialized services. While 75 percent of physician visits for lower income persons are to general practitioners, only 65 percent of physician visits of higher income persons are to such physicians.
>
> Those poor persons covered by both Medicare and Medicaid receive substantially more medical services than other poor persons not covered by Medicaid.

The lesson to be learned from this experience is that uniform cost-sharing provisions will yield a pattern of benefits that systematically favors higher income persons. If properly designed, however, cost-sharing provisions could actually channel a greater proportion of benefits to those most in need both of medical care and assistance in paying for such care. This requires, however, that cost-sharing features be carefully graduated with income—rather than set at a uniform level for all persons.

RACE

Inequalities in Medicare benefits on the basis of race also exist to a substantial degree. Furthermore, the lower utilization of medical services by blacks is not attributable to their lower average incomes or poor education, but to other factors associated with race such as discrimination. It should be noted, however, that the Medicare program has contributed to the reduction of discriminatory barriers to medical care for all persons through its insistence that hospitals provide services on a nondiscriminatory basis as a prerequisite for participation in the Medicare program. In spite of the notable achievements in the area of access to hospital care for minority persons, however, the program has been less successful in assuring equality in treatment for other types of medical services, particularly physicians' services and nursing home services. The difficulties faced by elderly blacks in receiving equal access to these services is particularly regrettable in view of their poorer health status and limited supporting services in the home.

The magnitude of racial differences in Medicare benefits is indicated in

TABLE 1

**Medicare Reimbursement per Enrollee for Selected Services,
by Region and Race, 1968**

	White	Black and Other	Ratio, White to Other
Inpatient hospital services (all areas)	$175.00	$136.98	1.278
Northeast	186.75	216.28	.863
North central	178.27	194.45	.917
South	156.99	101.87	1.541
West	197.71	181.34	1.090
Physicians' services (all areas)	78.76	48.44	1.626
Northeast	84.05	64.22	1.309
North central	64.44	51.85	1.243
South	76.80	39.37	1.951
West	102.86	80.17	1.283
Extended care facility services (all areas)	17.03	7.84	2.172
Northeast	18.28	8.81	2.075
North central	13.37	10.96	1.220
South	13.01	5.23	2.488
West	30.37	18.98	1.600

Source: Unpublished tabulations from the 1968 medicare summary based on bills for reimbursed services for a five-percent sample of the enrolled population, Office of Research and Statistics, Social Security Administration, U.S. Department of Health, Education, and Welfare.

Table 1. In 1968, whites received 30 percent more payments for inpatient hospital care per person enrolled than elderly blacks, 60 percent more payments for physicians' services.[1] and more than twice the payments for extended care facility services. In the South, disparities in benefits between races are even wider; whites received 55 percent more inpatient hospital care, 95 percent more payments for physicians' services, and more than two and one half times the payments for extended care services received by elderly blacks enrolled in Medicare.

Virtually all of the difference in average payments is a consequence of difference in quantity of services received—rather than in the average price of services. Only in the case of physicians' services is a small portion of the difference attributable to a difference in average reimbursement levels. This reflects in part the fact that elderly whites receive a greater portion of their medical care from specialists than do elderly blacks.

Numerous factors could account for the wide disparities between Medicare benefits available for whites and those received by blacks. Low income and poor education, while important in reducing utilization of medical services by elderly whites, have little impact on the use of physician services by elderly blacks. The most obvious explanation of the low utilization by elderly blacks is discrimination on the part of the medical system toward blacks. This could occur in any number of forms—refusal of some physicians to treat black patients, undignified treatment of black patients to discourage frequent utilization, refusal of hospitals to grant hospital staff privileges to black physicians, and discrimination by medical schools in the types of students admitted resulting in a shortage of physicians willing to practice in minority neighborhoods.

If national health insurance is to provide equal access to medical care for blacks and other minority groups, two things must be done. First is rigorous enforcement of nondiscriminatory practices on the part of all providers of medical services, including physicians as well as institutional providers. The second is supplementation of national health insurance with specific supply programs designed to increase access of minorities to medical care. Expanded medical school scholarships for persons willing to practice in minority neighborhoods, subsidies to neighborhood health centers serving disadvantaged persons, and paramedical training programs designed to increase the supply of supporting medical personnel in minority neighborhoods are all promising approaches to reducing disparities in access to care.

* * * * *

---

[1] These average benefits are based on persons enrolled and eligible for services. Since a lower proportion of elderly blacks are covered under the supplementary medical insurance plan, the disparities in physician payments per elderly person are even wider than indicated by average payments per enrollee.

INSURANCE AND MEDICAL CARE INFLATION

Several studies in the last few years have shown that the decline in out-of-pocket payments for hospital care and the dramatic increase in total hospital costs are not simply coincidental. Professor Martin Feldstein was the first to show that the hospital sector responds to increases in demand for hospital care (induced by expanding insurance coverage or rising income) by raising costs and prices to the highest level consistent with maintaining a desired level of occupancy.[2] Hospitals "break even," not by keeping their prices down to minimum cost levels, but by increasing their costs to equal the maximum revenue which they are able to collect without adversely affecting hospital utilization.

TABLE 2
Hospital Costs and 3-Party Payments, 1950–72, Selected Years

Fiscal years	Direct Consumer Payments as a Percent of Personal Hospital Expenditures	Total Expenses per Patient Day in Community Hospitals	Direct Payments for Hospital Care per Patient Day	Direct Payments for Hospital Care per Patient Day in 1950 Dollars
1950	34.2	$ 15.62	$ 5.34	$5.34
1955	23.6	23.12	5.46	4.91
1960	18.6	32.23	5.99	4.87
1966	18.5	48.15	8.91	6.62
1967	12.3	54.08	6.65	4.80
1968	10.7	61.38	6.57	4.55
1969	11.3	70.03	7.91	5.19
1970	13.3	81.01	10.77	6.68
1971	11.4	92.31	10.52	6.25
1972	8.4	105.21	8.84	5.09

Source: Barbara S. Cooper and Nancy L. Worthington, "National Health Expenditures, 1929–72," *Social Security Bulletin*, vol. 36, no. 1 (January 1973); American Hospital Association, *Hospital Statistics 1972*; and Bureau of Labor Statistics, Consumer Price Index.

Even though hospitals respond to expanding insurance coverage—whether public or private—by raising costs, there is little evidence that hospitals take this opportunity to become more inefficient. Instead, hospitals respond to pressures from staff physicians and patients to provide a "higher quality" or at least more expensive style of hospital care. Most of

---

[2] Martin S. Feldstein, "Hospital Cost Inflation: A Study of Nonprofit Price Dynamics," *American Economic Review*, vol. 61, no. 5 (December 1971), pp. 853–872; and *The Rising Cost of Hospital Care* (Washington, D.C.: Information Resources Press, 1971).

the increase in expenses has occurred in the provision of ancillary hospital services—such as laboratory expenses—rather than in the provision of basic room-and-board services or administrative expenses.[3] Over time, hospitals have also used more and more inputs—such as labor and specialized capital facilities—to provide a day of hospital care. As shown in Table 3, approximately half of the increase in hospital costs is accounted for by an increase in inputs used to provide a day of hospital care.

TABLE 3

Cost per Day per Patient in Short-Term Community Hospitals:
Average Annual Rate of Increase and Percentage Distribution
of Increase, Selected Periods, 1951–70

Item	1951–70	1951–55	1955–60	1960–66	1966–70
	Annual Percentage Increase				
Total	8.6	8.4	6.9	6.9	13.9
Increase in wages and prices	4.2	3.7	3.8	3.1	7.8
Wage rates	5.8	5.8	4.9	4.1	9.8
Price levels	2.1	.8	2.0	1.5	4.8
Income in inputs	4.4	4.7	3.1	3.8	6.1
Labor	2.9	4.4	2.2	2.5	2.8
Nonlabor	6.4	4.8	4.5	6.0	11.0
	Percentage Distribution				
Total	100.0	100.0	100.0	100.0	100.0
Increase in wages and prices	49.4	44.7	54.9	44.7	56.3
Wage rates	39.1	40.9	44.0	36.4	42.4
Price levels	10.4	3.8	11.0	8.3	13.9
Income in inputs	50.6	55.3	45.1	55.3	43.7
Labor	19.5	31.4	19.8	22.2	12.1
Nonlabor	31.1	23.9	25.3	33.1	31.7

Source: Saul Waldman, "The Effect of Changing Technology on Hospital Costs," Research and Statistics Note 4, Washington, D.C., Social Security Administration, 1972.

A study I recently completed for the Social Security Administration found that hospitals reacted to the Medicare program in much the same way as they had reacted to the earlier growth in private insurance.[4] The Medicare program had little additional impact on hospital costs beyond that attributable to reduction in out-of-pocket payments generally.

The concomitant growth of third-party payments and the rise in physicians' fees parallels that of the hospital industry. In 1950, patients paid

[3] See Karen Davis, "Hospital Costs and the Medicare Program," *Social Security Bulletin*, vol. 35, no. 8, August 1973; and Karen Davis and Richard W. Foster, Community Hospitals: *Inflation in the Pre-Medicare Period*, U.S. Department of Health, Education, and Welfare, Social Security Administration, Research Report no. 41 (Washington, D.C.: U.S. Government Printing Office, 1972).

[4] Davis, op. cit.

TABLE 4

Physician Fees and 3d-Party Payments, 1950–72, Selected Years

	Direct Consumer Payments as a Percent of Personal Physician Expenditures	BLS Physicians' Fees (1967 = 100)	Index of Physician Fee Paid Directly by Consumers[1] (1967 = 100)	Index of Physician Fee Paid Directly by Consumers in Constant Dollars[2] (1967 = 100)
Fiscal years				
1950	84.8	54.7	89.3	124.1
1955	71.2	65.4	89.7	112.1
1960	66.0	76.1	96.6	110.0
1966	62.1	90.2	107.8	112.8
1967	55.9	96.9	104.3	106.0
1968	48.3	102.8	95.7	94.0
1969	45.6	109.1	95.7	89.7
1970	43.5	117.0	98.0	86.7
1971	42.5	125.8	103.0	86.7
1972	41.1	132.3	104.7	85.0

[1] Calculated by multiplying col. 1 by col. 2 and scaling to an index value of 100 in 1967.

[2] Calculated by deflating col. 3 by the Consumer Price Index, all items, and scaling to an index value of 100 in 1967.

Source: Barbara S. Cooper and Nancy L. Worthington, "National Health Expenditures, 1929–72," *Social Security Bulletin*, vol. 36, no. 1 (January 1973); and Bureau of Labor Statistics, Consumer Price Index.

nearly all (about 85 percent) of their physician bills directly (see Table 4). By 1972, third-party payers—either public or private insurance—paid almost 60 percent of physician charges. Over that 22 year period, physicians' fees, as measured by the Bureau of Labor Statistics consumer price index, increased to two and one half times the 1950 level. However, because of the growth of insurance the amount paid directly by patients out-of-pocket only increased by less than 20 percent. If translated into constant dollars, the physician fee paid directly by the patient actually declined substantially over the past last two decades.

As a result of the Medicare and Medicaid programs, we have learned in a very costly and painful way that all insurance is inflationary. This poses a very difficult problem in designing further initiatives in financing medical care. And yet the remaining unmet needs are very real. Only one third of the poor have any health insurance coverage, compared with nine tenths of families with incomes over $10,000. Many middle-income persons are inadequately protected against large medical expenses. In 1970, only half the population was covered by major medical plans, and even for persons with such coverage, limits are frequently placed on the amounts that will be paid by the insurance plan.

There are essentially four alternatives to this dilemma. First is a do nothing approach. Realizing that any further extension of insurance is inevitably inflationary, remaining unmet needs can simply be forgotten. This is, of course, not an equitable or effective solution.

The second alternative is to extend insurance coverage to meet major unmet needs and counter these increases in insurance with incentives to reduce "excessive" insurance on the part of others. This could be accomplished, for example, by changing the existing tax structure which actually subsidizes the purchase of comprehensive insurance or by promulgating universal national health insurance with more out-of-pocket payments (or cost-sharing features) than currently exists. Any attempt to increase direct payments for medical care for some persons, however, would have to be carefully designed to insure that no one was subjected to out-of-pocket payments that posed a financial burden or assumed an unreasonable fraction of the family's income.

The third alternative is to design an effective set of incentives and/or controls which will keep costs down even in the face of further expansions in insurance coverage. Wage and price controls, areawide planning bodies, reimbursement incentives for hospitals, development of health maintenance organizations, utilization review, and professional standards review organizations are all possible ways of achieving this objective.

The fourth alternative is to replace all existing insurance coverage with a single system covering virtually all medical expenditures. Costs would then be controlled through negotiated contracts and budgets for medical care providers.

The third alternative is on the surface undoubtedly the most attractive. Unfortunately, we have little evidence to date that such attempts to control costs directly will be effective in the face of further reduction in consumer payments for medical care. Experience with wage and price controls for the health industry, while encouraging in many respects, have not been in effect during a period of major changes in insurance coverage. Undoubtedly, the strategy of controlling costs which will have to be pursued will be some combination of the second and third alternatives—retaining some direct market incentives for cost control, and supplementing these incentives with regulatory controls, review procedures, or organizational incentives.

Irene Till (1906–   )

DRUG PROCUREMENT: HIGH
ON PROFITS*

*Various public agencies buy a large share of drugs.
By effective purchasing strategies, they could force the
prices down sharply for their own purchases and for
the market generally. This may ultimately be the only
way to abate drug industry profits, which have long
averaged around 20 percent in investors' capital. But it
has not happened, as Till here shows. What would an
optimal treatment be?*

The federal government is not only a supplier of services to its citizens.
It is also a mass purchaser of goods. Military hardware is one example.
Drugs is another. The federal government currently spends about $1.5
billion a year for drugs, usually on high-priced brand name products
bought in the most costly manner. As any competent procurement expert
will attest, buying in large volume is the best way to obtain low prices.
This is particularly true where the buyer is dealing with an oligopolistic
industry such as drug manufacturing; big buyers must countervail big
sellers. Yet centralized purchasing accounts for less than $150 million, or
about 10 percent, of all drugs purchased by the federal government.

A primary offender in this respect is the Department of Health, Education, and Welfare (HEW), the largest single buyer of drugs in the
United States. Its total expenditures covering drugs amounted to $1.04
billion in 1971. About half of this amount represented actual product cost,
and the remainder constituted "overhead costs" such as pharmacy fees
for prescriptions, hospital expenses in drug administration, and the like.
Yet HEW buys no drugs directly. Under the Medicare program, costing
over $540 million, the agency has nothing more than a check-writing func-
tion. The Social Security Administration simply pays whatever bills are
submitted by hospitals and nursing homes through fiscal intermediaries
such as Blue Cross and the large insurance companies. Medicaid, a pro-

---

* Irene Till, "Drug Procurement: High on Profits." From *The Monopoly Makers*
by Mark J. Green. Copyright © 1971, 1973 by Center for Study of Responsive Law.
Reprinted by permission of Grossman Publishers. Excerpted from pp. 257–59, 262,
267, 276, and 282–85.

gram complementary to Medicare, is administered through grants to the states with no real supervision by HEW of how the money is spent. (In addition to the $455 million contributed by the federal government, state and local governments paid out $446 million for drugs under the Medicaid program in 1971.)

The two agencies with experience in buying drugs directly from manufacturers in volume are the Department of Defense and the Veterans Administration. The low prices they pay indicate the significant economies that can be achieved under centralized procurement. Only a portion of their purchases, however, are made in this manner. A substantial volume constitutes local procurement at high prices either through purchases from drug wholesalers or under Federal Supply Schedule contracts. This pattern is a tribute to the drug industry's ingenuity in maintaining its enviable reputation for high profits. Traditionally, it leads all manufacturing industries in the rate of profits. In 1971 its return on investment, after taxes, was 17.9 percent. For all manufacturing, the figure was 9.7 percent.

Unless there is an overhauling of the federal government's buying practices in drugs, this profit situation will continue indefinitely. The government is expected to play an ever-larger role in buying or paying for drugs. When Medicare is expanded to include the outpatient drug bills of the elderly—those not in hospitals or nursing homes—almost half of the industry's output will be accounted for by government expenditures. And when a federal health insurance program is enacted, covering the entire population, the federal government will foot virtually the entire bill for the products of the drug industry. . . .

An example or two will suffice. One of the most dramatic moments in the Kefauver hearings occurred in connection with prednisone, then widely used in the treatment of arthritis. While Schering's price to the druggist in 1960 was $170 per thousand (about $290 to the patient with the inclusion of the pharmacy markup), its bid on business to the military was $23.63 for the same quantity. It lost out to a small firm, Premo Laboratories, whose bid was $20.98. Schering retaliated on a later round with a price of $17.97 only to be beaten out by the same firm with a price of $11.79.

A similar situation occurred with reserpine, still widely used in the treatment of hypertension. While Ciba's price to the druggist was $39.40 for one thousand tablets (about $65 to the patient), the pressure of competition made it bid $.60 to the military for the same quantity. At the time the president of Ciba's U.S. subsidiary appeared before Senator Kefauver, he expressed regret in offering this bid. He remarked, "When we bid 60 cents for bottles of 1,000 here, we didn't anything like recover our out-of-pocket costs. . . . In retrospect it was perhaps a mistake that we did that." However, after his testimony, Ciba's bid on another procurement was $.58 and still later went to $.52 while the price to druggists remained at $39.40.

In all three cases, the business was awarded to other companies bidding below Ciba prices. . . .

TABLE A

Price Comparisons—VA Centralized Purchases, Federal Supply
Schedule Contracts, and Prices to Druggists

	VA Centralized (Fiscal 1969)	Federal Supply Schedule (1970)	Price to Druggist (1970)
Ritalin (Ciba)			
10 mg. 1,000's	$ 17.34	$ 44.97	$ 54.51
Doriden (Ciba)			
0.5 gm. 1,000's	18.04	32.01	40.01
Placidyl (Abbott)			
500 mg. 100's	2.09	4.84	5.00
Mysoline (Ayerst)			
0.25 gm. 1,000's	25.25	36.36	44.52
Compazine (SKF)			
10 mg. 5,000's	180.16	229.50	576.00
Griseofulvin (Ayerst)			
250 mg. 500's	11.06	40.10	52.00
Coly-Mycin (Warner)			
5 ml. (bottle)	1.73	1.99	2.40
Furadantin (Eaton)			
100 mg. 1,000's	75.537	199.992	270.00
Macrodantin (Eaton)			
50 mg. 1,000's	38.115	84.996	114.76
Thiosulfil Forte (Ayerst)			
0.5 gm. 100's	3.24	4.61	5.64
Ismelin (Ciba)			
25 mg. 100's	5.75	7.84	9.50
Peritrate (Warner)			
20 mg. 500's	9.05	14.50	16.88
Maalox Susp. (Rorer)			
6 oz.	.0934	.20	.59
Gelusil (Warner)			
1,000's	7.60	12.04	14.50
Rio-Pan (Ayerst)			
400 mg. 12 fl. oz.	.20	.88	1.02
Choledyl (Warner)			
200 mg. 1,000's	21.26	26.89	32.40
Diuril (Merck)			
0.5 gm. 1,000's	20.90	44.69	48.45

. . . As in the case of VA, DPSC has elected not to explore the possibilities of more competitive drug procurement from foreign sources of supply. Indeed this effort, originally started by MMSA, the predecessor agency, has all but been abandoned. For fiscal 1968 and 1969, only three products were purchased by DPSC from European firms. In each instance, prices were also sought from U.S. suppliers, and the contrast is striking.

In view of the marked price savings available, why has DPSC failed to explore foreign prices for other drugs controlled by patent monopoly in this country? Its predecessor agency had found that a mere expression of intent to do so had a beneficial effect: American suppliers reacted defensively with quotations of lower prices. DPSC officials say they cannot act because of the Buy American Act. Under this law government agencies are directed to buy U.S. products unless their prices are "unreasonable."

TABLE C
Price Comparisons—Foreign and U.S. Companies
on Drugs Imported by DPSC, 1969

Product	Successful Foreign Bidder	Lowest U.S. Price Bid
Meprobamate 400 mg., 500's	$ 1.68 (A/S Syntetic, Denmark)	$ 9.50 (Carter)
Tetracycline 250 mg., 100's	.90 (Carlo Erba, Italy)	2.09 (Pfizer)
Nitrofurantoin 100 mg., 1,000's	18.50 (Zambon, Italy)	76.30 (Morton-Norwich)

The executive order governing this provision defines an unreasonable U.S. price as one that exceeds 10 percent of the foreign price, exclusive of duty. But then the Department of Defense adds another hurdle. This is the 50 percent "evaluation factor" contained in the Armed Services Procurement Regulations (ASPR). . . .

There are still other hurdles. These center around the regulations of the Food and Drug Administration. No firm can qualify as a bidder on a particular product for DPSC—and also for VA—unless it has an approved New Drug Application. This involves inspection of the manufacturing plant as well as submission of acceptable data showing the drug's safety and efficacy. For foreign firms, plant inspection is no real problem. Many of the European plants are newer than those in the United States, and fully meet American standards. The real difficulty arises from the FDA requirement that animal and human testing data must include detailed studies conducted in the United States. . . .

Finally, it is customary for the major drug firms, just prior to the expiration of an important product patent, to bring out a slight molecular modification of the older drug. In this manner effective patent protection can be continued indefinitely. The new product is promoted intensively to physicians as a significant technological advance; and they respond by shifting their prescriptions to the new brand name. Although there is little therapeutic difference, extended experience with patients is often required before physicians recognize this fact. In the meantime the older drug has fallen into disuse as obsolete. . . .

... The result is that the United States taxpayer foots the bill each year for unnecessarily high drug costs incurred by our federal government. But the ultimate effect extends far beyond government procurement, reaching the structure of prices prevailing for the general public. Were the federal agencies to insure competition in their purchases, these prices could serve as a yardstick for the reasonableness of prices charged in the civilian market. At the present time, the public is incensed over rising health costs as well as the prices they must pay for drugs filled under doctors' prescriptions. But in the absence of specific knowledge, there is little they can do about it. And, unless the situation is remedied, future consequences will be great. When a federal health insurance program is enacted, the government will purchase most of the drugs used in this country. If it continues its present obeisance to monopolistic practices in the drug industry, the cost burden to the public under the program will be intolerable.

Roger G. Noll (1940–   )

GOVERNMENT AND THE SPORTS BUSINESS*

Sports have become big business since the 1950s and they now pose many familiar issues of monopoly, pricing, profits, subsidies, and allocation. Noll's book is an instant landmark, raising and testing many of these issues. The passages here convey some of the tentative findings about matters which will continue to vex this remarkable sector.

The professional sports industry provides a fascinating subject for students of the relationship between government and business. Virtually every major public policy toward business—antitrust, labor relations, taxation, even the constitutional prohibition against slavery—has a potentially significant application to sports.

---

* Roger G. Noll, ed., *Government and the Sports Business* © 1974 by The Brookings Institution, Washington, D.C., excerpted from Noll's introduction and epilogue, pp. 1–4, 7–9, and 414–20. A former collegiate basketball player, Noll is also an expert on regulation of industry and a professor at California Institute of Technology.

THE OPERATION OF TEAM SPORTS

A professional sports league is essentially a cartel, with the purpose of restricting competition and dividing markets among firms in the industry.[1] Each league has three types of restriction: one dealing with interteam competition for players, another with the location of league franchises, and a third with the sale of broadcasting rights. . . .

The Player Reservation System

The target of nearly all the antitrust cases in professional team sports has been the player reservation system, which limits competition among teams for players. This system includes rules governing the signing of new players, the promotion of players from minor to major leagues (of primary importance only in hockey and baseball), and the transfer of players from one major-league roster to another. These rules differ in detail from sport to sport, but their intention is everywhere the same—to limit, if not prevent, the competitive bidding among teams for the services of players.

The Reserve Clause. The component of the player reservation system that receives the most public attention is the so-called reserve clause—that is, a clause in the contract of each player that assigns to a specific team the exclusive right to deal with him for his entire playing life. Technically, only baseball and hockey actually have a reserve clause. In these sports a player can change teams only if his current team grants another team the right to deal with him or releases him from the obligations of his contract. Football and basketball have rules that appear less restrictive than the reserve clause. In both sports a player may "play out his option" according to the provisions of the "option clause" in his contract. . . .

While in theory the option system gives the player more opportunity to decide for himself where he will play, in practice it is almost as restrictive as the reserve system. The most important reason for this is the "Rozelle rule," which provides that a team signing a player who has played out his option must indemnify the player's former team. . . .

The key to the successful operation of the player reservation system is an agreement among the teams in a league not to compete for players. Each sport has an elaborate set of operating rules governing relations

---

[1] The fact that leagues are cartels has no policy significance by itself. As sports entrepreneurs have long contended, restrictions on competition in business practices may be necessary in order to promote competition on the playing field. The validity of this contention is at the heart of the policy debate over the social justification for restrictive business practices in professional sports.

among teams, including prohibitions against negotiating with players whose rights are held by other teams. A team that contacts a player to determine if he might be interested in changing teams is guilty of "tampering" and can be severely punished by the league. . . .

Exclusive Marketing Rights

Just as league rules limit competition in the acquisition of players, so, too, do they limit competition in selling the product of the industry. Teams have three important sources of income: admissions, broadcasting, and concessions. In all three areas, teams are essentially monopolistic: for each sport, only one team in any city normally has the right to sell tickets to major-league professional contests, to offer broadcasts of contests, and to sell food, beverages, and souvenirs to those in attendance at its games. . . .

Team Franchises. Each professional sport has rules governing the location of teams in the league. Although the rules vary among the leagues, the general effect is to prohibit a member team from locating in a city that another team has already designated as its home unless the latter gives its approval. Thus, each team has an exclusive right to sell admissions to major professional contests in the sport in its home territory. Leagues also control the movement of existing franchises to cities without teams. A team wishing to relocate its franchise must obtain the approval of most of the other teams in its league (though the details differ from sport to sport). . . .

Conclusions

As the preceding discussion makes clear, professional sports leagues have a remarkably complex set of rules and practices that all but eliminate business competition among their members. The extent of the anticompetitive practices is made especially apparent by the contrast between normal operations and conditions during the occasional periods when a new league emerges, when, until one league fails or a merger is consummated, competition prevails. During these "wars," player salaries, especially for rookies and superstars, are considerably higher, team profits appear to be much lower, and the number of major-league teams is greater.

❖   ❖   ❖   ❖   ❖

With these thoughts in mind, several other possibilities for dealing with the franchise problem emerge. All appear to make more sense than either the present system or direct government prohibition of or restriction on the relocation of teams.

1. Government could require some minimum degree of revenue sharing among teams in a league. This would at least partially alleviate the

wide disparities in the economic potential of franchise sites that contribute to the instability of franchises.

2. Government could eliminate or severely restrict the extent to which franchise costs could be allocated to players and depreciated. The upper limit should be the reasonable profit expectations of teams in a sport. This would eliminate the present incentive to use ownership of a sports enterprise as a shelter from income taxation revenues earned in other business activities. It would also tend to return sports ownership to individuals whose primary motivation for owning a team is to operate the team successfully, and who are thus less interested in selling the team within a few years. But to preserve many of the existing teams, this measure would have to be accompanied by more even revenue sharing.

3. Government could insist that leagues expand whenever someone is willing to put up a reasonable amount of money for a franchise. What would be "reasonable" is, of course, debatable. Existing owners have some claim to compensation, to the extent that expansion reduces the income of existing teams. This will happen if more teams share in a fixed national broadcasting contract, if attendance at games in the expansion city is below the league average (the existing teams then receive a diminished visitor's share for games in the new city), or if the new team goes bankrupt, forcing the league to operate the franchise until a new owner can be found or the team can be disbanded in an orderly fashion (certainly not in the middle of a season).

None of the empirical or theoretical analysis in this book, even by authors who favor maintaining some form of reservation system, lends any support to the view that player reservation has a significant effect on the balance of competition. The theoretical conclusion is that the reserve clause could balance competition only if player trades and sales were prohibited—certainly an undesirable and unenforceable proposition. Empirical investigations find no discernible relation between the closeness of competition on the field and the degree of competition in the market for players. They also find no evidence that the prime motivation of the vast majority of owners is any consideration other than profits. . . .

Perhaps more important than the debate over the exact effects of the reserve clause is the fact that all three of its alleged benefits—more balanced competition, greater financial security for weaker teams, player salaries more in line with a player's value to a league—could be obtained by mechanisms other than the reserve clause.

All three objectives would be served if teams divided income more evenly. In order to preserve an owner's incentive to maintain the quality of a team, a team's financial success must depend heavily on its ability to attract fans. But the dependence need not be total, as it is in most sports. At the minimum, other sports might be required to copy football's lead, by sharing gate receipts relatively evenly between home and visiting teams.

For sports that are heavily dependent on local broadcasting fees, similar sharing arrangements could be required for these revenues. Even more effective than splitting revenues between the home and visiting teams would be to divide a share of the revenues equally among all teams. . . .

Interteam financial disparities could also be reduced by increasing competition among teams for revenues. More teams could be placed in the most lucrative markets, and prohibitions on broadcast competition could be removed. . . . In any event, it is difficult to see the justification for preventing an owner from attempting to capture a share of a big-city market should he want to try. If he fails, the team can always move back to a smaller market. If he succeeds, the effect on league financial and playing balance can only be beneficial.

An effective mechanism for preventing an overzealous owner from monopolizing playing talent is to place a ceiling on a team's total budget for player salaries. Suppose that no team could spend more for player salaries than 150 percent of the league average expenditure in the previous year, and that each year every player was free to play for any team that offered him a job. The limit on total salaries would prevent a single team from signing a large number of superior players, would still permit substantial annual growth in the average compensation of players, and would substantially narrow the spread among teams in total player salaries (and, presumably, playing quality). . . .

Another complicated issue is the restriction on broadcast competition. The principal effect of the current arrangements—pooled national rights, exclusive local markets—is to create a series of broadcast monopolies that increase broadcast revenues for sports and advertising costs for sponsors, while reducing the number of broadcasts available to the fan. Although national broadcast revenues are evenly split among the teams in a league, the overall effect of broadcast practices probably contributes to disparities in the financial health of teams. This is because a team's monopoly in broadcasting in its home territory is more important the larger the broadcasting market in which the team is located. The wide variance among teams in local broadcasting revenues, which reflects market sizes, also increases financial disparities, particularly since the visiting team does not receive a share of the revenues from local broadcasts. . . .

The preceding discussion suggests the following arrangement as a reasonable alternative to the present system, or to the present system modified by a prohibition of blackouts.

Relatively even sharing of broadcast revenues, along the lines recommended above for gate receipts: either a 60–40 split between home and visiting teams, or a 50–25–25 split among the home team, the visiting team, and a fund to be divided equally among all teams.

Repeal of the 1961 sports broadcasting act, which exempts leagues from antitrust laws when they pool broadcasting rights to form a single national package, the 1973 bill that lifts the blackouts of sold-out home games, and the rules that inhibit placing home games on STV.

Prohibition of league rules that grant each team the right to exclude the broadcasts of other teams from its home territory. . . .

James R. Kurth (1948–   )

THE POLITICAL ECONOMY OF WEAPONS PROCUREMENT: THE FOLLOW-ON IMPERATIVE*

The buying of large-scale weapons is an ongoing process involving military officials and a relatively few supplying companies. Their factories are regarded as a national defense resource, to be kept in being. Kurth analyses how the eight major aerospace production lines were kept busy during 1960–72 with almost clockwork precision, despite the seeming existence of turbulent competition for orders. Kurth says this lock-step system is past; but is it?

❊   ❊   ❊   ❊   ❊

In contrast to the two cases of missile procurement, MIRV and ABM, the two major cases of manned aircraft procurement in the 1960s, the F-111 fighter-bomber and the C-5A jumbo transport, were less important strategically but as much debated politically. Both aircraft became famous, even notorious, because of "cost overruns," mechanical failures, prolonged groundings, and Congressional investigations. Further, in June 1970 the Air Force awarded a contract to produce prototypes of a new, large, manned bomber, the B-1, which begins anew the numbering of the bomber series and which would go into operational deployment in the late 1970s. By that time, given the efficiency of strategic missiles and anti-aircraft missiles, the new B-1 would seem to be about as useful and about as obsolete as the first B-1 of the 1920s.

Why does the United States buy such aircraft? There are, of course, the official, strategic explanations: The F-111 is needed for a variety of

* James R. Kurth, "The Political Economy of Weapons Procurement: The Follow-on Imperative," *American Economic Review*, May 1972, excerpted from pp. 306–10. Kurth is a faculty member at Swarthmore.

tasks, such as tactical bombing, strategic bombing, and air defense; the C-5A is needed for massive airlifts of troops and supplies; and the B-1 is needed for strategic bombing and post-attack reconnaissance. But these explanations neglect the fact that the respective tasks can be performed by a variety of ways and weapons, and that these particular manned aircraft are not clearly the most cost-effective way to do so.

There are, also, the possible bureaucratic explanations: the F-111 was needed by the Tactical Air Command to preserve its power and prestige within the overall balance of the military bureaucracies; the C-5A was needed similarly by the Military Airlift Command; and the B-1 is desired by the aging commanders of the Air Force and of the Strategic Air Command within it, who look back with nostalgia to their youth and to the manned bomber in which they rode first to heroic purpose and then to bureaucratic power. But these explanations are not fully satisfactory. . . .

An alternative explanation, more economic in emphasis and more general in scope, can be constructed by drawing some relations between two variables for the period since 1960: (1) aerospace systems which are military or military-related (i.e., military aircraft, missiles, and space systems) and (2) aerospace corporations which produce such systems.

AEROSPACE SYSTEMS

The major military aerospace systems produced at some time during the period since 1960 have been the following: the B-52, B-58, and B-70 large bombers; the Minuteman and Polaris missiles and their MIRV successors or "follow-ons," Minuteman III and Poseidon; the F-111 and F-4 fighter-bombers; and the C-130, C-141, and C-5A transports. In addition, there has been the military-related Apollo moon program. Major military aerospace systems planned for production in the mid or late 1970s are the B-1, which can be seen as a long-delayed follow-on to the canceled B-70; the Undersea Long-Range Missile System (ULMS), which will be a follow-on to Poseidon; the F-14 and F-15, which will follow the F-4; the ABM system including the Spartan and Sprint missiles; and the military-related space shuttle program.

These various aerospace systems can be grouped into six functional categories or production sectors: (1) large bombers, (2) missile systems, (3) antimissile systems, (4) fighter-bombers, (5) military transports, and (6) space systems.

AEROSPACE CORPORATIONS

At the beginning of our period, in 1960, there were a large number of aerospace corporations which produced military aircraft, missiles, or space systems. Four stood out, however, in the sense that each received in fiscal year (FY) 1961 military and space "prime contract awards" of some $1 billion or more: General Dynamics, North American, Lockheed, and Boeing.

During the decade after 1960, each of these four corporations continued normally to receive each year $1 billion or more in military and space contracts, although Boeing's awards occasionally dropped below that amount. . . . There are now six aerospace corporations which produce military aircraft, missiles, or space systems and which each normally receive some $1 billion or more in military and space contracts each year; in FY 1971, Lockheed, General Dynamics, Grumman, McDonnell Douglas, and North American Rockwell were each awarded contracts amounting to almost $1 billion or more; Boeing was awarded some $800 million.

We can analytically split Lockheed, which is normally the largest military contractor, into its two main military divisions, Lockheed-Missiles and Space, located in California, and Lockheed-Georgia. Similarly, we can split McDonnell Douglas into its McDonnell division in Missouri and its Douglas division in California. There are thus eight major production lines.

We can then chart the major military aerospace systems according to the production line to which the U.S. awarded the contract and according to the years when major development or production phased in or out or is scheduled to do so. Some interesting patterns result (see Table 1).

About the time a production line phases out production of one major government contract, it phases in production of a new one, usually within a year. In the cases of new aircraft, which usually require a development phase of about three years, the production line normally is awarded the contract for the new system about three years before production of the old one is scheduled to phase out. In the case of new missiles, the development phase usually is about two years. Further, in most cases, the new contract is for a system which is structurally similar but technically superior to the system being phased out, i.e., the new contract is a follow-on contract. (An exception is Apollo, but even here North American was NASA's largest contractor before the Apollo contract was awarded; in the case of the B-1, the follow-on is one step removed from the B-70.)

A large and established aerospace production line is a national resource —or so it seems to many high officers in the armed services. The corporation's managers, shareholders, bankers, engineers, and workers, of course, will enthusiastically agree, as will the area's Congressmen and Senators. The Defense Department would find it risky and even reckless to allow one of only eight or less large production lines to wither and die for lack of a large production contract.[1] There is at least latent pressure upon it

---

[1] This is especially so because for each of the aircraft production sectors (large bombers, fighter-bombers, and military transports), there are actually only four or

TABLE 1

Military Aerospace Systems and Major Production Lines

	General Dynamics	North American Rockwell	Boeing	Lockheed-M & S	Lockheed-Georgia	McDonnell	Douglas	Grumman
1960	B-58	B-70	B-52 Minuteman	Polaris	C-130	F-4	Nike Zeus d.	Misc.
1961		Apollo d. in	Minuteman build-up	Polaris build-up	C-141 d. in			
1962	B-58 out F-111 d. in		B-52 out					F-111 sub. d. in Apollo sub d. in
1963								
1964		B-70 out			C-141 p. in C-5A d. in			
1965							Nike Zeus out Spartan d. in	
1966	F-111 p. in	Apollo p. in	Minuteman III d. in	Poseidon d. in				F-111 sub. p. in Apollo sub. p. in
1967				Polaris out	C-141 out			
1968			Minuteman out Minuteman III p. in	Poseidon p. in	C-5A p. in			
1969						F-15 d. in		F-14 d. in
1970		B-1 d. in						
1971								
1972	F-111 out	Apollo out			C-5A out	F-4 out	Spartan p. in	F-111 sub. out Apollo sub. out F-14 p. in
1973	?	B-1 p. in	Minuteman III out Super-MIRV or SST in?	Poseidon out ULMS in?	?	F-15 p. in		

Note: d. = development; p. = production.

from many sources to award a new major contract to a production line when an old major contract is phasing out. Further, the disruption of the production line will be least and the efficiency of the product would seem highest if the new contract is structurally similar to the old, in the same functional category or production sector, i.e., is a follow-on contract. Such a contract renovates both the large and established aerospace corporation that produces the weapons system and the large and established military organization that deploys it.

This latent constraint or rather compulsion imposed on weapons procurement by industrial structure might be called the follow-on imperative and contrasted with the official imperative. The official imperative for weapons procurement might be phrased as follows: if a military service needs a new weapons system, it will solicit bids from several competing companies; ordinarily, the service will award the contract to the company with the most cost-effective design. The follow-on imperative is rather different: if one of the eight production lines is opening up, it will receive a new major contract from a military service; ordinarily, the new contract will be structurally similar to the old, i.e., a follow-on contract. Relatedly, the design competition between production lines is only a peripheral factor in the award.

The follow-on imperative would have predicted and can perhaps explain the production line and the product structure of nine out of the ten major contracts awarded from 1960 to 1970: (1) Minuteman III follow-on to Minuteman, (2) Poseidon follow-on to Polaris, (3) C-141 follow-on to C-130, (4) C-5A follow-on to C-141, (5) F-14 follow-on to F-111 major subcontract, (6) F-15 follow-on to F-4, (7) Spartan follow-on to Nike Zeus, (8) F-111 after B-58, a somewhat less certain case, (9) B-1 delayed follow-on to B-70. In regard to the tenth contract, Apollo, North American might have been predicted to receive the award, because it was already NASA's largest contractor.

The imperatives of the industrial structure are reinforced, not surprisingly, by the imperatives of the political system, as would be suggested by a democratic explanation. Five of the production lines are located in states which loom large in the Electoral College: California (Lockheed-Missiles and Space, North American Rockwell, and Douglas division of McDonnell Douglas), Texas (General Dynamics), and New York (Grumman). The three others are located in states which in the 1960s had a Senator who ranked high in the Senate Armed Services Committee or

---

five potential production lines out of the eight major lines we have listed. Large bombers are likely to be competed for and produced by only General Dynamics, North American Rockwell, Boeing, and perhaps Lockheed-Georgia; fighter-bombers by only General Dynamics, North American Rockwell, Boeing, McDonnell division, and Grumman; and military transports by only Boeing, Lockheed-Georgia, Douglas division, and, for small transports, Grumman.

Appropriations Committee: Washington (Boeing, Henry Jackson), Georgia (Lockheed-Georgia, Richard Russell), and Missouri (McDonnell division of McDonnell Douglas, Stuart Symington). . . .

The table indicates that there has been considerable pressure on the Nixon administration. In 1969–70, the administration confronted two impending phase-outs, the F-4 Phantom program of the McDonnell division of McDonnell Douglas, which was expected to phase out in 1972, and the Apollo program of North American Rockwell, whose funding was scheduled to decline sharply after the first two or three manned landings on the moon. The administration resolved the problem in the easiest and most incremental way, by a follow-on contract, the F-15, to the McDonnell division in December 1969, and by a delayed follow-on, the B-1, to North American Rockwell in June 1970. Seen in this perspective, the other competitors for the F-15 (Fairchild Hiller and North American Rockwell) and for the B-1 (General Dynamics and Boeing) were never really in the running.

❊   ❊   ❊   ❊   ❊

Whatever will be the Nixon administration's solution to the contract gap, however, the follow-on imperative in its strict form is dead. With the F-14 and F-15 nearing production, there can be no fighter-bomber to follow-on the F-111, unless it be the Air Force lightweight fighter, now being planned. With the C-5A nearing deployment, there can be no conceivable need for more military transport capacity, unless it be for the STOL transport, also now being planned. And so the analysis of the follow-on imperative presented in this paper, like the B-1 itself, may have appeared at the very moment that it has become obsolete.

VI. Questions for Review: Special Cases

How large a share of the economy is exempted from antitrust and regulation? Is this share growing? Should it be?

Are there good, cost-benefit reasons for the restrictions which now cover scores of "professions"?

Did the 1971–74 price controls work? What are their lessons for the future?

Why did U.S. price control during World War II work so well?

"The resort to 'economics by admonition'—government officials exhorting businessmen to do the right thing—simply reflects weak antitrust enforcement to ensure market competition." Do you agree?

Name *three* significant nontariff trade barriers which reduce import competition.

"Completely free international trade would provide the acid test of American industrial efficiency and would assure competition." Is this right?

Describe three government-backed cartels and evaluate their net social benefits.

Describe three public agencies which insure private risks (e.g., housing mortgages). What efficiency and equity benefits do they provide? Are they worth it?

Are federal maritime subsidies for building and operating ships remotely worth their cost? Outline the costs and benefits.

Is the FTC "policing" of advertising claims an optimal use of those resources?

Why does *farm* demand for food products have a lower income elasticity than *final* demand for food products?

"Farm programs banked millions of acres and large surpluses of farm products. These were available to be put to use when scarcity hit after 1971. Therefore farm programs made good long-run sense." Do you agree?

New food scarcities have swept away much of the old farm programs. What remaining supports are still warranted, at least for parts of the farm sector?

What is the social rate of interest (define the concept, not its magnitude)? Explain the relevance of this concept to the solution of a conservation problem. Why might the social rate of interest diverge from interest rates available in the private sector?

"Free private competitive-market choices will optimize the use of natural resources over time. Public intervention will only distort." Under what conditions is this *not* true?

"Competition and free entry have ruined the salmon, lobster and many other fishing industries, and it will soon blight the fish supply for the whole world." Why might this be true? What steps are needed to avoid it?

"Oil policies have caused a large waste of drilling resources *and* an inadequate use of American oil." How might this have happened?

Do unique features of the health services "industries" justify cartel behavior and entry barriers?

What main controls do medical doctors maintain on the health care sector? What is their rationale? What revisions in these controls would be justified?

Should hospitals be "regulated" in order to stop the rise in hospital charges? What other approaches are there?

"Each sport is a natural monopoly internally, but in stiff competition externally with other sports. Leagues should have a free hand to organize as they wish."

How do the present tax and franchise rules cause inferior performance and unstable franchises in pro sports?

Should cities be permitted to own teams in the pro leagues?

What kinds of subsidies do most pro sports teams receive?

How would an equal-gate-sharing rule foster better competition within pro sports leagues?

Do public subsidies for the performing arts tend to benefit only the elite? Is it possible to foster the arts in a fair (e.g., broad-based) way?

How is marginal cost a key factor in explaining the patterns of bidding and contracting for large weapons systems?

"Since a fixed-price contract applies the highest marginal incentive for efficiency, the Defense Department can optimize its procurement strategy by putting all contracts on that basis." Evaluate.

Are there good prospects for making Defense purchasing and R&D support more competitive in process, more efficient, and more favorable to competition in the economy? What specific steps do you think should be taken to make it so?

DATE DUE
